Jefferson's Fine Arts Library
His Selections for
the University of Virginia
Together with
His Own Architectural Books

Jefferson's Fine Arts Library

His Selections
for the University of Virginia Together
with His Own Architectural Books

William Bainter O'Neal

University Press of Virginia

Charlottesville

The publication of this work
has been made possible by a grant
generously made through
the Committee on the Bicentennial of
the University of Virginia.

THE UNIVERSITY PRESS OF VIRGINIA
Copyright © 1976 by the Rector and Visitors
of the University of Virginia

First published 1976

Library of Congress Cataloging in Publication Data

O'Neal, William Bainter.
  Jefferson's fine arts library.

  Based on the author's earlier ed. published under
title: Jefferson's fine arts library for the University
of Virginia, with additional notes on architectural
volumes known to have been owned by Jefferson.
  Includes index.
  1. Art—Bibliography—Catalogs.   2. Architecture—Bibliography—Catalogs.   3. Virginia.
University. Library. 4. Jefferson, Thomas, Pres.
U.S., 1743–1826. I.   Title.
Z5939.05 [N5300]   016.7   75–33229
ISBN 0–8139–0647–4

Printed in the United States of America

For
E. F. O.

Preface

This study had its genesis in my 53-page pamphlet of 1956, *Jefferson's Fine Arts Library for the University of Virginia: With Additional Notes on Architectural Volumes Known to Have Been Owned by Jefferson*, published on behalf of the Alderman Library and the Bibliographical Society of the University of Virginia by the University of Virginia Press. That text was based largely on a study of records rather than the actual books and became, in the long run, a desiderata list for a collection which would illuminate a particularly important facet of Jefferson's creative life, that is, his architecture and his attitudes on the fine arts generally.

Since that 1956 publication, the Thomas Jefferson Memorial Foundation has most generously helped the Alderman Library of the University of Virginia collect as many of the books that appeared in that study as possible.

This present study, although perhaps technically a second edition of the earlier work, has been largely based on the books themselves now gathered together at the University. I am tempted to say, then, "that this Work may in some sort be rather consider'd as an Original, than an Improvement," as Giacomo Leoni wrote about his own contributions to his splendid edition of Palladio (No. 92a). Certainly it has grown far beyond the bounds of the 1956 pamphlet.

It has been my purpose to give the reader not only accurate information about the books but also some knowledge of their structure and flavor so that it might be possible for him to form an idea of the architectural thought which surrounded Jefferson, who based his own architectural inspiration on them and who derived many of his architectural forms from them. Although architectural books and the architecture of the University of Virginia have been emphasized here, an emphasis peculiarly appropriate because of Jefferson's desire that the two should interact, the fine arts volumes also give us a glimpse of his background in painting and sculpture and, sometimes, a direct connection with his own collections.

It has seemed best to let the books speak for themselves. After a transcription of the title page, a physical description of each book, and background information about its authors, engravers, and subscribers, pertinent quotations from the books are inserted, for it was found that many of the authors gave very clear statements of their intentions and sometimes equally clear summaries of their theses. The quotations, in order not to weaken their impact, have been kept in their original languages.

Finally, the relationship between Jefferson, architecture, and the particular book is pointed out, a relationship which is inevitably closer in some cases than others. For this information no one can work today without consulting the writings of Fiske Kimball, the pioneer in the study of Jefferson's architecture, whose 1916 monograph has recently been reissued with an introduction by Frederick Doveton Nichols, and E. Millicent Sowerby's 1952–59 catalogue of the library Jefferson sold to Congress, a study which is so magnificently complete. Both have been acknowledged whenever used, and both appear frequently. One other source must be mentioned as being of the greatest help. Nichols's systematization of Jefferson's architectural drawings enormously simplifies problems of dating and identification.

The completion of this work has been made possible through the award of one of the University of Virginia's Summer Research Fellowships. The staff of the Alderman Library of the University, and particularly that of its Rare Book Department, has been invariably kind. The late John Cook Wyllie, the curator of rare books before becoming Librarian of the University, was both mentor and friend; Francis L. Berkeley, Jr., a former curator of manuscripts, was an ideal guide during the early stages of my research; William Runge, the present curator of the Tracy W. McGregor Collection, continued the many helpful acts of Mr. Wyllie and Mr. Berkeley; and Julius P. Barclay, the present curator of rare books, has spurred the publication of this study with his enthusiasm and very great technical and administrative knowledge. I also wish to thank Judy Nelson and Cynthia Sinnott of the staff of the Rare Book Department for their suggestions, their editorial services, and their searches for obscure copies of the books cited. Pauline Page of the Graphic Communications Services of the library has made the photographic portion of this study a delight. William L. Beiswanger, of the staff of the Thomas Jefferson Memorial Foundation, has kindly supplied additional facts about Nos. 11, 81, 109, and 117, as well as arranging for the photographs needed from Monticello.

It remains only to thank Thomas Jefferson for having led me into such a fascinating path of research. To have read these titles was to gain an insight not only into Jeffersonian thought but also into the best architectural minds of the years before the opening of the University.

WILLIAM B. O'NEAL

Charlottesville, Virginia
January 1976

Contents

Plates

Photographic Credits

The Massachusetts Historical Society supplied the photographs for Plates XX and XXI.

The Thomas Jefferson Memorial Foundation supplied those for Plates XXVII, XXIX, XXXI, LXX, CXVIII, and CXXXIX.

All other photographs were executed by the Graphic Communications Services of the University of Virginia Library.

Abbreviations

Bruce   Philip Alexander Bruce. *History of the University of Virginia.* 5 vols. New York, 1926.

DNB   *Dictionary of National Biography.*

1828 *Catalogue*   *A Catalogue of the Library of the University of Virginia. Arranged Alphabetically under Different Heads, with the Number and Size of the Volumes of Each Work, and Its Edition Specified. A Notice of Such Donations of Books as Have Been Made to the University.* Charlottesville, Va., 1828.

1829 sale catalogue   *Nathaniel P. Poor. Catalogue: President Jefferson's Library. . . .* Washington, D.C., 1829.

Kean   John V. Kean. "Catalogue of the Library of the University of Virginia," May 16, 1825. Manuscript, U. Va. Library.

Kimball   Fiske Kimball. *Thomas Jefferson, Architect.* Boston, 1916.

N   Frederick Doveton Nichols. *Thomas Jefferson's Architectural Drawings: Compiled and with Commentary and a Check List.* 2d ed. Boston and Charlottesville, Va., 1961.

Sowerby   E. Millicent Sowerby. *Catalogue of the Library of Thomas Jefferson.* 5 vols. Washington, D.C., 1952–59.

Note: The capsule biographies of engravers, authors, and translators have been derived from standard reference works. It has not been deemed necessary to cite these references except when a direct quotation was made.

Parentheses enclosing the abbreviation "No." and an Arabic numeral indicate one of the titles in this study.

In the Descriptive Catalogue, the books from Jefferson's personal library are indicated with an M. Those that were ordered for the University of Virginia or present before May 1825 are indicated with a U. Va.

An asterisk appearing before the library number of a title now owned by the University indicates that it is located in the Rare Book Department of the University Library.

Jefferson's Fine Arts Library

His Selections for
the University of Virginia
Together with
His Own Architectural Books

Introduction

I

As recently as March 9, 1975, the nation's leading architectural critic, Ada Louise Huxtable, has pointed out that "Jefferson was 'fixated' on books and on 'fishing' his designs out of them, according to Benjamin Latrobe, his friend and America's outstanding architect at that time."[1] Fiske Kimball said much the same thing sixty years earlier when he pointed out that "to know what architectural books were at hand is particularly important in Jefferson's case on account of his dependence on books for his inspiration."[2]

Colonel Isaac A. Coles gives us an eyewitness account of this use of books by Jefferson. In writing on February 23, 1816, to General John Cocke, who had asked Coles to consult with Jefferson about Cocke's proposed new dwelling at Bremo, Colonel Coles said that Jefferson pointed out that Palladio "was the bible. He has sent all his Books &c. &c. to Washington, or he would have drawn yr. House for you—it would have been a pleasure to him—but now he could not undertake to do it before the fall, when he expected other Books from Paris."[3]

With his wide personal experience of architecture through books, Jefferson also realized the importance of architectural experience through actual examples, and when he began the design of the University of Virginia, he wrote on April 13, 1817, that he wanted the buildings there to be "of various forms, models of chaste architecture, as examples for the school of architecture to be formed on."[4] Thus the University's holdings in architectural books, for which he made the want list, and the physical aspect of the University were to reinforce one another architecturally, a process which has taken place throughout the University's existence.

In the spring of 1825 Jefferson spent what must have been a happy

---

[1] "Thomas Jefferson's Grand Paradox," *New York Times*, March 9, 1975.
[2] P. 90.   [3] Shields-Wilson Collection, U. Va. Library.
[4] Jefferson to James Dinsmore, April 13, 1817, U. Va. Library.

time compiling a catalogue of books for the proposed library of the University. Although he had some help, notably from Bishop James Madison for the section on theology,[5] when he worked with the list for architecture, gardening, painting, sculpture, and music he was on firm ground, since he himself had owned one of the largest such fine art collections in the country.

When Jefferson sold his "great library" to Congress in 1815, he started reassembling this fine arts collection to include what was for the time a respectable number of architectural books. Forty-nine works on architecture alone were sold in 1815, while at least six, and possibly eleven, on the same subject were in Jefferson's library at his death.[6]

Comparable libraries in the United States usually contained fewer such books. Samuel McIntire had seven works on architecture at his death in 1811.[7] Charles Bulfinch had in his possession about fifteen architectural books before his death in 1844.[8] William Byrd's library at Westover showed some twenty-seven architectural entries when it was offered for sale in 1777.[9] The catalogue of the Carpenter's Company of Philadelphia lists only thirty-two architectural books printed before 1826.[10]

Some version of Palladio was the most commonly owned architectural book, both by gentlemen as well as by those more actively engaged in building. Joseph Coolidge presented a Palladio to the young University, as did James Madison, its second Rector.[11] There is also a letter from James Oldham, a master carpenter, to Jefferson mentioning his own copy of Palladio and telling how it lacked certain information: "J. Oldham sends Mr. Jefferson the Draughts of the window frames for his examination. The Dorick of Diocletians baths, Chambray, is not in the Book of Palladio which I have, and I must aske the favor of Mr. Jefferson to lone me the book to lay down my cornice and I will immediately return it safe."[12]

---

[5] Bruce, II, 40.   [6] Kimball, pp. 90–101.

[7] Fiske Kimball, *Mr. Samuel McIntire, Carver, Architect of Salem* (Portland, Me., 1940), p. 23.

[8] Charles A. Place, *Charles Bulfinch, Architect and Citizen* (Boston, 1925), pp. 285–86.

[9] Advertisement in *Virginia Gazette*, Dec. 19, 1777, reprinted in *The Writings of Colonel William Byrd*, ed. John Spencer Bassett (New York, 1901), and Kimball, p. 20.

[10] Carpenter's Company of the City and County of Philadelphia, *Finding List of the Library* (Philadelphia, 1894).

[11] 1828 *Catalogue*, pp. 105, 108.

[12] Oldham to Jefferson, June 21, 1819. See also Jefferson to Thomas Appleton, April 16, 1821, in which Jefferson specified certain orders by the numbers of specific plates in the Leoni, 1721 edition of Palladio. Both letters are in U. Va. Library.

The University of Virginia Library has a manuscript copy of Jefferson's want list of books for the institution. It is labeled "President Jefferson's Catalogue of Books for the University of Virginia Library. 1825." Written in what is probably the hand of Nicholas Trist, Jefferson's secretary, it is endorsed by Jefferson: "The preceding catalogue is that of the books with the purchase of which Mr. Wm. Hilliard is charged on behalf of the University of Virginia. Th: Jefferson Rector June 3. 1825."

The catalogue is arranged in the order Jefferson had devised for his own library. This method divided knowledge into the three faculties of Memory, Reason, and Imagination, subtitled respectively History, Philosophy, and Fine Arts. These are further subdivided into a total of forty-two headings, of which several contain books in the fields of building and the fine arts. Such books are found under "Hist-Civil-Antient," "Technical Arts" (a subdivision of "History, Civil"), "Architecture" (a subdivision of "Fine Arts"), "Gardening. Painting. Sculpture. Music." (also a subdivision of "Fine Arts"), and "Polygraphical," a section which fell outside the three main subdivisions.

Jefferson's signed endorsement of the existing catalogue and his mention of it in a letter of June 3, 1825, to Hilliard ("The copying of our Catalogue was finished yesterday and I now inclose it") [13] attest to its use for ordering his original selections for the library of the new University.

F. W. Page, a former librarian of the University, described an earlier want list, evidently in Jefferson's hand:

We have a manuscript volume, without date, but evidently prepared by him between the years 1820 and 1825, which he styles A Catalogue of Books Forming the Body of a Library for the University of Virginia, prefaced by an explanation of the views on which it is based, and by his classification into forty-two chapters, embracing 6,860 volumes, estimated to cost $24,076.50.

A Catalogue of Books Forming the Body of a Library for the University of Virginia, to be afterwards enlarged by annual additions—An explanation of the Views on which this Catalogue has been Prepared.

1. Great standard works of established reputation, too voluminous and too expensive for private libraries, should have a place in every public library, for the free resort of individuals.

2. Not merely the best books in their respective branches of science should be selected, but such also as were deemed good in their day, and which consequently furnish a history of the advance of the science.

3. The *opera omnia* of writers on various subjects are sometimes

[13] U. Va. Library.

placed in that chapter of this Catalogue to which their principal work belongs, and sometimes referred to the Polygraphical chapter.

4. In some cases, besides the *opera omnia*, a detached tract has been also placed in its proper chapter, on account of editorial or other merit.

5. Books in very rare languages are considered here as specimens of language only, and are placed in the chapter of Philology, without regard to their Subject.

6. Of the classical authors, several editions are often set down on account of some peculiar merit in each.

7. Translations are occasionally noted, on account of their peculiar merit or of difficulties of their originals.

8. Indifferent books are sometimes inserted, because none good are known on the same subject.

9. Nothing of mere amusement should lumber a public library.

10. The 8vo form is generally preferred, for the convenience with which it is handled, and the compactness and symmetry of arrangement on the shelves of the library.[14]

11. Some chapters are defective for want of a more familiar knowledge of their subject in the compiler, others from schisms in the science they relate to. In Medicine, e.g., the changes of theory which have successfully prevailed, from the age of Hippocrates to the present day, have produced distinct schools, acting on different hypotheses, and headed by respected names, such as Stahl, Boerhaave, Sydenham, Hoffman, Cudden, and our own good Dr. Rush, whose depletive and mercurial systems have formed a school, or perhaps revived that which arose on Harvey's discovery of the circulation of the blood. In Religion, divided as it is into multifarious creeds, differing in their bases, and more or less in their superstructure, such moral works have been chiefly selected as may be approved by all, omitting what is controversial and merely sectarian. Metaphysics have been incorporated with Ethics, and little extension given to them. For, while some attention may be usefully bestowed on the operations of thought, prolonged investigations of a faculty unamenable to the test of our senses, is an expense of time too unprofitable to be worthy of indulgence. Geology, too, has been merged in Mineralogy, which may properly embrace what is useful in this science, that is to say, a knowledge of the general stratification, collection and sequence of the different species of rocks and other mineral substances, while it takes no cognisance of theories for the self-generation of the universe, or the particular revolutions of our own globe by the agency of water, fire, or other agent, subordinate to the fiat of the Creator.[15]

[14] Practically the same rule is in Jefferson's letter to Hilliard of Sept. 16, 1825; see Elizabeth Cometti, *Jefferson's Ideas on a University Library* (Charlottesville, Va., 1950), p. 22.

[15] Page, "Our Library," dated Sept. 10, 1895, in *Alumni Bulletin of the University of Virginia*, II (Nov. 1895), 79.

The manuscript described by Page has disappeared, presumably as a result of the disastrous library fire of 1895.[16]

We have two ways of knowing which of the books ordered by Jefferson for the University were actually delivered in his lifetime. One source is a manuscript catalogue of the library compiled even before the date the Hilliard list was completed, and the other is a printed catalogue that appeared two years after Jefferson's death.

The slight manuscript list, "Catalogue of the Library of the University of Virginia" by John V. Kean, a student and Jefferson's first appointee to the post of librarian, was dated May 16, 1825, and thus was completed some two months after the University had opened its doors and before any books recommended by the faculty could have been added to the collection. This source and the 1828 *Catalogue* are both noted with the relevant books in the descriptive catalogue.

When one remembers that Jefferson was eighty-two when he completed a list of more than six thousand volumes for the University's library, one realizes the magnitude of his achievement. When one finds further that, in the area of the fine arts, many of the volumes are still considered as monuments in their field, Jefferson's choices become even more remarkable.

When it is also remembered that Jefferson's architectural achievements are second only to his political contributions to the United States, the importance of the group of books dealt with here can be appreciated. Without these books it is impossible to understand fully either Jeffersons' philosophy of architecture or his sources for the visual forms with which he gave objective life to that philosophy.

II

One fact needs to be emphasized here. The present catalogue has been made up of fine arts items culled from the list prepared by Jefferson for the University and from the Kean list, and has been supplemented by *architectural* [17] books from his private libraries. A listing of Jefferson's

---

[16] *A Catalogue of the Library of the University of Virginia* (Charlottesville, Va., 1828; 1945 facsimile edition by W. H. Peden), p. 2.

[17] Kimball's implicit definition of an architectural book has in general been followed in the present listing (thus the omission from the present lists, for example, of books in the private library on gems), but the boundary line between an architectural book and one on engineering or mathematics is sometimes shadowy. Books on surveying have generally been included, but otherwise the books on ap-

personal books on music, painting, and sculpture has been placed outside this discussion except for those titles which appeared in both collections. The information for his personal architectural books has been taken from Sowerby's catalogue of his "great" library which was sold to Congress and from the catalogue of the 1829 sale of those volumes he had assembled for his own use after the 1815 sale, and two which appear only in a manuscript catalogue now at the Massachusetts Historical Society.

Those volumes not owned by the University at this time have been assigned numbers in order that they may fall into the right place in the descriptive catalogue, but they are clearly indicated as not being present. There are twenty-three of these titles, but two (Nos. 31 and 77) are almost or wholly impossible to reassemble, and three (Nos. 12, 41, and 50) are owned in microprint, except for a few volumes of No. 41. Of the remaining eighteen another two (Nos. 16 and 17) are price books, almost the most fugitive of all, for they were normally worn out with use. Four have to do with structures (Nos. 9, 30, 79, and 82), and others are a surveying manual (No. 57), a guidebook (No. 74), an elements of architecture handbook (No. 103), a book on gems (No. 65), a work on public monuments (No. 62), a treatise on geometry (No. 70), and a study of naval architecture (No. 115). One (No. 125b) is a copy of Vitruvius duplicated in two other editions included in the scope of this catalogue, as are two (Nos. 43a and 61a) with single duplicates each, also within the scope of this study. Only the remaining two are of prime importance; both Nos. 11 and 81 are not only works of considerable worth in themselves but both were referred to by Jefferson in his notes.

Of the books themselves it is possible to say that, though there is a wide range in dates, they all share a very strong sense of clarity. The purpose is normally stated, sometimes on the title page (the longer the title page, the more important it usually becomes, and the more neces-

---

plied mathematics have generally been excluded. Books on shipbuilding have been omitted, with two exceptions which have been included arbitrarily as a concession to titles containing the word "Architecture." Books on dikes, bridges, and fortifications have been omitted as being more strictly of an engineering nature. The selection of architecturally important books from Jefferson's headings of "Geography," "History," and the like, has been peculiarly difficult. Not many additions, however, will in the future be made in the field of Jefferson's interests in Roman antiquities. In a slightly different category, Maucomble's *Histoire abrégée de la ville de Nîmes* obviously needed to be added to former lists, and has been added here, but perhaps others will want to make further additions to the northern European group. In American architecture, only William Birch's *City of Philadelphia* has been added to correct a formerly conspicuous omission, and it seems doubtful that much else could conceivably be added in this field without embracing the problem of isolated plates in otherwise largely irrelevant books.

sary it is to read it), and the development of the book follows the most direct and logical course.

The vocabularies used are often strange to our eyes and ears. The word *art* is especially troublesome for the present-day reader, for it could often mean, in the centuries covered by these books, either a craft and the pursuit of a craft or a *fine* art, whereas modern usage implies *fine* whenever *art* is used. But the tone and intent of words as well as the qualities described by them were frequently very different in the early writing Jefferson knew. Words such as *sublimity, magnitude, grandeur, beauty, magnificence, elegance,* and even *terror* are just beginning to creep back into architectural language after a long absence. Phrases such as "a glowing Pile of Beauty," "justness in proportion," "singularity in manner," "an astonishing projection" of a cornice, a feature "to wound the eye of a savant," "the grandeur of an entablature," "proper ornaments," "a flowery imagination," "a delicate fancy," and "grand and pompous edifices which always mark the glory of those for whom they were raised" display a world of architectural thought which raises many difficulties to our appreciation but which helps to explain the attitudes of the designers of the time, attitudes that are often reflected in their architecture.

From the books themselves a glimpse of the architectural book market may be seen. Availability is, of course, fundamental to anyone's choice of books. As late as 1804 Jefferson pointed out that there had never been a copy of Palladio in Washington until he brought the London, 1700 edition there (No. 94). In the preface to that particular edition of Palladio, the translator said there are "few books we can recommend to you besides the excellent Discourses of Sir *H. Wotton* and *John Evelin,* Esq." This was written, presumably, for the book's first edition of 1663. Although the translator for Leoni's 1715 edition of Palladio claims that its illustrations are the first to have been engraved (as opposed to the use of woodcuts) for any Palladio (No. 92a), he is mistaken since our earlier one also has engraved plates. The earlier one comprises, however, only the first book rather than the entire text of Palladio, whereas the 1715 issue is complete.

This rather slow start of the English architectural book market changed quickly, since in 1724 it was necessary for an author to apologize for bringing out another volume "at a Time when the Town is already burthened with Volumes" (No. 53a). At some time before 1788 I. and J. Taylor had established a publishing house and book shop called the Architectural Library at 56 High Holborn in London. Their catalogue included in a 1788 book had 59 entries, primarily of the handbook variety (No. 16). The speed at which architectural publishing was growing is shown by the Architectural Library's 1793 catalogue (No. 89), which listed over 100 items, including books by John Soane, James Paine, Hepplewhite, John Wood, Sir William Chambers, Stuart and Revett, Brook Taylor, and Batty Langley as well as an expanded group of handbooks.

Jefferson, then, had access to a narrow selection at home but a comparatively wide one abroad. Millicent Sowerby is especially careful in giving the sources of his purchases, and there is little need to amplify that information here. We know, also, from Kimball (pp. 92–101) that of the 49 architectural titles in Jefferson's own library no less than 23 were purchased during his stay abroad between 1785 and 1789.

A cursory examination of the subscription lists included in so many eighteenth-century books turns up further, and sometimes surprising, information about the book market. Gentlemen, that is, people of title or persons dignified with an "Esq.," were very much in the majority, a fact which certainly corroborates the widely held opinion that architecture was a gentlemanly interest during the late seventeenth, the eighteenth, and the early nineteenth centuries. The next largest group of subscribers seems to have been clergymen and physicians, of whom the clergymen were usually and the physicians sometimes included in the ranks of gentlemen. After them come the architects, who are often a very small minority. The crafts—carpenters, carvers, glaziers, joiners, masons, and plasterers—also subscribed but usually in comparatively small numbers. It would seem, then, that a book large enough or important enough to carry a subscription list reached an audience most of whose members were not engaged in the practice of architecture.

We have no way, of course, of tracing the purchasers of handbooks, but since many of the surviving copies are in a very worn condition, it may be assumed that they were in daily use by craftsmen as well as by architects.

In the minute book of the Board of Visitors of the University of Virginia under the date of October 15, 1825, Thomas Jefferson recorded in his own hand the resolution "that the board approves of the advance of 18,000. Dollars to William Hilliard, agent for procuring the library." [18] A letter of May 22, 1825, from Jefferson to Hilliard shows that this approval was given after the money had been deposited to Hilliard's account: "Our money is deposited in the Virginia and Farmer's banks at Richmond and our Bursar will write by the next mail (of the 25th) to have the sum of 18,000 D. immediately deposited to your credit in the bank of the U.S. at Philadelphia. I have added 3000. D. to the 15. M.

[18] U. Va. Library.

originally agreed upon. Further than this our funds do not admit us to go at present with convenience, and moreover I confidently expect that that sum may cover the whole purchase." [19]

This $18,000 was a portion of the $50,000 received from the "central government" [20] as a partial compensation to the Commonwealth of Virginia for its advances during the War of 1812. [21] As early as 1820 Jefferson was dealing with budgetary matters concerning the purchase of books, for in that year he proposed uses for hypothetical revenues of $15,000 and $30,000 a year. For the first amount he included an item "Books, say 150. vols. a year @ 10.D.–1,500," or 10 percent of the total budget, while for the second he suggested "Books, suppose 600. vols. a year @ 10.D.–6,000," [22] or 20 per cent of the total budget.

Bruce stated that "all the volumes [in Jefferson's catalogue] descriptive of architecture, sculpture, painting, and music were written in Italian." [23] That this was incorrect is seen when one examines the list itself or considers Jefferson's explanation to Hilliard dated November 4, 1825: "in foreign books a strong regard to the edition named except where a newer and obviously better has been published, and a discretionary latitude as to recent editions of English books, and in no case a translation unless expressly specified. In general I wrote the title in the language described, but where I did not understand the language, I was not always exact in doing that, but the face of the catalogue shows that originals in all languages are what we want." [24] As we have seen Jefferson also preferred the octavo size, but in the field of the fine arts a great variety of sizes had to be purchased.

Only seventeen of the titles originally purchased survived the 1895 fire in the Library of the University, and some of these survived only in part, but under the seventeen titles are fifty-seven volumes.

Many, if not all, of the books on the manuscript want list were already known to Jefferson. His own library, either before or after the sale to the Library of Congress, or both, contained most of the architectural titles that also appeared in the catalogue sent to Hilliard, [25] and these have frequently helped to identify the editions Jefferson must have had in mind for the University.

To reconstruct the fine arts library as it was proposed in the cata-

[19] Cometti, p. 22.

[20] Minutes of the Board of Visitors, Oct. 15, 1825, U. Va. Library.

[21] Bruce, II, 38, 40.

[22] "Notes for the Consideration of the Board of Visitors," 1820?, U. Va. Library.

[23] Bruce, II, 188.   [24] U. Va. Library.

[25] Kimball, pp. 90–101. But see also note 17.

logue sent to Hilliard is not as difficult a task as it first appeared. Such a reconstruction was begun by the late E. S. Campbell, Chairman of the School of Art and Architecture at the University from 1927 until his death in 1950. Campbell had purchased a dozen titles as they became available and as funds permitted. Since his death and before the 1956 desiderata list was issued, another dozen items had been acquired. With the titles surviving from Jefferson's original purchase and with replacements, the University of Virginia was at that time already numerically in almost as strong a position as it was in 1828 toward establishing the collection in the fine arts that had been proposed. Since then all but twenty-three titles have been acquired, all but two of them the generous gift of the Thomas Jefferson Memorial Foundation. Thus a large proportion of the total is available in the University's collection.

It has been a much smaller step to attempt a complete reconstruction of Jefferson's personal architectural library. Of the books listed by Kimball,[26] the library owned a few, including two of the Palladios. In addition, the library also had a copy of Palladio not listed by Kimball, the Leoni edition of 1721, which Jefferson used in building the University,[27] though it is uncertain whether the copy used by Jefferson was his personal property.[28] To complete the collection of the entire section on architecture in the personal library will be an important step, and the titles in architecture from the personal list have been added to this study as being relevant to a discussion of Jefferson's sources for architecture and knowledge of the field of architectural books.[29]

[26] Kimball, pp. 90–101.   [27] See note 12.
[28] Kean lists a Leoni edition of Palladio and adds the marginal note "(at Monticello)." Thus the book appears to have been the property of the University on May 16, 1825, but whether it had been purchased by the University or given to it by Jefferson is uncertain.
[29] The titles that have been so supplied will be apparent from the annotations to the descriptive catalogue. A word on the sources of information concerning Jefferson's personal libraries, however, is in order. Kimball's, pp. 90–101, was the pioneer effort at listing the architectural books in all of Jefferson's private libraries. Other than manuscript lists, there were formerly available only three important printed sources of information on the library Jefferson sold to Congress: *Catalogue of the Library of the United States* (Washington, D.C., 1815); *Catalogue of the Library of Congress* (Washington, D.C., 1830); and *Catalogue of the Library of Congress, in the Capitol of the United States of America* (Washington, D.C., 1840). That these need to be used with caution may be evidenced by a single example. The 1840 *Catalogue* assigned to Jefferson's library the congressional copy of Claude Leopold Geneté's *Nouvelle construction de chiminées* (Liege, 1760), which apparently never belonged to Jefferson. Fortunately, the work of E. Millicent Sowerby has superseded the earlier and less reliable printed catalogues. For the last of Jefferson's libraries, no such similar study exists, and recourse still has

An examination of Sowerby shows that there are only nineteen additional titles needed to complete a duplication of Jefferson's personal books on music, painting, and sculpture. The University already owns six of these and two different editions of the seventh and eighth. This leaves only eleven titles unrepresented on the library's shelves.[30]

Of one entry in the descriptive catalogue there is some doubt. It was thought at one time that the notation in Jefferson's want list "Portfeuille des artistes ou dessins de chateaux etc. [4to] Leips. 1800" was intended to be identical with No. 117, Christian Ludwig Stieglitz, *Plans et dessins tirés de la belle architecture . . .* , Leipzig, 1800. It now appears that this may not be exact. For a fuller discussion of this point, see the entry in the text.

III

The sources used for the inclusion of titles in the descriptive catalogue follow.

Pertinent volumes from "President Jefferson's Catalogue of Books for the University of Virginia Library, 1825": Nos. 1, 2, 3, 6, 9, 10, 11, 15, 18b, 19, 21, 23, 24, 25, 27, 29, 31, 33, 35, 36, 38, 39, 40, 41, 42, 43b, 45, 46, 47, 48, 49a, 51b, 52, 54, 55, 56, 59b, 61b, 62, 63, 64, 65, 66, 67, 69, 71, 72, 73, 75, 76, 78, 81, 83, 84, 86, 88, 89, 90, 91, 95, 96a, 97, 98a, 99, 100, 102, 104, 106, 107, 108, 109, 111c, 112, 114b, 115, 116, 117, 118b, 119, 120, 121, 122, 123a, 124, 125c, 125d, 126a or 126b, 127a or 127b, 128b, 129, and 130.

Pertinent volumes from John V. Kean's "Catalogue of the Library of the University of Virginia" (May 16, 1825): Nos. 5, 7, 8, 13, 22, 32, 34, 60, 92b, 93, and 114b.

Pertinent volumes from the 1828 *Catalogue:* Nos. 1, 6, 10, 13, 24, 25, 27, 32, 34, 36, 39, 40, 41, 43b, 48, 52, 56, 59b, 60, 61b, 67, 68, 70, 71, 73, 75, 76, 78, 93, 95, 96a, 98b, 100, 102, 104, 114b, 116, 118b, 120, 124, 125d, 127a or 127b, 129, and 130.

Pertinent volumes from the Monticello "great" library, taken from Sowerby: Nos. 4, 6, 11, 12, 14, 15, 16, 18a, 19, 20, 21, 23, 24, 26, 28, 29, 30, 31, 35, 36, 37, 38, 39, 41, 42, 43a, 45, 46, 48, 49b, 50, 53a or 53b, 55, 58, 59a, 61a, 62, 63, 64, 65, 66, 67, 68, 69, 70, 71, 72, 73, 74, 75, 77, 79,

---

to be made to the 1829 sale catalogue, of which a facsimile was issued by the Clements Library in 1944 without annotation.

[30] Books on music, painting, and sculpture in Jefferson's personal library not included in this study are listed in the Appendix.

80, 81, 82, 84, 87, 92a, 92c, 92d, 95, 96b, 97, 99, 101, 103, 105, 107, 108, 109, 110, 111a, 111b, 112, 113, 114a, 116, 117, 118a, 119, 120, 122, 123b, 125d, 127a, 128a, and 129.

Pertinent volumes from the 1829 sale catalogue: Nos. 2, 17, 46, 51a, 57, 77, 83, 85, 123a, 125a or 125b, 126a or 126b, and 127a or 127b.

Pertinent volumes from the manuscript catalogue of Jefferson's library in the Massachusetts Historical Society: Nos. 44 and 94.

Descriptive Catalogue

1. Aberdeen, George Hamilton Gordon, 4th earl of.

AN / INQUIRY / INTO THE / PRINCIPLES OF BEAUTY / IN / GRECIAN ARCHITECTURE; / WITH / AN HISTORICAL VIEW / OF / *THE RISE AND PROGRESS OF THE ART IN / GREECE.* / BY GEORGE, EARL OF ABERDEEN, K. T. &c. / LONDON: / JOHN MURRAY, ALBEMARLE-STREET. / 1822.

8vo. Title page (1 leaf); note (1 leaf); text ([1]–217).

The fourth earl of Aberdeen (1784–1860) was a diplomat, the foreign secretary under the duke of Wellington, and the holder of various other governmental offices. A trip to Greece in 1803 made him an ardent philhellenist, and he became a founder of the Athenian Society.

His *Inquiry into the Principles of Beauty in Grecian Architecture* was first published as an introduction to William Wilkins's translation of *The Civil Architecture of Vitruvius* (London, 1812) and was called there "An Introduction Containing an Historical View of the Rise and Progress of Architecture amongst the Greeks." It was printed separately in London in 1822 and again in 1860 as No. 130 of Weale's series of Rudimentary Works for the Use of Beginners.

The book is not quite as rudimentary as the title of Weale's series might suggest. Aberdeen examines Homer and other literary sources for architectural information and describes surviving monuments, proportions, and the origin of the arch. He sets out to analyze sublimity as follows:

Indeed, as I think in all cases of the moral sublime, it may be justly stated that whatever tends to create ideas of superior energy and force, producing thereby an elevation and expansion of mind, is its real and efficient cause; I am persuaded, also, that in visible objects, all such qualities as are capable of exciting similar sensations must be considered as the only true source of sublimity. Of these qualities in monuments of architecture, magnitude is the principal, and perhaps single one, which is indispensable: but its effect may be much increased by the height of the building, and by the solidity of the materials which compose its mass. Height, it may be said, is only extension in a particular direction; but it produces increased sublimity in architecture, because it most forcibly suggests ideas of great effort, and of great power, as well as of difficulty overcome. The solidity of the materials also, confirms and strengthens the first impressions of admiration suggested by magnitude and height; and, in addition to the sense of original difficulty overcome, gives an appearance of eternal stability to the building. [Pp. 5–7]

Although he notes that Edmund Burke (1729–97) in *The Philosophical Inquiry into the Origin of Our Ideas on the Sublime and the Beautiful* observes "that uniformity and succession of parts, as the great causes of the artificial infinite, tend mainly in architecture to produce sublimity" (p. 9), he is, in actuality, anti-Burke, anti–flowing line, a proponent of angularity, and a supporter of neoclassicism.

His note on the value of the Greek remains is illuminating both for its description of the state of archaeology then and for its condemnation of the copyist:

The precious remains of Grecian art were long neglected, and the most beautiful were, in truth, nearly inaccessible to the Christian world. . . . Henceforth, therefore, these exquisite remains should form the chief study of the architect who aspires to permanent reputation; other modes are transitory and uncertain, but the essential qualities of Grecian excellence, as they are founded on reason, and are consistent with fitness and propriety, will ever continue to deserve his first care. These models should be imitated, however,—not with the timid and servile hand of a copyist; but their beauties should be transferred to our soil, preserving, at the same time, a due regard to the changes of customs and manners, to the difference of our climate, and to the condition of modern society. [Pp. 215–16]

Jefferson ordered the book for the University in the section on "Architecture" of the want list and a copy had been received by 1828. This copy subsequently disappeared, but another has recently been acquired, the gift of the Thomas Jefferson Memorial Foundation.

U. Va.
*NA270.A2.1822

2. Adam, Alexander.

ROMAN ANTIQUITIES: / OR, AN / ACCOUNT / OF THE / MANNERS AND CUSTOMS / OF THE / ROMANS; / RESPECTING THEIR / GOVERNMENT, MAGISTRACY, LAWS, JUDI-

CIAL PROCEEDINGS, RELIGION, GAMES, / MILITARY AND NAVAL AFFAIRS, DRESS, EXERCISE, BATHS, MARRIAGES, DI- / VORCES, FUNERALS, WEIGHTS AND MEASURES, COINS, METHOD OF WRITING, / HOUSES, GARDENS, AGRICULTURE, CARRIAGES, PUBLIC BUILDINGS, &C. &C. / DESIGNED CHIEFLY / TO ILLUSTRATE THE / LATIN CLASSICS, / BY EXPLAINING WORDS AND PHRASES, FROM THE RITES AND / CUSTOMS TO WHICH THEY REFER. / BY ALEXANDER ADAM, LL. D. / RECTOR OF THE HIGH SCHOOL OF EDINBURGH. / RE-VISED, CORRECTED, AND ILLUSTRATED WITH NOTES AND ADDITIONS, / BY P. WILSON, LL. D. / PROFESSOR OF LANGUAGES IN COLUMBIA COLLEGE. / *NEW-YORK:* / PRINTED BY WILLIAM A. MERCEIN, NO. 93 GOLD-STREET, / For Kirk & Mercein, W. B. Gilley, C. Wiley & Co. John Sayre, Scott & Seguine, John Tie-/bout, L. & F. Lockwood, E. Bliss, Samuel Campbell & Son, A. T. Goodrich & Co. G. A. / Banks, New-York, and Cushing & Jewett, and F. Lucas, jun. Baltimore. / Sept. 1819.

8vo. Title page ([i]); preface to first ed. ([iii]-vii); note to 2d ed. (viii); table of contents ([ix]-xii); (1–16 skipped); text ([17]–548); Latin index (549–56); index of proper names and things (557–65).

Title page inscribed: 'S. A. Elliot's – 1829 – Bought at the sale of Mr. Jefferson's library.'

Alexander Adam (1741–1809) was the son of a farmer. He learned Latin at the parish school, then went to Edinburgh where he attended lectures at the university and at nineteen became the headmaster of Watson's Hospital. He later was the tutor to the family of a Mr. Kincaid, and finally rector of the High School. Lord Cockburn said of him, "He was born to teach Latin, some Greek, and all virtue."

He was paid £600 for *Roman Antiquities*, which was first published in 1791 and subsequently went into several editions, being issued both in England and in America. Although its architectural passages are minor, it does treat, in descriptions taken from Roman literature, of libraries (pp. 492–93), houses (pp. 493–96, 499–503), villas and gardens (pp. 504–6), and public buildings (pp. 543–47).

A sample description follows:

2. The PANTHEON, built by Agrippa, son-in-law to Augustus, and dedicated to Jupiter Ultor, *Plin.* xxxvi. 15. or to Mars and Venus, *Dio.* liii. 27. or, as its name imports, to all the gods, *see p.* 309.[1] repaired by Adrian, *Spartian.* 19. consecrated by Pope Boniface IV. to the Virgin Mary, and All Saints, A.D.

---

[1] The note on p. 309 of Adam says: "A temple built by Agrippa in the time of Augustus, and dedicated to all the gods, was called *Pantheon*, Dio. liii. 27."

607. now called the *Rotunda*, from its round figure, said to be 150 feet high, and of about the same breadth. The roof is curiously vaulted, void spaces being left here and there for the greater strength. It has no windows, but only an opening in the top for the admission of light, of about 25 feet diameter. The walls in the inside are either solid marble or incrusted. The front on the outside was covered with brazen plates gilt, the top with silver-plates, but now it is covered with lead. The gate was of brass of extraordinary work and size. They used to ascend it by twelve steps, but now they go down as many; the earth around being so much raised by the demolition of houses. [P. 535]

Laid in the University of Virginia's copy is a letter, dated February 24, 1950, from E. Millicent Sowerby:

On June 8, 1821 Jefferson wrote a letter to his kinsman and agent, Captain Bernard Peyton, and on the polygraph copy retained by himself added a note:

June 25. wrote to him for Adam's Roman antiquities & Valpy's Gr. grammar, to come by mail.

Three days later, on June 28 (received by Jefferson at Monticello on July 2) Peyton wrote from Richmond:

I send herewith, agreeable to your request, Adam's Roaman [sic] Antiquities & Valpy's Greek Grammar, both of which I wish safe to hand.

. . . The book, as you know was lot no. 60 at the sale in 1829.

The originals of the above letter and note are in the Coolidge Collection in the MHS.

"The book" refers to the specific copy of the book now in the library. Thus, although the University has Jefferson's own copy of Adam (see Plate I), acquired in recent years by the McGregor Library, there is no record that the copy he ordered for it, in the section on "History-Civil-Antient" of the want list, was ever received. Since Jefferson ordered his copy during June 1821 and his drawings for the Rotunda were approved by the Board of Visitors on April 2, 1821, the book cannot have had any influence on the design of the University.[2]

U. Va.   M
*A1819.A332

3. Adam, Robert.

RVINS OF THE PALACE / OF THE EMPEROR DIOCLETIAN / AT SPALATRO IN DALMATIA / BY R. ADAM F.R.S. F.S.A. /

[2] William B. O'Neal, *Jefferson's Buildings at the University of Virginia: The Rotunda* (Charlottesville: University of Virginia Press, 1960), p. 20.

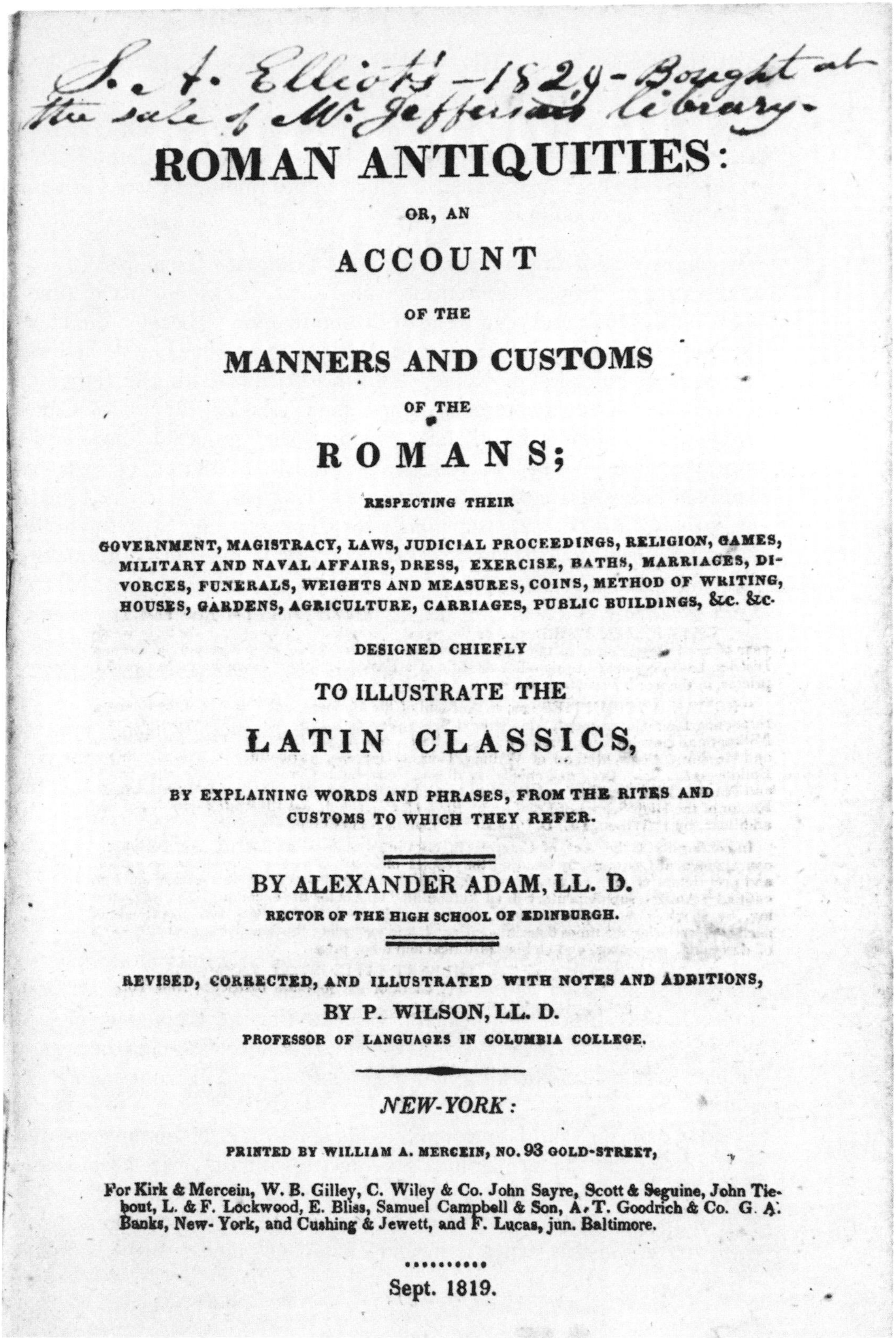

S. A. Elliot's — 1829 — Bought at the sale of Mr. Jefferson's library —

ROMAN ANTIQUITIES:

OR, AN

ACCOUNT

OF THE

MANNERS AND CUSTOMS

OF THE

ROMANS;

RESPECTING THEIR

GOVERNMENT, MAGISTRACY, LAWS, JUDICIAL PROCEEDINGS, RELIGION, GAMES, MILITARY AND NAVAL AFFAIRS, DRESS, EXERCISE, BATHS, MARRIAGES, DIVORCES, FUNERALS, WEIGHTS AND MEASURES, COINS, METHOD OF WRITING, HOUSES, GARDENS, AGRICULTURE, CARRIAGES, PUBLIC BUILDINGS, &c. &c.

DESIGNED CHIEFLY

TO ILLUSTRATE THE

LATIN CLASSICS,

BY EXPLAINING WORDS AND PHRASES, FROM THE RITES AND CUSTOMS TO WHICH THEY REFER.

BY ALEXANDER ADAM, LL. D.

RECTOR OF THE HIGH SCHOOL OF EDINBURGH.

REVISED, CORRECTED, AND ILLUSTRATED WITH NOTES AND ADDITIONS,

BY P. WILSON, LL. D.

PROFESSOR OF LANGUAGES IN COLUMBIA COLLEGE.

NEW-YORK:

PRINTED BY WILLIAM A. MERCEIN, NO. 93 GOLD-STREET,

For Kirk & Mercein, W. B. Gilley, C. Wiley & Co. John Sayre, Scott & Seguine, John Tiebout, L. & F. Lockwood, E. Bliss, Samuel Campbell & Son, A. T. Goodrich & Co. G. A. Banks, New-York, and Cushing & Jewett, and F. Lucas, jun. Baltimore.

....

Sept. 1819.

Plate I. *From No. 2.* Title page. Copy originally owned by Jefferson.

ARCHITECT TO THE KING / AND TO THE QUEEN / PRINTED FOR A. MILLAR / MDCCLXIIII

Folio. Title page ([i]); dedication ([iii]-iv); list of subscribers (4 leaves); introduction ([1]-4); text ([5]-17); explanation of plates ([19]-33); 60 engraved plates, of which 11 are folding (Plate I of a total of 61 plates is missing).

The engravers for this notable work were Francesco Bartolozzi (1725 or 1727–1813 or 1815), a Florentine who came to England just in time to work on the book and who went to Lisbon in 1802 to become director of the National Academy there; James Basire (1730–1802), who had studied with Dalton and in Rome, and who became both the father and grandfather of engravers also named James Basire; Domenico Cunego (1727–94), Italian, who, though a painter, distinguished himself as an engraver; Peter Mazell (fl.1761–97), English; F. Patton (fl.1754–64), English; Edward Rooker (*ca.* 1712–74), English, who worked on several architectural books, particularly for Chambers and Stuart as well as Adam; P. Santini; Anthony Walker (1726–65), one of a family of Scottish engravers who settled in London, Anthony studying at St. Martin's Lane Academy and working largely for Boydell; and Zucchi, a member of an Italian family of engravers which originated in Venice, flourished during both the seventeenth and eighteenth centuries, and worked in many Italian and foreign centers.

The professionals among the subscribers include four architects, three booksellers, two carpenters, a carver, the Clerk of the Signet, fourteen doctors, eight ecclesiastics, an engineer, two merchants, six painters, two printers, and two statuaries. Charles-Louis Clérisseau, Adam's assistant; Adam's three brothers, John, James, and William; Giovanni Battista Piranesi; James Dawkins; Thomas Whatley; and Joshua Kirby, the "Designer in Perspective to his Majesty," all appear on the list. But also included is a "Major General Julius Caesar"!

Robert Adam (1728–92) was not only an architect himself but the son of the architect William Adam and the brother of the architects John, James, and William Adam. Educated at the University of Edinburgh, he went to Italy in 1754. On his return to England he was appointed architect to the king and queen and in 1762 became both F.R.S. and F.S.A.

He describes in his introduction his entourage for his investigations at Spalatro, the modern Split: "Having prevailed on Mr. Clerisseau, a French artist, from whose taste and knowledge of antiquities I was certain of receiving great assistance in the execution of my scheme, to accompany me in this expedition, and having engaged two draughtsmen, of whose skill and accuracy I had long experience, we set sail from Venice on the 11th of July, 1757, and on the 22nd of that month arrived at Spalatro" (p. 2). There is a figure of one of the draughtsmen at work in his Plate XXXIII, the "View of the Inside of the Temple of Jupiter" (see Plate II).

He also gives a description of his methods of work at the palace: "By good fortune its remains are, in many places, so intire, as to be able to fix, with the utmost certainty, the form and dimensions of the principal apartments. The knowledge of these, leads to the discovery of the corresponding parts; and the descriptions given us by Pliny and Vitruvius [1] of the Roman villas, enable us to assign each apartment its proper name, and to discover its use" (p. 7). This literary method was followed by other authors, notably by the two preceding and Robert Castell (No. 21).

The *DNB* article on Adam says that the *Ruins of the Palace of Diocletian* was published "because of its residential character, classical architecture being studied in England exclusively from the remains of public buildings." That this was a desirable procedure is corroborated by Adam when he says:

THE buildings of the Ancients are in Architecture, what the works of Nature are with respect to the other Arts; they serve as models which we should imitate, and as standards by which we ought to judge: for this reason, they who aim at eminence, either in the knowledge or in the practice of Architecture, find it necessary to view with their own eyes the works of the Ancients which remain, that they may catch from them those ideas of grandeur and beauty, which nothing, perhaps, but such an observation can suggest. [P. 1]

The *Ruins of the Palace of Diocletian* has also been called "a work of incalculable importance in the development of the European neoclassical movement." [2]

Although Jefferson himself did not own a copy of this book, he may very well have known it from the time of his stay in France where he, too, worked with Charles-Louis Clérisseau (No. 29). In any case Adam's "General Plan of the Palace restored" (see Plate III) would have been to his liking with its many octagonal forms.

Jefferson ordered the *Spalatro* for the University in the section on "Architecture" of the want list, but there is no record of its having been

---

[1] The references to Pliny and Vitruvius are noted as: "Plinius Junior, L. 2. Ep. 17; & L. S. Ep. 6." and "Vitruvius, L. 6."

[2] *A Catalogue of a Collection of Illustrated Books and Volumes of Prints, mostly of the Eighteenth Century* (London: Sotheby Parke Bernet and Co., 1975), p. 99.

Plate II. *From No. 3.* "View of the Inside of the Temple of Jupiter" in Diocletian's Palace (Pl. XXXIII).

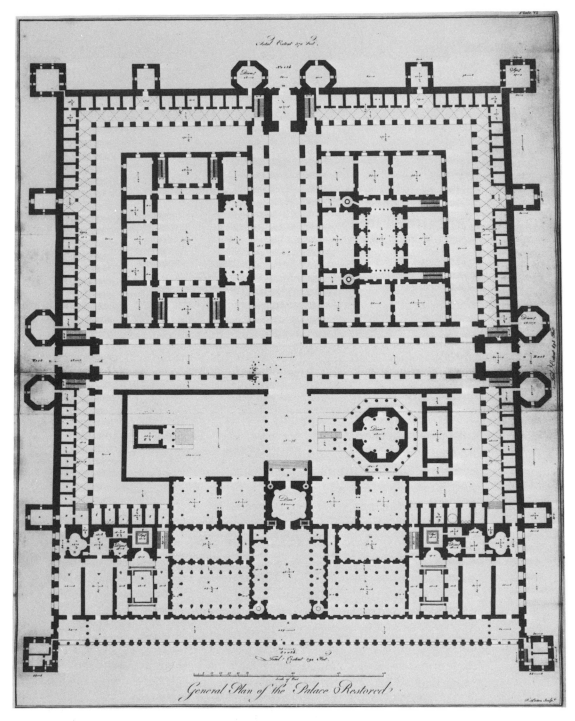

Plate III. *From No. 3.* "General Plan of the Palace [of Diocletian] Restored" (Pl. VI).

received during his lifetime. The library's present copy was acquired during this century.

U. Va.
*NA320.A3.1764

4. Alberti, Leon Battista.

L'ARCHITETTVRA / DI   LEONBATTISTA / ALBERTI / TRA-DOTTA IN LINGVA / Fiorentina da Cosimo Bartoli, / Gentilhuomo, & Academico / Fiorentino. / Con la aggiunta di Disegni. / IN VENETIA, *Appresso Francesco Franceschi*, Sanese. 1565.

Small 4to. Title page (1 unnumbered p.); woodcut portrait (1 unnumbered p.); dedication (1 leaf); poem ([1–2]); 2d dedication ([3]–4); Alberti's preface (5–8); text, with 48 woodcut plates, of which 1 is folding, all in numbered pagination, and with 35 additional woodcut figures (9–404); index (14 unnumbered leaves).

Leon Battista Alberti (1404–72) was born in Genoa. He wrote easily in Latin, was considered a fine organist, and was the author of *Della statua*, *De Pictura*, and *De re aedificatoria*. His importance, not only in the fifteenth century but also in the following centuries, may be partially measured by the fact that all his books went into many editions, while the *De re aedificatoria*, one of the monuments of architectural literature, was translated into Italian, English, French, Spanish, and German.[1] It was first printed by Alemanus in Florence in 1485. This translation into Italian by Cosimo Bartoli (ca.1503–ca.1572), an Italian architect and scholar, was first published in 1550.

There are two illustrations in the book which may have had some influence on Jefferson. The first is an arcade which, in its simple form, may have helped to suggest the simplicities of the arcades on the Ranges at the University of Virginia (see Plate IV), though the book was no longer in Jefferson's hands at the time he designed them. The second, taken from Book VII, whose title may be translated as "On Ornaments of Sacred Temples," would have reinforced Jefferson's argument with

[1] See John Bennett Schwartzman, *Leon Battista Alberti: A Bibliography* (Charlottesville, Va.: American Association of Architectural Bibliographers, 1962).

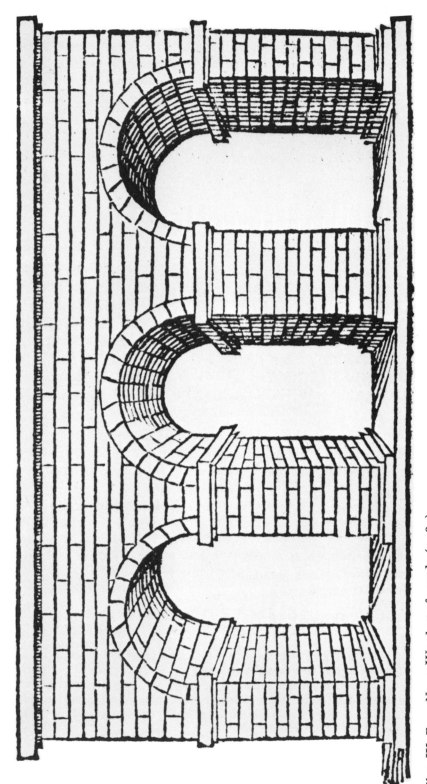

Plate IV. *From No. 4.* Woodcut of arcade (p. 67).

his ornamentist, William Coffee, about the appropriateness of ornament in domestic and public use (see Plate V).[2]

Sowerby points out that Jefferson paid "4." (dollars?) for his own copy, which Kimball says was purchased between 1785 and 1789 (p. 92). That copy was sold to Congress. The book was not ordered for the University. The present copy in the library is the gift of the Thomas Jefferson Memorial Foundation.

M

*NA2515.A33.1565

Sowerby 4199

5. Aldrich, Henry.

THE / ELEMENTS / OF / CIVIL ARCHITECTURE, / ACCORDING TO / Vitruvius and other Ancients, / AND THE / MOST APPROVED PRACTICE OF MODERN AUTHORS, / ESPECIALLY PALLADIO. / BY HENRY ALDRICH, D. D. / FORMERLY DEAN OF CHRIST CHURCH. / TRANSLATED BY / THE REV. PHILIP SMYTH, LL. B. / FELLOW OF NEW COLLEGE. / SECOND EDITION. / OXFORD, / *PRINTED BY W. BAXTER*, / FOR J. PARKER: / MESSRS. PAYNE AND FOSS, PALL MALL; AND MESSRS. LAW AND / WHITTAKER, AVE MARIA LANE, LONDON. / 1818.

8vo. Engraved portrait ([ii]); title page ([iii]); preface to 2d ed. ([v]-vi); note ([vii]-viii); introduction by Philip Smyth (1–75); First Part of text ([77]–124); Second Part of text (125–51); 55 engraved plates.

Inscribed on page v: 'University Library / June 1840 / John Beaford / London.'

Of Henry Aldrich (1647–1710), who was born at Westminster and educated at Westminster School and Christ Church, Oxford, his translator says in his introduction:

The Author of the ensuing Elements died Dean of Christ Church in 1710. . . . [In Italy] he became impassioned for Architecture and Music. . . .

[2] Jefferson, Monticello, to Coffee, July 10, 1822 (Coolidge Collection, MHS): "You are right in what you have thought and done as to the Metops of our Doric pavilion. Those of the baths of Diocletian are all human faces, and so are to be those of our Doric pavilion. But in my middle room at Poplar Forest, I mean to mix the faces and ox-sculls, a fancy which I can indulge in my own case, altho in a public work I feel bound to follow authority strictly."

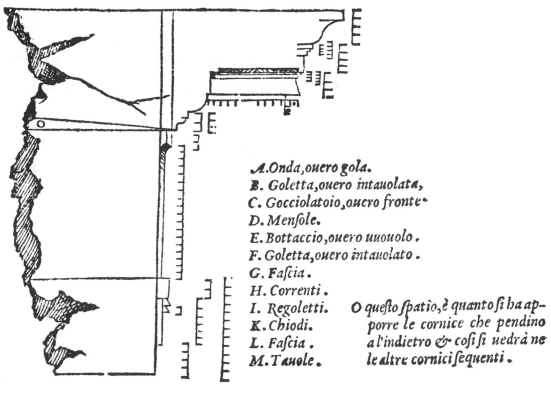

A. Onda, ouero gola.
B. Goletta, ouero intauolata,
C. Gocciolatoio, ouero fronte.
D. Mensole.
E. Bottaccio, ouero uuouolo.
F. Goletta, ouero intauolato.
G. Fascia.
H. Correnti.
I. Regoletti.
K. Chiodi.
L. Fascia.
M. Tauole.

O questo spatio, è quanto si ha apporre le cornice che pendino al'indietro & cosi si uedrà ne le altre cornici sequenti.

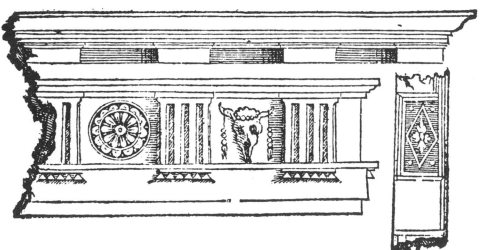

Plate V. *From No. 4.* Woodcut of an entablature (p. 228).

That the impression was not merely local and momentary, his executed designs [1] in the one, and his yet daily recited compositions [2] in the other, would enable his historian to prove . . . the suavity of his manners, the hilarity of his conversation, the variety and excellence of his talents, in conjunction with a fine person, conciliated and attached all committed to his superintendence to such a degree, that his latest surviving disciples, of the first rank, have been seen unable to speak, recollectedly, of their intercourse with him, without the tenderest indications of affection to his memory . . . in favour of the few, whose happier fortunes permit them to join elegant with solid information, he compiled the rudiments of Architecture now offered to the public. [Pp. 73–74]

Aldrich says that he wrote for students who might follow "this study from particular inclination . . . and [I] shall so explain to him the language and most approved precepts of Architecture, that he may either rest satisfied with my instructions, to be able by his own application to study my omissions" (p. 78).

Aldrich's original scheme was for the volume to be divided into two parts, each having three books: "The first book will contain general rules: the second will speak of public and private edifices: the third of the ornaments of building; the fourth will describe fortification: the fifth naval Architecture: the sixth instruments of war" (p. 78). In this edition, however, only the first two books were printed. They are as described above, the first part basing its rules on the tripartite admonition for utility, strength, and beauty and the second part expanded to include descriptions of those buildings illustrated, among which are some by Bramante, Raphael, Romano, Peruzzi, Palladio, and Vignola.

A copy of this book was presented by Joseph Coolidge to Jefferson for the library at the University, as listed in the Kean catalogue; it disappeared, however, and was replaced in 1840 by the present volume.

U. Va.
*NA2515.A4.1818

6. Arteaga, Esteban.

Vol. I. *LE RIVOLUZIONI* / DEL / TEATRO MUSICALE / ITALIANO / DALLA SUA ORIGINE FINO AL PRESENTE / *OPERA*

---

[1] Aldrich note: "The Peckwater Quadrangle at Christ Church, the Church and beautiful Campanile of All Saints in Oxford, are of the number, and, most probably, Trinity Chapel. See Mr. Warton's Life of Dr. Bathurst, p. 71."

[2] Aldrich note: "Those of the devotional kind are still current in all our best choirs."

/ DI STEFANO ARTEAGA / MADRIDENSE / TOMO PRIMO. / *Il faut se rendre a ce Palais magique,* / *Ou les beaux vers, la dance, la musique,* / *L'art de tromper les yeux par les couleurs,* / *L'art plus heureux de seduire les coeurs,* / *De cent plaisirs font un plaisir unique.* / BOLOGNA MDCCLXXXIII / Per la Stamperìa di Carlo Trenti all' Insegna / di Sant' Antonio. / *Con licenza de' Superiori.*

Small 8vo. Title page ([i]); dedication (iii-x); note (xi); table of contents (xii-xiv); license (1 leaf); text (1–411); errata (1 leaf).

Vol. II. *LE RIVOLUZIONI* / . . . / MADRIDENSE / TOMO SECONDO. / BOLOGNA MDCCLXXXV. / . . .

Small 8vo. Title page ([iii]); dedication (v-xii); table of contents (xiii-xiv); license (1 leaf); text (1–207).

Vol. III. *LE RIVOLUZIONI* / . . . / MADRIDENSE / TERZO ED ULTIMO TOMO / Arricchito delle Repliche fatte alle / Osservazioni dell' Autore intorno / ad un' Estratto del Tomo II. / BOLOGNA MDCCLXXXVIII / . . . .

Small 8vo. Title page ([iii]); dedication (v-ix); note (x-xii); errata (xiv); imprimatur (unnumbered p.); half title (1 leaf); folded leaf of music; text ([1]–216).

Esteban Arteaga (1747–99), a Spanish Jesuit, emigrated to Italy on the suppression of his order. He went later to Paris where he died. He wrote, in addition to the *Rivoluzioni*, the *Investigaciones filosoficas sobre la belleza ideal* (Madrid, 1789) and *Dell' influenza degli Arabi sull' origine della poesia moderna in Europa* (Rome, 1791).

The first edition of the *Rivoluzioni* was issued in 1783 in two volumes. It was later expanded into three, and letters on the subject by François Arnaud (1721–84) and Vicenzo Manfredini (1737–99) were included. The first volume discusses such subjects as the nature of musical drama, the origins of sacred music, profane music, opera seria, and opera buffo, the progress of melody, and the introduction of eunuchs into music, as well as giving a survey of the Italian musical scene. The second volume discusses the decadence of Italian opera, the causes lying in the vanity and ignorance of the singers and the abandonment of musical poetry. The third volume is a continuation of the discussion in Vol. II and includes letters from Arnaud and Manfredini. The entire work has been called an acute and diligent book.

Jefferson owned and sold to Congress the three-volume edition of Arteaga which was published in Venice in 1785, but the date of purchase is not known. He ordered all three volumes for the University, in the section on "Gardening. Painting. Sculpture. Music" of the want list, but only two were received and these have not survived. The library's present set, with the volumes dated 1783, 1785, and 1788, is a recent acquisition, the gift of the Thomas Jefferson Memorial Foundation.

U. Va.   M
*ML1733.3.A7.1783   Sowerby 4256

7. Atwood, George.

A / DISSERTATION / ON THE / CONSTRUCTION AND PROPERTIES / OF / ARCHES. / BY / G. ATWOOD, ESQ. F.R.S. / LONDON: / PRINTED BY W. BULMER AND CO. / CLEVELAND-ROW, ST. JAMES'S. / FOR LUNN, OXFORD-STREET, AND EGERTON, WHITEHALL. / 1801.

4to. Title page ([i]); preface ([iii]-viii); text ([1]–51); 6 folding engraved plates (Plate VI, of a total of 7 plates, is missing).

George Atwood (1746–1807), a mathematician, was educated at Westminster and Trinity College, Oxford.

He gives a clear account of the geometrical and trigonometrical approach to his book and an equally clear account of the bases on which the book is grounded:

An arch being formed (according to the usual modes of construction) by the apposition of wedges, or sections of a wedge-like form, the properties of arches seem to be naturally derived from those of the wedge, on which principle the inquiries in the ensuing Tract are founded.

By considering the subject on this ground, it appears that the theory of arches may be inferred from geometrical construction, depending only on the known properties of the wedge and other elementary laws of mechanics, without having recourse to the more abstruse branches of geometry in explaining this practical subject, to which a more direct and obvious method of inference seems better adapted. [P. iii]

In the course of this inquiry, exclusive of the general principles which have been here described, sundry other properties are investigated, which, it is presumed, may be of use in the practice of architecture, in the construction of arches of every kind, as well as in explaining some particulars relating to the subject, which have not hitherto been accounted for in a satisfactory manner. [P. v]

The object of the ensuing tract appears to consist principally in the solutions of two statical problems, which may be briefly expressed in the following terms: 1st, from having given the angles contained by the sides of the wedges which form an arch, together with the weight of the highest or middle section, to infer the weights of the other sections; and conversely, from the weights of each wedge given, together with the angle of the first section, to determine the angles between the sides of the other sections, so as to form an arch perfectly balanced in all its parts. [P. 5]

In 1804 a supplement was "written at the request of a committee of the House of Commons, then engaged in considering Telford's plan for replacing London Bridge with a one-arched iron construction" (*DNB*).

The copy now in the library lacks the 1804 supplement, as apparently did the copy received by Jefferson for the University, as shown in the Kean catalogue.

U. Va.
*TG327.A88.1801

8. Baldinucci, Filippo.

Vol. I. COMINCIAMENTO / E / PROGRESSO / DELL' ARTE DELL' INTAGLIARE IN RAME / COLLE VITE / Di molti de'più eccellenti Maestri / della stessa Professione / *OPERA* / DI FILIPPO BALDINUCCI / FIORENTINO / *ACCADEMICO DELLA CRUSCA* / Con Annotazioni / DEL SIG. DOMENICO MARIA MANNI / MILANO / Dalla Società Tipografica DE'CLASSICI ITALIANI, / contrada di s. Margherita, No. 1118. / ANNO 1808.

8vo. Engraved portrait ([iv]); title page ([v]); editor's preface (vii-xii); author's preface (1–14); text (15–268); index (269–87); errata (1 unnumbered p.).

Vol. II. VOCABOLARIO TOSCANO / DELL' ARTE / DEL DISEGNO / DI / FILIPPO BALDINUCCI / FIORENTINO. / VOLUME PRIMO. / MILANO / Dalla Società Tipografica DE'CLASSICI ITALIANI, / contrada di s. Margherita, No. 1118. / ANNO 1809.

8vo. Title page ([3]); dedication (5–8); preface (9–19); text (21–370); errata (1 unnumbered p.).

Vol. III. VOCABOLARIO TOSCANO / . . . / VOLUME SECONDO. / . . .

8vo. Title page ([3]); text (5–255); additions (257–69); lecture (271–319); letter (321–59); errata (1 unnumbered p.).

Vol. IV. NOTIZIE / DE' PROFESSORI DEL DISEGNO / DA CIMABUE IN QUA / *OPERA* / DI FILIPPO BALDINUCCI / FIORENTINO / ACCADEMICO DELLA CRUSCA / CON NOTE ED AGGIUNTE. / MILANO / Dalla Società Tipografica DE'CLASSIGI [*sic*] ITALIANI / contrada dal Cappuccio. / ANNO 1811.

8vo. Title page ([iii]); editor's note (v-viii); dedication (ix-xii); author's note (xiii-xxxii); text (1–541); index (543–82); errata (1 unnumbered p.).

Vol. V. NOTIZIE / . . .

8vo. Title page ([3]); publisher's note (5–9); text (11–528); index (529–45); errata (547).

Vol. VI. NOTIZIE / . . .

8vo. Title page ([3]); note by Giuseppe Piacenza (5–13); text (15–403); index (405–16); errata (1 unnumbered p.).

Vol. VII. NOTIZIE / . . .

8vo. Title page ([3]); text (5–642); index (643–62); errata (663).

Vol. VIII. NOTIZIE / . . .

8vo. Title page ([3]); text (5–570); notes (571); index (573–90); errata (1 unnumbered p.).

Vol. IX. NOTIZIE / . . . / ANNO 1812.

8vo. Title page ([3]); text ([5]–568); index (569–81); errata (583).

Vol. X. NOTIZIE / . . .

8vo. Title page ([3]); text (5–478); index (479–86); errata (487).

Vol. XI. NOTIZIE / . . .

8vo. Title page ([3]); text (5–495); index (497–512); errata (1 unnumbered p.).

Vol. XII. NOTIZIE / . . .

8vo. Title page ([3]); text (5–491); index (493–98); errata (499).

Vol. XIII.   NOTIZIE / . . .

8vo. Title page ([3]); text (5–521); index (523–30); errata (531).

Vol. XIV.   NOTIZIE / . . .

8vo. Title page ([3]); dedication (5–8); text (9–298); index (299–312); errata (1 unnumbered p.).

Filippo Baldinucci (1624–96) was born at Florence. He was a writer on the history of the arts, but he had the fault of attempting to derive all Italian art from the schools of Florence.

This edition is the first collected edition of his works. Volume I treats of the lives of engravers from all countries and contains 157 entries; Vol. II is the first part of a dictionary of the terms used in pictorial design, from Ab to Nu; Vol. III contains the continuation of the dictionary from Ob to Zu, a section of additions from A to V and ends with a lecture Baldinucci gave at the Accademia della Crusca on December 29, 1690, and January 5, 1691; Vols. IV–XIV contain essays on the works of various artists, some few by other authors. These last volumes are not very well arranged, for they are not alphabetical internally or from volume to volume. There are no illustrations in the set beyond the initial portrait.

This is a set that was already in the library in the spring of 1825 when Jefferson was making up his want list.

U. Va.
*N27.B2.1808

9. Barlow, Peter.

An Essay on the Strength and Stress of Timber. 2d ed. London, 1818. Not now owned by the University.

The University only has the third edition of this work, whereas Jefferson presumably ordered the second edition. The third edition (of 1826) contains 6 engraved plates, all folding and dated August 12, 1817, 250 pages of text, and an appendix of 55 pages. Interestingly enough, there are also 26 pages of advertisements.

Peter Barlow (1776–1862), born at Norwich, was largely self-taught. He kept a school, attained a considerable degree of scientific knowledge, and eventually taught at the Royal Military Academy. He was elected F.R.S. in 1823 and was an honorary member of the Cambridge Philosophical Society and the Society of Civil Engineers.

His first book was *An Elementary Investigation of the Theory of Numbers*, 1811; his second *A New Mathematical and Philosophical Dictionary*, 1814; and his third was this book, first issued in 1817. Its second edition was in 1818, the edition of 1826 was the third, and it went into its sixth edition in 1867.

In his text Barlow examines previous theories of strength and stress, experiments most carefully, then sets up new theories based on his experiments. He seems to have been one of the first to pronounce theories of the strength of materials based on sufficient and valid experiments. One should note, too, his early interest in iron as a structural material.

The third edition, with its preface dated January 16, 1826, was issued after Jefferson's list was made up and may well not have been available in this country until after Jefferson's death. Since Jefferson normally wanted the latest edition of a work, it may be assumed that it was the second edition of 1818 which he ordered for the University, in the section on "Technical Arts" of the want list. There is no record of the library's having acquired any edition in Jefferson's lifetime.

U. Va.
[*TA405.B3.1826]

Bartoli, Pietro Santi. *See* La Chausse, Michel Ange de (No. 64).

10. Basan, Pierre François.

DICTIONNAIRE / *DES GRAVEURS* / ANCIENS ET MODERNES / *DEPUIS L'ORIGINE DE LA GRAVEUR;* / AVEC / UNE NOTICE / *DES PRINCIPALES ESTAMPES* / *Qu'ils ont gravées.* / SUIVI / Des Catalogues des OEuvres de Jacques / Jordans, & de Corneille Visscher. / *Par F. BASAN, Graveur.* / PREMIERE PARTIE. / *A PARIS*, / Chez / DE LORMEL, rue de Foin. / SAILLANT, rue S. Jean de Beauvais. / VEUVE DURAND, rue des Noyers. / DURAND NEVEU, rue S. Jacques. / DESSAINT, rue du Foin. / M.DCC.LXVII. / Avec Approbation & Privilege du Roi.

12mo. Half title (1 leaf); title page (1 leaf); note (i-iv); dictionary, 1st part (1–342⁺, since the pagination 245–64 appears twice); [Half title for 2d part missing;] dictionary, 2d part (343–572); supplement (573–92); errata, 1st part (1 leaf); errata, 2d part (1 leaf); [new pagination;] supplement (1–192); index (193–227). (The catalogues are missing.)

Pierre François Basan (1723–97), French, studied under Etienne Fessard and J. Daullé. He was an engraver and a seller of prints and objets d'art. Of his more than 1,200 plates it is said that "la valeur . . . est mediocrement cotée."

He says he will be "trop heureux si les soins que je me suis donné pour parvenir à mon but, peuvent procurer aux Amateurs quelques-unes des connoissances qui sont l'objet de leurs recherches" (pp. ii-iii). He describes the structure of his work: "L'Ouvrage est divisé en deux Volumes, & un toisieme faisant suite & contenant seul le Catalogue de l'OEuvre de P. P. Rubens, d'une édition beaucoup plus ample & plus correct que celui qui en avoit été publié en 1751, par le sieur Hecquet" (p. iv).

The dictionary was first published in 1767, again in a very much more handsome edition in 1789, and finally in 1809.

Jefferson ordered the 1767 edition for the University, in the section on "Gardening. Painting. Sculpture. Music" of the want list, contrary to his usual practice of buying the latest edition. It was in the library by 1828, but it has not survived. The recently acquired copy the gift of the Thomas Jefferson Memorial Foundation, is still missing the catalogues of Jordans and Vischer.

U. Va.
*NE800.B3.1767

11. Becker, Wilhelm Gottlieb.

Neue Garten und Landschafts-Gebaüde. Leipzig: Voss und Cie., 1798–99.
Not now owned by the University.

Sowerby, who had no opportunity to examine a copy, describes the book as a folio volume with four parts and thirty-four plates. She gives the date of purchase by Jefferson for his own library as June 21, 1805, its price as $17.00, and the cost of its binding at $2.00.

Although references to Becker are few, Sowerby says he was a German landscape artist and antiquarian.

Jefferson, in a study of garden pavilions with notes (Kimball, Fig. 164 and N-182), cites the Becker work: "Chinese model. wood   Becker pl. 10-a." The Chinese designs in the book were drawn by the architect Schäffer and included detailed explanations.

Jefferson's French title, "Becker. Plans d'architecture," is not on the book, but that this was the book ordered for the University, in the section on "Architecture" of the want list, seems certain from Jefferson's use of the same title for the copy of the same work that he sold to Congress. No record of its receipt at the library during his lifetime exists.

U. Va.   M

Sowerby 4223

12. Birch, William, and Son.

The / CITY OF PHILADELPHIA, / *in the State of Pennsylvania* / North America; / as it appeared in the Year 1800 / *consisting of TWENTY EIGHT Plates* / Drawn and Engraved by W. BIRCH & SON. / Published by W. Birch, Springfield Cot, near Nethaminy Bridge on the Bristol Road, Pennsylvania. Decr. 31st. 1800.

Folio. Engraved frontispiece (1 leaf); engraved title page (1 leaf); 28 engraved plates; list of subscribers (1 unnumbered p.).

The University owns a microprint copy only.

William Birch (1755–1834) was born in Warwickshire and educated in Bristol and London. In England he exhibited miniatures at the Royal Academy, in 1785 received a medal from the Society of Arts, and published a series of views called *Delices de la Grande Bretagne* (London, 1789). Emigrating to this country in 1794, he worked on the *City of Philadelphia* between 1798 and 1800 and included in it a series of views of the city and of its prominent buildings. He published a view of New York in 1803, issued a series of plates of American country seats in 1808, and executed a number of miniatures.

On the page of subscribers for the *City of Philadelphia* he says:

The price of the Work, in boards, is 28 Dollars; bound, 31 dollars; if coloured, in boards, 41½ Dollars; bound, 44½ Dollars. Also may be had, a large Print of the Frontispiece, 25¼ inches by 21½ engraved in an elegant and bold style, for the purpose of framing: Price 6 Dollars plain, and 9 coloured. A companion to which is now engraving, to be the City of New-York, which will, together compose an elegant pair of Prints of the two principal Cities of North-America.

The list of subscribers includes "Thomas Jefferson, Vice-President of U. States" and "Mr. B. Henry Latrobe, Richmond, Virginia."

Jefferson's own copy was sold to Congress. The work was not ordered for the University.

M
Sowerby 4161

13. Borghini, Raffaello.

Vol. I. IL / RIPOSO / DI / RAFFAELLO BORGHINI. / VOLUME PRIMO. / MILANO / Dalla Società Tipografica DE'CLASSICI ITALIANI, / contrada di s. Margherita, No. 1118. / ANNO 1807.

8vo. Half title ([i]); title page ([iii]); foreword (v-ix); preface by Monsignor Bottari (xi-xxiv); text (1–288); errata (1 unnumbered p.).

Vol. II. IL / RIPOSO / . . . / VOLUME SECONDO. / . . .
8vo. Half title ([1]); title page ([3]); text (5–261); errata and notes (1 leaf).

Vol. III. IL / RIPOSO / . . . / VOLUME TERZO. / . . .
8vo. Half title ([1]); title page ([3]); text (5–234); index (235–58); errata (1 unnumbered p.).

Raffaello Borghini (1541–88) was born in Florence. He wrote comedies such as the *Diana pietosa*, 1585, as well as *Il Riposa*, which was first issued in 1584.

Il Riposo, concerning Italian artists, was partially drawn from Vasari (No. 122) and B. Varchi, but it has, in addition, interesting information on Florentine mannerism. It is a work in four books bound in three volumes, printed partly because of "la squisitezza della lingua," as the publisher says.

Although a set was in the University's library before Jefferson made up his want list and was well identified in the 1828 *Catalogue*, that set did not survive. It has recently been replaced by the present set, the gift of the Thomas Jefferson Memorial Foundation.

U. Va.
*N7420.B7.1807

14. Brusco, Giacomo.

DESCRIPTION / DES BEAUTÉS / DE GENES / ET DE SES EN- VIRONS / Ornée de differentes Vuës, / de tailles douce, et de la Carte / Topographique de la Ville. / *A GENES MDCCLXXXI / CHEZ YVES GRAVIER / Libraire sous la Loge des Banquie.*

12mo. Engraved, folding map; title page (1 leaf); preface (1–2); text, with 20 engraved plates, of which 17 are folding, inserted (3–138); in- dex (139–42); list of plates (1 unnumbered p.).

Fifteen of the folding plates are surprisingly vigorous views of Genoa engraved by Guidotti (see Plate VI), and the other two are maps. The three single-page plates, presumably by another hand, are of Genoese costumes and are more hackneyed than the plates of views. One of the maps is labeled in Italian.

Practically nothing is known of Giacomo Brusco. He wrote this handsome guide with its interesting views of the city and its buildings because "le grand nombre de Morceaux de peinture, de sculpture, & d'architecture, que j'ai vus dans cette superbe Ville, & qui ne sont pas assez connus, m'a fait naître l'idée d'en dresser un mémoire, que je crois devoir rendre public" (p. 1).

Although Jefferson visited Genoa during April 1787, the date of his purchase of this book is not known. His copy was sold to Congress. It was not ordered for the University. The library's present copy is the gift of the Thomas Jefferson Memorial Foundation.

M
*DG632.B7.1781   Sowerby 3910

15. *Builder's Dictionary.*

Vol. I. THE / Builder's Dictionary: / OR, / Gentleman and Archi- tect's / COMPANION. / Explaining not only the / TERMS of ART /

Vue Du Pont Royal : 1. Banc de St George. 2 Port franc.

Plate VI. *From No. 14.* "Vue du Pont Royal" at Genoa.

In all the several / PARTS of ARCHITECTURE, / But also containing the / THEORY and PRACTICE / Of the / Various BRANCHES thereof, requisite to be known by /

MASONS,	PLAISTERERS,	TURNERS,
CARPENTERS,	PAINTERS,	CARVERS,
JOINERS,	GLAIZIERS,	STATUARIES,
BRICKLAYERS,	SMITHS,	PLUMBERS, &C.

Also Necessary Problems in / ARITHMETIC, GEOMETRY, MECHANICS, PERSPECTIVE, / HYDRAULICS, and other MATHEMATICAL SCIENCES. / Together with / The Quantities, Proportions, and Prices of all Kinds of MATERIALS / used in BUILDING; with DIRECTIONS for Chusing, Preparing, / and Using them: The several Proportions of the FIVE ORDERS of / ARCHITECTURE, and all their Members, according to VITRUVIUS, / PALLADIO, SCAMOZZI, VIGNOLA, M. LE CLERC, &c. / With RULES for the Valuation of HOUSES, and the EXPENCE calculated / of Erecting any FABRICK, Great or Small. / The Whole Illustrated with more than Two Hundred FIGURES, many of / them curiously Engraven on COPPER-PLATES: Being a Work of great / Use, not only to ARTIFICERS, but likewise to GENTLEMEN, and others, / concerned in BUILDING, &c. / *Faithfully Digested from the most Approved Writers on these Subjects.* / In TWO VOLUMES. / *LONDON*: / Printed for A. BETTESWORTH and C. HITCH, at the *Red-Lion* in *Pater-noster- / Row;* and S. AUSTEN, at the *Angel* and *Bible* in *St. Paul's Church-Yard.* / M. DCC. XXXIV.

8vo. Engraved frontispiece (1 leaf); title page (1 unnumbered p.); endorsement (1 unnumbered p.); preface (4 leaves); text, with 15 engraved plates inserted, and numerous woodcut figures (242 leaves).

Vol. II.   THE / Builder's Dictionary / . . . / Vol. II / . . .

8vo. Endorsement (1 leaf); title page (1 leaf); text with numerous woodcut figures (see Plate VII) and 18 engraved plates inserted (247 leaves and 1 unnumbered p.); advertisement (1 unnumbered p.); errata (1 unnumbered p.).

The endorsement says:

January 11. 1731/4.
We have perused these Two Volumes of the Builder's Dictionary, *and do think they contain a great deal of useful Knowledge in the Building Business.*
Nicholas Hawksmoor,
John James
James Gibbs.

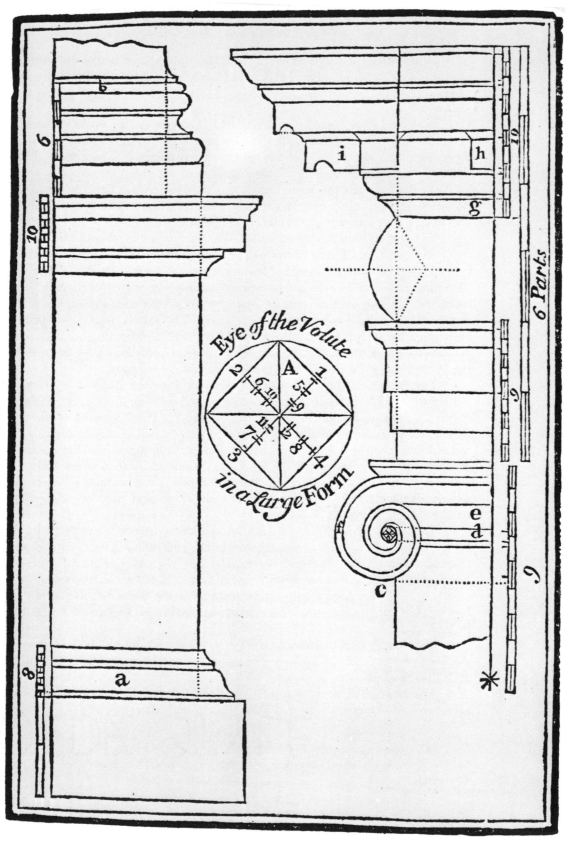

Plate VII. *From No. 15.* "The Proportions of the Ionic Order, by equal Parts" (Vol. II, p. IO).

While the title page describes the contents of the book, the preface contains much sound advice and is certainly worthy of the endorsement of Hawksmoor, James (see No. 37), and Gibbs (Nos. 48, 49a, and 49b):

Architecture is one of those Arts which Necessity has made universal: From the Time that Men first felt the Inclemencies of the Seasons, it had its Beginning; and accordingly it has spread wheresoever the Severities of the Climate demanded Shelter or Shade. . . .

As Distress was the Parent of it, so Convenience was the first Object it regarded: Mangificence and Decoration were the Result of long Refinement, and designed to flatter the Ostentation of the Owners. . . .

'Tis easy to conclude from hence, That *Convenience* should still be the Builder's first View: Every Structure is raised to answer some particular End; and the most obvious and simple Means are always the best to obtain it. . . . Many an excellent Workman has proved himself a mere Mechanick, and many a surprising Genius, that he was ignorant of the very Principles of the Art he made it his Profession to understand. To make a thorough Master, both must be united; for the Propriety of a Plan is seldom attended to, and seldomer understood; and a glaring Pile of beauty, without Use, but mocks the Possessor with a Dream of Grandeur he can never enjoy.

The Design of this DICTIONARY is chiefly, for the Assistance of such, who study the Mechanical Part of Building, and will be of the greatest Service to all Professions that have any Relation to it: The Elements of the Art will be fully explained, and in so regular a Method too, that it can hardly be in the Power even of a Novice to mistake. Neither is it impossible that the most finish'd Artist, or most perfect Critick, should stand in need of its Help: It will serve, at least, as a kind of Remembrancer, or Common Place-Book, where all their Knowledge lies regularly digested, and may be referred to with Ease and Pleasure.

To do this more effectually, all the valuable Authors which have wrote on the Subject have been examin'd, consulted, and reduced into Method and Consistency with each other: We may quote a great Variety of eminent Names; but as *Le Clerc* has been referred to the most, we shall content ourselves with his Authority only, and recommend the Steps he, in particular, has pointed out,[1] as the surest Methods to attain to any Degree of Perfection in this Art. . . .

But though Genius cannot be learn'd, it may be improv'd: And though the Gift of *Designing* is born with a Man, it may be methodized by Study and Observation.

The principal Points, therefore, that the *Designer* should have in view, are first Convenience, . . . and then Beauty and Magnificence. . . .

---

[1] The steps pointed out are arithmetic, geometry, masonry, leveling, hydraulics, mechanics, sketching, drawing, and the "Science of Designing." See Le Clerc (No. 69).

SIMPLICITY is generally understood to be the Groundwork of Beauty, and Decoration of Magnificence.

Entries in the *Dictionary* often run to several pages, as in the case of that for Water, which is thirty-eight pages long, or sometimes are comparatively simple, as follows:

RULE of THREE
RULE of PROPORTION
commonly call'd the GOLDEN RULE is a Rule which teaches how to find a fourth Proportional Number to three others given.

Sowerby points out that Kimball (on p. 134) proves that Jefferson used this book before 1771. Jefferson sold his own copy to Congress and then ordered this book for the University in the section on "Architecture" of the want list. Though not directly associated with Jefferson, the library's present copy is from the books of Joseph C. Cabell, one of the original Visitors of the University, and is thus intimately associated with the beginnings of the University.

U. Va. M
*NA 31.B82.1734 Sowerby 4187

16. *Builder's Price Book.*

The Builder's Price-Book. . . . 5th ed., corrected. London, 1788.

The University does not own the fifth edition of this book but has recently acquired a copy of the sixth edition.

THE / BUILDER'S / *PRICE-BOOK;* / CONTAINING / A CORRECT LIST OF THE PRICES / ALLOWED BY THE MOST EMINENT / SURVEYORS IN LONDON, / TO THE SEVERAL / ARTIFICERS CONCERNED IN BUILDING; / INCLUDING / THE JOURNEYMEN'S PRICES. / THE SIXTH EDITION, / CORRECTED. / BY AN *EXPERIENCED SURVEYOR.* / LONDON: / Printed for I. and J. TAYLOR, at the Architectural Library, / No. 56, opposite Great Turnstile, Holborn. / MDCCLXXXVIII.

Small 8vo. Title page (1 leaf); foreword (1 unnumbered p.); table of contents (1 unnumbered p.); text ([1]–176); [new pagination:] catalogue of books ([1]–8).

Although Sowerby had no copy of the fifth edition for examination, she describes it as a small quarto of eighty-three leaves; as having been entered in Jefferson's undated manuscript catalogue with no price, as having been bound for Jefferson during August 1805, and as having been printed for I. and J. Taylor. Its original price was 2.6. sewed.

The editor says of his book in his foreword to the sixth edition:

The increased reputation which each impression of this work has experienced, particularly the last, (the whole being sold within a few months) tends more to evince its real utility, than any words possibly can; at the same time, it affords the most pleasing reflection to the Proprietors, that the attention paid to the addition of new articles, the correcting of old ones, and carefully examining every reprinting, has been rewarded with the satisfaction of the Public.

It is hoped, the favourable opinions already obtained, will at least be continued, if not increased, by the present corrected edition.

Prices are for units of work for blacksmiths, bricklayers, carpenters, carvers, gilders, glaziers, joiners, masons, painters, pavers, "Plaisterers," plumbers, sawyers, and slaters. These are given in a series of tables with the prices for the work, at various levels of skill, for each trade.

The catalogue of books at the end of the sixth edition ("Catalogue of Modern Books on Architecture, &c.") lists fifty-nine titles from the Architectural Library at No. 56, Holborn.

Jefferson's copy of the fifth edition was sold to Congress. The book was not ordered for the University.

[*TH435.B82.1788]

M
Sowerby 1181

17. *Builders' Prices.*

Builders' Prices, Philadelphia, Washington, and Pittsburgh. [Philadelphia?, *ca.*1815–26.]
Not now owned by the University.

The secrecy which surrounded price books and their destruction through use in computing their owners' estimates make them some of the most difficult of books to find. Their use, however, was widespread. In a letter of January 26, 1819, now in the University collection, from Alexander Garrett to Jefferson, it is stated, for example, that James Dinsmore agreed to work by Latrobe's price book.

This title, otherwise identified only as an octavo, is from the 1829 sale catalogue, lot 243, and was in Jefferson's library at the time of his death. It was not ordered for the University.

M

18a. Burney, Charles.

THE / PRESENT STATE / OF / MUSIC / IN / FRANCE and ITALY: / OR, / The JOURNAL of a TOUR through those / Countries, undertaken to collect Materials for / A GENERAL HISTORY OF MUSIC. / By CHARLES BURNEY, Mus D. / Ei cantarono allor si dolcemente, / Che la dolcezza ancor dentro mi suona. / DANTE, Purg. Canto 2do. / LONDON, / Printed for T. BECKET and Co. in the Strand. / MDCCLXXI.

8vo. Title page (i); explication of some musical terms, etc. (iii-vii); introduction (1–8); text (9–369); index (5 leaves); advertisement (1 unnumbered p.); errata (1 unnumbered p.).

Charles Burney (1726–1814) grew up at Shrewsbury under the care of an old nurse. He was later educated at the free school in Chester, then studied music with his elder brother James at Shrewsbury. In London he continued his musical studies under Arne. He later became a well-known London figure, a critic and composer, and a lively and busy man. He was elected F.R.S. in 1773.

He began his journey to Italy "in the beginning of June 1770." In his introduction he states most clearly the reasons for writing his book:

Among the numerous accounts of Italy, published by travelers who have visited that delightful country, from different motives of interest or curiosity; it is somewhat exraordinary [*sic*] that none have hitherto confined their views and researches to the rise and progress, or present state of music in that part of the world, where it has been cultivated with such success. [P. 1]

In hopes, therefore, of stamping on my intended history some marks of originality, or at least of novelty, I determined to allay my thirst of knowledge at the source, and take such draughts in Italy, as England cannot supply. It was there I determined to hear with my *own* ears, and to see with my *own* eyes; and, if possible, to *hear* and *see* nothing but *music*. [Pp. 6–7]

Dr. Burney describes his musical experiences under the headings of the various localities where they occurred and in the order of his arrival at the various towns.

Sowerby points out that Jefferson met Burney in London and, in 1786, asked him to supervise the making of a harpsichord ("mahogany, solid not veneered, without any inlaid work"). Burney was delighted to execute the commission, and Jefferson, in thanking him, spoke of "the reading of your account of the state of music in Europe" (Sowerby 4254).

Jefferson ordered the work for the University, in the section on "Gardening. Painting. Sculpture. Music" of the want list, without specifying whether he wanted this edition or a second one, of 1773 (No. 18b). Although neither edition was received, it may be presumed that he would have preferred that of 1773. Nevertheless it was a copy of the 1771 edition, the first, that he sold to Congress.

The library's present copies of both editions are in the Mackay-Smith Collection.

U. Va.?   M
*ML195.B96.1771   Sowerby 4253

18b. Burney, Charles.

THE / PRESENT STATE / OF / MUSIC / . . . / THE SECOND EDITION, CORRECTED. / . . . / Printed for T. Becket and Co. Strand; J. Robson, New Bond-Street, and G. Robinson, Paternoster-Row, 1773.

8vo. Advertisements (i-ii); title page (iii); explication of some musical terms, etc. (v-viii); introduction (1–8); text (9–409); index, with errata at bottom of last page (5 leaves).

For information about Charles Burney and general information about the book, see No. 18a. This, the second edition, seems to have been reset and is slightly expanded from the first. The original errata have been corrected, but some new ones have crept in.

U. Va.?
*ML195.B96.1773

19. Burney, Charles.

Vol. I. THE / PRESENT STATE / OF / MUSIC / IN / GERMANY, / THE NETHERLANDS, / AND / UNITED PROVINCES.

/ OR, / The JOURNAL of a TOUR through those / Countries, undertaken to collect Materials for / A GENERAL HISTORY OF MUSIC. / By CHARLES BURNEY, Mus. D. F.R.S. / IN TWO VOLUMES. / VOL. I. / Auf Virtuosen sen stolz, Germanien, die du gezeuget; / In Frankreich und Welschland sind grosere nicht. / Zacharia. / THE SECOND EDITION CORRECTED. / LONDON, / Printed for T. Becket, Strand; J. Robson, New Bond-/Street; and G. Robinson, Paternoster-Row. 1775.

8vo. Title page (i); introduction (iii-viii); text (1–372); index (373–80).

Vol. II. THE / PRESENT STATE / OF / MUSIC / IN / GERMANY, / . . . / VOL. II / . . .

8vo. Title page (1 leaf); advertisement (1 unnumbered p.); proposals for printing by subscription a general history of music (1 unnumbered p.); text (1–344); index (345–52).

For information about Dr. Burney and his relationship with Jefferson, see No. 18a.

This present work was written almost as a continuation of the preceding volume. Burney says,

as I have, in a late publication, endeavored to do justice to the talents and attainments of the present musicians of France and Italy, I shall now make the same attempt, with respect to those of Germany, hoping that the testimony of one who has himself been witness of the particulars he relates, will have a weight which integrity itself cannot give to hear-say evidence, and that the mind of the reader will be more entertained, in proportion as it is more satisfied of the truth of what is written. For if *knowledge* be *medicine for the soul*, according to the famous inscription on the Egyptian Library, it seems as much to concern us to obtain it genuine, as to procure unadulterated medicine for the body. [P. iv]

Though Italy has carried *vocal* music to a perfection unknown in any other country, much of the present excellence of *instrumental* is certainly owing to the natives of Germany, as wind and keyed instruments have never, perhaps in any age or country, been brought to a greater degree of refinement, either in construction or use, than by the modern Germans. [Pp. vi-vii]

This work follows the same organization as that on France and Italy. It was first published in 1773.

Jefferson ordered the work for the University, in the section on "Gardening. Painting. Sculpture. Music" of the want list, without specifying the edition, though his general instructions to Hilliard would certainly have produced the corrected edition if they had produced either. No copy of this, however, is known to have been acquired in Jefferson's lifetime. The copy Jefferson sold Congress was the 1773 edition. The library's present copy of the 1775 edition is in the Mackay-Smith Collection.

U. Va.?
*ML195.B963.1775

M [1773]
Sowerby 4254

20. Caslon, William, and Son.

A / SPECIMEN / OF / Printing Types, / BY / W. Caslon and Son, / *Letter Founders*, / London. / Printed by JOHN TOWERS, / MDCC-LXIV.

Small 8vo. Engraved portrait added; title page (1 leaf); text (37 leaves).

William Caslon (1692–1766) was born in Worcestershire. Apprenticed to an engraver of gun locks and barrels there, he set up shop in 1716 in London, where he began cutting type punches at the request of John Watts, the printer. Watts then backed a small foundry for Caslon where he cut type in the "English Arabic," pica roman, italic, Hebrew, and Coptic. From 1742 he worked with his son William (1720–78). The firm was continued by William II's wife after his death, and by their two sons, William III and Henry. William III removed to Sheffield, where his new firm, later known as Stephenson, Blake, and Co., has had a very long life. Henry's firm, under the later name of A. W. Caslon and Co., has had an equally long tenure.

The book of type samples ranges from a very clear Roman to a series of non-Roman alphabets—Greek, Hebrew, Coptic. "Aethiopick," Etruscan, Syriac, "Arabick," Armenian, Samaritan, and Saxon—as well as music and typographical ornaments.

Sowerby points out that Jefferson bought his copy at the sale of the library of the Rev. Samuel Henly in March 1785, a copy which must have been either the 1763 or 1764 edition, since it seems too early for the 1785 edition to have reached this country. Since Jefferson usually preferred a later edition, it is supposed that the 1764 edition would be the more suitable.

Jefferson's own copy was sold to the Library of Congress. It was not ordered for the University. The library's present copy is a gift of the Thomas Jefferson Memorial Foundation.

21. Castell, Robert.

THE / VILLAS / OF THE / ANCIENTS / ILLUSTRATED. / BY / Robert Castell. / *Vos sapere & solos aio bene / vivere, quorum / Conspicitur nitidis fundata pecunia Villis.* / Hor. / *LONDON:* / Printed for the AUTHOR. / MDCCXXVIII.

Folio. Title page (1 leaf); dedication (1 leaf); preface (1 leaf); list of subscribers (1 leaf); text (1–128); index (1 leaf); 13 engraved plates, of which 6 are folding.

The engravers were P. Fourdrinier, who may be supposed to be either Paul or Pierre Fourdrinier (fl.1720–60), Paul being known as "Old" Fourdrinier and Pierre as "Young" Fourdrinier, both having worked in London; and G. King, who may be George King, an English engraver said to have flourished ca.1740, though that date seems a little late for this book.

The crafts or professions are not listed on the pages of subscribers, but a copy went to Paul Foudrinier and to a clergyman, and two copies to James Oglethorpe.

Very little is known about Robert Castell other than the evidence of this book. It has been lately established that he was not the German architect who settled in Ireland in the second decade of the eighteenth century under the name of Robert Castele, Castle, Cassel, or Cassels.

Castell says that he

resolved to take for my Subject the Rules that were observed in the situating and disposing of the *Roman Villas,* . . . and to this End I have been at the Pains to peruse many ancient Authors, who have treated more at large of that Part, not the meanest of the Architect's Business.

Most of the *Roman* Writers upon Agriculture that are remaining, have thought fit, at the Beginning of their Works, to tell us what were to be consider'd in the Situation and Disposition of *Villas. Cato,* the eldest of them left the fewest Rules on that Head . . . ; but *Varro* that was the next after him, has been more ample and judicious in his observations. . . .

Pliny the Younger alone has exceeded *Varro* in this Particular; he has left us two Epistles, containing an exact Description of his *Villas* of *Laurentinum* and *Tuscum*, and tho' we find not in him any direct Rules for the Disposition of the *Villa Urbana* or Country House of Pleasure, yet he gives us to understand, that those Buildings were contriv'd according to the strictest. Rules of Art. . . . He speaks only of the Situation, and Disposition of those Buildings, knowing his Friends to whom he wrote, could not but be sensible that the Rules laid down by *Vitruvius* with respect to Beauty and Proportion were equally to take Place in the City and Country. . . .

The whole Work consists of three Parts. The first contains the Description of a *Villa Urbana*, or Countrey House of Retirement near the City, that was supplied with most of the Necessaries of Life from a neighbouring Market-Town. The second sets forth the Rules that were necessary to be observed by an Architect, who had the Liberty to chuse a Situation, and to make a proper Distribution of all Things in and about the *Villa;* but particularly with relation to the Farm-House, which in this Sort of Buildings, according to the more ancient *Roman* Manner, was always join'd to the Master's House, or but very little remov's from it. In the third Part is shewn the Description of another *Villa Urbana*, on a Situation very different from the former, with the Farm-House and its Appurtenances so far remov'd as to be no Annoyance to it, and at the same Time so near as to furnish it conveniently with all necessaries. [Preface]

He also tells us that "the Antients esteem'd four Things essential to that of a good one [i.e., situation], viz. good Roads for themselves and Carriages, or the Conveniency of a navigable River; next, fertile Land to produce what was necessary for the Support of Man and Beast; wholesome Water; and, lastly, an healthy Air; which last-mentioned, as it immediately regarded the Life of the Inhabitant, was chiefly to be considered" (p. 17).

It is not known at what date this rather literary work, with its restorations based on ancient texts (see Plate VIII), came into Jefferson's hands. Sowerby suggests that he probably bought it in England, and Kimball (p. 92) states that he bought it between 1785 and 1789. His own copy was sold to Congress. Although it was ordered for the University in the section on "Architecture" of the want list, there is no record of its having been acquired during Jefferson's lifetime. The present copy has come into the collection recently, the gift of an anonymous donor.

U. Va.
*NA324.C3.1728

M
Sowerby 4191

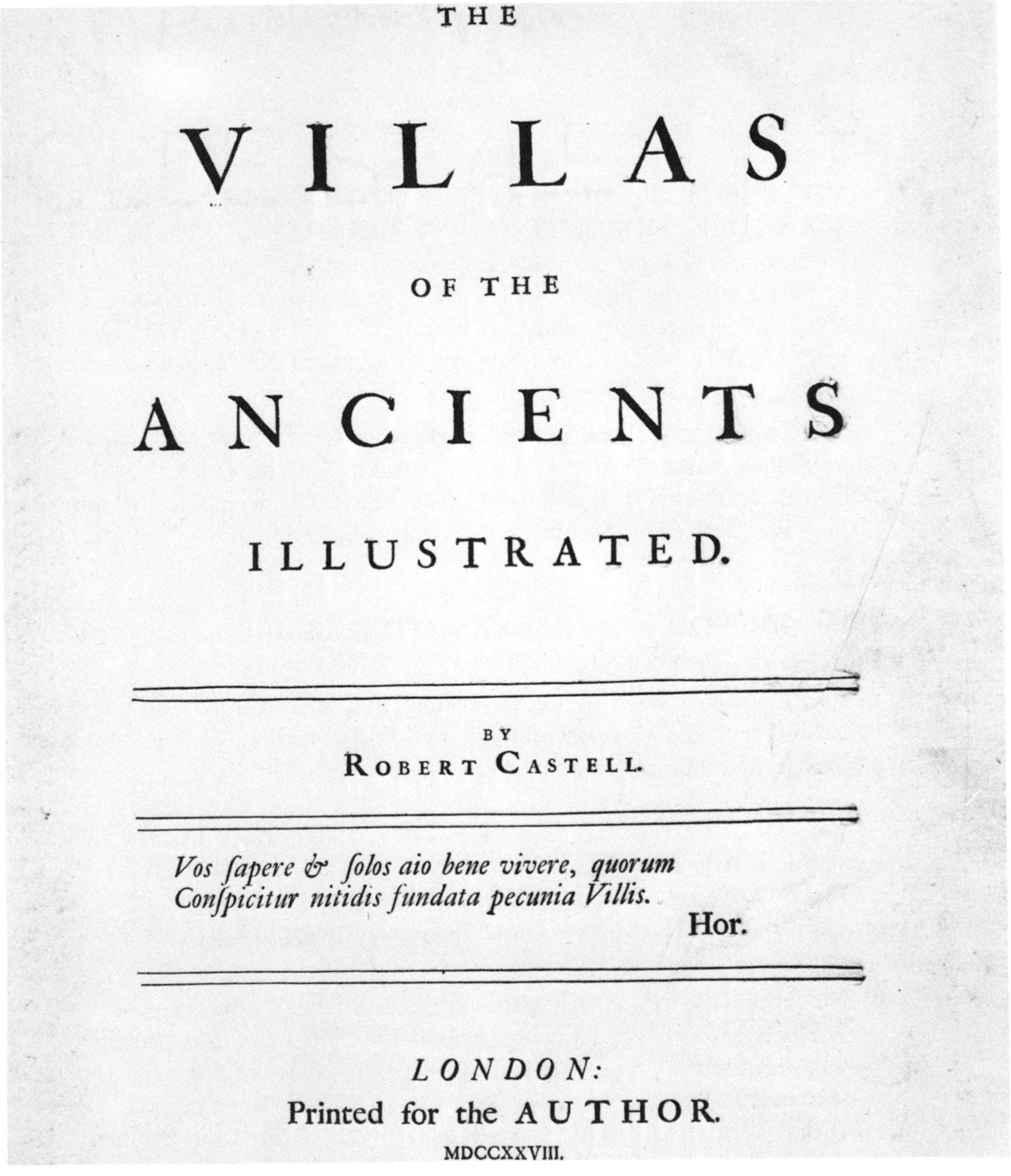

THE

VILLAS

OF THE

ANCIENTS

ILLUSTRATED.

BY
ROBERT CASTELL.

Vos sapere & solos aio bene vivere, quorum
Conspicitur nitidis fundata pecunia Villis.

Hor.

LONDON:
Printed for the AUTHOR.
MDCCXXVIII.

Plate VIII. *From No. 21.* Title page.

22. Cellini, Benvenuto.

Vol. I. VITA / DI / BENVENUTO CELLINI / OREFICE E SCULTORE FIORENTINO / DA LUI MEDESIMO SCRITTA / Nella quale si leggono molte importanti notizie / appartenenti alle Arti ed alla Storia del Secolo XVI. / *Ora per la prima volta ridotta a buona lezione / ed accompagnata con note* / DA / GIO. PALAMEDE CARPANI. / MILANO / Dalla Società Tipografica de'Classici Italiani, / contrada di s. Margherita, No. 1118. / Anno 1806.

8vo. Half title ([i]); engraved portrait of Cellini (ii); title page (iii); publisher's note (v); preface by Antonio Cocchi (vii-xxiv); letter of Cellini (xxv-xxvi); sonnet by Cellini (xxvii); note on Laurentian Ms. (xxviii); text (1–453); chronology (454–65); appendix (1 unnumbered p.).

Vol. II. VITA / DI / BENVENUTO CELLINI /. . . . / VOLUME II. /. . . / Contrada del Cappuccio. / ANNO 1811.

8vo. Engraved frontispiece (Perseus); half title ([i]); title page (iii); publisher's note (v); chronology (vii-xlvi); text (1–496); notes (497–502); emendation (1 unnumbered p.).

Vol. III. DUE TRATTATI / DI / BENVENUTO CELLINI / SCULTORE FIORENTINO / UNO / DELL' OREFICERIA / L'ALTRO / DELLA SCULTURA. / *Coll'aggiunta di altre operette del medesimo.* / MILANO. / Dalla Società Tipografica de'Classici Italiani / contrada del Cappuccio. / ANNO 1811.

8vo. Half title ([i]); title page (iii); publisher's note (v-viii); preface of Florence, 1731 edition (ix-xlvii); dedication (xlix-lii); prormeio (liii-lx); oreficeria (1–151); on sculpture (153–217); fragment on the art of drawing (219–29); letters, discourses, and poems (233–99); executed works of sculpture, etc. (300–310); travels (311–14); exploits (315–21); illnesses (322–23); index (324–417); errata (1 unnumbered p.).

Benvenuto Cellini (1500–1571), born in Florence, was apprenticed to Andrea di Sandó Marcone, a goldsmith. He completed many important works both as goldsmith and sculptor in spite of his turbulent life. He wrote a treatise on sculpture and dictated his famous autobiography to a secretary. It was first printed in Italian in 1728, in English in 1771, in German in 1796, and in French in 1822.

The first two volumes of this edition, comprising the *Vita*, were edited by Gio. Palamede Carpani. The third volume includes the *Due trattati* as well as a series of miscellaneous works.

There was a set of this edition already in the University's collection when Jefferson made up his want list, but it subsequently disappeared. It has been replaced in recent years by the present set, the gift of the Thomas Jefferson Memorial Foundation.

U. Va.
*NB623.C3.1806

23. Chambers, Sir William.

DESIGNS / OF / CHINESE / BUILDING, / FURNITURE, DRESSES, / MACHINES, and UTENSILS. / Engraved by the Best Hands, / From the ORIGINALS drawn in CHINA / BY / Mr. CHAMBERS, Architect, / Member of the Imperial Academy of Arts at FLORENCE. / To which is annexed, / A DESCRIPTION of their TEMPLES, HOUSES, GARDENS, &c. / LONDON: / Published for the AUTHOR, and sold by him next Door to Tom's Coffee-house, Russel-street, / Covent-Garden: Also by Mess. Dodsley, in Pall-mall; Mess. Wilson and Durham; / Mr. A. Millar, in the Strand, and Mr. R. Willock, in Cornhill. / MDCCLVII.

Folio. Title page (1 leaf); dedication (1 leaf); list of subscribers (1 leaf); preface (2 leaves); text (1–19); title page in French (1 leaf); dedication in French (1 leaf); preface in French (2 leaves); [new pagination:] text in French (1–19); 21 engraved plates.

The plates were engraved by P. Fourdrinier (see No. 21); J. Fougeron, an engraver in London whose first name was Ignace; Charles Grignion (1716–1810), who was born in London of French parents, did some work with Hogarth (No. 56), was a founder member of the Royal Academy, and had a son, also named Charles, who was an engraver as well; Edward Rooker (see No. 3); and P. Sandby, who may have been Paul (1725–1809) or Pierre (1732–1808).

Among the subscribers were architects, a "Bookseller at Bath," a builder, a carver, ecclesiastics, an engraver, the "Master of Perspective to HRH, Prince of Wales," a professor of moral philosophy, and a sculptor. Listed with the architects were John and James Adam, James Payne, and John Vardie. "J. Reinolds" was among the painters, and both

Plate IX. *From No. 23.* Pavilion in the Court of the Pagoda of Ho-nang, Canton (Pl. II).

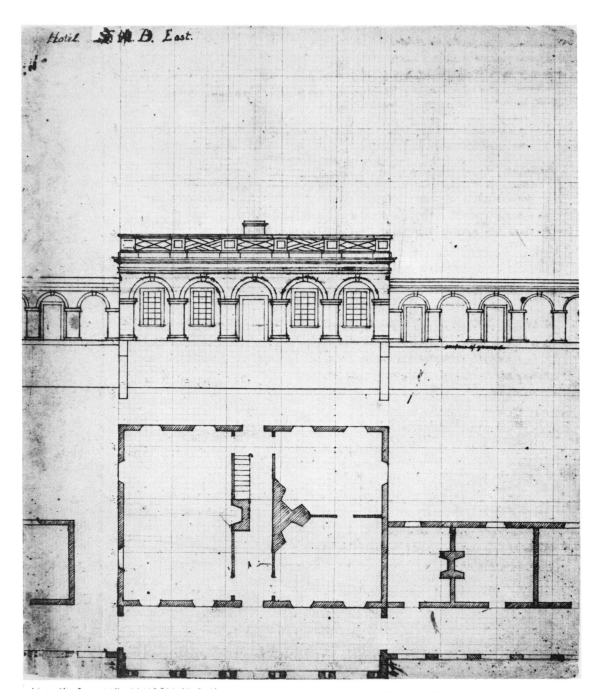

Plate X. Jefferson's drawing for Hotel D East, University of Virginia (N-362).

Paul and Thomas Sandby were listed, Thomas being identified as "draughtsman to HRH, the Duke."

William Chambers (1726–96) was born at Stockholm where his grandfather was a prosperous English merchant. His father returned to England in 1728, but William, at sixteen, went to China with the Swedish East India Company, where he made a series of sketches which were later published in this book in 1757. At eighteen he went to Italy to study architecture and while in Rome lived with Charles-Louis Clérisseau (No. 29).

After his return to England he became architectural tutor to the Prince of Wales (afterwards George III), to whom this book is dedicated, a founding member and the first treasurer of the Royal Academy, and the comptroller of His Majesty's works. He was eventually knighted and was buried in Westminister Abbey, in the Poet's Corner. His books include, in addition to *Designs for Chinese Buildings*, the *Treatise of Civil Architecture* (1759; 2d ed., 1768; 3d ed., 1791); the *Buildings at Kew*, 1763 (No. 24); and the *Dissertation on Oriental Gardening*, 1772.

He introduces his *Designs of Chinese Buildings* by saying:

I AM far from desiring to be numbered among the exaggerators of Chinese excellence . . . yet they must be allowed to claim our notice as a distinct and very singular race of men; as the inhabitants of a region divided by it's situation from all civilized countries; who have formed their own manners, and invented their own arts, without the assistance of example. . . . Our notions of their architecture are very imperfect . . . and no designs worth notice have yet been published.

THESE which I now offer the publick are done from sketches and measures taken by me at Canton some years ago, chiefly to satisfy my own curiosity. . . .[1]

WHATEVER is really Chinese has at least the merit of being original: these people seldom or never copy or imitate the inventions of other nations . . . but their architecture has this farther advantage that there is a remarkable affinity between it and that of the antients, which is the more surprising as there is not the least probability that the one was borrowed from the other.

IN both the antique and Chinese architecture the general form of almost every composition has a tendency to the pyramidal figure: In both, columns are employed for support; and in both, these columns have diminution and bases, some of which bear a near resemblance to each other: fretwork, so

---

[1] In a later footnote Chambers says "I do not pretend to give this as a very accurate plan of that building: exact measures of Chinese structures are of small consequence to European Artists: and it is a matter of great difficulty to measure any publick work in China with accuracy, because the populace are very troublesome to strangers, throwing stones, and offering other insults."

common in the buildings of the antients, is likewise very frequent in those of the Chinese; . . . the Atrium, and the Monopteros and Prostyle temples, are forms of building that nearly resemble some used in China. . . .

Though I am publishing a work of Chinese Architecture, let it not be suspected that my intention is to promote a taste so much inferior to the antique, and so very unfit for our climate: but a particular so interesting as the architecture of one of the most extraordinary nations in the universe cannot be a matter of indifference to a true lover of the arts, and an architect should by no means be ignorant of so singular a stile of building: at least the knowledge is curious, and on particular occasions may likewise be useful; as he may sometimes be obliged to make Chinese compositions, and at others it may be judicious in him to do so. For though, generally speaking, Chinese architecture does not suit European purposes; yet in extensive parks and gardens, where a great variety of scenes are required, or in immense palaces, containing a numerous series of apartments, I do not see the impropriety of finishing some of the inferiour ones in the Chinese taste. Variety is always delightful; and novelty, attended with nothing inconsistent or disagreeable, sometimes takes [the] place of beauty. . . .

THE buildings of the Chinese are neither remarkable for magnitude or richness of materials; yet there is a singularity in their manner, a justness in their proportion, a simplicity, and sometimes even beauty, in their form, which recommend them to our notice. I look upon them as toys in architecture: and as toys are sometimes, on account of their oddity, prettyness, or neatness of workmanship, admitted into the cabinets of the curious, so may Chinese buildings be sometimes allowed a place among compositions of a nobler kind. [Preface]

This book (as well as Chambers's *Dissertation on Oriental Gardening*) was extremely influential in spreading a taste for things Chinese. Kimball (p. 126) states that Jefferson knew the book as early as 1771. It is supposed to have been a source for what Jefferson called "Chinese railings," and certainly Plates II, III, VI, and XI show railings which do relate to the ones he designed, the first three most closely (see Plates IX and X). Jefferson used the term on an early scheme for the pavilions at the University of Virginia (N-309), a drawing which may be dated before May 1817, as well as on subsequent drawings for the University.

Jefferson ordered the book for the University in the section on "Architecture" of the want list, but there is no record of its having been received by the library during his lifetime. The present copy was recently acquired, the gift of an anonymous donor. Jefferson's own copy was sold to Congress.

U. Va   M
*DS708.C4.1757   Sowerby 4220

24. Chambers, Sir William.

Plans, Elevations, / Sections, and Perspective Views / OF THE / GAR-DENS / AND / BUILDINGS / At KEW in Surry, / The Seat of Her ROYAL HIGHNESS / The Princess Dowager of Wales. / BY / WILLIAM CHAMBERS, / MEMBER / Of the Imperial Academy of Arts at Florence, and of the Royal Academy of Architecture at Paris, / ARCHITECT / *To the KING, and to Her Royal Highness the Princess Dowager of WALES.* / LONDON, / Printed by J. Haberkorn, in Grafton Street, St. Anne's Soho; / Published for the Author, / And to be had at his House in Poland Street; / Likewise of A. Millar, D. Wilson, and T. Becket, all in the Strand; and of R. and J. Dodsley / in Pall-Mall; R. Sayer in Fleet-Street, A. Webley in Holborn, J. Walter at Charing-/Cross, and Dorothy Mercier at the Golden Ball, Windmill Street, Golden Square. / MDCCLXIII.

Folio. Engraved frontispiece (1 leaf); title page (1 leaf); dedication (1 leaf); description of plates (1–8); 41 engraved plates, of which 2 are folding (2 of a total of 43 are missing).

The engravers were James Basire (see No. 3); Charles Grignion (see No. 23); Tobias Miller, or Müller (fl.1763–90), born in Nuremburg, but working in London where he had a brother, Johann Sebastian Miller, or Müller, also an engraver; James Noual; F. Patton (see No. 3); Edward Rooker (see No. 3); P. Sandby (see No. 23); and William Wollett (1735–85), of Dutch descent but English birth, who became engraver to the king in 1775.

The frontispiece, an allegory on architecture with the royal coronet, the Prince of Wales feather, and the badge of the Garter being used to form a kind of "Corinthian" capital, was drawn by William Hogarth (No. 56) and engraved by William Wollett. It was first used in Kirby's *Perspective of Architecture*, 1761 (No. 63).

For a note on Chambers, see No. 23. In 1762 Chambers built for Augusta, Dowager Princess of Wales, several temples and what were called "unmeaning falballas of Turkish and Chinese chequerwork" at Kew. Among these was the famous pagoda, which survives, and is illustrated in this work. Chambers had sketched in Canton and later published a Chinese pagoda in Plate I of his *Designs of Chinese Buildings* (No. 23).

He endorses this book by saying: "All the architectural designs and ornaments were done by me with the greatest care and accuracy, the figures drawn by Signor Cipriani, and the views by Messieurs [Jos.] Kirby [No. 63], Thomas Sandby, and [Wm.] Marlow, all of them excellent draftsmen. The whole work is engraved by the most eminent of our Artists."

Plate VIII of this work shows an elevation of a garden seat by William Kent, while Plate XXXIV shows its plan (see Plates XI and XII). These were copied in pen and ink and wash by Cornelia Jefferson Randolph while she was at Monticello with her grandfather Thomas Jefferson (see Plate XIII).

Many of the plates in this book are in the Chinese taste, especially Plates IX, XI, XV, XXIII, XXV, XXXII, XXXVIII, XXXIX, and XL, but Plate XV, "the House of Confucius," is especially good for railings and may have strengthened Jefferson's liking for this form. In addition, some of the plates show pavilions in a neoclassic manner.

Sowerby points out that Jefferson, on his visit to Kew, was primarily interested in the Archimedes screw for raising water and went so far as to illustrate it in his notes.

Jefferson's own copy of this work, which Kimball (p. 93) says was acquired before 1783, was sold to Congress. He ordered it for the University in the section on "Architecture" of the want list, but it has not survived. It has recently been replaced by the present copy, the gift of the Thomas Jefferson Memorial Foundation.

U. Va.   M
*NA7746.K4C4.1763   Sowerby 4225

Chambray, Fréart de. *See* Fréart de Chambray (No. 46).

25. Charnock, John.

Vol. I. [Engraved title page:] HISTORY / of / Marine / ARCHI-TECTURE. / By John Charnock Esqr. FSA. / LONDON. / MDCCCI.

Vol. I. [Printed title page:] AN / HISTORY / OF / MARINE AR-CHITECTURE. / INCLUDING AN / ENLARGED AND PRO-GRESSIVE VIEW / OF THE / NAUTICAL REGULATIONS AND NAVAL HISTORY, / BOTH CIVIL AND MILITARY, / OF ALL NATIONS, / *ESPECIALLY OF GREAT BRITAIN;* / DERIVED CHIEFLY FROM / Original Manuscripts, / AS WELL IN PRIVATE

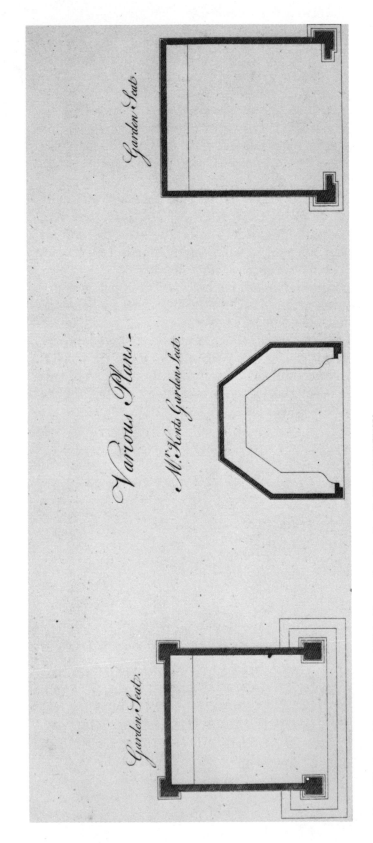

Plate XI. *From No. 24.* Plan of "Mr. Kents Garden Seat" (Pl. [XXXIV]).

Garden Seat

M. Kent Architectus.   E. Rooker Sculp.

Plate XII. *From No. 24.* "Garden Seat" (Pl. [VIII]).

Plate XIII. Cornelia Jefferson Randolph's drawing for a garden seat (N-497).

COLLECTIONS AS IN THE GREAT PUBLIC REPOSITORIES: / AND DEDUCED FROM / THE EARLIEST PERIOD TO THE PRESENT TIME. / IN THREE VOLUMES. / VOL. I. / *By JOHN CHARNOCK, ESQ*. F.S.A. / London: / Printed for R. FAULDER, Bond-street; G. G. and J. ROBINSON and Co. Paternoster-row; A. and J. BLACK, and H. PARRY, Leaden-/hall-street; T. EGERTON, Charing Cross; G. NICOLL, Pall Mall; C. LAW, Ave Maria-lane; J. SEWELL, Cornhill; J. WHITE, Fleet-/street; W. J. W. RICHARDSON, Royal Exchange; LEIGH and SOTHEBY, York-street; CADELL and DAVIES, and W. OTRIDGE and / Son, Strand; I. and J. BOYDELL, Cheapside; F. and C. RIVINGTON, St. Paul's Church-yard; T. PAYNE, Mews Gate; HEATHER / and Co. Leadenhall-street; LONGMAN and REES, J. WALLIS, and H. D. SYMONDS, Paternoster-row; J. DEBRETT and J. WRIGHT, / Picadilly; J. and A. ARCH, Gracechurch-street; VERNOR and HOOD, Poultry; J. HOOKHAM, and J. CARPENTER and Co., Bond-/street; J. BELL, Oxford-road; CROSBY and LETTERMAN, Stationer's-court; BUNNEY and GOLD, Shoelane; DARTON and HARVEY, / Gracechurch-street; D. STEEL, Tower-hill; J. HARDY and Sons, Ratcliffe Highway; LACKINGTON, ALLEN and Co. Finsbury-/square; E. LLOYD, Harley-street; and S. DEIGHTON, Cambridge: / By Bye and Law, St. John's-square, Clerkenwell. / MDCCC.

4to. Engraved title (1 leaf); printed title page ([[i]]); dedication (iii-vi); preface (vii-xcv); list of plates (xcvi); advertisement (xcvii-c); test, with 18 engraved plates inserted (1–368).

Vol. II. AN / HISTORY / OF / MARINE ARCHITECTURE. / . . .

4to. Title page (1 leaf); list of plates (1 leaf); text, with 36 engraved plates inserted, of which 19 are folding (1–496).

Vol. III. AN / HISTORY / OF / MARINE ARCHITECTURE. / . . . / MDCCCII.

4to. Title page (1 leaf); list of plates (1 leaf); text, with 46 engraved plates, of which 1 is folding, inserted (1–412); general table of contents (413–36).

The engraved title page of Vol. I has a medallion designed by Benjamin West and D. Serres, engraved by Shipster (see Plate XIV). The engravings in Vol. I, a few of which are touched with acquatint, are charming drawings of ships. The engravers were Thomas Hall (fl.1800), an English painter, engraver, and user of acquatint; James Newton (1748–ca.1804); and R. Shipster (fl.1796–99), English, a student of Bartolozzi see No. 3). The engravings in Vol. II are by James Newton and Charles Tomkins, and the engravings in Vol III are by Barlow, James Newton, and Charles Tomkins.

John Charnock (1756–1807) was educated at Winchester and Trinity College, Oxford. After a break with his father, he devoted himself entirely to naval affairs. His first book, *The Rights of a Free People*, 1792, was quickly followed by the six-volume work *Biographia Navalis: Impartial Memoirs of the Lives and Characters of the Navy of Great Britain from the Year 1660*, 1794–98. These were then succeeded by *A Letter on Finance and on National Defense*, 1798; this work, the *History of Marine Architecture*, 1800–1802; and the *Life of Lord Nelson*, 1806.

There is, perhaps, a question of the actual date of issue of the *History of Marine Architecture*. The title page is dated 1800, the engraved title page is dated 1801, the dedication is dated December 31, 1800, and the advertisement in Vol. I is dated April 6, 1802. Since the title page of Vol. II is dated 1801 and that of Vol. III 1802, it may very well be that the entire work was issued in 1802. Or perhaps this set is a second printing of the first edition.

In referring to the wartime uses of marine architecture and the improvements those uses may have brought, Charnock shows himself both thoughtful and sensitive. He says:

Degrading as it may appear to what is called the dignity of human nature, we fear it is a truth, too firmly established to be controverted, or even disputed, that many of those arts, the discovery and perfection of which are thought to have contributed most eminently to the benefit and advantage of mankind, owe their existence and progress in a much greater degree to the depravity of the human mind, than to any of those virtuous principles of enquiry which can alone adorn and exalt it. [I, 1]

The set ordered by Jefferson for the University in the section on "Technical Arts" of the want list is still in the library, though it now lacks a frontispiece.

U. Va.
*VM15.C48.1801

26. Chippendale, Thomas.

THE / GENTLEMAN / AND / CABINET-MAKER'S / DIRECTOR. / BEING A LARGE / COLLECTION / OF THE MOST / Elegant and Useful Designs of Household Furniture / IN THE /

HISTORY

OF

Marine

ARCHITECTURE

By JOHN CHARNOCK Esqr. FSA.

LONDON.

MDCCCI.

Plate XIV. *From No. 25.* Engraved title page.

GOTHIC, CHINESE and MODERN TASTE: / Including a great VARIETY of / BOOK-CASES for LIBRARIES or Private / Rooms. COMMODES, / LIBRARY and WRITING-TABLES, / BUROES, BREAKFAST-TABLES, / DRESSING and CHINA-TABLES, / CHINA-CASES, HANGING SHELVES, / TEA-CHESTS, TRAYS, FIRE-SCREENS, / CHAIRS, SETEES, SOPHA'S, BEDS, / PRESSES and CLOATHS-CHESTS, / PIER-GLASS SCONCES, SLAB FRAMES, / BRACKETS, CANDLE-STANDS, / CLOCK-CASES, FRETS, / AND OTHER / ORNAMENTS. / TO WHICH IS PREFIXED, / A Short EXPLANATION of the Five ORDERS of ARCHITECTURE, / and RULES of PERSPECTIVE; / WITH / Proper DIRECTIONS for executing the most difficult Pieces, the Mouldings being exhibited / at large, and the Dimensions of each DESIGN specified: / THE WHOLE COMPREHENDED IN / One Hundred and Sixty COPPER-PLATES, neatly Engraved, / Calculated to improve and refine the present TASTE, and suited to the Fancy and Circumstances of / Persons in all Degrees of Life. / *Dulcique animos novitate tenebo.* OVID. / *Ludentis speciem dabit & torquebitur.* HOR. / BY / *THOMAS CHIPPENDALE,* / Of St. *MARTIN'S-LANE,* CABINET-MAKER. / THE SECOND EDITION. / *LONDON,* / Printed by J. HABERKORN, in Gerard-Street, / For the AUTHOR, and sold at his House in St. Martin's-Lane. / Also by T. OSBORNE, Bookseller, in Gray's-Inn; H. PIERS, Bookseller, in Holborn; R. SAYER, Print-/seller, in Fleetstreet; J. SWAN, near Northumberland House, in the Strand. At EDINBURGH, by / Messrs. HAMILTON and BALFOUR: And at DUBLIN, by Mr. JOHN SMITH, on the Blind-Quay. / M DCCLV.

Folio. Title page in red and black (1 leaf); engraved dedication (i); preface (iii-vi); list of subscribers (vii-x); description of plates, with pp. 25–27 misbound (1–27); 160 engraved plates.

The engravers were Matthew Darly (fl.1754–72), English engraver and caricaturist; Johann Sebastian Miller, or Müller (1715–85), also known as John Miller and sometimes caled L'Espérance, born in Nuremburg but working principally in England where he arrived in 1744; and Tobias Miller, or Müller (see No. 24).

There was only one architect among the subscribers, James Payne. But four booksellers, one bricklayer, eighty-six cabinetmakers, four carpenters, ten carvers, one chemist, two engravers, two founders, one jeweler, thirteen joiners, one merchant, one organmaker, two painters, one picture-frame maker, two plasterers, two professors of philosophy, seventeen "upholders," five "upholsterers," and one watchmaker were included.

Thomas Chippendale (d.1779) was born in Worcestershire. By 1752 he had become a cabinetmaker and upholsterer in London, and his reputation was great enough by 1754, the date of the first issue of his *Gentleman and Cabinet-Maker's Director*, that his book was stocked by booksellers in London, Edinburgh, and Dublin. This edition (1755) is the second, and the third was published in 1762. Its contents are well outlined on the title page.

By 1793, however, the book had gone out of fashion. Sheraton said of it at that time that "as for the designs themselves, they are now wholly antiquated and laid aside, though possessed of great merit according to the times in which they were executed" (*DNB*).

Chippendale must have been rather used to disparaging statements, though he did not live to hear Sheraton's, for he says at the end of his preface:

Upon the whole, I have here given no design but what may be executed with advantage by the hands of a skillful workman, tho' some of the profession have been diligent enough to represent them (especially those after the Gothic and Chinese manner) as so many specious drawings, impossible to be work'd off by any mechanic whatsoever. I will not scruple to attribute this to malice, ignorance and inability: And I am confident I can convince all Noblemen, Gentlemen, or others, who will honour me with their commands, that every design in the book can be improved, both as to beauty and enrichment, in the execution of it by

Their Most Obedient Servant.
Thomas Chippendale.

Just as his plates begin with an examination of the orders, so we find him placing the relation between architecture and cabinetmaking first in importance in his preface:

Of all the ARTS which are either improved or ornamented by Architecture, that of CABINET-MAKING is not only the most useful and ornamental, but capable of receiving as great assistance from it an any whatever. I have therefore prefixed to the following designs a short explanation of the five Orders. Without an acquaintance with this science, and some knowledge of the rules of Perspective, the Cabinet-maker cannot make the designs of his work intelligible, nor shew, in a little compass, the whole conduct and effect of the piece. These, therefore, ought to be carefully studied by everyone who would excell in this branch, since they are the very soul and basis of his art.

Chinese adaptations permeate the book, even in furniture designated Gothic or French, as in Plate XVII on the frets of "French Chairs." It is especially strong in Plates XCIII, CX, CXI, CXV, and CLVII–CLX (see Plates XV and XVI). The three plate descriptions that follow are

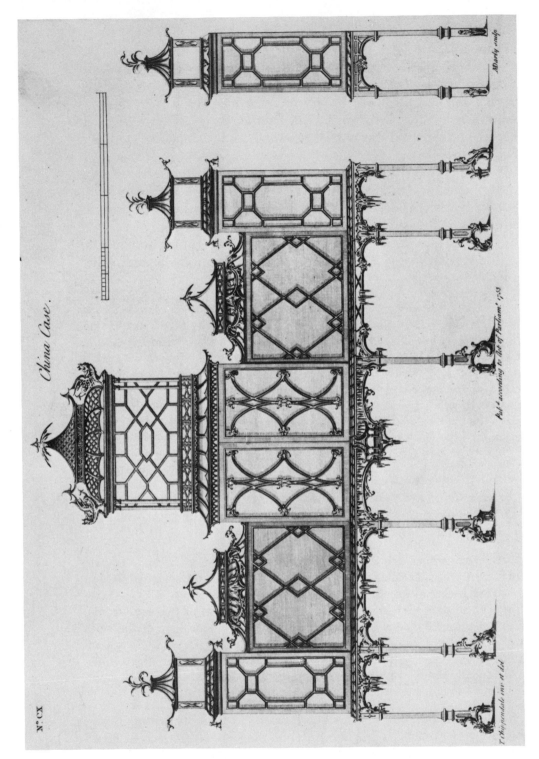

China Case.

Plate XV. *From No. 26.* "China Case" (No. CX).

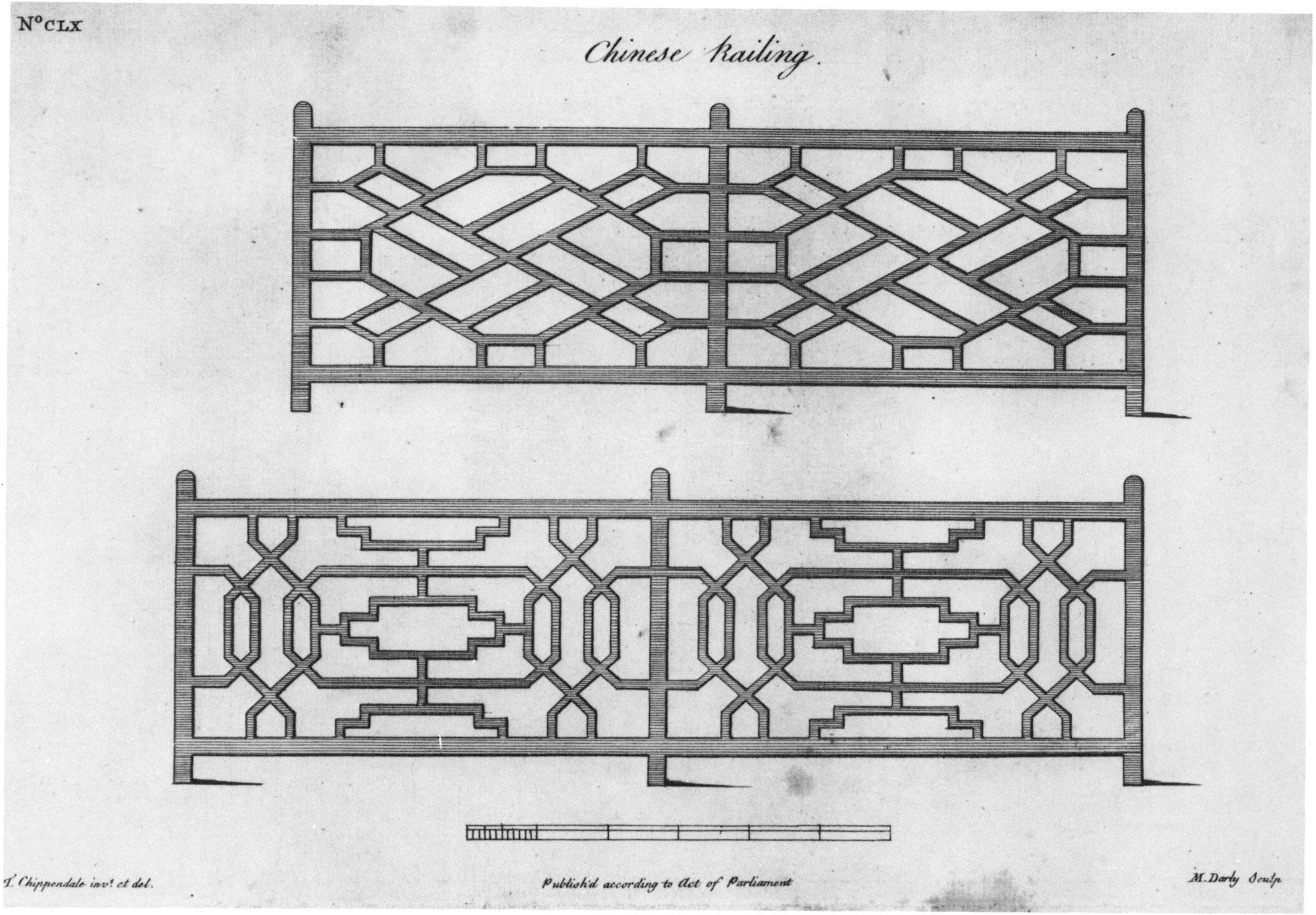
N^o CLX
Chinese Railing.
T. Chippendale inv^t et del.
Publish'd according to Act of Parliament
M. Darly Sculp.

Plate XVI. *From No. 26.* "Chinese Railing" (No. CLX).

typical and may very well have strengthened Jefferson's interest in Chinese forms:

Plate XCIII. Is a Chinese cabinet with drawers in the middle part, and two different sorts of doors at each end. The bottom drawer is intended to be all in one; the dimensions and mouldings are all fixed to the design. This Cabinet, finished according to the drawing, and by a good workman, will, I am confident, be very genteel. [P. 19]

Plate CXI. A China Case, not only the richest and most magnificent in the whole, but perhaps in all Europe. I had a particular pleasure in retouching and finishing this design, but should have much more in the execution of it, as I am confident I can make the work more beautiful and striking than the drawing. The proportion and harmony of the several parts will then be view'd with advantage, and reflect mutual beauty upon each other. The ornaments will appear more natural and graceful, and the whole construction will be so much improv'd under the ingenious hand of a workman, as to make it fit to adorn the most elegant apartment. [P. 22]

Plates CLVII. CLVIII. CLIX. and CLX. A Variety of Chinese railing, very proper for gardens and other places, and may be converted (by the ingenious workman) to other uses. [P. 27]

Jefferson sold his copy to Congress, an edition which Kimball incorrectly called the third, saying Jefferson had acquired it after 1789. The copy now at the University duplicates Jefferson's and is the gift of the Class of 1952. Jefferson did not order it for the University.

M

*NK2542.C5A3

Sowerby 4221

27. Clarke, Edward Daniel.

GREEK MARBLES / BROUGHT / FROM THE SHORES / OF THE / EUXINE, ARCHIPELAGO, and MEDITERRANEAN, / AND DEPOSITED IN THE / *VESTIBULE OF THE PUBLIC LIBRARY* / OF THE / UNIVERSITY OF CAMBRIDGE, / BY / EDWARD DANIEL CLARKE, LL.D. / LATE FELLOW OF JESUS COLLEGE, / AND PROFESSOR OF MINERALOGY IN THAT UNIVERSITY. / *CAMBRIDGE:* / PRINTED BY ORDER OF THE SYNDICS OF THE PRESS. / SOLD BY PAYNE, PALL MALL, CADELL AND DAVIES, STRAND, LONDON, AND THE / BOOKSELLERS OF THE TWO UNIVERSITIES. / M.DCCC.IX.

Small 4to. Engraved frontispiece; title page (1 leaf); advertisement (1 leaf); preface ([i]-vii); text (1–79); postscript (81); 3 engraved plates inserted.

Three of the plates were drawn by John Flaxman (1755–1826), who was born at York, the son of a maker and seller of plaster casts who worked principally in London. Flaxman, although a child prodigy gaining a first prize from the Royal Society of Arts at the age of twelve, also studied at the Royal Academy Schools and spent some time in Rome. He returned to England to execute an immense amount of work, both sculpture and drawings. Pettro William Tompkins (1760–1840), the engraver, was born in England. He studied with Bartolozzi (see No. 3) and became a distinguished engraver in the chalk and dotted manner. Many small prints that bear his name may have been engraved by scholars under his direction. For Sir William Gell, who drew the fourth plate, see No. 47.

Edward Daniel Clarke (1769–1822), a traveler, antiquary, and mineralogist, was born in the vicarage at Willingdon, Sussex, the grandson of William Clarke, the antiquary. He was educated at Tonbridge Grammar school and Jesus College, Cambridge. He received his B.A. in 1790, his M.A. in 1794, and his L.L.D. in 1803. He later traveled in Italy, Germany, Scotland, Scandinavia, Russia, and Asia Minor before he found himself in Greece in 1801. There he arranged the removal of the colossal statue of Ceres, now generally called a Kistophoros, but it was necessary to bribe the waiwode of Athens, purchase the statue, and obtain a firman. The boat bearing the statue and the other marbles sank just off the coast of England, but the crates were salvaged. After Clarke's return to England, he was given two livings on the occasion of his ordination. In 1808 he was appointed the university professor of mineralogy at Cambridge and in 1817 was made the librarian of the University.

He published some sixteen works in all, such as *Testimonies of Different Authors Respecting the Colossal Statue of Ceres . . . at Cambridge*, 1802, and the six-volume quarto work *Travels in Various Countries of Europe, Asia, and Africa*, 1810–23, as well as this book, which was first published in 1809 at the expense of Cambridge University.

In his preface Clarke says: "The Collection, such as it is, must be considered, after all, merely a gleaning. . . . But, if future travelers from the University, hereafter visiting the territories in which these monuments were found, contribute also their portion, Alma Mater will have no reason to blush for her poverty in documents so materially affecting the utility and dignity of her establishment. The foundation, at least, of a Collection of Greek Marbles may be said to have been laid" (pp. i-ii).

The text is a catalogue of the collection, chiefly fragments with inscriptions, but the centerpiece of the collection was the remains of what was thought to be the colossal statue of Ceres of Eleusis.

Jefferson's "4" annotation on the order for this book for the University, in the section on "History-Civil-Antient" of the want list, either indicates an error on his part as to the number of volumes or else doubt as to whether the format was quarto or octavo. The book was in the collection by 1828 but has not survived. The present copy on the library's shelves, a gift from the Thomas Jefferson Memorial Foundation, is from the collection of Baron Northwick.

U. Va.
*NB87.C53.1809

28. Clendinin, John.

THE / PRACTICAL SURVEYOR's / ASSISTANT. / *IN TWO PARTS.* /

Part the I. being a Table of Difference of Latitude and Departure, fitted to every Degree of the Quadrant, and continued from one tenth of a Perch to a Mile.	Part the II. a like Table fitted to every quarter of a Degree of the Quadrant and continued from one tenth of a Perch to Four hundred and fifty Perches.

CALCULATED BY / *JOHN CLENDININ*, / LAND SURVEYOR. / *PHILADELPHIA:* / *PRINTED* by BENJAMIN JOHNSON, / *FOR THE AUTHOR.* / M,DCC,XCIII.

8vo. Title page (1 leaf); subscription list (2 leaves); tables ([1]–45).

Sowerby points out that John Clendinin, a surveyor of 47 Sugar Alley, appears in the Philadelphia directory only in 1793. She had seen no copy of the *Assistant* for collation. The book contains only two series of tables, as described on the title page.

Jefferson sold his copy of the *Assistant* to Congress. He did not order it for the University, whose present copy is a part of the Stone Collection.

M
Sowerby 3709

*TYP1793.C54

29. Clérisseau, Charles-Louis.

ANTIQUITÉS / *DE* / LA FRANCE, / *Par M.* CLERISSEAU, *Archi-tecte, de l'Académie Royale de Peinture* / *& Sculpture de Paris, Mem-bre de la Société Royale de Peinture,* / *Sculpture & Architecture de Londres.* / PREMIERE PARTIE. / *A PARIS,* / De l'Imprimerie de PHILIPPE-DENYS PIERRES, rue S. Jacques. / *Et se vend* / Chez / L'AUTEUR, au Louvre, Porte de la Colonnade. / Le Sieur POULLEAU, Graveur, à l'Estrapade. / Le Sieur JOULLAIN, Md d'Estampes, Quai de la Mégisserie, à la ville de Rome. / M. DCC. LXXVIII.

Folio. Half title ([i]); title page ([iii]); dedication ([v-vi]); preface (vii-xiv); table of plates (xv-xxii); list of subscribers (1 leaf); en-graved frontispiece (1 leaf); 41 engraved plates.

The engraver was C. R. G. Poulleau, who also acted as one of the sellers of the book.

The list of subscribers included fourteen architects, four men of law, four doctors, one engineer, one engraver, one engraver of medals, seven painters, and one sculptor.

Charles-Louis Clérisseau (1721–1820), born in Paris, was edu-cated at the Académie de Peinture et de Sculpture there and later at Rome after he had won the Prix de Rome in 1746. While in Rome he knew Winckelmann (Nos. 128a & b); Robert Adam, whom he accom-panied to Spalatro (No. 3); Chambers, who lived with him in Rome (Nos. 23 & 24); and Piranesi (No. 99). He went to London to work with the Adam brothers in 1771, but their bankruptcy sent him back to France in 1778. Although he was appointed first architect to Catherine II of Russia in 1783, he returned to France before the Revolution and he settled in the country, gaining membership in the Legion d'honneur un-der the Empire. He had been an Academician as early as 1769 and also was a member of the Academy of St. Petersburg.

This work was first issued in 1778 (see Plate XVII). The second edition of 1806 had a text by J. G. Legrand. Plates I–IX illustrate the "Maison quarrée," Plates X–XIX the amphitheater at Nîmes, and Plates XX–XLI a temple near the baths at Nîmes and fragments found nearby.

Clérisseau prefers the spirit of the ancient monuments to exact copies and tells us why:

Pour arriver à ce point de perfection, il nous reste donc encore à faire sur l'antique de nouvelles observations non moins intéressantes aux celles qui nous

ANTIQUITÉS

DE

LA FRANCE,

Par M. CLERISSEAU, Architecte, de l'Académie Royale de Peinture
& Sculpture de Paris, Membre de la Société Royale de Peinture,
Sculpture & Architecture de Londres.

PREMIERE PARTIE.

A PARIS,

De l'Imprimerie de PHILIPPE-DENYS PIERRES, rue S. Jacques.

Et se vend

Chez { L'AUTEUR, au Louvre, Porte de la Colonnade.
{ Le Sieur POULLEAU, Graveur, à l'Estrapade.
{ Le Sieur JOULLAIN, Md d'Estampes, Quai de la Mégisserie, à la ville de Rome.

M. DCC. LXXVIII.

Plate XVII. *From No. 29.* Title page.

ont occupé jusqu'à présent. Si nos édifices n'ont point cette majesté & cette sage convenance, qui caractérisent les Monumens des Anciens; n'est-ce point parce qu'en copiant exactement les formes de leurs masses, & les proportions de leur détails, nous n'etudions pas assez l'esprit dans lequel ces Monumens étoient composés, & nous ne recherchons pas ce qui a pu leur imprimer ce caractère imposant qui nous étonne encore aujourd'hui dans leurs vestiges? [Pp. xi-xii]

He had several reasons for starting with Nîmes in general and with the "Maison quarrée" in particular:

Les Monumens de Nismes tiennent le premier rang parmi les Antiquités de la France. C'est donc leur assigner la place qui leur convient que de commencer par eux le Recueil de tous les Monumens anciens que je me propose de donner au Public. Les Artistes & les Gens de Lettres sont tous convenus que Rome n'avoit point de Monument plus parfait que la *Maison quarrée*. [P. vii]

Si nous sommes une fois bien convaincus, que les colonnes en péristile, ne portent un caractère majestueux que lorsqu'elles sont espacées à deux diamètres un quant au plus, nous conviendrons facilement qu'il faut les supprimer par-tout où elles ne sont pas de nécessité absolue, & ou il est impossible de les employer dans ce rapport.

C'est à cette justesse de proportion dans leur espacement, que les colonnes de la Maison quarrée doivent toute leur grace, & le caractère imposant qu'elles portent malgré leur petit diamètre, ce qui m'a determiné à en donner au public les mesures & les dessins dans le plus grand détail; & avec toute l'exactitude possible. [P. xiii]

Clérisseau assisted Jefferson with his designs for the Capitol at Richmond, and, of course, the "Maison quarrée" was chosen by Jefferson as his model. The resemblance between the two buildings, beyond the use in both of the rectangular, porticoed temple form, is not great, however, due primarily to the change in orders from the Corinthian of the original to the Ionic of the Capitol (see Plates XVIII, XIX, XX, and XXI). The introduction of windows in the Capitol also lessens the resemblance to the original temple in both Jefferson's drawings and in the model made under Clérisseau's supervision and sent to Richmond from Paris (N-280). (See also No. 80 for further information on Jefferson and the temple.)

Sowerby points out that Jefferson bought this book from Clérisseau himself in 1786, a year before his famous visit to Nîmes. Jefferson "pd. Clerissault for a book 72 f." according to his notebook for June 2, 1786. But Jefferson had known about the building before that, since he was using it in his designs for the Capitol as early as September 20, 1785, as stated in a letter to James Madison.

Facade de la maison quarree à Nismes.

Plate XVIII. *From No. 29.* "Facade de la maison quarree à Nismes" (Pl. II).

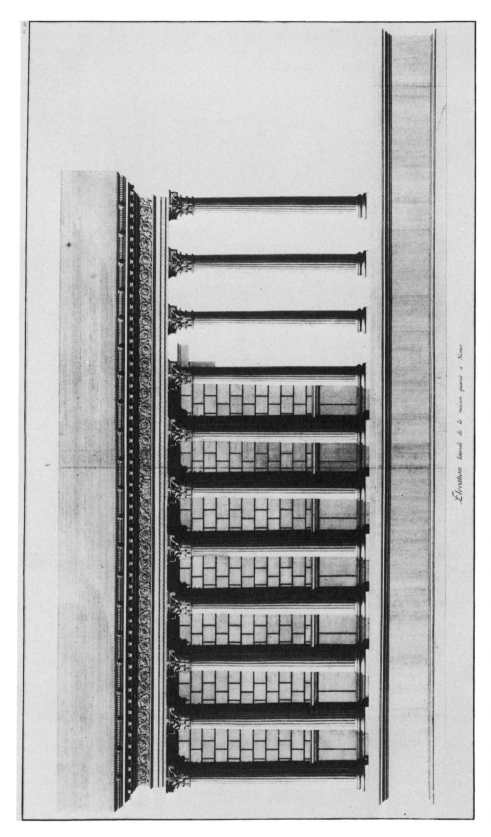

Élévation laterale de la maison quarrée a Nismes

Plate XIX. *From No.* 29. "Elevation laterale de la maison quarrée à Nismes" (Pl. III).

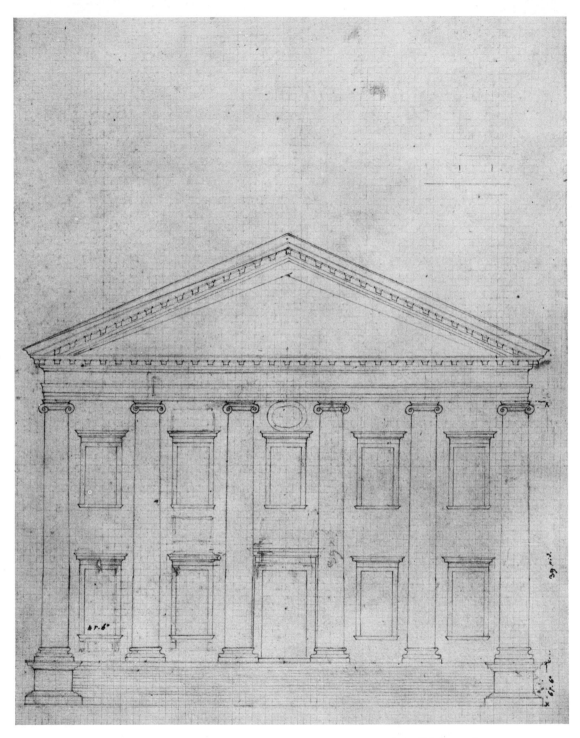

Plate XX. Jefferson's drawing for the front elevation of the Capitol, Richmond
(N-273–79). See Plate XVIII.

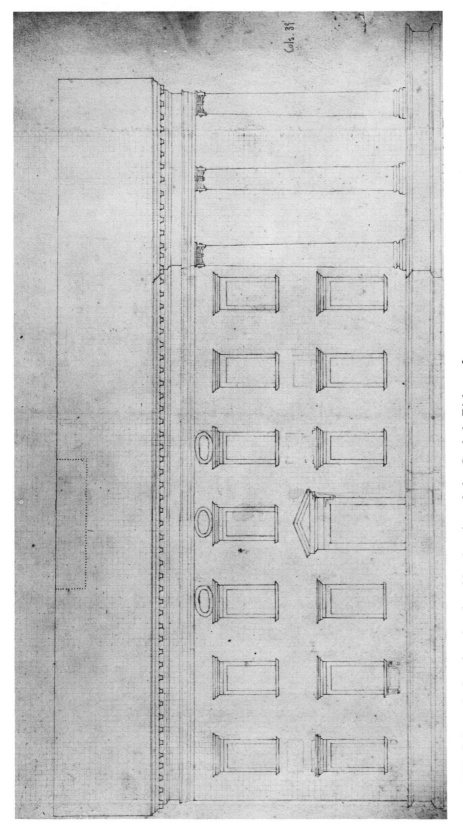

Plate XXI. Jefferson's drawing for the side elevation of the Capitol, Richmond (N-273–79). See Plate XIX.

The half title of this book is "Monumens de Nismes." The book is called "Première Partie," but this volume is all that was ever published. This edition was printed by P. D. Pierres, who a few years later was to print the first edition of Jefferson's *Notes on Virginia*.

Jefferson's own copy of the book was sold to Congress. He ordered it for the University in the section on "Architecture" of the want list, but there is no record that it was acquired in his lifetime. The copy in the library now was acquired soon after 1950.

U. Va.   M
*NA335.N5C6.1778   Sowerby 4209

Coetnempren, Armand-Guy Simon de, comte de Kersaint. *See* Kersaint, Armand-Guy Simon de Coetnempren, comte de (No. 62).

30. Cointeraux, François.

Ecole d'architecture rurale. Paris, 1791.

The University owns only Henry Holland's translation and condensation of the work, titled:

PISÉ, / Or the Art of Building strong and durable / Walls, to the Height of several Stories, with / nothing but Earth, or the most common Ma-/terials. Drawn up and presented to the / Board of Agriculture, by Henry Holland, / Esq.

The translation appeared in the *American Farmer*, Baltimore, for March 30, April 6, April 13, and April 27, 1821. It is an essay on the method of building with tamped earth. The University's copy consists of loose quarto sheets torn from the original journal.

François Cointeraux (b. 1739) worked at Lyons where the use of pisé had been known for centuries.

Sowerby describes the French work as a first edition and an octavo in four parts. She also points out that Jefferson "had seen buiding in this way near Lyons" and "had known the author at Paris, where he raised some walls to shew his manner," as Jefferson wrote in a letter of April 13, 1800, to William Short in Paris; that Jefferson had told Washington that Cointeraux was not entitled to any particular answer when

Cointeraux had asked to be brought to this country; and that Jefferson had made a précis called "Pisé walls. Cointeraux's new method of 1808."

Jefferson sold his copy to Congress. He did not order it for the University.

[*TH1421.C675.1821]

M
Sowerby 1177

31. *Collection of Papers.*

Collection of Papers on Naval Architecture, Originally Communicated through the Channel of the European Magazine. 2d ed. 2 vols. London, 1791–1800.

Not now owned by the University.

This was ordered by Jefferson for the University in the section on "Technical Arts" of the want list, but there is no record of the library's ever having received a copy. Jefferson sold his own copy, or at least a part of it, to Congress. The British Museum description, rather than Sowerby's annotation on the above edition, has been given here.

U. Va.

M
Sowerby 1227

32. Cresswell, Daniel.

THE / ELEMENTS / OF / LINEAR PERSPECTIVE, / DESIGNED / FOR THE USE OF STUDENTS / IN THE / UNIVERSITY. / By D. CRESSWELL, A.M. / FELLOW OF TRINITY COLLEGE, CAMBRIDGE. / CAMBRIDGE: / *Printed by FRANCIS HODSON,* / FOR J. DEIGHTON; / AND SOLD BY LONGMAN, HURST, REES, ORME, AND BROWN, / PATERNOSTER-ROW, LONDON: AND PARKER, OXFORD. / 1811.

8vo. Title page ([i]); preface (iii-x); table of contents (1 leaf); text (1–66); errata (1 leaf); 9 engraved, folding plates.

The engraver, Wilson Lowry (1762–1824), was born in Whitehaven but worked in London. He was the son of Strickland Lowry, the portraitist and illustrator, and the pupil of John Brown.

Daniel Cresswell (1776–1844) was educated at Cambridge. In addition to the *Perspective* he also wrote a *Treatise on Spherics*. He gives his reasons for the *Perspective*, notes the uses of the camera lucida, and points out what is new in his book in its preface:

The following pages originated in the supposed want of a concise treatise on Perspective, adapted to the system of education established in the University of Cambridge. Perhaps no subject, within the whole range of mathematical enquiry, is in itself more attractive. . . . It is not so readily conceived how the business of delineation can be reduced to a science, certain and demonstrable as that of arithmetic. The principles, by means of which this is effected, although few, and plain, and familiar to the studious, lie beyond the limits of common observation; neither is such an application of them very likely to occur to those who know them best. The bare enunciation, therefore, of the problem, *so to represent an object upon a given surface, that the picture and its original shall excite the same sensations*, is sufficient to stimulate the curiosity of a young and ingenuous mind. Whether, indeed, the doctrine of Perspective be considered only as a remarkable instance of ingenious speculation, or as forming the basis of correct design, and instructing the judgement of the connoisseur in painting, it comes sufficiently recommended to the man of liberal education. [Pp. iii-iv]

They who wish to copy accurately and expeditiously the scenery of nature, will probably have recourse to mechanical means; and the Camera Lucida, the recent invention of Dr. Wollaston, will be found well suited to their purpose. Still, whoever employs himself in drawing will find his advantage in learning the principles of Perspective. [P. vii]

If the investigations here offered to the University should appear difficult to any student of the second year, . . . it can only be attributed to one, or both, of these two causes; the newness of the terms employed, and the want of a familiar acquaintance with the first principles of the geometry of solids. [P. ix]

It only remains formally to acknowledge, what would doubtless be inferred from the history of Perspective, that the following is chiefly to be considered as a new work in what regards its language, the formation and connexion of its propositions, and its general arrangement. They who have read the admirable essay of Dr. Brook Taylor [see No. 63], will no more expect any thing which really deserves the name of originality here, than they would in a treatise on Optics, written after that of Sir Isaac Newton: And this is a subject the utmost limits of which are discovered at a first view. [P. ix-x]

This treatise on perspective is a straightforward exposition of the subject with diagrammatic plates, except for the last, which shows a simple, rendered interior.

There are two copies of the text at the University (QA515 and QA535). In each the *Elements of Linear Perspective* is bound with the

Treatise on Spherics, the *Elements of Linear Perspective* first in QA515 and second in QA535. The spine of QA515 is labeled "Cresswell's Sup. to Euclid."

There is evidence from the nature of the 1825 Kean entry and the 1828 *Catalogue* printed entry that the binding for QA535 was done between these years. A copy of this book was already at the University before Jefferson made up his want list.

U. Va.
*QA515.C7.1811; *QA535.C7

33. Cutbush, James.

Vol. I. THE AMERICAN / ARTIST'S MANUAL, / OR / DIC-TIONARY OF PRACTICAL KNOWLEDGE / IN THE / AP-PLICATION OF PHILOSOPHY / TO / THE ARTS AND MANUFACTURES. / *Selected from the most complete European Systems*, / WITH / ORIGINAL IMPROVEMENTS / AND / APPRO-PRIATE ENGRAVINGS. / ADAPTED TO / THE USE OF THE MANUFACTURERS OF THE UNITED STATES. / BY JAMES CUTBUSH. / *IN TWO VOLUMES–VOL. I.* / PHILADELPHIA: / PUBLISHED BY JOHNSON & WARNER, AND R. FISHER. / W. Brown Printer, Church Alley. / 1814.

8vo. Title page (1 unnumbered p.); copyright (1 unnumbered p.); dedication ([i]); preface ([iii]-iv); text with 14 engravings, of which 1 is folding, inserted and with numerous figures (336 leaves).

Vol. II. THE AMERICAN / ARTIST'S MANUAL / . . . / *IN TWO VOLUMES–VOL. II.* / . . .

8vo. Title page (1 unnumbered p.); copyright (1 unnumbered p.); text, with 22 engravings inserted and with many figures in the text (348 leaves).

The engravers were Hugh Anderson (fl.1811–24), a Philadelphian; Joseph H. Seymour (fl.1719–1822), who worked at Worcester, Boston, and Philadelphia; and either Benjamin Tanner (1775–1848) or his brother Henry S. Tanner (1786–1858), both of whom worked along the eastern seaboard.

James Cutbush (1788–1823), an American chemist, introduces his book by saying:

It was not to be expected that the United States, possessing such an extensive territory, and with a population so small compared with the older countries of Europe, where the number of inhabitants insures manual labor at a moderate price, could have, hitherto, made equal advances in the arts and manufactures. Recent experience has however shewn us what the united efforts of industry and enterprize, conducted by the inventive talents of our countrymen, are capable of effecting. The time has already arrived, when a general diffusion of the knowledge of Europe on these subjects, cannot fail of being highly interesting and beneficial amongst us. [P. iii]

His book is, in actuality, a dictionary of crafts, which is a synonym for the word "arts" as used in the title. The entries on the following subjects, however, are pertinent to the fine arts—bricks, bricklayers, building, cement, color making, engraving, etching, gaslight, nails, pencils, stucco, and whitewash. It is interesting to note in connection with this list that Jefferson wished to have the possibility of using gaslights at the University of Virginia investigated, as seen in a letter of May 20, 1826, to John H. Cocke, although the suggestion seems to have come from the first faculty members.

Cutbush defined building as

the art of constructing and raising an edifice: in which sense it comprehends as well the expenses, as the invention and execution of the design.

In the practice of this useful art, there are five particulars to be principally attended to: 1. Situation; 2. Contrivance, or design; 3. Strength and solidity; 4. Convenience and utility; and 5. Elegance. . . .

The modern rage for building, however, is apparently attended with this unfavourable effect, that little attention is paid to the quality of the materials, and the strength of the edifice, if speculative monied men attain their object, in erecting houses that may be let at a certain rent. [N.p.]

Jefferson ordered this book for the University in the section on "Technical Arts" of the want list, but there is no evidence that a set was acquired before 1828. The library's present set was the gift of A. C. Taylor.

U. Va.
*T9.C95.1814

34. Dati, Carlo Roberto.

VITE / DE' PITTORI ANTICHI / SCRITTE ED ILLUSTRATE / DA CARLO DATI / *NELL' ACCADEMIA DELLA CRUSCA* / LO SMARRITO. / *Colle postille della prima edizione e con quelle che scritte*

/ *in margine dello stesso Autore furono publicate* / *nella seconda.* /
MILANO / Dalla Società Tipografica de' Classici Italiani, / contrada
di s. Margherita, No. 1118. / ANNO 1806.

8vo. Engraved portrait of Dati (1 leaf); title page ([1]); note on the
author ([3]–15); dedication (16–18); note to the reader (19–25); text
(27–294); index (1 unnumbered p.); errata (1 unnumbered p.).

Carlo Roberto Dati (1619–76) was born in Florence. He was an author,
a philosopher, a scientist, and a disciple of Galileo. From 1663 he was
secretary of the Academia della Crusca. His numerous linguistic and
scientific writings, as well as the *Vite* for which he is perhaps best
known, were praised for both style and language.

The *Vite* was first issued in 1667 at Florence. The book is a compilation of the lives of the painters of antiquity, such as Apelles, Par-
rhasius, and Zeuxis.

It was in the University library before Jefferson made up his want
list. Although it appeared in the Kean catalogue, it was more fully identified in the 1828 *Catalogue*. That copy has not survived, but a duplicate
has been acquired recently, the gift of the Thomas Jefferson Memorial
Foundation.

U. Va.
*ND110.D3.1806

35. Delorme, Philibert.

NOVVELLES / INVENTIONS / POVR BIEN BASTIR ET / A
PETITS FRAIZ, TROVVEES / N'AGVERES PAR PHILIBERT
DE / L'orme Lyonnois, Architecte, Con-/seiller & Aumosnier ordinaire /
du feu Roy Henry, / & Abbé de S. Eloy / les Noyon. / A PARIS, /
De l'Imprimerie de Hierosme de Marnef, & / Guillaume Cauellat, au
mont S. Hilaire / à l'enseigne du Pelican. / 1576.

Folio. Title page (1 leaf); dedication (2 leaves); letter to reader (3 unnumbered pp.); poem (1 unnumbered p.); text (1–94); table of contents (2 leaves); colophon (1 leaf). Full-page woodcuts appear on pp.
12, 18, 26, 30, 32, 35, 42, 44, 50, 52, 55, 57, 66, 69, 72, 78, 83, and 85, and
numerous woodcut figures appear in the text.

Philibert Delorme, or de l'Orme (*ca.*1510–70) was born at Lyons, the
son of a master workman, Jehan de l'Orme, who taught him the arts of

building. He then studied in Italy and returned to France under the patronage of Cardinal du Bellay. In 1545 he was *maistre architect et conducteur général des bastiments et édifices, ouvrages, et fortifications* in Brittany, under royal appointment. By 1548 he was at Fontainbleau under Henri II, but he lost his appointments in 1559. A French judgment of Delorme calls him "un des plus grands maitres en l'art de bâtir, non seulement de France, mais du monde entire."

The first edition of this work was in 1561, and the dedication in the 1576 edition is still dated September 8, 1561 (see Plate XXII). The book is primarily a study of timber and timber framing, especially for large, and often barrel-vault-shaped, roofs. It first examines the best kinds of wood and then progresses into the uses of wood in framing. Delorme's other book, *Le premier tome de l'architecture*, 1567, is an entirely different text.

On the back of the drawing of the framing plan of the dome of the Rotunda for the University of Virginia (see Plate XXIII), Jefferson noted "on the top of the wall lay a curbed plate, in Delorme's manner, consisting of 4. thicknesses of 3.i. each. 22.i. wide, pieces 12.f. long, breaking joints every 3.f. bolted through with bolts of iron having a nut & screw at their end. On this curved plate the ribs of the roof are to rest." He also specifies on the same drawing that "the ribs are to be 4. thicknesses of 1.i. plank, in pieces 4.f. long, breaking joints at every foot." There are several illustrations in Delorme showing similar constructions (pp. 12, 18, 32, 35, and 42), but the illustration on page 14 shows a rib made up of short pieces of wood such as Jefferson specified (see Plate XXIV).

The book was ordered for the University in the section on "Architecture" of the want list but was not received during Jefferson's lifetime, although he wrote General Joseph Smith, June 21, 1825: "I was much indebted to you for the kind loan of De Lorme's Architecture. It is now packed up in readiness to be returned. It is one of those of the Catalogue given to Mr. Hilliard, and which he would probably be very willing to take at a reasonable price" (U. Va. Library).

Jefferson sold his own copy to Congress. Kimball (p. 90) says it was acquired between 1785 and 1789. A duplicate has only recently entered the library's collections, the gift of the Thomas Jefferson Memorial Foundation.

U. Va.   M
*NA2517.D4.1576   Sowerby 4183

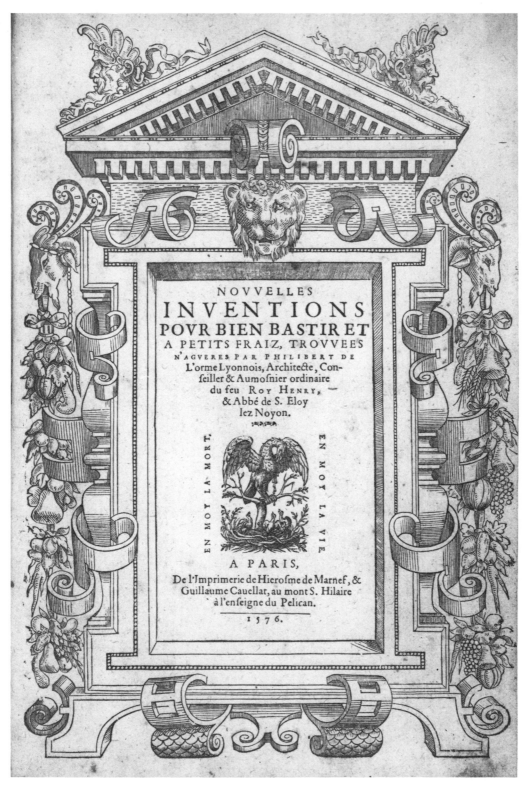

Plate XXII. *From No. 35.* Title page.

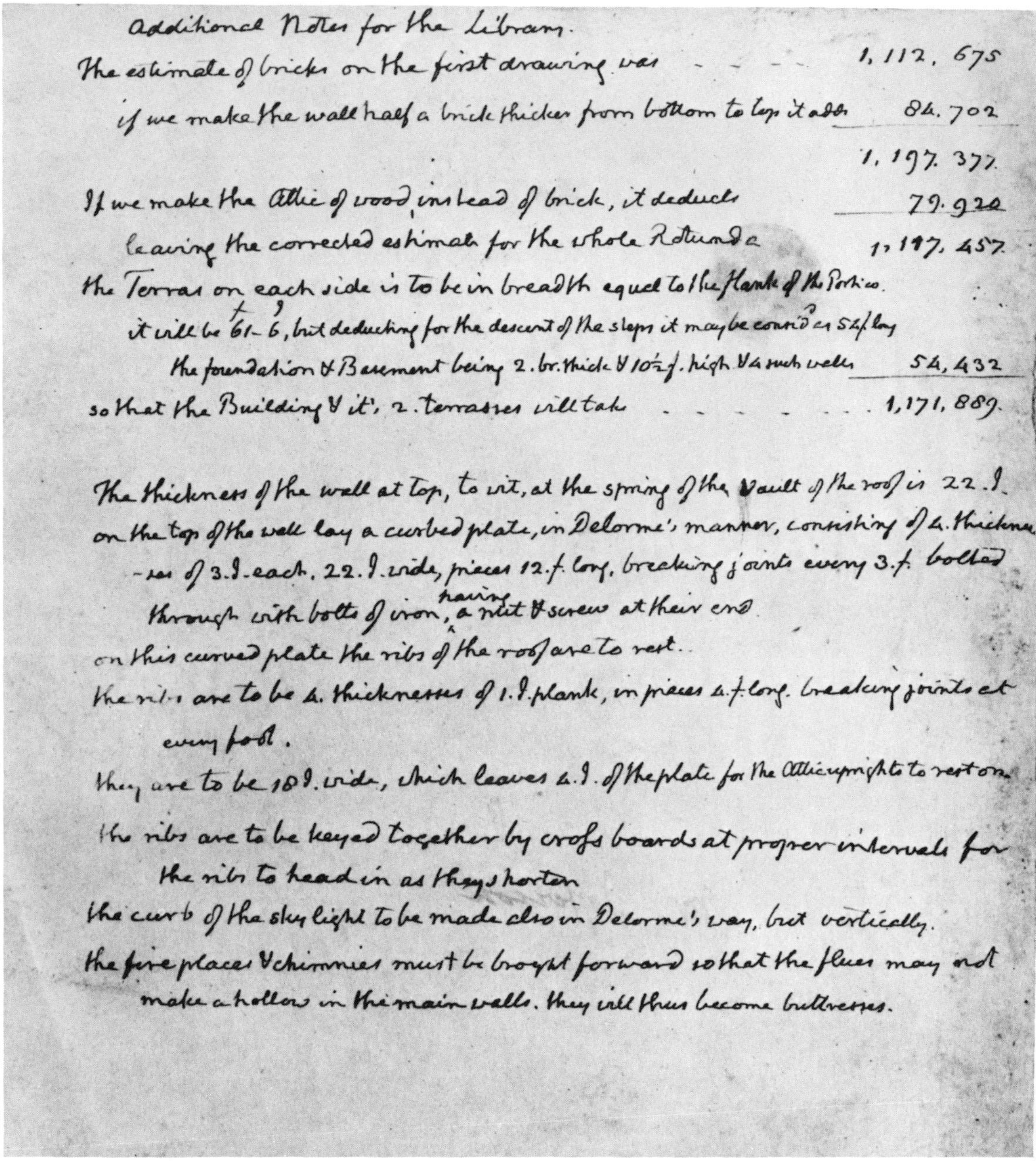

additional Notes for the Library.

The estimate of bricks on the first drawing was   — — — —   1,112,675

if we make the wall half a brick thicker from bottom to top it adds   84,702

                                                           1,197,377

If we make the Attic of wood, instead of brick, it deducts   79,920

leaving the corrected estimate for the whole Rotunda   1,197,457

the Terras on each side is to be in breadth equal to the flank of the Portico.

it will be 61–6, but deducting for the descent of the steps it may be consid'd 54 f long

the foundation & Basement being 2. br. thick & 10½ f. high & as such walls   54,432

so that the Building & it's 2. terrasses will take — — — — —   1,171,889.

The thickness of the wall at top, to wit, at the spring of the Vault of the roof is 22. I.

on the top of the wall lay a curved plate, in Delorme's manner, consisting of 4. thicknesses of 3. I. each. 22. I. wide, pieces 12.f. long, breaking joints every 3.f. bolted through with bolts of iron, having a nut & screw at their end.

on this curved plate the ribs of the roof are to rest.

the ribs are to be 4. thicknesses of 1. I. plank, in pieces 4.f. long. breaking joints at every foot.

they are to be 18 I. wide, which leaves 4. I. of the plate for the Attic uprights to rest on.

the ribs are to be keyed together by cross boards at proper intervals for the ribs to head in as they shorten

the curb of the sky light to be made also in Delorme's way, but vertically.

the fire places & chimnies must be brought forward so that the flues may not make a hollow in the main walls. they will thus become buttresses.

Plate XXIII. Jefferson's specifications for the framing of the Rotunda, University of Virginia (N-332, recto).

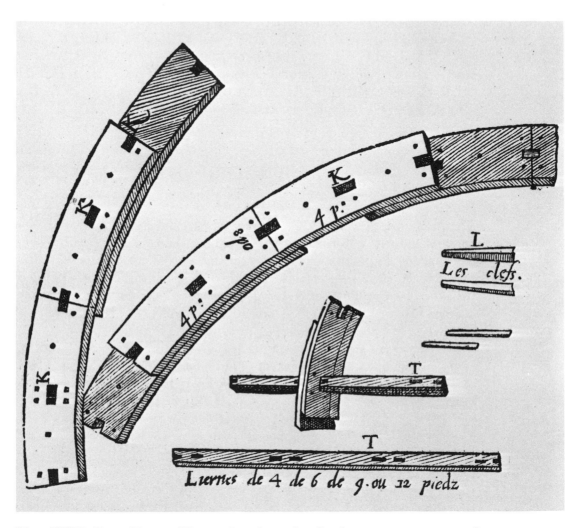

Plate XXIV. *From No. 35.* "Comme les pieces des Courbes se monstrent quand ells sont toutes assembles" (p. 14).

36. Desgodetz, Antoine Babuty.

LES / ÉDIFICES ANTIQUES / DE ROME, / MESURÉS ET DES-SINÉS TRES-EXACTEMENT / SUR LES LIEUX / PAR FEU M. DESGODETZ, / ARCHITECTE DU ROI. / NOUVELLE ÉDITION. / A PARIS, RUE DAUPHINE, / Chez CLAUDE-ANTOINE JOMBERT, File aîné, / Libraire du ROI pour le Génie & l'Artillerie. / DE L'IMPRI-MERIE DE MONSIEUR. / M.DCC.LXXIX. / AVEC APPROBA-TION, ET PRIVILÈGE DU ROI.

Folio. Engraved title page (1 leaf); title page ([i]); dedication ([iii]-iv); note on new edition ([v]-viii); preface of original edition ([ix]-xi); table of chapters (1 unnumbered p.); text (1–140); 137 engraved plates, of which 21 are folding.

The plates were drawn by Desgodetz. The engravers were Nicolas Bonnart (1646–1718), the brother of two painters and the father of a second Nicolas who was both a painter and an engraver; J. B. Brebes (fl.1682), French; De la Boissier; Louis, or Ludwig, de Chastillon, or Chatillon, Chaillon, or Chaillot (1639–1734), French, a painter and engraver; Nicolas Guerard (1648–1719), French, who had a son Nicolas, also an engraver; Sébastien Le Clerc (No. 69); Jean Le Pautre (1618–82), who began life as a carpenter, executed plans and ornaments, and went on to become famous as an engraver; Pierre Le Pautre (1660–1744), son of Jean Le Pautre, both a sculptor and an engraver and holder of the Prix de Rome; le Potre (a misspelling for Le Pautre?); A. D. Marotte; and Jean Jacques Tournier (1604–ca.1670), or perhaps Georges Tournier (fl.1650–84), although some say they were the same person.

The engraved title in this edition (see Plate XXV) is the same as that for the 1682 edition, except that the date has been removed and 1779 inserted. The other plates are restrikes of those in the 1682 edition.

Antoine Babuty Desgodetz (1653–1728), born in Paris, was educated at the Académie and, in 1674, became a *pensionnaire du roi* at the French academy in Rome. On his return to France he became *contrôleur des bâtiments de Chambord*, 1680; *contrôleur des monuments de Paris*, 1694; and a professor at the Académie, 1707.

His eighteenth-century editor gives a good account of Desgodetz and the reasons for reissuing his book:

Antoine Desgodetz naquit à Paris en Novembre 1653, & s'adonna, dès ses premières années, a l'étude de l'Architecture, pour laquelle il avoit un goût

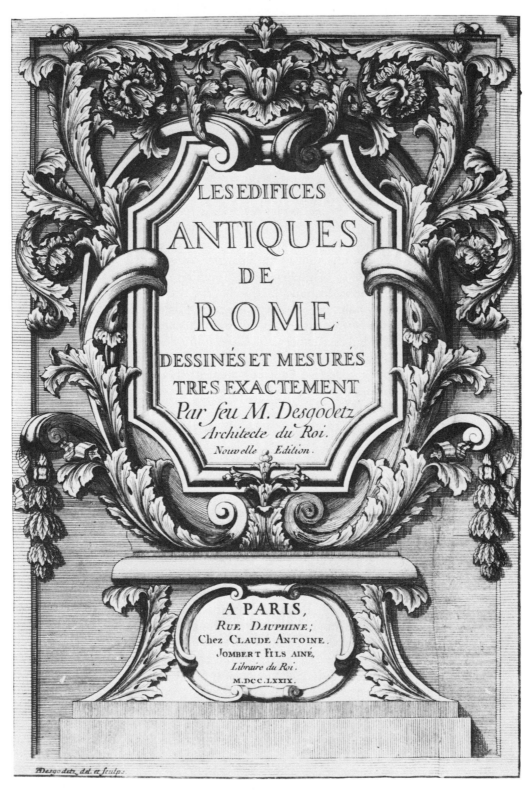

LES EDIFICES ANTIQUES DE ROME
DESSINÉS ET MESURÉS TRES EXACTEMENT
Par feu M. Desgodetz
Architecte du Roi.
Nouvelle Edition.

A PARIS,
RUE DAUPHINE,
Chez CLAUDE ANTOINE
JOMBERT FILS AÎNÉ,
Libraire du Roi.
M.DCC.LXXIX.

Desgodetz del. et sculps.

Plate XXV. *From No. 36.* Engraved title page.

décidé. Il se livra à cet Art avec tant d'ardeur, qu'à l'âge de dix-neuf ans (1672) il obtint la permission d'être présent aux conférences de l'Académie. Deux ans après (1674), M. Colbert l'envoya en Italie pour l'exécution du projet dont nous venons de parler. De retour dans sa patrie (1677), il rassembla tous les dessins qu'il avoit faits de ces somptueux Edifices, dont les vestiges ont encore aujourd'hui tant d'admirateurs. Il ajouta une description historique & critique sur chacun de ces objets, & en fit un recueil qu'il publia (1682) à Paris en un volume in-folio sous ce titre, *Les Edifices antiques de Rome*, &c:, &c c'est ce même Ouvrage dont nous donnons aujourd'hui une Edition nouvelle. [P. vi]

Lorsque M. Desgodetz revint à Paris, il rendit compte de ses travaux à M. Colbert, qui en fut se satisfait qu'il chargea de choisir les meilleurs Graveurs en Architecture, pour faire exécuter ses dessins aux dépens de Sa Majesté: il ordonna que rein ne fût épargne pour rendre cet Ouvrage digne de la grandeur & de la magnificence de Louis XIV. Ce Monarque fit présent de l'Edition à l'Auteur, laquelle, à la vérité, fut tirée à petit nombre & bientôt épuisée. Après la mort de M. Desgodetz, ces Planches sont passée dans les mains d'un de ses neveux, qui n'a point voulu qu'elles vissent le jour tant qu'il a vécu. Depuis nombre d'années, ce Livre infiniment recherché étoit devenu d'un prix excessif; . . . Des héritiers plus traitables viennent heureusement de consentir à les céder; ce sont ces mêmes Planches que l'on s'empresse d'offrir aux Curieux instruits, avec le texte de l'Auteur, que l'on redonne sans aucun changement. [Pp. (v)-vi]

Desgodetz himself says

Je ne doute point que mon entreprise ne paroisse bien téméraire, de vouloir traiter un sujet sur lequel les plus savans Architectes ont déja travaillé, & qu'ils semblent avoir entièrement épuisé: je ne le fais aussi qu'avec beaucoup de répugnance, ayant de la peine à me persuader qu'il se puisse rien ajouter aux Ouvrages excellens que Palladio [No. 91], Serlio [No. 113] & Labacco nous ont laissés des Edifices anciens, & à ce que M. de Chambray en a remarqué dans son Parallèle de l'Architecture antique avec la moderne [No. 46].

Ma premiere intention a donc été, lorsque j'ai entrepris de mesurer avec précision les Antiquités de Rome, de savoir lequel de ces Auteurs qui sont en réputation devoit être suivi, comme ayant donné les véritables mesures. Mais lorsqu'étant sur les lieux j'ai employé tout le soin nécessaire pour être éclairci sur ce doute, j'ai été bien surpris de trouver un autre éclaircissement que je ne cherchois pas, qui a été de voir que ceux qui ont mesuré jusqu'à présent les Edifices antiques, ne l'ont pas fait avec précision; & qu'il n'y a aucun de tous les dessins que nous en avons, où il ne se trouve des fautes très-considérables. [P. ix]

Ayant communiqué ces dessins à Messieurs de l'Académie Royale d'Architecture, lorsque j'ai été de retour, & à quelques autres personnes intelligentes pour les examiner, ils m'ont témoigné de les approuver assez pour me donner la confiance de les présenter a Monseigneur Colbert, qui m'ordonna de les mettre en état d'être gravés par les plus habiles de ceux qui gravent l'Architecture pour le Roi, & d'être imprimés; voulant que le tout fût fait aux dépens de Sa Majesté, afin que rien ne manquât de sa part à la perfection de cet Ouvrage. [P. x]

Mais je n'ai pas cru que pour éviter le reproche d'une vaine ostentation d'exactitude, je dusse m'absentir d'exposer les choses telles que je les ai trouvées, puisque cette exactitude est la seule chose dont il s'agit ici. [P. xi]

The accuracy of Desgodetz's measurements, the brilliance of his drawings, and the beauty of the engraved plates have made this a most respected and desired book.

Of the twenty-five buildings dealt with, at least six may be traced as influences in Jefferson's work. The orders of four, the Pantheon, the baths of Diocletian, the theater of Marcellus, and the temple of Fortuna Virilis, were used as models for buildings at the University of Virginia, though at the time the University was built Jefferson no longer owned Desgodetz and went to Palladio (No. 92b) and Fréart de Chambray (No. 46) for details. Desgodetz devotes no less than twenty-three plates to the Pantheon and describes very elaborately and carefully the frieze ornaments for the temple of Fortuna Virilis.

Jefferson had also used Desgodetz earlier to derive the frieze ornaments for the entrance hall, the parlor, and his own bedroom at Monticello.[1] That for his bedroom was taken from the fourth plate for the temple of Fortuna Virilis (see Plates XXVI and XXVII) and that for the entrance hall from the fourth plate for the temple of Antonin and Faustina (see Plates XXVIII and XXIX). The frieze in the parlor is taken from the temple of Jupiter the Thunderer (see Plates XXX and XXXI). Only a portion of the entablature of the last temple remained, but as the plates show, Jefferson faithfully copied Desgodetz's rendering, and Desgodetz's description of the temple applies equally to the frieze at Monticello: "Du Temple de Jupiter tonnant. . . . Dans la frize, les têtes de boeuf ne répondent pas au droit du milieu des colonnes; & les instrumens des sacrifices sont semés sans ordre & sans symétrie. On ne peut savoir ce qui étoit à l'angle de la frise, parce qu'il est ruiné" (p. 59).

Sowerby points out that Jefferson's copy was ordered on July 20, 1791. It was the Jombert edition that Jefferson owned and later sold to Congress. It was also this edition which he ordered for the University in the section on "Architecture" of the want list. A copy was at the University before the 1828 *Catalogue* was compiled, but it is listed there as

---

[1] "All the interior friezes Jefferson took from Desgodetz *Les edifices antiques de Rome*" (Frederick D. Nichols and James A. Bear, Jr., *Monticello* [Monticello, Va.: The Thomas Jefferson Memorial Foundation, 1967], p. 24).

Plate XXVI. *From No. 36.* "Du temple de la Fortune Virile, à Rome" (Pl. IV, p.44).

Plate XXVII. Frieze in Jefferson's bedroom, Monticello. See Plate XXVI.

ornements de la frise

4 modules   5 parties

Chapiteau des colonnes dessiné sur l'angle du tailloir

plan du chapiteau des Colonnes

Soffite de l'architrave

1. module   23 parties ½

Desgodetz delin.

Plate XXVIII. *From No. 36.* "Du portique du temple d'Antonin et de Faustine, a Rome" (Pl. IV, p. 50).

Plate XXIX. Frieze in entrance hall, Monticello.

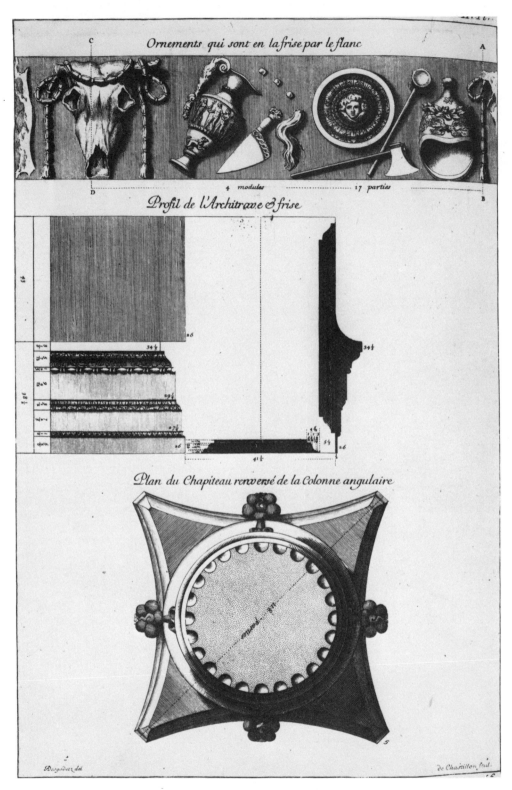

Ornements qui sont en la frise par le flanc

Profil de l'Architrave & frise

Plan du Chapiteau renversé de la Colonne angulaire

Plate XXX. *From No. 36.* "Du temple de Iupiter Tonant, à Rome" (Pl. II, p. 59).

Plate XXXI. Frieze in parlor, Monticello.

"1729" presumably a misreading of the Roman numerals. That copy has not survived, but a duplicate, the gift of the Thomas Jefferson Memorial Foundation, has replaced it.

U. Va.   M
*NA311.D4.1779   Sowerby 4198

37. Dezallier d'Argentville, Antoine Joseph.

THE / *THEORY* and *PRACTICE* / OF / GARDENING: / Wherein is fully handled / All that relates to Fine GARDENS, / COMMONLY CALLED / PLEASURE-GARDENS, / Consisting of / PARTERRES, GROVES, BOWLING-GREENS, &c. / CONTAINING / Several PLANS, and general DISPOSITIONS of GARDENS, New Designs / of Parterres, Groves, Grass-plots, Mazes, Banqueting-Rooms, Galleries, / Portico's, and Summer-houses of Arbour-work, Terrasses, Stairs, Fountains, / Cascades, and other Ornaments of use in the Decoration and Embelish-/ ment of Gardens. / WITH / The Manner of making the GROUND, forming DESIGNS suitable to the Place, / and putting them in Execution, according to the Principles of Geometry. / The Method of Setting and Raising in little time, all the PLANTS requisite in fine GARDENS: / Also the Way to find WATER, to convey it into Gardens, and to make Basons and Fountains / for the same. / Together with REMARKS and GENERAL RULES in all that concerns the ART of / GARDENING. / By *Le Sieur* ALEXANDER LE BLOND. / *Done from the late Edition printed at* Paris, / By *JOHN JAMES* of *Greenwich.* / The Second Edition. / With very large ADDITIONS, and a new TREATISE of FLOWERS / and ORANGE-TREES. / *LONDON:* / Printed for BERNARD LINTOT, at the *Cross-Keys*, between the / *Temple-Gates*, in *Fleet-street.* 1728.

4to. Title page in two colors ([i]); table of contents (ii-vii, with ii-iv missing, and v-vi partially torn away); advice to the binder and errata (1 unnumbered p.); text (1–297); index (6 leaves); 24 engravings (of a total of 38; 14 have been cut or torn out), all folding.

The engraver signs himself "Ver. Gucht." He might have been Michael van der Gucht (1660–1725) or either of his sons, Gerard (1696–1776) or Jan, or John (1697–1776), both of whom trained with their father. Jan became a friend of Hogarth (No. 56).

As a French work, *Théorie et practique du jardinage*, this book was first published in 1709 under the initials L. S. A. J. D. A., for Le Sieur

A. J. Desallier d'Argentville. The second edition (1713) and third edition (1722) came out under the name of Alexander Le Blond, who had done some drawings for it. His name was retained, even in translation, until 1747, when, as Sowerby points out, Dezallier d'Argentville brought out an edition under his own name and explained the earlier confusions.

Antoine Joseph Dezallier d'Argentville (1680–1765) was born in Paris. He studied with B. Picart, de Piles, and Le Blond and also studied natural history. He published, in addition to the *Théorie*, an *Histoire naturelle*, 1742, the three-volume *Abrégé de la vie des plus fameux peintres*, 1745–52, and *Ennumerationis fossilium*, 1751.

John James (d.1742) worked under Wren, Vanbrugh, Campbell, and Ripley. He was clerk of the works at Greenwich Hospital, 1705; master carpenter at St. Paul's Cathedral, 1711; surveyor of Westminster Abbey, 1725; Master of the Carpenter's Company, 1724; and, it is thought, surveyor of His Majesty's works, 1736. He was especially active in the field of architectural publishing and translation. In addition to the *Theory*, whose first edition in English was before 1712, he published a translation from the Italian of Pozzo's *Rules and Examples of Perspective*, 1707; a translation from the French of Claude Perrault's *A Treatise of the Five Orders of Columns in Architecture*, 1708 (see No. 96a); and *A Short Review of the Several Pamphlets and Schemes That Have Been Offered to the Publick in Relation to the Building of a Bridge at Westminster*, 1736.

Jean Baptiste Alexander Le Blond (1679–1719) was a French architect especially interested in gardens.

The book is:

divided into four Parts, which contain, in all, twenty two Chapters.

IN the first Part is taught all the *Theory of Gardening*, it being necessary, as every one knows, to learn the Theory before the Practice. . . .

THE second Part teaches the *Practice of Gardening*. . . .

THE third Part contains the Manner of planting and raising in little time, the Plants and Flowers proper for Pleasure-Gardens.

THE fourth and last Part shews the Method of searching out Water, conveying it into Gardens, and of making Basons, Fountains, and Cascades. [Pp. 5–6]

It does not conceal the fact that wealth is needed in order to have a handsome garden, it is full of good advice, and it is most interesting on the relations between the architect and the client, relations which apparently have not changed much over the centuries:

SUPPOSING, then, that a private Person, wealthy, and curious in the Art of Gardening, would be at the necessary Expence of planting a handsome Garden, I lead him, step by step, from the Choice he ought to make of a good Soil, to the Execution and highest Perfection of his Garden, instructing him in whatever he ought to know, that he be not impos'd upon by the Countrymen and Artificers he shall have occasion to employ. [P. 4]

The first Thing, and the most essential to be observed is chusing a Place to plant a Garden in, is the Situation and Exposition of the Ground. [P. 7]

To make a complete Disposition and Distribution of a general Plan, respect must be had to the Situation of the Ground: For the greatest Skill in the right ordering of a Garden, is, thoroughly to understand, and consider the natural Advantages and Defects of the Place; to make use of the one, and to redress the other: Situations differing in every Garden. . . .

Tis, therefore, the great Business of an Architect, or Designer of Gardens, when he would contrive a handsome Plan, with his utmost Art and good OEconomy to improve the natural Advantages, and to redress the Imperfections, Bevellings, and Inequalities of the Ground. With these Precautions he should guide and restrain the Impetuosity of his Genius, never swerving from Reason, but constantly submitting, and conforming himself to that which suits best with the natural Situation of the Place.

An Architect has sometimes great cause to complain, that he is oblig'd to subject his Genius and good Taste to the wrong Notions of the Gentlemen he has to do with, who are often so fond of their own Opinions, as to spoil many good Designs. This, without Enquiry into the Cause, is by Criticks generally, though unjustly, thrown upon the Architect, unless he may be said to have deserv'd it for his blind Complaisance. [P. 15]

The design of gardens in 1709 was still primarily worked out "according to the Principles of Geometry," as the title page says, an approach which may be seen in the book's discussion of parterres:

The Name of *Parterre* has its Original from the *Latin* Word *Partiri*, to *divide;* and according to some, a Parterre denotes a flat and even Surface.

The Compartiments and Borders of Parterres are taken from Geometrical Figures, as well rightlined, as circular, mix'd, &c. [P. 39]

Parterres of Embroidery are so called, because the Box wherewith they are planted, imitates Embroidery upon the Ground. These are the finest and most magnificent of all, and are sometimes accompanied with Knots and Scrolls of Grass-work. Their Bottom should be sanded, the better to distinguish the Foliage and Flourish'd-work of the Embroidery, which is usually filled with Smiths-Dust, or black Earth. [P. 41]

The book does not seem to have had an influence on Jefferson, since there is almost no evidence that he used this formal kind of garden design. The library's present copy duplicates the one Jefferson sold to Congress. He did not order it for the University.

M

*SB461.D48   Sowerby 4226

38. Donati, Alessandro.

ALEXANDRI DONATI / E SOCIETATE JESU / ROMA / VETUS AC RECENS / Utriusque AEdificiis / ILLUSTRATA. / *In multis locis aucta, castigatior reditta, indice locupletissimo,* / & *Figuris AEneis illustrata.* / EDITIO ULTIMA. / AMSTELAEDAMI, / *Prostant* apud Janssonio-Waesbergios / & Joannem Wolters. 1695. / *Cum Privilegio.*

4to. Engraved frontispiece (1 leaf); two-color title page (1 leaf); dedication (2 leaves); note to reader (1 unnumbered p.); index of chapters, with notes to binders and note of privilege, each 1 leaf, misbound within index (3 unnumbered pp.); text, with 90 engravings, of which 3 are folding maps (1–356); poetic quotations (1 unnumbered p.); indexes (19 unnumbered pp.).

Alessandro Donati (1584–1640) was an Italian professor and antiquary.

The first edition of this book was in 1633. It gives a description of ancient Roman buildings with many quotations from ancient authors. The engraved plates, all unsigned, show the buildings both in their seventeenth-century condition and in the author's restorations, with some illustrations from coins. The frontispiece is an allegory of Rome, pagan and Christian (see Plate XXXII).

Jefferson's own copy, acquired about 1778 according to Kimball (p. 93), was sold to Congress. He ordered the book for the University in the section on "Architecture" of the want list, but there is no record of its having been received before his death. The library's present copy is a recent acquisition, the gift of the Thomas Jefferson Memorial Foundation.

U. Va.
*DG63.D67.1695

M
Sowerby 4195

Plate XXXII. *From No. 38.* Frontispiece.

39. Dossie, Robert.

Vol. I. THE / HANDMAID / TO THE / ARTS, / VOL. THE FIRST. / TEACHING, /

I. A perfect knowledge of the MATERIA PICTORIA; or, the nature, use, preparation, and composition, of all the various substances employed in PAINTING, as well *vehicles*, *dryers*, &c. as *colours;* including those peculiar to enamel and painting on glass.

II. The means of delineation, or the several DEVICES employed for the more easily and accurately making DESIGNS FROM NATURE, or DEPICTED REPRESENTATIONS; either by *off-tracing*, *calking*, *reduction*, or other means; with the methods of taking *casts*, or *impres*sions, from *figures*, *busts*, *medals*, *leaves*, &c.

III. The various manners of GILDING, SILVERING, BRONZING, with the preparation of the genuine GOLD and SILVER *powders*, and the imitations of them, as also of the *fat oil*, *gold sizes*, and other necessary compositions; —the art of JAPANNING, as applicable not only to the former purposes, but to coaches, snuffboxes, &c. in the manner lately introduced;—and the method of STAINING DIFFERENT KINDS OF SUBSTANCES, *with all the several colours.*

The whole being calculated, as well for conveying a more / accurate and extensive knowledge of the matters treated of / to professed artists, as to initiate those who are desirous to / attempt these arts, into the method of preparing and using / all the colours, and other substances employed in *painting* in / *oil*, *miniature*, *crayons*, *encaustic*, *enamel*, *varnish*, *distemper*, and *fresco*, as also in *gilding*, &c. / The SECOND EDITION, with considerable Additions and / Improvements. / LONDON: / Printed for J. NOURSE, Bookseller in Ordinary to his / MAJESTY. / MDCCLXIV.

8vo. Title page ([i]); dedication ([iii-iv]); preface ([v]-xxvii); table of contents (9 unnumbered pp.); text ([1]–522); index (10 leaves).

Vol. II. THE / HANDMAID / TO THE / ARTS, / VOL. THE SECOND. / TEACHING, /

I. The preparation of *inks, cements,* and *sealing-wax,* of every kind.
II. The art of *engraving, etching,* and *scraping mezzotintos;* with the preparation of the *aqua fortis,* varnishes, or other grounds, &c. in the best manner now practised by the French; as also the best manner of *printing copper-plates;* an improved method of producing *washed prints,* and of *printing* in *chiaro obscuro,* and *with colours,* in the way practised by Mr. *Le Blon.*
III. The nature, composition, and preparation of *glass* of every sort; as also the various methods of counterfeiting *gems* of all kinds, by *coloured glass, pastes, doublets,* or the use of *foils.*

IV. The nature and composition of *porcelain,* as well according to the methods practised in China, as in the several European manufactories; with the best manner of burning, glazing, painting, and gilding the ware.
V. Preparation of *transparent* and *coloured glazings,* for stone or earthen-ware.
VI. The manner of preparing and moulding *papier mache,* and whole paper, for the forming boxes, frames, festoons, &c. and of varnishing, painting, and gilding the pieces of each kind; with the method of making the light Japan-ware.

To which is added an APPENDIX; / CONTAINING / Several supplemental articles belonging, in some manner, to / heads before treated of, either in this or the first volume; / particularly, the method of *marbling paper,* of *taking off / paintings from old and transferring them to new cloths;* of / *weaving tapestry,* both by the *high* and *low warp;* and of / manufacturing *paper hangings* of every kind. / The SECOND EDITION, . . .

8vo. Title page ([i]); preface ([iii]-xiv); table of contents (7 leaves); text ([1]–409); half title for appendix ([411]); appendix (413–62); index (5 leaves).

Robert Dossie (d. 1777) was English, some say an apothecary.

The first edition of his book is given as 1758. It is essentially a how-to-do-it book, and its title pages indicate the fields it investigates (see Plate XXXIII). Dossie notes the camera obscura, a device used by Jefferson whose own camera obscura still exists at Monticello, as follows: "In the drawing after nature . . . some reflected image is obtained by means of a *camera obscura,* which affords an opportunity both of drawing the figure, and imitating the natural colour of the objects" (I, 386). And again: "The second method used to facilitate the drawing after nature, to wit, by the reflected image of the object, is performed by the

THE
HANDMAID
TO THE
ARTS,

VOL. THE FIRST.

TEACHING,

I. A perfect knowledge of the MA-TERIA PICTORIA; or, the nature, use, preparation, and composition, of all the various substances employed in PAINTING, as well *vehicles*, *dryers*, &c. as *colours*; including those peculiar to enamel and painting on glass.

II. The means of delineation, or the several DEVICES employed for the more easily and accurately making DESIGNS FROM NATURE, or DEPICTED REPRESENTATIONS; either by *off-tracing*, *calking*, *reduction*, or other means; with the methods of taking *casts*, or *impres-*sions, from *figures*, *busts*, *medals*, *leaves*, &c.

III. The various manners of GILDING, SILVERING, BRONZING, with the preparation of the genuine GOLD and SILVER *powders*, and imitations of them, as also of the *fat oil*, *gold sizes*, and other necessary compositions; —the art of JAPANNING, as applicable not only to the former purposes, but to coaches, snuff-boxes, &c. in the manner lately introduced;—and the method of STAINING DIFFERENT KINDS OF SUBSTANCES, *with all the several colours.*

The whole being calculated, as well for conveying a more accurate and extensive knowledge of the matters treated of to professed artists, as to initiate those who are desirous to attempt these arts, into the method of preparing and using all the colours, and other substances employed in *painting* in *oil*, *miniature*, *crayons*, *encaustic*, *enamel*, *varnish*, *distemper*, and *fresco*, as also in *gilding*, &c.

The SECOND EDITION, with considerable Additions and Improvements.

LONDON:

Printed for J. NOURSE, Bookseller in Ordinary to his
MAJESTY.

MDCCLXIV.

Plate XXXIII. *From No.* 39. Title page (Vol. I). Copy received on Jefferson's order.

camera obscura, of which a portable kind adapted to this purpose is commonly made by the opticians. It is needless, therefore, to give any description of these instruments" (I, 394).

Sowerby points out that Jefferson's own set, later sold to Congress, was entered in his undated manuscript catalogue as having cost "9/6." He ordered the same edition for the University in the section on "Technical Arts" of the want list, and the library still owns the set acquired on his order.

U. Va.   M
*TP144.D72.1764   Sowerby 1094

40. Durand, Jean-Nicolas-Louis.

RECUEIL ET PARALLÈLE / DES ÉDIFICES DE TOUT GENRE, ANCIENS ET MODERNES, / *REMARQUABLES PAR LEUR BEAUTÉ, PAR LEUR GRANDEUR OU PAR LEUR SINGULARITÉ, ET DESSINÉS SUR UNE MÊME ÉCHELLE.* / Par J. N. L. DURAND, Architecte et Professeur d'Architecture à l'Ecole Polytechnique. /

Il importe extrêmement aux Architectes, aux Ingénieurs civils et militaires, aux / Peintres d'histoire et de paysage, aux Sculpteurs, aux Dessinateurs, aux Décorateurs / de téâtres, en un mot, à tous ceux qui doivent construire ou représenter des édi-/fices et des monumens, d'étudier et de connoître tout ce qu'on a fait de plus / intéressant en architecture dans les pays et dans tous les siècles. /

Mais les édifices qui méritent quelque considération se trouvent confondus avec une / foule d'autres qui ne sont remarquables en rien; il sont de plus dispersés dans près de / trois cents volumes, la plupart in-folio, dont la collection monteroit à un prix / énorme; et il est impossible aux artistes de s'en procurer la connoissance entière, / par une autre voie que celle des bibliothèques. /

Ce moyen-là même exige un tems infini, et n'est d'ailleurs practicable que pour les artistes / qui habitent les grandes villes. De plus, quand ils seroient tous à portée d'en faire usa-/ge; peut-être que les avantages qu'il leur procureroit ne les dédommageroit que foi-/blement de leurs peines. En voici la raison: souvent un volume n'est composé que d'objets / de différent genres; tandi que ceux qui sont du même genre se trouvent disséminés / dans un grand nombre de voulmes. Or on sent combien, dans ce cas-là, les comparaisons, / qui, seules peuvent amener à juger et à raisonner, doivent être longues, pénibles, impar-/faites et peu fructueuses. La différence des échelles ajoute encore à ces inconvé-niens. /

Dans cet état de chose, j'ai pensé que si détachant des trois cents volumes dont je / viens de parler, les seuls objets qui sont essentiels à connoître, je les rassemblois dans un / seul volume d'un prix tout au plus égal à celui d'un ouvrage ordinaire d'architecture; / ce seroit offrir aux artistes un tableau général et peu coûteux de l'architecture, un / tableau qu'ils pourroient parcourir en peu de tems, examiner sans peine, étudier a-/vec fruit; surtout, si classois les édifices et les monumens par genres; si je les / rapprochois selon leur degré d'analogie; si je les assujetissois en outre à une même / échelle: et c'est ce que j'ai entrepris de faire. Pour arriver plus sûrement à ce but, j'ai / rejeté de ce recueil, nonseulement tous les objets qui n'offroient aucun intérêt en eux-/mêmes, mais encore ceux qui ressemblant plus ou moins à d'autres morceaux d'un / intérêt majeur n'auroient fait que grosser le volume, sans augmenter la masse des idées. /

Peutre-être, trouvera-t-on dans ce recueil, quelques édifices qui paroîtront peu / intéressans; mais comme ce sont presque les seuls de ce genre qui existent, j'ai / cru devoir les y placer afin d'appeler l'attention sur ce genre d'architecture. /

On y trouvera aussi des restaurations peu authentiques, telles que celles des / thermes par Palladio, et de plusiers édifices de l'ancienne Rome par Piranèse, / Pirro Ligorio &c.; mais je n'ai pas voulu priver les architectes des beaux / partis que ces restaurations présentent, et dont il peuvent faire de fréquentes / et d'heureuses applications. /

Je me suis même permis, non-seulement de les simplifier, mais encore d'en / offrir qui sont presque entièrement de ma façon, j'espére qu'on me pardonnera / d'avoir osé me ranger à côté de ces grands mai-tres; pour peu que l'on fasse / attention que loin d'avoir voulu les cor-riger, je ne me suis attaché qu'à manifester d'u-/ne mannière plus évidente, l'esprit qui règne dans leur magnifiques productions. /

Cet ouvrage composé de quatre-vingt-douze planches se trouve à l'Ecole Polytechnique, chez l'Auteur. Prix 180 francs. / *Les artistes pourront le prendre par cahier. Chaque cahier est de six feuilles.* Prix 12 francs. / Paris, an ix [1800].

Folio. Engraved double title page; engraved double index plate; plates 1–90, all double engravings.

The engravers were Louis-Pierre Baltard (1764–1846), architect, en-graver, and painter who trained, partially, in Rome after 1786; Coquet, an early nineteenth-century French engraver; J. J. De la Porte, French; Antoine-Joseph Gaitte (1753–ca.1835), French engraver, principally of monuments; Lepagellet, or Lepagelet, or le Pagelet, French, working in Paris; Charles Pierre Joseph Normand (1765–1840), Prix de Rome, 1792, an architect and engraver and a member of the Académie des Beaux-Arts; Pierre Nicolas Ransonnette (1745–1810), student of Choffard, *dessinateur et graveur de Monsieur, frère du roi*, and a painter as well as an engraver (see also No. 64); and Jean-Baptiste Réville (1767–1825), a student of Berthault.

Jean-Nicolas-Louis Durand (1760–1834) was the son of Nicolas Durand (1739–1830), who was the *architecte de la Province de Champagne* and the *architecte des Dames de France*. Jean-Nicolas-Louis studied with Boulée and at the École des Beaux-Arts, eventually holding a professorship at the École Polytechnique from 1795 to 1830. In addition to the *Recueil* he also issued his *Précis des leçons d'architecture*, 1801–5.

The only "text" in the *Recueil* is that on the title page. The plates show historic building types drawn to the same scale for comparative purposes. Both the drawing and the restorations are very neoclassic.

The date on the title page reads "An IX," which the compiler of the University's 1828 *Catalogue* took to mean 1801 instead of 1800. Although it was in the University's collection by 1828 as a result of Jefferson's order in the section on "Architecture" of the want list, it did not survive. The library's present copy is a recently acquired duplicate, the gift of the Thomas Jefferson Memorial Foundation.

U. Va.
*NA202.D8.1800

41. Encyclopédie méthodique.

Encyclopédie méthodique, ou par ordre de matieres, par une Societé de Gens de Lettres. Paris, 1782–1832.

Not now owned by the University, except for some volumes outside the fine arts and a microfilm copy of the volumes on *Musique*.

Not completed until 1832, this encyclopedia was eventually to reach 102 numbers, or 337 parts, comprising 166½ volumes of quarto text and 51 parts of illustrations with a total of 6,439 plates. Jefferson's own set, which he sold to Congress, contained 136½ volumes.

In 1828 the library had 162 of the volumes, probably all that had been issued to that date. Of these, only the volumes concerning mathematics are now in the collections, but these alone are enough to confirm that the dating of the set in the printed *Catalogue* is wrong. The beginning date of 1787 given there is almost certainly a misprint for 1782, when the printing of the encyclopedia actually began.

Jefferson, presumably to distinguish the set from the alphabetically arranged work of Diderot and D'Alembert, referred to it under the name of its first publisher, Panckoucke. Since the present listing concerns the fine arts, the following sections are relevant, and indeed, as Brunet pointed out long ago, the volumes on the different subject matters have for more than a century usually been sold separately:

Antiquités et mythologie. 10 parts in 5 vols., plus 2 vols. of 380 plates.

Architecture. 3 vols.

Art oratoire et jardinage. 1 vol. and 54 plates.

Arts et métiers. 16 parts in 8 vols., and 1,509 plates.

Beaux-arts. 2 parts in 4 vols., and 1 vol. of 115 plates.

Musique. 3 parts in 2 vols., with 188 plates.

U. Va.   M
                                                                           Sowerby 4889

42. Etienne, Jean d'.

MEMOIRE / SUR LA DÉCOUVERTE / D'UN CIMENT / IMPÉNÉTRABLE A L'EAU; / ET SUR L'APPLICATION DE CE MÊME CIMENT / A UNE TERRASSE DE LA MAISON DE L'AUTEUR. / *Par M. D'Etienne, Chevalier de l'Ordre Royal,* / & *Militaire de S. Louis, &c. &c.* / Prix, trois livres. / A PARIS, / De l'Imprimerie de Ph.-D. PIERRES, Imprimeur Ordinaire du Roi. / *Et se vend* chez l'Auteur, rue de Mesnil-montant, près le Boulevard du Temple. / *M. DCC. LXXXII.*

Small 4to. Title page (1 leaf); dedication (1 leaf); text ([1]–19); engraved headpiece; 1 woodcut tailpiece.

Jean d'Etienne (1725–98) was a French engineer and mathematician. The cement is, as the title of the book states, "impénétrable a l'eau." Etienne gives its composition and the preparation of the floor to receive it. The book is a paperbound pamphlet.

Sowerby described the book as the first edition, a quarto of fourteen leaves. Jefferson acquired his copy between 1785 and 1789, according to Kimball (p. 93), and sold it to Congress. This edition was printed by Philippe-Denys Pierres, who a few years later was to print Jefferson's *Notes on Virginia*.

Jefferson ordered the book for the University in the section on "Technical Arts" of the want list, but there is no record of its having been received by the library. It should be noted that Jefferson listed this book under "Architecture" in his catalogue of his own library. The present copy on the University's shelves has been recently acquired, the gift of the Thomas Jefferson Memorial Foundation.

U. Va.   M
*TP877.E7.1782   Sowerby 4204

43a. Félibien, André.

Entretiens sur les vies et sur les ouvrages des plus excellens peintres anciens et modernes. 5 vols. Amsterdam, 1706.

Not now owned by the University.

See No. 43b.

M
Sowerby 4248

43b. Félibien, André.

Vol. I ENTRETIENS / SUR LES VIES / ET / SUR LES OUVRAGES / DES PLUS / EXCELLENS PEINTRES / ANCIENS ET MODERNES; / *AVEC* / LA VIE DES ARCHITECTES / *PAR MONSIEUR FELIBIEN.* / NOUVELLE EDITION, REVUE, CORRIGÉE / & augmentée des Conferences de l'Académie Royale / de Peinture & de Sculpture; / *De l'Idée du Peintre parfait, des Traitez de la Miniature, / des Desseins, des Estampes, de la connoissance / des Tableaux, & du Goût des Nations;* / DE LA DESCRIPTION DES MAISONS DE / Campagne de Pline, & celle des Invalides. / TOME PREMIER. / A TREVOUX, / DE L'IMPRIMERIE DE S. A. S. / M. DCCXXV.

12mo. Engraved frontispiece (1 leaf); two-color title page (1 leaf); dedication ([1]–16); preface ([17]–48); text ([49]–364); table of contents (6 leaves).

Vol. II.   ENTRETIENS / . . . / TOME SECOND. / . . .

12mo. Engraved frontispiece (1 leaf); two-color title page (1 leaf); text ([1]–384); table of contents (4 leaves).

Vol. III.   ENTRETIENS / . . . / TOME TROISIÉME. / . . .

12mo. Two-color title page (1 leaf); text ([1]–537); table of contents (7 unnumbered pp.).

Vol. IV.   ENTRETIENS / . . . / TOME QUATRIÉME. / . . .

12mo. Two-color title page (1 leaf); text ([1]–467); table of contents (5 unnumbered pp.).

Vol. V.   ENTRETIENS / . . . / TOME CINQUIÉME. / . . .

and

[Half title:] CONFERENCES / DE / L'ACADEMIE ROYALE / DE PEINTURE / ET / DE SCULPTURE. / PAR *Mr. FELIBIEN*, / Sécrétaire de l'Académie des Sciences, & / Historiographe du Roi.

12mo. Two-color title page (1 leaf); dedication ([1]–12); preface ([13]–24); text ([25]–267); table of contents (19 unnumbered pp.); half title (1 leaf); dedication ([291]–97); preface ([298]–330); text ([331]–466).

Vol. VI.   ENTRETIENS / . . . / TOME SIXIÉME. / . . .

12mo. Two-color title page ([i]); dedication ([iii]-vi); note ([vii]-viii); 1st text ([ix]-cxvii); table of contents (3 unnumbered pp.); 2d text ([1]–283); table of contents (5 leaves); 5 engravings, of which 3 are folding.

André Félibien, sieur des Avaux et de Javercy (1619–95), was born in Chartres. He was educated in Paris and Rome and knew Fouquet, Colbert, and Nicolas Poussin, under whom he also studied. In 1666 he became *historiographe des batiments,* in 1671 the secretary of the Académie d'Architecture on its establishment during that year, and in 1673 the *garde du Cabinet des antiques.* He was the author of numerous works.

This book passed through many editions. Its first was in 1666 in Paris, and thereafter it appeared in four more editions before 1700. The first four volumes of this edition, 1725, deal with painters, the first part of the fifth with architects, the second part of the fifth with some lectures by Félibien, and the sixth volume embraces a series of short pieces.

Sowerby, who found no copy for examination, says that Jefferson's own set was in 12mo. and consisted of five volumes which had been issued in Amsterdam in 1706. This set was sold to Congress. Since Jefferson ordered a five-volume set in 12mo. for the University in the section on "Gardening. Painting. Sculpture. Music" of the want list, there is little doubt that he had the Amsterdam, 1706 edition in mind. What Hilliard bought for him, however, was the six-volume set of 1725 which was issued at Trevoux. This set is still in the library (see Plate XXXIV).

U. Va.
*N27.F3.1725

44. Ferguson, James.

THE / ART / OF / DRAWING in PERSPECTIVE / MADE EASY / To those who have no previous Knowledge of / the MATHEMATICS. / By JAMES FERGUSON, F.R.S. / Illustrated with PLATES. / LONDON: / Printed for W. STRAHAN; and T. CADELL in the Strand. / M DCC LXXV.

8vo. Half title ([i]); title page ([iii]); preface ([v]-xii); text ([1]-123); list of Ferguson's books (1 unnumbered p.); 9 engraved plates, all folding, inserted.

Ferguson drew all the plates. They were engraved by J. Lodge (d. 1796), who worked in London.

James Ferguson (1710–76) was born in Banffshire, the son of a day laborer. His formal education was gained at Keith Grammar School, but he was put to service as a shepherd and in various other menial positions. He was always studying, however, especially astronomy and painting. In 1743 he went to London where he supported himself by painting but continued working with astronomy and soon (1746) began scientific, chiefly astronomical, writing. He gave popular lectures about astronomy, was presented to the future George III in 1758, stopped portrait painting in 1760, and was elected F.R.S. in 1763. He often advised George III on mechanics and was considered one of the first elementary writers on natural philosophy.

He published many books, among them the titles *Astronomy Explained upon Sir Isaac Newton's Principles, and Made Easy to Those Who Have Not Studied Mathematics; An Easy Introduction to Astronomy, for Young Gentlemen and Ladies; Tables and Tracts Relative to Several Arts and Sciences; An Introduction to Electricity; Lectures on*

ENTRETIENS
SUR LES VIES
ET
SUR LES OUVRAGES
DES PLUS
EXCELLENS PEINTRES
ANCIENS ET MODERNES;
AVEC
LA VIE DES ARCHITECTES
PAR MONSIEUR FÉLIBIEN.

NOUVELLE EDITION, REVUE, CORRIGÉE
& augmentée des Conferences de l'Académie Royale
de Peinture & de Sculpture;

De l'Idée du Peintre parfait, des Traitez de la Miniature,
des Desseins, des Estampes, de la connoissance
des Tableaux, & du Goût des Nations;

DE LA DESCRIPTION DES MAISONS DE
Campagne de Pline, & de celle des Invalides.

TOME PREMIER.

A TREVOUX,
DE L'IMPRIMERIE DE

M. DCCXXV.

Plate XXXIV. *From No. 43b.* Title page (Vol. I). Copy received
on Jefferson's order.

Select Subjects in Mechanics, Hydrostatics, Pneumatics, and Optics, with the Use of the Globes, the Art of Dialling, and the Calculation of the Mean Times of the New and Full Moons and Eclipses; and *Select Mechanical Exercises, Shewing How to Construct Different Clocks, Orreries, and Sun Dials, on Plain and Easy Principles.*

The Art of Drawing in Perspective was first published in 1775 and went through five editions. At the time of writing Ferguson described himself as being in an "infirm state of health, a situation that is very apt to affect the mental faculties."

Ferguson says in his preface:

I need not observe how requisite it is for painters who put groupes [*sic*] of figures together, but also for those who draw landscapes, or figures of machines and engines for books, to know the rules of Perspective. [Pp. vi-vii]

I am far from considering the following Work as a complete system of *Perspective*, for *that* would require a very large volume. But I think I may venture to say, that, when the learner is fully master of what is there contained, he will not find any great difficulty in proceding to what length he pleases in the attainment of this science, without any further assistence. [Pp. x-xi]

It is very probable, that those who already understand Perspective, if they take the trouble of reading this small Treatise, may think I have been rather verbose in most of my descriptions. I only request of such to consider, that I never wrote any thing for those who are well skilled in the few branches of science whereof I have treated; but only for those who wish to attain a moderate knowledge of them; and to such, I think, everything ought to be made as plain and easy, and be as minutely described, as is possible. [Pp. xi-xii]

The evidence that a copy of this work belonged to Jefferson is in the manuscript library catalogue now at the Massachusetts Historical Society. The book was apparently not sold to Congress and does not appear in the 1829 sale catalogue. It would appear that the copy in Jefferson's library was the London, 1775 edition.

Jefferson did not order it for the University. The library's present copy has been recently acquired, the gift of the Thomas Jefferson Memorial Foundation.

M

*NC749.F5.1775

45. Ficoroni, Francesco de'.

Vol. I.   LE VESTIGIA, / E RARITÁ / *DI* / ROMA ANTICA / RICERCATE, E SPIEGATE / *DA* / FRANCESCO DE' FICORONI /

Aggregato alla Reale Accademia / di Francia. / LIBRO PRIMO / *DE*-DICATO / Alla Santita' di Nostro Signore / BENEDETTO XIV. / IN ROMA MDCCXLIV. / Nella Stamperia di Girolamo Mainardi. / CON LICENZA DE' SUPERIORI.

4to. Two-color title page (1 leaf); dedication (1 leaf); notes to reader (1 leaf); indexes (3 leaves); text (1–186); appendix (187–95).

bound with

Vol. II. [Half title:] LE / SINGOLARITÁ / *DI* / ROMA MODERNA / RICERCATE, E SPIEGATE / *DA* / FRANCESCO DE' FICORONI / Aggregato alla Reale Accademia di Francia.

4to. Half title (1 leaf); indexes (3 leaves); text (1–77).

In the two volumes there are 40 engravings, of which 4 are folding, bound in the text and, in addition, numerous engraved figures in the text.

The drawings for the illustrations were by Salvator de Franceschi and Franciscus Viera. The engravers, for those few engravings which are signed, were Io de Franceschi and Maximilian Joseph Limpach, an eighteenth-century engraver from Prague who worked in Rome.

Francesco de' Ficoroni (1664–1747), born in Lugnano nel Lazio, was a student of antiquity and a collector. Although he published several books before the *Vestigia*, his collections were considered better than his writings.

The *Vestigia* (see Plate XXXV) is a kind of guidebook with many views of buildings both old and new, including churches, and many statues and coins. Among the old buildings are the Pantheon and the temple of Fortuna Virilis, both used as precedents for the University of Virginia, although Jefferson no longer owned the book at the time he designed the University.

Jefferson sold his set of the *Vestigia*, which Kimball (p. 94) says was acquired between 1785 and 1789, to Congress. Sowerby notes that the cost was entered by Jefferson as "15.0" in his undated manuscript catalogue. Jefferson ordered the two volumes of this work in a single volume for the University in the section on "Architecture" of the want list, and it is apparently sometimes so bound. There is no record of the library's having acquired the book until recently, when a copy, with the two volumes bound in one, entered the collections, the gift of the Thomas Jefferson Memorial Foundation.

U. Va.
*DG62.5.F5.1744

M
Sowerby 4196

LE VESTIGIA,

E RARITÁ

D I

ROMA ANTICA

RICERCATE, E SPIEGATE

D A

FRANCESCO DE' FICORONI

Aggregato alla Reale Accademia
di Francia.

LIBRO PRIMO

DEDICATO

ALLA SANTITA' DI NOSTRO SIGNORE

BENEDETTO XIV.

IN ROMA MDCCXLIV.

NELLA STAMPERIA DI GIROLAMO MAINARDI.
CON LICENZA DE' SUPERIORI.

46. Fréart de Chambray, Roland.

PARALLELE / DE / L'ARCHITECTURE / *ANTIQUE* / AVEC LA MODERNE, / Suivant les dix principaux Auteurs / qui ont écrit sur les cinq Ordres. / Par MM. ERRARD & DE CHAMBRAY. / *NOUVELLE EDITION* / Augmentée des Piedestaux pour les cinq Ordres, / suivant les mêmes Auteurs, & du Parallel de / M. *Errard* avec M. *Perrault*, &c. / Par CHARLES-ANTOINE JOMBERT. / A PARIS, RUE DAUPHINE, / Chez L'AUTEUR, Libraire du Roi pour l'Artillerie / & le Génie, à l'Image Notre-Dame. / M. DCC. LXVI. / *Avec Approbation & Privilege du Roi.*

8vo. Engraved frontispiece ([ii]); title page ([iii]); note ([v]-vii); preface (viii-xvi); table of contents (xvii-xx); text, with 63 engraved plates inserted ([1]–132); glossary (133–39).

Roland Fréart, sieur de Chambray (d. ca. 1676), was born at Le Mans. He studied architecture in Italy where he knew Poussin. The *Parallèle*, 1650, was his first work. After that he translated the *Quatre livres d'architecture de Palladio*, 1651, and Leonardo da Vinci's *Treatise of Painting* (see No. 72), and issued the *Idée de la perfection de la peinture* (Le Mans, 1662) and the *Perspective d'Euclid* (Le Mans, 1663).

Charles Errard (1606–89) was the son of an elder Charles Errard, a painter, architect, and engraver. The younger Charles studied in Rome where he met Fréart. He took an early interest in the establishment of the French academies in both Paris and Rome and became the first director of the one at Rome. He, too, was both a painter and an architect, but of his many works only a small drawing of Fréart has survived.

The first (1650) edition of the *Parallèle* was in folio with plates which were very baroque, the heads in the triglyphs of the Doric of Diocletion having their hair arranged in a seventeenth-century fashion rather like the contemporary wigs, for example. It was issued again in 1689 and 1702 using the 1650 engravings. In 1733 it was translated into English by John Evelyn.

This edition was issued by Charles Antoine Jombert (1712–84), a Parisian author-publisher who was most knowledgeable in matters of mathematics, architecture, and iconography and who issued many reprints of earlier architectural works. The *Parallèle* in his edition (1766) was the fourth book in a collection entitled *Bibliothèque portative d'architecture élémentaire, à l'usage des artistes* (Paris, 1764–66). Although six parts were planned, only four volumes were published. The other three volumes were: 1. *Règles des cinq ordres d' architecture*, by Giacomo Barrozzio da Vignola (No. 123a); 2. *Architecture de Palladio* (no. 91); and 3. *Oeuvres d'architecture de Vincent Scamozzi* (No. 111c).

Jombert said in his note:

On trouvera donc ici tout ce qui a fait rechercher avec tant d'empressement les deux premiers éditions de ce Livre, l'une faite en 1650, sous les yeux de l'Auteur; & l'autre en 1702, après sa mort, sans aucun changement ni augmentation que celle des dix planches d'ornamens du piedestal de la colonne Trajane. Ansi l'on donne dans cette nouvelle édition le discours de M. *de Chambray* en entier & tel qu'il l'a composé sous le titre de *Parallele des dix principaux Auteurs qui ont écrit sur les cinq Ordres d'Architecture*, &c; on y trouvera de plus une continuation de ce même ouvrage pour les piedestaux des cinq Ordres, suivant les mêmes Architectes, avec la parallel des six dernier Auteurs pour les Ordres Toscan & Composite, que M. *de Chambray* avoit négligé de donner, & qui M. *Errard*, son collegue, se proposoit d'y ajouter dans une nouvelle édition qui n'a pas eu lieu. Enfin, pour faire voir que c'est avec justice que j'ai parlé avec éloge de M. *Errard* en différens endroits de ce Livre, je présente ici un choix de ses compositions sur les cinq Ordres d'Architecture, mises en parallele avec les profils du célebre *Perrault* pour les memes Ordres. [Pp. v-vi]

No less than twenty-five plates were added to this edition.

Kimball (p. 94) says Jefferson acquired his copy of the *Parallèle* sometime after 1789. Its influence on Jefferson needs further investigation. Not only had he used Plates 2, 3, 4, and 5 at Monticello, according to inscriptions in his own hand on each of those plates in his own copy, which has survived at the Library of Congress, but the book's orders may be traced in at least six of the pavilions at the University of Virginia, two of them directly and the other four indirectly.

On the reverse of Jefferson's drawing for Pavilion I (see Plate XXXVI), executed sometime between May 1817 and July 8, 1819, is inscribed in his hand "No. I. the Doric of Diocletion's baths. Chambray." Similar wording also appears in his manuscript notebook, called "Operations at & for the College" (p. 25, U. Va. Library). The plate in the *Parallèle* (facing p. 27) illustrating this order is labeled "Ordre Dorique: Au Termes de Diocletien à Rome" (see Plate XXXVII). Chambray has this to say about the order: "ce profil est d'une si noble composition & si régulier, qu'il ne cede en rien au précédent: enfin quoique les propriétés spécifiques de cet Ordre soient d'être simple & solide, néamoins les ornemens y sont si judicieusement appliqués sur chaque membre, qu'il conservent l'une sans blesser l'autre" (p. 27).

Although Jefferson on his drawing for Pavilion VIII (see Plate XXXVIII), executed between June 12 and June 27, 1819, said only "Pavilion No. VIII. East. Corinthian of Diocletian's Baths" and used similar wording on page 19 of "Operations at & for the College," he wrote in a letter of specifications to Thomas Appleton, the American consul at Leghorn, on April 16, 1821:

Corinthian capitels . . . to be copied from those of the Thermae of Diocletian at Rome. This is not in Palladio, but is given by other authors, and particularly by Errard and Chambray in their Parallele dal' Architecture antique et modern. Paris 1766. pa. 79. plate 33. I should prefer however to have only the ovolo of the abacus carved, and its cavetto plain . . . nor would I require it's volutes or caulicoles to be so much carved, as those of Diocletian's Baths, finding the simplicity of those in Palladio preferable. [U. Va. Library]

The plate in the *Parallèle* (facing p. 80) illustrating this is labeled "Ordre Corinthien: Des Termes de Diocletien" (see Plate XXXIX). Fréart de Chambray says: "Après cet example Corinthien il ne faut plus rien chercher de riche dans l'Architecture, mais il n'appartient qu'aux judicieux de le mettre en oeuvre, car l'abondance des ornemens n'est pas toujour estimable ni avantageuse à un édifice. . . . Il ne faut jamais en faire de profusion, parce qu'ils . . . sont naître entre les membres une confusion qui blesse l'oeil des savans & qui est antipathique au nom d'Ordre. On ne doit donc l'employer qu'aux grands ouvrages publics" (p. 79).

The evidence for the other four pavilions is not quite so direct, yet it would seem fairly safe to assume Fréart de Chambray served as a precedent.

On his drawing for Pavilion IV (see Plate XL), executed between June 12 and June 27, 1819, and again on page 17 of the "Operations at & for the College," Jefferson noted "Pavilion No. IV. East. Doric of Albano." Facing page 28 of the *Parallèle* there is a plate labeled "Ordre Dorique: A Albane pres de Rome" (see Plate XLI). Fréart de Chambray says of the order:

Ce rare chef-d'oeuvre Dorique fut découvert à Albane . . . parmi plusieurs autres vieux fragmens d'architecture très curieux. . . .

Ce que j'estime particulierement en celui-ci c'est une grandeur de maniere majestueuse. . . .

Ce qui est le plus digne d'être remarqué & admiré en cette composition, c'est la richesse & la forme extraordinaire des modillons . . . produisent un effet merveilleux, lequel est encore beaucoup augmenté par les rosons du sophite de la couronne, laquelle ayant une projecture étonnante, fait paroître l'Ordre tout gigantesque: & c'est proprement cela qu'on appelle la grande maniere. [Pp. 28–29]

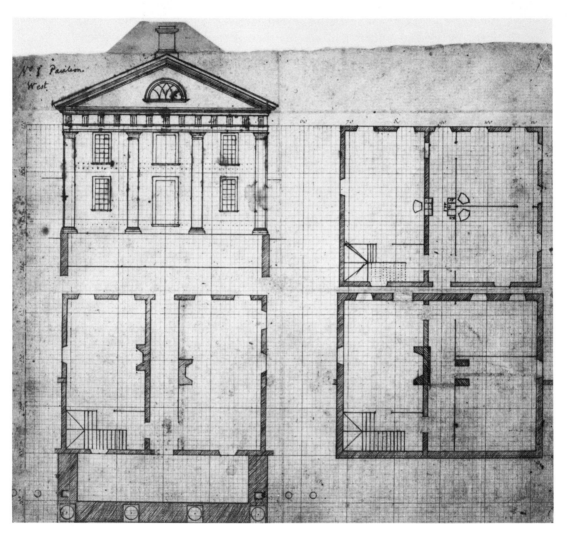

Plate XXXVI. Jefferson's drawing for Pavilion I, University of Virginia (N-355).

Au Termes de Diocletien à Rome

Ordre Dorique

Plate XXXVII. *From No. 46.* "Ordre Dorique: Au Termes de Diocletien à Rome" (Pl. 3).

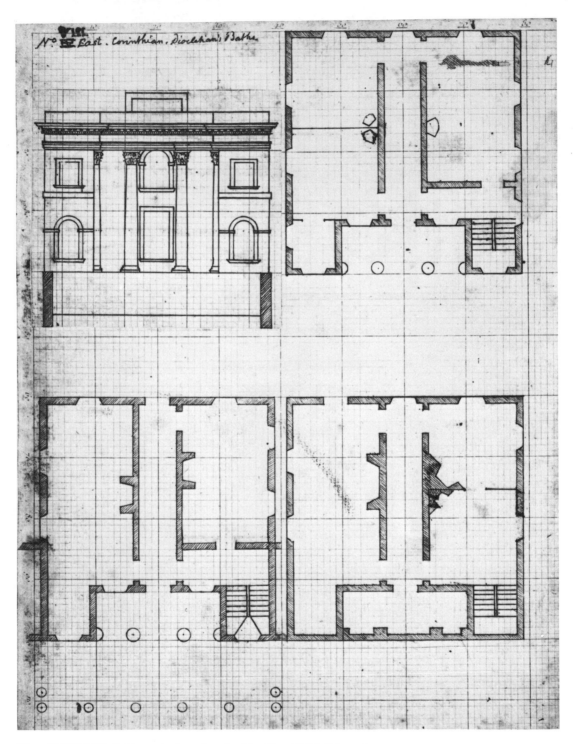

Plate XXXVIII. Jefferson's drawing for Pavilion VIII (N-325).

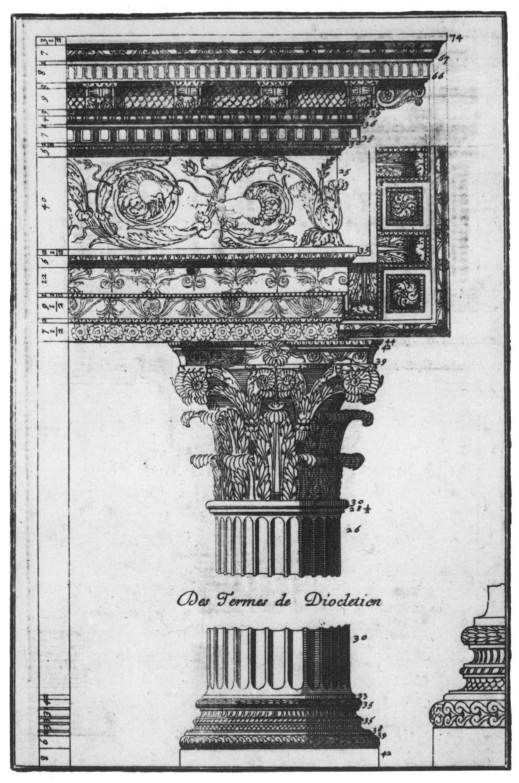

Des Termes de Diocletien

Plate XXXIX. *From No. 46.* "Ordre Corinthien: Des Termes de Diocletien" (Pl. 33).

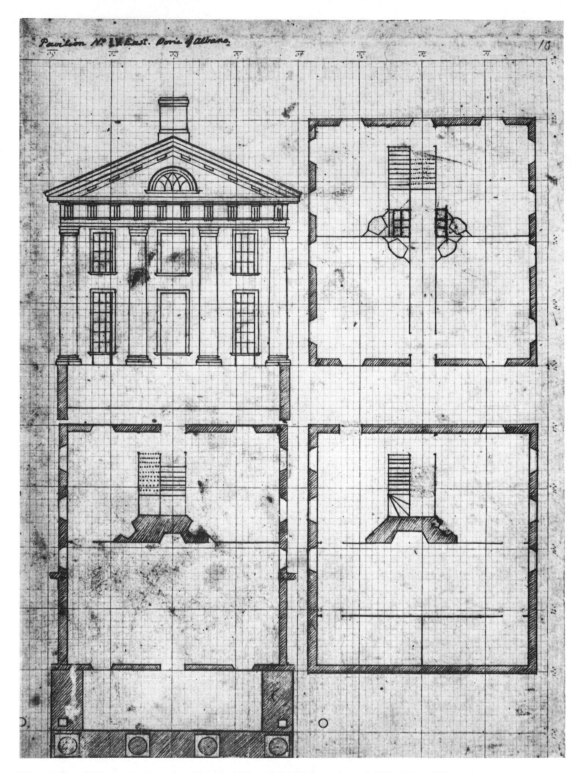

Plate XL. Jefferson's drawing for Pavilion IV, University of Virginia (N-322).

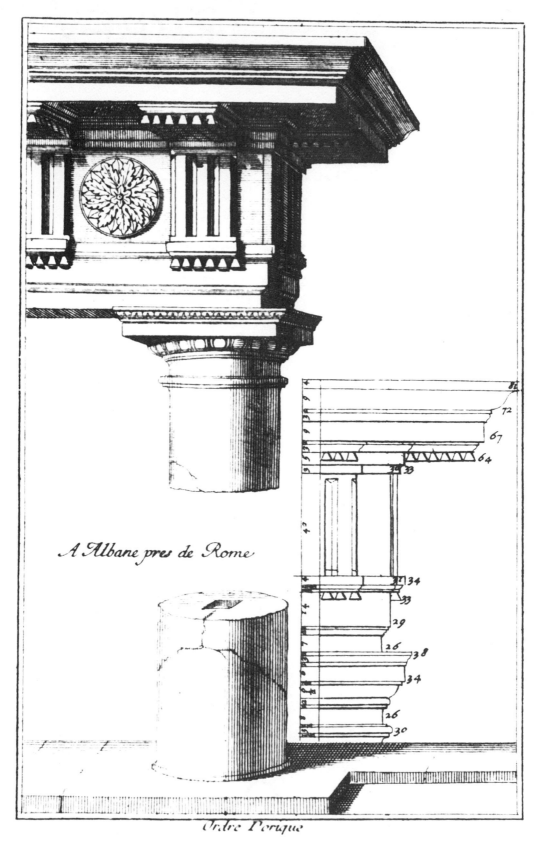

A Albane pres de Rome

Ordre Dorique

Plate XLI. *From No. 46.* "Ordre Dorique: A Albane pres de Rome" (Pl. 4).

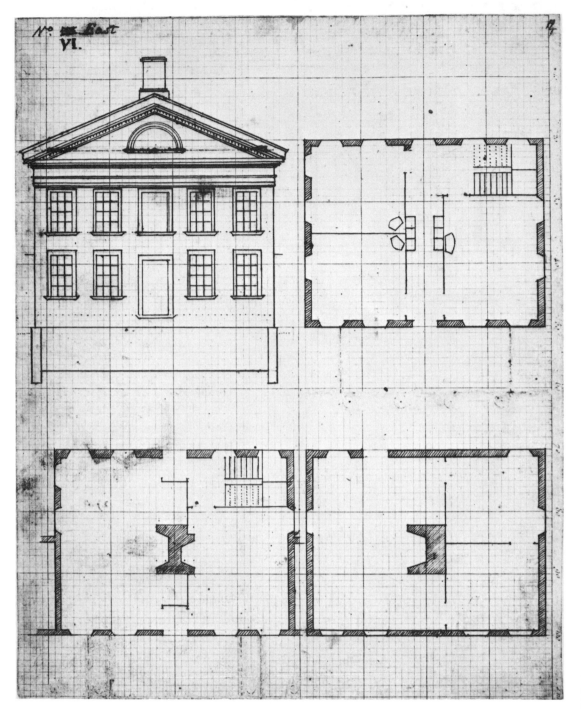

Plate XLII. Jefferson's drawing for Pavilion VI (N-324).

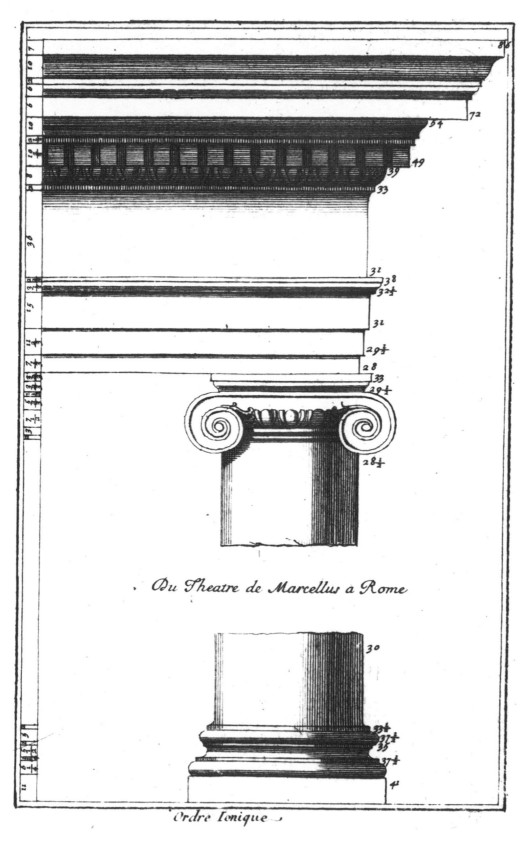

Du Theatre de Marcellus a Rome

Ordre Ionique

Plate XLIII. *From No. 46.* "Order Ionique: Du Theatre de Marcellus a Rome" (Pl. 16).

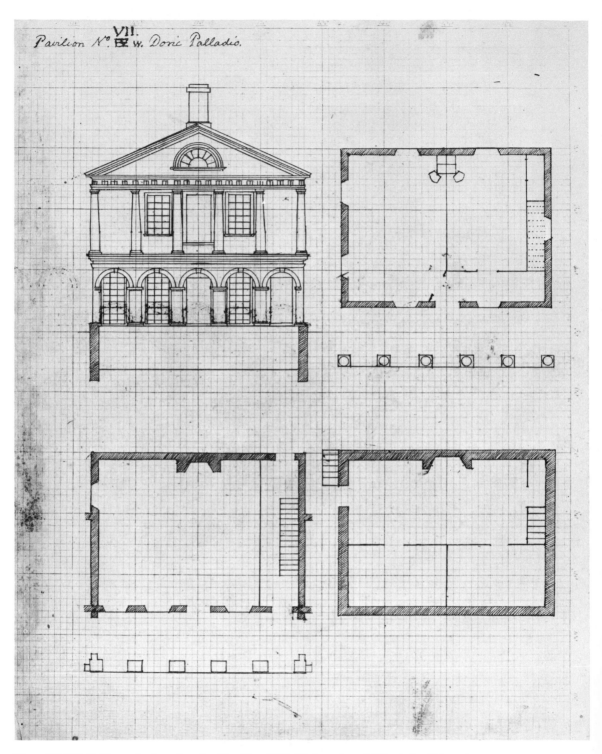

Plate XLIV. Jefferson's drawing for Pavilion VII, University of Virginia (N-311).

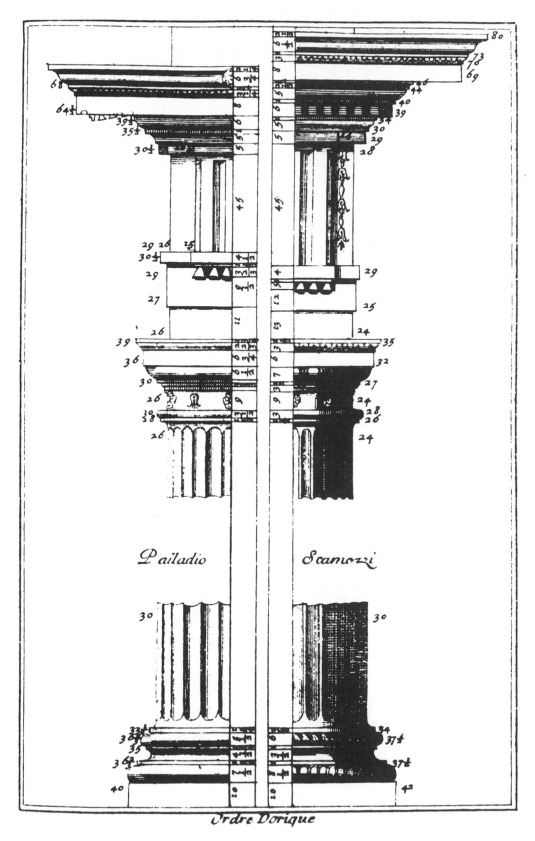

Palladio

Scamozzi

Ordre Dorique

Plate XLV. *From No. 46.* "Ordre Dorique: Palladio [and] Scamozzi" (Pl. 5).

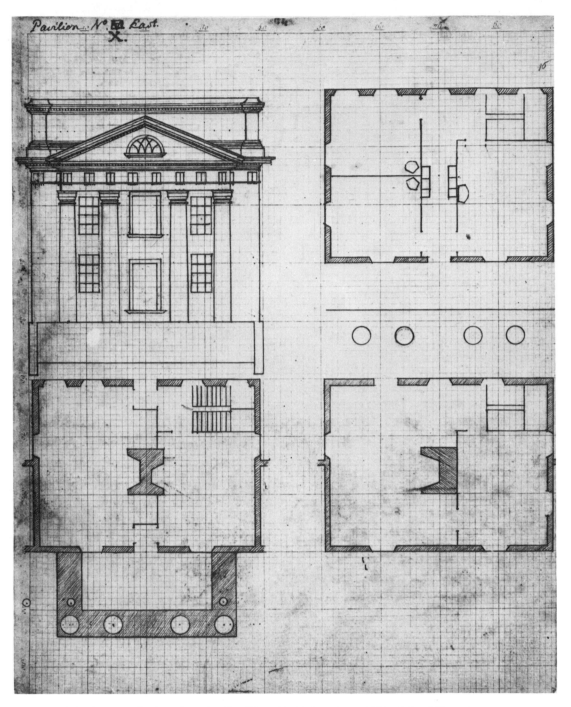

Plate XLVI. Jefferson's drawing for Pavilion X, University of Virginia (N-326).

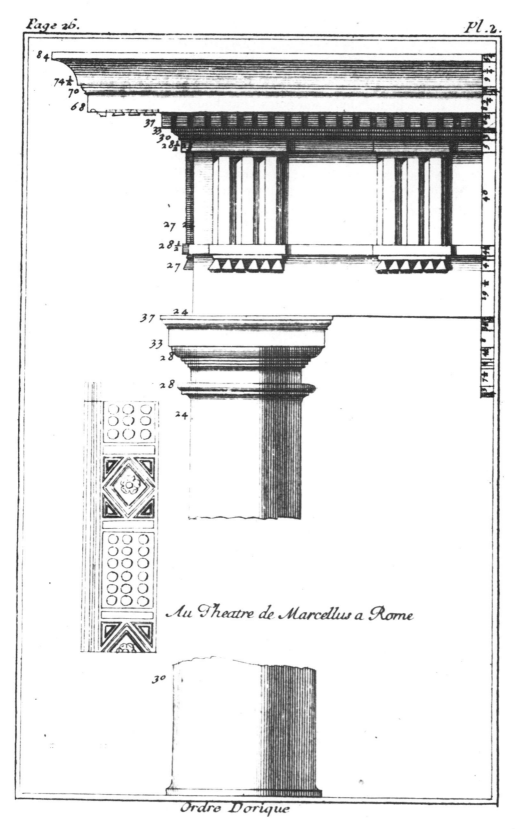

Au Theatre de Marcellus a Rome

Ordre Dorique

Plate XLVII. *From No. 46.* "Ordre Dorique: Au Theatre de Marcellus a Rome" (Pl. 2).

On his drawing for Pavilion VI (see Plate XLII), made between June 12 and June 27, 1819, and again on page 21 of the "Operations at & for the College," Jefferson notes "Pavilion No. VI. East. Ionic of the theatre of Marcellus." Facing page 50 of the *Parallèle* there is a plate labeled "Ordre Ionique: Du Theatre de Marcellus a Rome" (see Plate XLIII). Fréart de Chambray says: "j'ai considéré depuis que la grandeur de l'entablement, jointe à sa simplicité extraordinaire, étoit un effet particulier de la discrétion de l'Architecte, lequel voulant placer cet Ordre en un très grand édifice, & de plus en un lieu fort élevé" (p. 50).

On his drawing for Pavilion VII (see Plate XLIV), made between May and June 23–28, 1817, Jefferson noted "Pavilion No. VII. w. Doric Palladio." Although Plate XVI, Book I, of Leoni's *Palladio* (No. 92b) shows this order, it is drawn with ox skulls in the metopes, whereas the frieze of Pavilion VII is without ox skulls. It would seem, then, that the plate facing page 30 of the *Parallèle* labeled "Ordre Dorique: Palladio" (see Plate XLV), which is labeled in Jefferson's own hand in his copy at the Library of Congress as having been used in the dining room at Monticello, and which is without ox skulls, might very well have been the model for Pavilion VII.

And finally, the drawing for Pavilion X (see Plate XLVI), made between June 12 and June 27, 1819, and page 23 of "Operations at & for the College" have the notation in Jefferson's hand, "Pavilion No. X. East. Doric of the Theatre of Marcellus." Facing page 26 of the *Parallèle* there is a plate labeled "Ordre Dorique: Au Theatre de Marcellus a Rome" (see Plate XLVII).

From the comparative wording, the descriptions of the appropriate uses for these orders, and the uses to which Jefferson put them, as well as his previous use of Fréart de Chambray's plates as proved by his own notes on them in the Library of Congress copy, it would seem that they were more than probably the precedent for the orders for Pavilions IV, VI, and X, and very possibly for Pavilion VII.

The *Parallèle* is also one of the few architectural books which Jefferson replaced in his own library after his earlier collection had been sold to Congress. He had been well aware before that sale that the *Parallèle* formed only one of four parts in the *Bibliothéque portative*, as the correspondence in Sowerby shows, and after that sale he managed to obtain all four parts, which were still in his library at the time of his death. They were sold as lot 723 in the 1829 sale.

Jefferson ordered the complete multivolume set for the University in the section on "Architecture" of the want list, but there is no record of the library's having acquired it. The copy of the *Parallèle* in the library at the present time is a recent acquisition, the gift of the Thomas Jefferson Memorial Foundation.

U. Va. M
*NA2810.F8.1766 Sowerby 4216

47. Gell, Sir William.

Vol. I. POMPEIANA: / THE / TOPOGRAPHY, EDIFICES, / AND / ORNAMENTS / OF / POMPEII. / BY / SIR WILLIAM GELL, F. R. S. F. S. A. &c. / AND / JOHN P. GANDY, ARCHITECT. / LONDON: / PRINTED FOR / RODWELL AND MARTIN, / NEW BOND STREET. / 1817–1819.

4to. Half title ([i]); title page ([iii]); dedication ([v]); preface ([vii]-xxviii); list of plates ([xxix]-xxxi); note (1 unnumbered p.); descriptive text ([1]–273); emendations and note to binder (1 leaf).

Vol II. [Engraved title:] POMPEIANA BY SIR WILLIAM GELL AND JOHN P. GANDY ARCHITECT / London, Published July 1, 1819, by Rodwell & Martin, New Bond Street.

4to. Engraved title page (1 leaf); 92 engraved plates, some of which appear in 2 or even 3 states, making a total of 159 engravings.

The engravers were G. Cooke (1781–1834), a pupil of James Basire; Charles Heath (1785–1848), for whom mythological subjects were a forte; H. Hobson (fl.1814–22), English; George Hollis (1792–1842), born in Oxford and died in Walworth; John Le Keux (1783–1846), a Londoner; Frederick Christian Lewis (1779–1856), who studied at the Royal Academy and was a painter, a watercolorist, and an engraver; James Lewis, perhaps the architect who flourished ca.1774–1800; William Home Lizars (1788–1859), a Scot, the son and pupil of Daniel Lizars; Wilson Lowry (see No. 32); Henry Moses (1782–1870), one of the master engravers in England at the time; S. Porter; John Pye (b. 1745), a student of Major (see No. 76) who worked for the publisher Boydell; Shury; John Walker, Jr. (fl. ca.1800), a nephew of Anthony Walker, also an engraver; Robert Wallis (1794–1878), English; and W. Wise (fl.1817–76), who worked in London and Oxford.

Sir William Gell (1777–1835) was born in Derbyshire and educated at Jesus College, Cambridge, and at the schools of the Royal Academy. Knighted in 1803, he issued his first book, *Topography of Troy*, a folio illustrated by his own sketches, in 1804. This was followed by *Geography and Antiquities of Ithaca*, 1807; *Itinerary of Greece*, 1810, with a second edition in 1827; *Itinerary of the Morea*, 1817; *Narrative of a Journey in the Morea*, 1823; and *Topography of Rome and Its Vicinity*, 2 vols., 1834, with a second edition in 1846. Byron said of his sketching: "Rapid indeed! He topographised and topographised king Priam's dominions in three days" (*DNB*). Gell was a Fellow of the Society of Antiquaries, F.R.S., and F.S.A. and a member of the Academy of Berlin and the Institute of France.

J. P. Gandy (1787–1850) changed his name to J. P. Deering on receiving an inheritance from Henry Deering. He was the younger brother of Joseph and Michael Gandy, the architects. Educated at the Royal Academy, he went to Greece for the Dilettanti Society in 1813 and later with Gell to Pompeii. He was elected A.R.A. in 1826.

Gell says that the excavation at "Pompeii was begun upon in 1748; and it may at first excite our surprise, that from this date to the present day, no work has appeared in the English language upon the subject of its domestic antiquities, except a few pages by Sir William Hamilton, in the Archaeologia" (I, ix-x). One can understand how he could "topographise king Priam's dominions" so quickly after he tells us that "the authors of the present work . . . generally avoided entering into a scrupulous detail of measurement" (I, xi-xii). He goes on to say: "It may be proper to state, that the original drawings for this work were made with the *camera lucida*, by Sir WILLIAM GELL. To render the subject clearer, a slight alteration has in two or three instances been made, but always mentioned in the text. The literary part with the exception of the first essay, are [*sic*] by his coadjutor" (I, xvi).

This edition was the first. It was expanded in 1832 by two volumes called *Pompeiana: The Topography, Ornaments, &c.* that gave the results of the excavations after 1819. There was also a partial reprint in 1880 under the title *Pompeii, Its Destruction and Re-Discovery*.

One of the original paper covers for one of the volumes is bound in the University's recently acquired set. From it we learn that the original price per volume was 12 shillings. The views, though handsome, are a little on the romantic side (see Plate XLVIII).

Although Jefferson ordered *Pompeiana* for the University in the section on "Architecture" of the want list, there is no record of a set entering the collections until recently. The present set on the library's shelves is the gift of the Thomas Jefferson Memorial Foundation.

U. Va.
*DG70.P.7G3.1817

Plate XLVIII. *From No. 47.* "Pompeii. Peristyle or Inner Court of the House of Pansa" (Pl. 35).

48. Gibbs, James.

A / BOOK / OF / ARCHITECTURE, / CONTAINING / DE-
SIGNS / OF / BUILDINGS / AND / ORNAMENTS. / by JAMES
GIBBS. / *London:* / Printed MDCCXXVIII.

Folio. Title page (1 leaf); dedication (1 leaf); introduction (i-iii); description of plates (iv-xxv); list of subscribers (xxviii); 150 engravings,
of which 4 are double.

The engravers were Bernard Baron (1696–1762 or 1766), who, though
French and a pupil and son-in-law of Nicolas Tardieu, moved to London
where he worked largely for Boydell; H. Harris; John Harris (fl.1715–
39), who worked for John Kip and the publishers of *Vitruvius Britannicus;* I. (or J.) Mynde (fl.1728–70), English; and George Vertue
(1684–1756), a student of Michael van der Gucht (No. 37). Vertue's
notes for a history of English painting were purchased after his death by
Horace Walpole, who used them in writing *Anecdotes of Painting in
England.*

The list of subscribers does not give many professions or crafts. It
is possible to pick out, however, one bookseller, one carpenter, one carver,
two doctors, six ecclesiastics, one judge, one merchant, and one professor.
Nicholas Hawksmoor, William Adam, Henry Flitcroft, William Kent,
Thomas Ripley, and Christopher Wren the younger, all architects, are
listed, as well as Michael Rysbrack, the sculptor, and Sir James Thornhill, the painter.

James Gibbs (1682–1754) was born in the Links of Aberdeen. He
was educated at the grammar school, Marischal College of Aberdeen, in
Holland, and in Rome where he was a student of Carlo Fontana. He returned from the Continent in 1709 and began his practice in London with
his first public building, St. Mary-le-Strand, 1714. Of his publications
the *Book of Architecture*, 1728, was the first. It was followed by the
Rules for Drawing, 1732, with a second edition in 1738 (Nos. 49a & b);
and the *Bibliotheca Radcliviana, or A Short Description of the Radcliffe
Library at Oxford*, 1747, the library being a building Gibbs had designed.

The *Book of Architecture* was published as a design source. In the
introduction Gibbs makes this plain, as well as warning the client against
unreliable workmen and architects, saying that

such Gentlemen as might be concerned in Building, especially in the remote parts of the Country, where little or no assistance for Designs can be procured . . . may be here furnished with Draughts of useful and convenient Buildings and proper Ornaments; which may be executed by any Workman who understands Lines, either as here Design'd, or with some Alteration, which may be easily made by a person of Judgment; without which a Variation in Draughts, once well digested, frequently proves a Detriment to the Building, as well as a Disparagement to the person that gives them. I mention this to caution Gentlemen from suffering any material Change to be made in their Designs, by the Forwardness of unskilful Workmen, or the Caprice of ignorant, assuming Pretenders.

Some, for want of better Helps, have unfortunately put into the hands of common workmen, the management of Buildings of considerable expence; which when finished, they have had the mortification to find condemned by persons of Taste to that degree that sometimes they have been pulled down, at least alter'd at a greater charge than would have procur'd better advice from an able Artist; or if they have stood, they have remained lasting Monuments of the Ignorance or Parsimoniousness of the Owners, or (it may be) of a wrong-judged Profuseness.

What heaps of stone, and even Marble, are daily seen in Monuments, Chimneys, and other Ornamental pieces of Architecture, without the least Symmetry or Order? When the same or fewer Materials, under the conduct of a skilful Surveyor, would, in less room and with much less charge, have been equally (if not more) useful, and by Justness of Proportion have had a more grand Appearance, and consequently, have better answered the Intention of the Expence. For it is not the Bulk of a Fabrick, the Richness and Quantity of the Materials, the Multiplicity of Lines, nor the Gaudiness of the Finishing, that give the Grace or Beauty and Grandeur to a Building; but the Proportion of the Parts to one another and to the Whole, whether entirely plain, or enriched with a few Ornaments properly disposed. [Pp. i-iii]

All the plates were drawn by Gibbs and are of his design (see Plates XLIX and L). They show churches, collegiate buildings, houses, pavilions, obelisks, memorial columns, gates, mantels, doors, windows, monuments, sarcophagi, vases, cisterns for buffets, fonts, stone tables, sundials, and pedestals for busts. The designs are very Palladian.

Sowerby points out that Kimball (p. 129) says Jefferson was using this book as early as 1770 or 1771, and Kimball (p. 94) further says it was acquired about that time. It not only was ordered by Jefferson for the University in the section on "Architecture" of the want list but was actually received, though that copy has not survived. Jefferson's own copy was sold to Congress. The present copy came into the collections during the twentieth century.

U. Va.   M

*NA2620.G5.1728   Sowerby 4218

Prospectūs Templi Sᵗᵃ Mariæ Londini in vico dicto the Strand, architectura Iacobi Gibbs.

Ja: Gibbs Archi: inven: et del.   *Jo: Harris fec.*

Plate XLIX. *From No. 48.* St. Mary le Strand (Pl. 21).

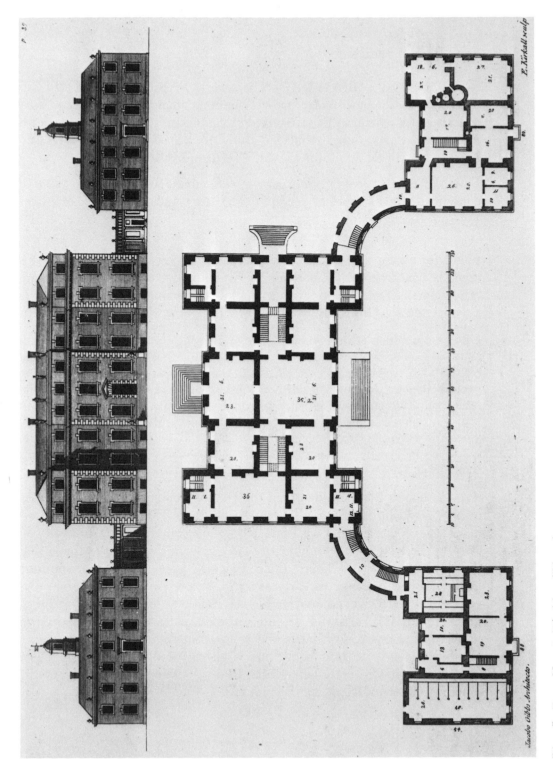

Jacobo Gibbs Architecto.   E. Kirkall sculp

Plate L. *From No. 48.* Ditchley (Pl. 39).

49a. Gibbs, James.

RULES / FOR / DRAWING / The several PARTS of / ARCHITEC-TURE, / IN A More exact and easy manner than has been here-/tofore practised, by which all FRACTIONS, in / dividing the principal MEMBERS and their Parts, / are avoided. / By *JAMES GIBBS.* / *LONDON* / Printed by W. BOWYER for the AUTHOR. / MDCCXXXII.

Folio. License (1 leaf); title page (1 leaf); dedication (1 leaf); table of contents (1 leaf); note to reader (1–2); text and description of plates (3–42); 64 engravings.

For information on Gibbs, see the preceding entry. Two-thirds of this book is concerned with methods of drawing the orders, the rest with other classical and Georgian forms such as rooms, mantels, and doors (see Plate LI). Gibbs says of the genesis of his work:

Upon examination of the common ways of drawing the Five Orders of Architecture, I thought there might be a Method found out so to divide the principal Members and their Parts, both as to their Heights and Projections, as to avoid Fractions. And having tried one Order with success, I proceeded to another, till at length I was satisfied it would answer my intention in all. . . .

. . . by this method of dividing the Orders Mechanically into equal parts, Fractions are entirely avoided; which will be found so beneficial to workmen in drawing any part at large . . . that when they are once accustomed to it, they will never follow any other. [Pp. 1–2]

Although Kimball identified the volume Jefferson sold to Congress as the 1753 edition, it was the 1738 edition (see No. 49b). Jefferson ordered the 1732 edition (see Plate LII), however, for the University in 1825 in the section on "Architecture" of the want list, perhaps forgetting that he had owned the later edition. Sowerby notes that though he may have acquired his copy as early as 1769, he certainly had it before December 20, 1798, when he wrote his son-in-law to lend his copy to Dinsmore, the master carpenter, and described it as "a large thin folio lying uppermost of a parcel of books laid horizontally on the shelf close to my turning chair. . . . It is bound in rough calf and one lid is off." The 1732 edition has recently entered the library's collections, the gift of the Thomas Jefferson Memorial Foundation.

U. Va.
*NA2841.G5.1732

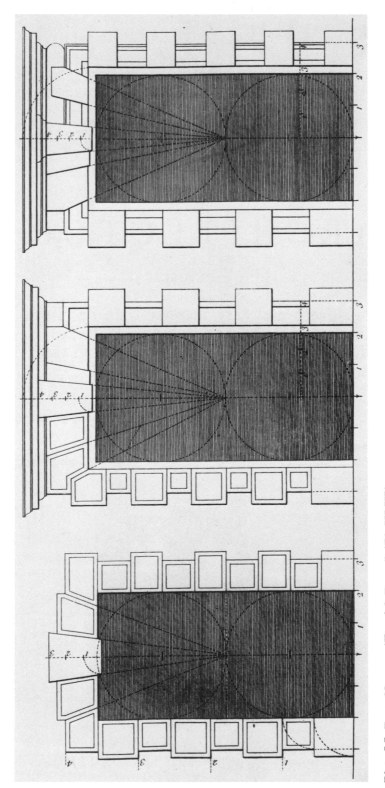

Plate LI. *From No. 49a.* "Rustick Doors" (Pl. XLIII).

RULES

FOR

DRAWING

The several PARTS of

ARCHITECTURE,

IN A

More exact and easy manner than has been here-
tofore practised, by which all FRACTIONS, in
dividing the principal MEMBERS and their Parts,
are avoided.

By *JAMES GIBBS.*

LONDON,
Printed by W. BOWYER for the AUTHOR.
MDCCXXXII.

Plate LII. *From No. 49a.* Title page.

49b. Gibbs, James.

RULES / FOR / . . . / By JAMES GIBBS. / The Second Edition. / LONDON: / Printed for A. Bettesworth and C. Hitch in Pater- noster-Row, / W. Innys and R. Manby at the West-end of St. Paul's, and / J. and P. Knapton in Ludgate-street. / MDCCXXXVIII.

Folio. License (1 leaf); title page (1 leaf); dedication (1 leaf); table of contents (1 leaf); note to reader (1–2); text and description of plates, with 64 engravings inserted (3–42).

See No. 49a. This copy of the 1738 edition of the *Rules for Drawing Architecture* has been recently acquired by the University library, the gift of the Thomas Jefferson Memorial Foundation.

M

*NA2841.G5.1738   Sowerby 4148

50. Gibson, Robert.

A Treatise of Practical Surveying. . . . 6th ed. Philadelphia, 1790.
Not now owned by the University, except in microprint form.

See No. 51a for information about Gibson.

M
Sowerby 3707

51a. Gibson, Robert.

THE / THEORY AND PRACTICE / OF / SURVEYING; / CON- TAINING / *All the Instructions requisite for the skilful practice / of this Art.* / BY ROBERT GIBSON. / ILLUSTRATED BY COPPER- PLATES. / THE WHOLE CORRECTED, NEWLY ARRANGED, AND / GREATLY ENLARGED, / WITH USEFUL SELECTIONS, / AND A NEW SET OF ACCURATE / MATHEMATICAL TA- BLES. / *BY D. P. ADAMS,* / TEACHER OF THE MATHEMAT-

ICS. / NEW-YORK: / PUBLISHED BY EVERT DUYCKINCK, / NO. 110 PEARL-STREET. / *George Long, printer.* / 1811.

8vo. Title page (1 unnumbered p.); copyright (1 unnumbered p.); table of contents (1 unnumbered p.); explanation of symbols (1 unnumbered p.); text ([1]–324); [new pagination:] mathematical tables ([1]–184); 13 engraved plates, all folding.

Robert Gibson (fl.1790–?) was a British mathematician whose work on surveying went through many editions. The University has no less than fourteen of these, the ones for 1792, 1796, 1798, 1803, 1806, 1811, 1814, 1816, 1818, 1821, 1828, 1834, 1835, and 1839.

The book is a straightforward text on surveying, a technique which the author defines as follows:

The word Surveying, in the Mathematics, signifies the art of measuring land, and of delineating its boundries on a map.

The Surveyor, in the practice of this art, directs his attention, at first, to the tracing and measuring of lines; secondly, to the position of these lines in respect to each other, or the angles formed by them; thirdly, to the plan, or the representation of the field, or tract which he surveys; and fourthly, to the calculation of its area, or superficial content. . . . Surveying, therefore, requires an intimate acquaintance with the several parts of the Mathematics, which are here inserted as an introduction to this treatise. [P. (1)]

After having sold his copy of Gibson's *A Treatise of Practical Surveying* (No. 50) to Congress, Jefferson acquired either the 1811 or 1814 edition of *The Theory and Practice of Surveying*. It was in his library at the time of his death, but the 1829 sale catalogue (lot 413) did not identify the volume exactly, except to show that it was one of the Adams editions. Either of the ones now in the University library, the 1811 edition or the 1814 edition—which with the exception of a reset title page, seems to contain identical information with the 1811 edition—could be a duplicate of the one Jefferson had. Furthermore, it was probably one of these editions Jefferson wished to order for the University in the section on "Geometry" of the want list in 1825.

In ordering the book for the University, however, Jefferson did not specify the edition. The 1821 edition, with the tables of James Ryan, is the one which was actually supplied, though the copy in the library is not the one purchased for it by Jefferson.

U. Va.?   M?
*TA545.G4.1811

51b. Gibson, Robert.

THE / THEORY AND PRACTICE / OF / SURVEYING; / CON-
TAINING / All the Instructions requisite for the skilful practice / of
this Art. / BY / ROBERT GIBSON. / ILLUSTRATED BY COP-
PER-PLATES: / THE / WHOLE CORRECTED, NEWLY AR-
RANGED, AND GREATLY ENLARGED, / WITH USEFUL
SELECTIONS, / AND A NEW SET OF ACCURATE / MATHE-
MATICAL TABLES. / By *D. P. Adams*, / TEACHER OF THE
MATHEMATICS. / NEW YORK: / PUBLISHED BY EVERT
DUYCKINCK, / NO. 102 PEARL-STREET. / G. Long, printer. /
1814.

See No. 51a for further information about No. 51b.

U. Va.?   M?
*TA545.G4.1814

51c. Gibson, Robert.

The Theory and Practice of Surveying. New York, 1821.

Owned by the University, but not available for examination.

See No. 51a for information on Gibson and further information on this
title.

U.Va.
*TA545.G4.1821

52. Grose, Francis.

RULES / FOR DRAWING / CARICATURAS: / WITH / AN ES-
SAY ON / COMIC PAINTING. / BY FRANCIS GROSE, Esq. F.R.S.
and A.S. / London: / PRINTED FOR SAMUEL BAGSTER, IN
THE STRAND. [1791?]

8vo. [Bound with Hogarth's *Analysis of Beauty;* see No. 56.] Engraved
portrait of Francis Grose ([ii]); [*Analysis of Beauty;*] 4 engraved plates

for *Rules for Drawing Caricaturas*, bound in the following order: IV, III, II, and I; title page ([1]); text ([3]–24).

Francis Grose (1731?–91), born at Greenford, Middlesex, was the son of a Swiss jeweler of Richmond, Surry. He studied at Shipley's school of drawing and became a member of the Society of Antiquarians in 1757 and the Society of Artists in 1766. His acquaintances called him an "inimitable boon companion." There were some fourteen of his works put in print. This book was first published in 1788 and was given a French edition in 1802.

Grose's system of drawing caricatures is based on the exaggeration of the parts of the body and their relation to one another. He says:

The art of drawing Caricaturas is generally considered as a dangerous acquisition, tending rather to make the possessor feared than esteemed; but it is certainly an unfair mode of reasoning, to urge the abuse to which any art is liable, as an argument against the art itself.

In order to do jutice to the art in question, it should be considered, that it is one of the elements of satirical painting, which, like poetry of the same denomination, may be most efficaciously employed in the cause of virtue and decorum, by holding up to public notice many offenders against both, who are not amenable to any other tribunal; and who, though they contemptuously defy all serious reproof, tremble at the thoughts of seeing their vices or follies attacked by the keen shafts of ridicule. [Pp. (3)–4]

In the essay on comic painting he says:

Various have been the opinions respecting the cause of Laughter. . . . Mr. Hobbes attributed it to a supposed consciousness of superiority in the laugher to the object laughed at. Hutceson seems to think that it is occasioned by a contrast or opposition of dignity and meaness; and Mr. Beattie says, "that the quality in things which makes them provoke that pleasing emotion of sentiment, whereof laughter is the external sign, is an uncommon mixture of relation and contrariety, exhibited or supposed to be united in the same assemblage. . . ."

This system clearly points out a very simple though general rule, applicable to all compositions of the ludicrous kind in painting – a rule comprised in these few words: let the employments and properties or qualities of all objects be incompatible; that is, let every person and thing represented, be employed in that office or business, for which by age, size, profession, construction, or some other accident, they are totally unfit. [Pp. (13)–14]

The library's copy is that which came into the collections on Jefferson's order. See No. 56.

U. Va.
*N70.H7.1791

53a. Halfpenny, William.

PRACTICAL ARCHITECTURE, / *or a* Sure Guide *to the* / *true working according to the* / Rules *of that* Science: / *Representing the* / FIVE ORDERS, / *with their several* / DOORS & WINDOWS / *taken from* Inigo Jones *& other* / Celebrated Architects / *to each Plate Tables Containing* / *the exact Proportions of the* / *several Parts are likewise fitted* / Very useful / *to all true Lovers of* / ARCHITECTURE, / *but particularly so to those* / *who are engag'd in ye* / Noble Art of Building / *By Willm. Halfpenny.* / *Printed for & Sold by Tho: Bowles Printseller next ye Chap-/ter House in St. Pauls Ch. Yard, by Jer. Batley Bookseller at* / *ye Dove in Pater Noster Row, & by J. Bowles Printseller aganst.* / *Stocks Market.* / *J. Church Sc.* 1724

12mo. Engraved title page (1 leaf); engraved dedication (1 leaf); engraved preface (1 leaf); 48 engraved plates.

William Halfpenny (fl.1724–52) was also known as Michael Hoare and was called by both names by Batty Langley (No. 68). He called himself both architect and carpenter and lived at Richmond and London.

This book, one which was entirely engraved, was his second. Its first edition was without date, with some subsequent editions in 1724, 1730, 1736, 1748, and 1751. He says, rather immodestly, in his preface:

It is altogether needless to say much concerning the Usefulness of this small Tract, or the motives which put me upon the Compiling of it, for its Serviceableness and Advantage to all who are employed in Buildings will appear at the first Inspection, & the general complaint of Workmen for want of something in this Nature, is Sufficient reason for my Undertaking it, tho' at a Time when the Town is already burthened with Volumes. True, Proportions are the Fundamentals, the Beauty and the very Life of Architecture, and yet tho' many and able Hands have treated of that Science, I know of none who have bestow'd their Labours in Calculating these first principles thereof: but now with great Exactness they are made Publick, neatly & distinctly Engraved on Copper and brought into such a size as without burthen may be carryed in the Pocket and be always ready for Use. They are calculated to the several Sizes which most often occur in Practice from the small gradually on to the Largest, so that after the Measure of one part is given by having recourse to these Tables, the Measures of ye other parts are seen at one view and the Time and Trouble of working the Proportions of every part by Figures are saved.

The edition sold to Congress by Jefferson has not been positively identified. Sowerby notes that the 1724 edition is Kimball's conjecture and that he further suggests (p. 94) that Jefferson's copy came from William Byrd of Westover *ca.*1778, but that is uncertain.

The University has recently acquired both the 1724 and the 1736 editions. With the exception of "The fifth Edition, 1736" being engraved on the title page of that edition, they are identical. Neither edition was ordered for the University. The library's present copy of the 1724 edition is the recent gift of the Thomas Jefferson Memorial Foundation.

M?

*NA2515.H35.1724   Sowerby 4186

53b. Halfpenny, William.

PRACTICAL ARCHITECTURE, / . . . / . . . 1736.

See No. 53a for further information about No. 53b. The 1736 edition of this book, recently acquired by the library, is the gift of the Thomas Jefferson Memorial Foundation.

*NA2515.H35.1736

54. Hancarville, Pierre Francois Hugues, chevalier d'.

Vol. I. RECHERCHES / SUR / L'ORIGINE, L'ESPRIT ET LES PROGRÈS / DES ARTS DE LA GRÈCE; / SUR LEUR CON-NEXION AVEC LES ARTS ET LA / RELIGION DES PLUS ANCIENS PEUPLES CONNUS; / *SUR LES MONUMENS AN-TIQUES DE L'INDE, DE LA PERSE, DU / RESTE DE L'ASIE, DE L'EUROPE ET DE L'ÈGYPT.* / TOME PREMIER. / A LON-DRES, / Chez B. APPLEYARD, LIBRAIRE, *Queen Ann Street West,* / *& Wimpole Street*, CAVENDISH SQUARE. M.DCC.LXXXV.

4to. Title page (1 leaf); preface ([i])-xxiv); discours préliminaire ([xxv]-xxviii); errata (1 leaf); text ([1]–510); 29 engraved plates, of which 1 is folding.

Vol. II. RECHERCHES / . . . / TOME SECOND / . . .

4to. Title page (1 leaf); text ([1]–480); 34 engraved plates, of which 7 are folding.

Vol. III. SUPPLÉMENT / AUX RECHERCHES / SUR L'ORI-
GINE, L'ESPRIT ET LES PROGRÈS / DES ARTS DE LA
GRÈCE; SUR LEUR CONNEXION AVEC LES ARTS ET LA RE-
LIGION / DES PLUS ANCIENS PEUPLES CONNUS; / *SUR LES
MONUMENS ANTIQUES DE L'INDE, DE LA PERSE, DU /
RESTE DE L'ASIE, DE L'EUROPE DE DE L'ÉGYPTE.* / Conte-
nant des Observations nouvelles, sur l'Origine des Idées employées
dans / les anciens Emblêmes religieux; sur les Raisons qui les firent
choisir; sur les / suites du Déluge universel; sur les Origines des Scythes,
des Chinois & des / Indiens; sur la Religion primitive de ces peuples;
sur celles des anciens Perses, / &c. &c. / A LONDRES, / Chez B. AP-
PLEYARD, LIBRAIRE, *Queen Ann Street West* / & *Wimpole Street*,
CAVENDISH SQUARE. / M.DCC.LXXXV.

4to. Title page ([i]); preface ([iii]-xii); reviews, etc. ([1]–64); text
([65]–175); 22 engraved plates, of which five are folding.

All the plates in Vol. I are anonymous except Plate XVIII, which was
drawn by Thomas Stothard and engraved by Charles Townley, to whom
the book is addressed. Those for Vols. II and III are also anonymous.

Pierre François Hugues Hancarville (1719–1805), known as d'Hancarville or the chevalier d'Hancarville, was an antiquarian. In spite of
his having written in French—he was also the author of *Antiquités
Etrusques, Greques et Romaines, tirées du cabinet de M. Hamilton*—he
seems to have had English connections in his literary efforts. This book
is interesting for its early representations of Near Eastern and Asiatic
antiquities.

It was ordered by Jefferson for the University in the section on
"Gardening. Painting. Sculpture. Music" of the want list, but there is
no record of the library's having received a set until this one recently
entered the collections. It is the gift of the Thomas Jefferson Memorial
Foundation.

U. Va.
*N5633.H25.1785

55. Heely, Joseph.

Vol. I. LETTERS / ON THE / BEAUTIES / OF / HAGLEY, EN-
VIL, / AND THE / LEASOWES. / WITH CRITICAL REMARKS:
/ AND OBSERVATIONS ON THE / MODERN TASTE IN GAR-

DENING. / By Joseph Heely, Esq. / FOR NATURE HERE / WANTONS AS IN HER PRIME, AND PLAYS AT WILL / HER VIRGIN FANCIES. / MILT / IN TWO VOLUMES. / VOL. I. / LONDON: / PRINTED FOR R. BALDWIN, PATER-NOSTER-ROW. / MDCCLXXVII.

12mo. Title page ([1]); note ([iii]-iv); table of contents ([v]-vii); text ([1]–231).

Vol. II. LETTERS / ON THE / BEAUTIES / . . . / VOL. II. / . . .

12mo. Title page ([1]); table of contents ([iii]-v); text ([1]–215).

Very little is known about Joseph Heely (fl.1777) except the evidence found in this book. After the first few of his letters of observations, the rest are concerned with descriptions of Hagley, Envil, and the Leasowes. He has a great deal to say about "the modern taste in gardening," which is to say the new picturesque as opposed to the old formal garden design:

I think, among all the recreations the country affords, Gardening is one of the most agreeable—that it is not only a commendable, and healthful employment, but a pleasing and entertaining study—that it fills the mind with every flattering sensation, charms the eye, and wherever introduced by the hand of taste, makes the face of nature smile in elegance and perpetual verdure. [P. 5]

Since gardening has emerged from its former vicious, and puerile state, the delightful scenery that has sprung from the pure principles of the modern practice, is really admirable. The science has been brought into such perfection, that in many places, the greatest difficulty is to discover where *art* has been busy to arrive at it; so simple, yet so elegant; every scene so beautifully characterised; so different, yet so configurative! [Pp. 11–12]

Architecture and gardening, may be called sister arts, though diametrically opposite in their principles; the excellencies of the first are founded in a mathematical exactness, and regularity: in the latter, on an assemblage of scenery without either: yet when both unite, each graces the other so powerfully, and affords so striking a contrast, that, it is much to be lamented, they are ever seen but in an inseparable connection. [Pp. 21–22]

But the time approached, when poor nature was to be intirely kicked out of doors; and in her room, to be substituted, every ridiculous absurdity, the caprice of low invention could suggest.—*Le Notre*, that celebrated but cruel spoiler, . . . mangled the sighing earth, with all that fire of genius which was then the prevailing mode, absurdly following, or perhaps beginning, the miserable fashion, of mutilating the trees, and in short, inverting the beauty of every thing he approached. [Pp. 32–33]

If this art [of designing gardens] is really to be learnt, nature only is the proper school for it—it depends not on the rules that comprehend science of any other kind; there are no abstruse problems to be worked by the compasses, or any mathematical instrument; its rules depend on other powers—on good sense, on an inventive genius, a flowery imagination, and a delicate fancy—it is these only, that can produce perfection—that can teach you to slide from one beauty to another, to characterise, combine, and give every scene a pleasing effect, from whatever point it is viewed. [P. 37]

The principles which every expert designer will work upon, have the force of exhibiting to the eye, the most finished pictures. [P. 48]

Sowerby (4228) quotes Jefferson's notes written after he had visited Hagley and the Leasowes in 1786. He says

Hagley. Now Ld. Wescot. 1000 as. No distinction between park & garden. Both blended, but more of the character of garden. Between 2. & 300. deer in it, some few of them red deer. . . .

Leasowes. In Shropshire. Now the property of Mr. Horne by purchase. 150 as. within the walk. The waters small. This is not even an ornamental farm. It is only a grazing farm with a path round it. Here and there a seat of board, rarely any thing better. Architecture has contributed nothing. The obelisk is of brick. Shenstone [the previous owner] had but 300 £ a year, & ruined himself by what he did to this farm.

One might also note that the ideas expressed in Heely are similar to those principles used by Jefferson when he designed his own garden at Monticello.

Jefferson's own set of Heely, which Kimball (p. 95) says was purchased between 1785 and 1789, was sold to Congress. He ordered it for the University in the section on "Gardening. Painting. Sculpture. Music." of the want list, but it was not received during his lifetime. The set now owned by the library was acquired during the twentieth century.

U. Va.   M
*DA660.H45.1777   Sowerby 4228

56. Hogarth, William.

THE / ANALYSIS OF BEAUTY. / WRITTEN / WITH A VIEW OF FIXING THE FLUCTUATING IDEAS/ /OF / TASTE. / BY WILLIAM HOGARTH. / *So vary'd he, and of his tortuous train /Cur'l many a wanton wreath, in sight of Eve, / To lure her eye.* Milton. / London: / PRINTED FOR SAMUEL BAGSTER, IN THE STRAND. [1791?]

8vo. [Bound with Grose's *Rules for Drawing Caricaturas;* see No. 52.] [Engraved portrait of Francis Grose ([ii]);] title page ([iii]); figures referred to in the work ([v]-vii);   new pagination:] preface ([i]-xxvi); note ([xxvii]); table of contents ([xxix]-xxx); text ([33]-240); [plates and text of *Rules for Drawing Caricaturas*].

William Hogarth (1697–1764) was born in London. He was apprenticed first to an engraver of silver and later studied at Sir James Thornhill's art school. He eloped with Sir James's daughter in 1729 and, after a reconciliation with his father-in-law, eventually succeeded him as head of the school.

The date of the first edition of this book was 1753. It had a German edition in 1754, an Italian in 1761, and a French in 1805. In the original edition it was accompanied by two folio plates called "Satuary's Yard" and "Country Dance" which with their numerous figures illustrated Hogarth's treatise.

Although it is said that the *Analysis* had a mixed reception, the importance of the treatise itself has not as yet ben sufficiently investigated. Hogarth's principles of beauty and his discussion of the various kinds of line seem to have been known to philosophers and designers as well as the dilettanti. He says:

I now offer to the public a short essay, accompanied with two explanatory prints, in which I shall endeavour to shew what the principles are in nature, by which we are directed to call the forms of some bodies beautiful, others ugly; some graceful, and others the reverse; by considering more minutely than has hitherto been done, the nature of those lines, and their different combinations, which serve to raise in the mind the ideas of all the variety of forms imaginable. . . . I have but little hopes of having a favourable attention given to my design in general, by those who have already had a more fashionable introduction into the mysteries of the arts of painting and sculpture. Much less do I expect or in truth desire, the countenance of that set of people, who have an interest in exploding any kind of doctrine, that may teach us to *see with our own eyes*. [Pp. (33), 35]

. . . I shall proceed to consider the fundamental principles, which are generally allowed to give an elegance and beauty, when duly blended together, to compositions of all kinds whatever; and point out to my readers, the particular force of each, in those compositions in nature and art, which seem most to *please and entertain the eye*, and give that grace and beauty, which is the subject of this inquiry. The principles I mean, are FITTNESS, VARIETY, UNIFORMITY, SIMPLICITY, INTRICACY, and QUANTITY;—*all which cooperate in the production of beauty, mutually correcting and restraining each other occasionally*. [Pp. 47–48]

It is to be observed, that straight lines vary only in length, and therefore are least ornamental.

That curved lines, as they can be varied in their degrees of curvature, as well as in their lengths, begin, on that account, to be ornamental.

That straight and curved lines, joined, being a compound line, vary more than curves alone, and so become somewhat more ornamental.

That the waving line, or line of beauty, varying still more, being composed of two curves contrasted, becomes still more ornamental and pleasing, insomuch that the hand takes a lively movement in making it with pen or pencil.

And that the serpentine line by its waving and winding at the same time different ways, leads the eye in a pleasing manner along the continuity of its variety, if I may be allowed the expression; and which by its twisting so many different ways, may be said to enclose (though but a single line) varied contents; and therefore all its variety, cannot be expressed on paper by one continued line, without the assistance of the imagination, or the help of a figure; see (Fig. 26, T. pl. 1) where that sort of proportioned winding line, which will hereafter be called the precise serpentine line, or *line of grace*, is represented by a fine wire properly twisted round the elegant and varied figure of a cone. [Pp. 83–84]

Although this book was not in Jefferson's personal library, some authorities attribute his liking for the serpentine line to its influence, either directly or indirectly through other authors.

The library's copy of the *Analysis*, bound with Francis Grose's *Rules for Drawing Caricaturas* (No. 52), is the copy purchased for the University on Jefferson's order in the section on "Gardening. Painting. Scultpure. Music" of the want list and is the one that the 1828 *Catalogue* dated 1776.

U. Va.
*N70.H7.1791

57. Jess, Zachariah.

A Compendious System of Practical Surveying. 2d ed. Philadelphia, 1814.

Not now owned by the University.

Jefferson had a copy of this book in his private library at the time of his death. The 1829 sale catalogue (lot 414) does not specify the edition, but it seems unlikely that Jefferson would have owned the Wilmington, 1799 first edition. He did not order it for the University.

M

58. Johnson, Stephen William.

RURAL ECONOMY: / CONTAINING / A TREATISE / *ON PISÉ BUILDING;* / As recommended by the Board of Agriculture in Great Britain, / with Improvements by the Author; / On Buildings in general; / Particularly on the Arrangement of those belonging to Farms: / *On the Culture of the Vine;* AND / ON TURNPIKE ROADS. / WITH PLATES. / *BY S. W. JOHNSON.* / New Brunswick, N.J. / Printed by William Elliot, / FOR I. RILEY & CO. NO. 1, CITY-HOTEL, BROADWAY, / NEW-YORK. / 1806.

8vo. Half title (1 leaf); title page ([i]); dedication ([iii]); preface ([v]-vi); table of contents ([vii]-viii); text ([1]–246); index (2 leaves); 8 anonymously engraved plates.

Stephen William Johnson was master in chancery at New Brunswick, N.J. See Plate LIII for his dedication of this book to Jefferson.

The volume is divided into a series of books on each of the subjects listed on the title page. That on pisé building has an acknowledgment of the author's debt to Cointeraux (No. 30) and gives the derivation of the term:

. . . As late only as the year 1791 a work was published at Paris, by M. FRANCOIS COINTERAUX, containing an account of a mode of building strong and durable houses with no other materials than earth; and which had been practised for ages in the province of Lyons, though little known in any other part of France or in Europe. [P. 1]

The French of the Lyonese terrotory [*sic*], in their vernacular idiom, call their mode of building *Pisé*, which . . . has its derivation from the name of the instrument with which the walls are rammed and made into a solid compact body, called in French, *Pisoir;* having a figure essentially different from any thing called in English a rammer. [P. 4]

In spite of the dedication, Jefferson sold his copy to Congress. He did not order the book for the University, whose copy is a recent acquisition, the gift of the Thomas Jefferson Memorial Foundation.

M

*TH1421.J7.1806   Sowerby 1178

Jombert, Charles Antoine. *Bibliothèque portative d'architecture élémentaire, à l'usage des artistes.* Paris, 1764–66. *See* Nos. 46, 91, 111c, and 123a.

TO THOMAS JEFFERSON, ESQ.

PRESIDENT OF THE UNITED STATES.

SIR,

It having been the leading principle of the greatest statesmen that have benefited mankind, to regard with peculiar respect the welfare and advancement of Agriculture; and from the attention and interest which you have hitherto manifested in its prosperity, by your own valuable improvement in the plough, I feel a confidence in presenting you with a testimony of my attachment to rural life, and an attempt at some improvements in it. With these impressions, I dedicate this small volume to you, as a tribute of the respect and esteem of

your humble servant,

S. W. JOHNSON.

Sonman's Hill, near New-Brunswick, N. J.

Plate LIII. *From No. 58.* Dedication page.

59a. Jones, Inigo.

Vol. I. THE / DESIGNS / OF / INIGO JONES, / Consisting of / PLANS and ELEVATIONS / FOR / *Publick* and *Private* Buildings. / Publish'd by WILLIAM KENT, / With some Additional Designs. / The FIRST VOLUME. / M. DCC. XXVII.

Folio. Engraved allegorical portrait of Jones (1 leaf); title page (1 leaf); dedication (1 leaf); note (1 leaf); list of plates (3 leaves); list of subscribers (1 leaf); 49 engravings, of which 7 are double and 5 are folding (listed as 73 plates, through multiple numbering on some plates).

bound with

Vol. II. THE / DESIGNS / OF / INIGO JONES / . . . / THE SECOND VOLUME / . . .

Folio. Title page (1 leaf); list of plates (3 leaves); 46 engraved plates, of which 17 are double (listed as 63 plates through multiple numbering on some plates).

The delineators of Vol. I were the architects William Kent and Henry Flitcroft. Flitcroft (1697–1769) was the son of Jefferey Flitcroft, the gardener to William III at Hampton Court. Apprenticed to a joiner for seven years, the younger Flitcroft worked as a carpenter for the earl of Burlington, but, having broken a leg, was used as a draftsman on this book issued at the earl's expense. Success as an architect came quickly to Flitcroft after that, and by 1758 he was comptroller of the works. The engravers were I. Cole (fl. ca.1720), who engraved many buildings; Pierre or Paul Foudrinier (No. 21); Antoine Herisset (1685–1769), who often worked with plans and who was the father and grandfather of engravers; and Hendrich Hulsberg (d.1729), Dutch, who worked in London. Of the designs included the earl of Burlington "inv." (devised) four and William Kent six.

Flitcroft was the delineator of Vol. II, while Hulsburg and Cole were the engravers. Burlington was credited with five of the designs and Palladio with four.

The list of subscribers shows one bricklayer, one cabinetmaker, six carpenters, one carver, one doctor, three ecclesiastics, five joiners, six masons, two painters, three plasterers, one schoolmaster, one statuary, and one timber merchant. The architects included Colin Campbell,

James Gibbs, Nicholas Hawksmoor, Christopher Wren the younger, and Isaac Ware. The engraver Fourdrinier was a subscriber, as was also the improbably named Christopher Horsenail.

Inigo Jones (1573–1654) was born in London and educated in Italy as a painter. He was in Italy a second time about 1613. On his return he served as both architect and set designer and generally brought many Italianate architectural and theatrical ideas to England. By 1615 he was surveyor general of the works and continued to be an influential figure until his death. For portraits of him, see Plates LIV and LV.

Wiliam Kent (1684–1748), born in Yorkshire, was apprenticed to a coach painter. He made his way to London and later went to Rome to study as a painter. There he met Richard Boyle (1695–1753), third earl of Burlington, who became his patron and who furthered his interest in architecture and landscape architecture.

This book is the result of Burlington's interest in Jones and his possession of many of Jones's drawings. The note in the 1727 edition tells us:

THE Character of *Inigo Jones* is so universally known, that his Name alone will be a sufficient Recommendation of the following Designs; the Originals of which (drawn by himself and Mr. *Webb*) belong to the *Earl of Burlington*. . . .

If the Reputation of this *Great Man* doth not rise in proportion to his Merits in his own Country, 'tis certain, in *Italy*, (which was his School) and other parts of *Europe*, he was in great esteem; in which places, as well as in *England*, his own Works are his Monument and best Panegyrick; which together with those of *Palladio*, remain equal Proofs of the Superiority of those two Great Masters to all others.

To this Collection are added Designs of Doors, Windows, Gates, Peers, Chimneys, Insides of Rooms, and Ceilings; as also some few Designs of Buildings by the Earl of Burlington.

Sowerby points out that Kimball (pp. 133, 134) says Jefferson must have had or known *The Designs* by 1779, since he refers to it several times in his notes for some of the decorative structures proposed in that year at Monticello. One of the plates specifically mentioned is Plate LXXIII of Vol. I, a plate which reproduces a garden house at Chiswick (see Plate LVI).[1]

---

[1] The specifications on a drawing, reproduced by Kimball as No. 62, are quoted by him (p. 133) as saying in Jefferson's hand, "The form and proportions of this building are taken from Jones's designs, pl. 73 only that this one is square." The same drawing is reproduced as Fig. 5 in Nichols and is indexed there as N–91–92, where Nichols says of the specifications on the back that they "indicate Jefferson's composite method of designing."

Plate **LIV**. *From No. 59a.* Frontispiece.

THE
DESIGNS
OF
INIGO JONES,

Confifting of

PLANS and ELEVATIONS

FOR

Publick and *Private* Buildings.

Publifh'd by WILLIAM KENT,
With fome Additional Defigns.

The FIRST VOLUME.
M. DCC. XXVII.

Plate LV. *From No. 59a*. Title page (Vol. I).

Plate LVI. *From No. 59a*. Elevation of a temple in the garden at Chiswick (Vol. 1, Pl. 73).

The 1727 edition was the first. It was the one owned by Jefferson and sold by him to Congress. The more expansive edition of 1770 (see No. 59b) was ordered by Jefferson for the University in the section on "Architecture" of the want list. It was the one actually bought, having been received before the 1828 *Catalogue* was compiled. The University presently owns both editions, the 1727 one being the gift of the Thomas Jefferson Memorial Foundation.

*NA997.J7K4.1727

M
Sowerby 4217

59b. Jones, Inigo.

Vol. I. THE / DESIGNS / OF / INIGO JONES, / CONSISTING OF / PLANS AND ELEVATIONS / FOR / PUBLIC AND PRI-VATE BUILDINGS. / PUBLISHED / BY WILLIAM KENT, / WITH SOME ADDITIONAL DESIGNS. / VOLUME I. / LON-DON: / PRINTED FOR BENJAMIN WHITE, AT HORACE'S HEAD, FLEET-STREET. / MDCCLXX.

Folio. Engraved allegorical portrait of Jones (1 leaf); title page (1 leaf); list of plates (3 leaves); title page in French (1 leaf); list of plates in French (3 leaves); 74 engraved plates.

bound with

Vol. II. THE / DESIGNS / OF / INIGO JONES / . . . / VOL-UME II. / . . .

Folio. Title page (1 leaf); list of plates (3 leaves); title page in French (1 leaf); list of plates in French (3 leaves); 64 engraved plates.

In Vol. I the frontispiece and seventy-three of the engraved plates are the same as those in the 1727 edition. The seventy-fourth plate is a perspective of the proposed Whitehall Palace. In Vol. II an engraved perspective of Wentworth House has been added to the sixty-three plates that appeared in the 1727 edition.

See No. 59a for further information. This 1770 edition was acquired by the library during the twentieth century.

U. Va.
*NA997.J7K4.1770

60. Kelsall, Charles.

Phantasm / OF / AN UNIVERSITY: / WITH / Prolegomena. / BY / CHARLES KELSALL, ESQ. / AUTHOR OF "A LETTER FROM ATHENS," AND OF "A TRANSLATION OF / THE TWO LAST PLEADINGS OF CICERO AGAINST VERRES." / "MINIME MIRUM EST SI SCIENTIAE NON CRESCANT, CUM / "A *RADICIBUS SUIS* SINT SEPARATAE." / FRANCISC. BACON, *Nov. Org. Aphor.* lxxx. / LONDON: / PRINTED BY J. MOYES, GREVILLE STREET, HATTON GARDEN, / FOR WHITE, COCHRANE, AND CO. FLEET STREET. / M.DCCC.XIV.

Large 4to. Half title (1 leaf); title page (1 leaf); dedication (1 leaf); half title for Part the First (1 leaf); text ([1]–123); 2 engraved plates; half title for Part the Second (1 leaf); text ([127]–74); engraved plate; list of engravings (1 leaf); 15 engravings, all folding.

The plates were designed by Charles Kelsall. The engravers were Henry Moses (No. 47); J. Rolfe; and Charles Wild (1781–1835), an architectural painter and engraver.

In his *Phantasam*, Charles Kelsall (fl.1812–20), a writer who used three pseudonyms—Zachary Craft, Arpinas Laurea, and Britannicus Mela—as well as his own name, gives his proposals for a new university, saying that the "great art of education is not to *immerse* minds in science, but to store them so far, that an elastic reaction and play of the intellectual powers may remain" (p. 25).

He suggests that a university should consist of six colleges, for Civil Polity and Languages, Fine Arts, Agriculture and Manufactures, Natural Philosophy, Moral Philosophy, and Mathematics. At a proposed cost of £5,000,000 he would build a complex of these six colleges, each in a single building in the center of its own courtyard, edged with dormitories, the courtyards grouped so that there is a large central court containing a chapel and a library.

He says that his "main object . . . is the architectural disposition of a new University. . . . With the hope of but rarely violating the Vitruvian rules, of abiding generally by the spirit of the Grecian school, and of indulging occasionally in the display of the best parts of the Italian style, I have undertaken the following designs, and submit them to the candid decision of the public" (pp. 127–28).

He goes on to describe in neoclassic, but somewhat pompous, terms the ideal university's senate house, public library, and museum:

The Ionic columns are from the Temple of Erechtheus at Athens, with the omission of the flutings. The Doric are after Vitruvius, as delineated by Galiani. The Apollo of Belvedere, and Pallas of Velletri, one of the best statues of the goddess transmitted from antiquity, stand on each side of the portico of the Public Library. I know not whether my having introduced two windows in the intercolumniations of the wings will be approved. The araeo-style disposition has, however, been there adopted. The windows are rather larger than I could have wished. [P. 133]

He then suggests that the subjects for the pedimental scultpure of this group should be "Ptolemy Lagus lays the first stone of the Alexandrian Library" and "Sylla orders the Library of Apellicon, the Peripatetic, to be removed to Rome." In spite of these neoclassic directions, he also gives alternate elevations for his institution in the Saxon and Norman and Gothic Revival modes (see Plate LVII). The second part of the *Phantasm* contains the architectural detail.

The copy received by Jefferson for the University before he made up the want list was the gift of James Madison, but it has not survived. A duplicate has been recently acquired, the gift of the Thomas Jefferson Memorial Foundation.

U. Va.
*LA637.K5.1814

61a. Kennett, Basil.

Romae Antiquae Notitia, or The Antiquities of Rome. London, 1746.
Not now owned by the University.

See No. 61b.

M
Sowerby 114

61b. Kennett, Basil.

Romae Antiquae Notitia; / OR THE / ANTIQUITIES OF ROME. / IN TWO PARTS. / TO WHICH ARE PREFIXED / TWO ESSAYS, / CONCERNING THE / ROMAN LEARNING AND THE ROMAN EDUCATION. / BY BASIL KENNETT, of C. C. C. Oxon.

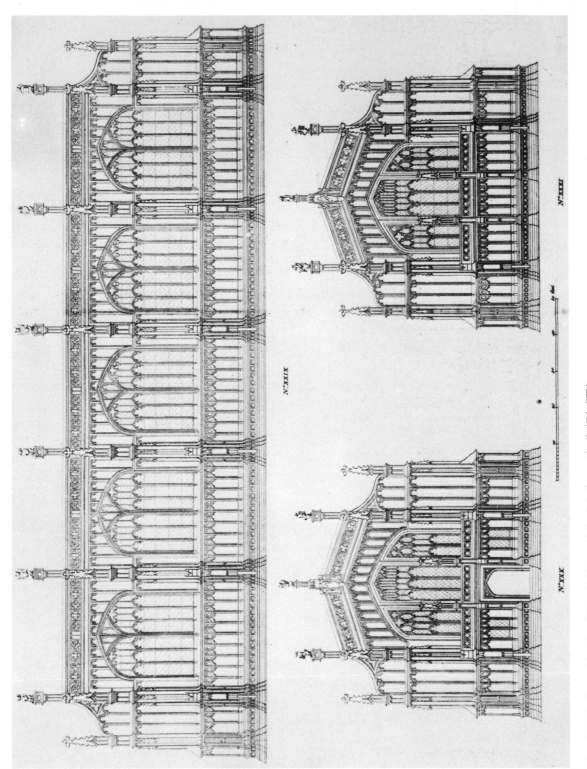

N.ºXXXV

N.ºXXXII

N.ºXXX

Plate LVII. *From No. 60.* "The College of the Mathematics" (Pl. XI).

/ *Ne desinat unquam* / *Tecum Graia loqui, tecum Romana vetustas.* /
CLAUDIAN. / FIRST AMERICAN EDITION, / EMBELISHED
WITH FIFTEEN ENGRAVINGS. / *PHILADELPHIA:* / HICK-
MAN & HAZZARD NO. 121, CHESTNUT STREET. / 1822

8vo. Folding engraving; title page ([i]); dedication ([iii]-iv); preface
([v]-vii); table of contents ([ix]-xii); text ([1]–356); index (7 leaves);
scriptores (4 leaves); 14 engravings, of which 5 are folding.

Basil Kennett (1674–1715) was born at Postling, Kent. He was educated by his brother, the bishop of Peterborough; at a school at Bicester;
at the house of Sir William Glynne; and at Oxford. In 1697 he was a
fellow and tutor at Corpus Christi, Oxford, but in 1706 he was appointed
chaplain at the English factory at Leghorn. He did not return to Oxford
until 1714.

He published many works and many translations from the Greek
and Latin. This work was first issued in 1696 and went into many editions, among them one in 1746 as well as this American edition of 1822.

The text included descriptions of various buildings of ancient Rome,
including the Pantheon. The University owns a 1726 edition, and the
plates in the American, 1822 edition are the same as those in the earlier
editions.

Jefferson sold his own copy, which was the 1746 edition, to Congress. The library received the Philadelphia, 1822 edition on Jefferson's
order in the section on "History-Civil-Antient" of the want list, and that
copy survives.

U. Va.
*DC76.K34.1822

62. Kersaint, Armand-Guy Simon de Coetnempren, comte de.

*Discours sur les monumens publiques, prononcé au Conseil du Départe-
ment de Paris, le 15 decembre 1791, par Armand-Guy Kersaint.* Paris,
1792.

Not now owned by the University.

Armand-Guy Simon de Coetnempren, comte de Kersaint, (1742–93),
entered the French navy in 1755. He had an active part in the early
stages of the French Revolution and became a deputy for the Départe-
ment de Paris, but was beheaded on December 4, 1793.

Sowerby describes the book as the first edition, a quarto of forty-seven leaves with twelve plates engraved by Poulleau (see No. 29).

The book was sold by Jefferson to Congress. He had acquired it after 1792 according to Kimball (p. 95). It was ordered by Jefferson for the University in the section on "Architecture" of the want list, but there is no record of the library's ever having acquired it.

U. Va.   M

Sowerby 4212

63. Kirby, John Joshua.

Vol. I. THE / PERSPECTIVE / OF / ARCHITECTURE. / A WORK ENTIRELY NEW; / DEDUCED FROM THE PRINCIPLES OF / DR. *BROOK TAYLOR:* / And PERFORMED by / TWO RULES only of Universal Application. / BEGUN BY / Command of His Present MAJESTY / WHEN / PRINCE OF *WALES* / BY / JOSHUA KIRBY, Designer in Perspective to His MAJESTY. / LONDON: / PRINTED FOR THE AUTHOR, / By R. FRANCKLIN, in *Russel-Street, Covent-Garden:* / and SOLD by T. PAYNE, at the *Mews-Gate;* Messrs. KNAPTON and HORSEFIELD, in *Ludgate-Street;* / Messrs. DODSLEY, in *Pall-Mall.* T. LONGMAN, in *Paternoster-Row;* T. DAVIES, in *Russel-Street,* / *Covent-Garden;* and J. GRETTON, in *Bond-Street.* 1761.

Folio. Engraved frontispiece; title page (1 leaf); dedication (1 leaf); preface (2 leaves); introduction ([i]-ii); text (1–60); index and errata (1 leaf).

Vol. II.   [No title page.]

Folio. 73 engraved plates.

The engraved frontispiece by Hogarth (see Plate LVIII) was used in Vol. I of this book first, although it was also used two years later in No. 24. The engravers were James Basire (see No. 3); Samuel Boyce (d. 1775), English; J. Fougeron (see No. 23); C. Grignion (see No. 23); John Joshua Kirby, Jr. (see below); Peter Mazell (fl.1761–97), English; F. Patton (see No. 3); and John Ryland (fl.1757–90), English.

John Joshua Kirby the younger (1716–74) was the eldest son of John Kirby, a schoolmaster and topographer. The younger Kirby was born at Wickham Market, Suffolk. He was trained first as a coach and

Plate LVIII. *From No. 63. Frontispiece* (Vol. I).

house painter. He knew Gainsborough at Ipswich, tried landscape, then studied linear perspective at St. Martin's Lane Academy, where he later taught it. He was a friend of Hogarth, who designed the frontispiece for this book. Gainsborough remained Kirby's friend and asked to be buried beside him at Kew.

Besides being the designer in perspective to His Majesty (George III) and clerk of the works at Kew Palace, he was elected F.R.S. in 1767, F.S.A. in 1768, and was both secertary and president (1768) of the Society of Artists.

In addition to this work, which was first issued in 1761, Kirby had earlier published *Dr. Brook Taylor's Method of Perspective Made Easy, Both in Theory and Practice*, 1754. This book was based on Dr. Taylor's (1685–1731) two treatises, *Linear Perspective*, 1715, and *New Principles of Linear Perspective*, 1719. Kirby later published *Dr. Brook Taylor's Method of Perspective Compared with the Examples Lately Published . . . as Sirifatti's by J. Ware . . . Being a Parallel between Those Two Methods of Perspective. In Which the Superior Excellence of Taylor's Is Shown*, ca.1767.

Kirby scrupulously differentiates between his and Dr. Taylor's contributions to this work:

All the figures, which are produced as general rules in this work, I have ventured to call my own; not having had any other assistance herein, than some elegant designs for the Perspective; and likewise all the prints which particularly relate to the architectonic sector, which is an instrument of a new and curious construction; and by which, persons wholly unacquainted with architecture, may be enabled to delineate any part of it, with elegance and exactness.

Now if any one should say, that my rules (strictly speaking) may all be obtained from the study of Dr. Taylor, I would answer, that the same kind of remark will hold good against every mathematician, that has wrote since the time of Euclid. . . .

I make no doubt, however, that the method for drawing many of the finished examples, will at least be considered as new. [Preface]

It shall be our business to strike into a new path, and endeavour to establish such principles for this part of perspective as shall have a rational theory, and fully answer the end proposed by them. [P. i]

He then describes the organization of his book:

This volume is divided into four books, and each of these into several sections. In the first book we have given a few simple, but general rules. In the second book we have shewn how, with these rules, to put all the five orders of architecture into perspective. The third book relates wholly to the doctrine of light and shadow, which explains this part of perspective in a new and familiar manner. In the fourth and last book, we have shewn the application of our general rules, beginning with simple colonnades, and ending with elegant structures. [P. ii]

This is a sumptuous work, surely one of the most handsome of all the books on perspective that have been published. In addition to his textual acknowledgment of his debt to Dr. Taylor, Kirby made a pictorial acknowledgment, for he includes a plate, No. LV, which shows a shrine to Dr. Taylor. This plate is dedicated to Dr. Taylor's daughter (see Plate LIX). It is also said that George III contributed the design for the house engraved on Plate LXIV of Kirby's book.

Although we do not know exactly when the set came into Jefferson's library, Kimball (p. 95) points out that it was purchased sometime between 1785 and 1789 and that the method of perspective described is that used by Jefferson in his bird's-eye view of the University of Virginia (N-335). One must, however, admit the view is not completely successful.

Jefferson specifically ordered this edition for the University in the section on "Architecture" of the want list, though there is no record of the library's having acquired it during Jefferson's lifetime. His own set was sold to Congress. The library's present set entered the collections recently, the gift of the Thomas Jefferson Memorial Foundation.

U. Va.   M
*NA2710.K6.1761   Sowerby 4207

64. Krafft, Johann Karl.

PLANS, COUPES, ÉLÉVATIONS / DES PLUS BELLES / MAISONS ET DES HOTELS / CONSTRUITS A PARIS ET DANS LES ENVIRONS. / PUBLIÉS PAR J.-CH. KRAFFT, ARCHITECTE, ET N. RANSONNETTE, GRAVEUR. / *A PARIS* / Chez / LES deux Associés, KRAFFT, Architecte, rue de Bourgogne, No. 1463, fauxbourg Saint-Germain; / et RANSONNETTE, Graveur, rue du Figuier, No. 43, quartier Saint-Paul; / CH. POUGENS, Imprimeur-Libraire, quai Voltaire, No. 10; / FUCHS, Libraire, rue des Nathurins Saint-Jacques, No. 334; / CALIXTE VOLLAND, Libraire, quai des Augustins, No. 25; / LEVRAULT, Libraire, quai Malaquais, au coin de la rue des Petits-Augustins./ GRUNDRISSE, DURCHSCHNITTE UND AUFRISSE / DES SCHOENSTEN IN PARIS / UND DER UMLIEGENDEN GEGEND BEFINDLICHEN HAEUSER UND PALLAESTE. /

To Mrs Younge, Daughter of Dr Brook Taylor; This Plate as a Tribute Due to her Fathers Merit, is Dedicated, by Her unknown, but (Most Respectfull humble Servant, Joshua Kirby.

Plate LIX. *From No. 63*. Dedication plate (Vol. II, Pl. LV).

HERAUSGEGEBEN VON J. CH. KRAFFT, BAUMEISTER, UND N. RAN-
SONNETTE, KUPFESTECHER. / *PARIS* / Bey / IM Verlage bey den
Herausgebern, dem Baumeister KRAFFT, rue de Bourgogne, No. 1463,
fauxbourg / Saint-Germain; und dem Kupferstecher RANSONNETTE, rue
du Figuier, No. 43, quartier / Saint-Paul; / CARL POUGENS, Buch-
drucker und Buchhaendler, quai Voltaire, No. 10; / FUCHS, Buch-
haendler, rue des Maturins Saint-Jacques, No. 334; / CALIXTE
VOLLAND, Buchhaendler, quai des Augustins, No. 25; / LEVRAULT,
Buchhaendler, quai Malaquais, au coin de la rue des Petits-Augustins. /
PLANS, FORMS, ELEVATIONS / OF THE MOST REMARK-
ABLE / HOUSES AND HOTELS / ERECTED IN PARIS AND
ITS ENVIRONS / PUBLISHED BY J. CH. KRAFFT, ARCHITECT, AND
RANSONNETTE, ENGRAVER. / *PARIS,* / By / SOLD by the Editors,
KRAFFT, Architect, rue de Bourgogne, No. 1463 fauxbourg Saint-Ger-
main; / and RANNSONNETTE, Engraver, rue du Figuier, No. 43, quartier
Saint-Paul; / CH. POUGENS, Bookseller, quai Voltaire, No. 10; / FUCHS,
Bookseller, rue des Mathurins Saint-Jacques, No. 334; / CALIXTE VOL-
LAND, Bookseller, quai des Augustins, No. 25; / LEVRAULT, Bookseller,
quai Malaquais, au coin de la rue des Petits-Augustins. / De l'Impri-
merie de CLOUSIER, rue de Sorbonne, No. 390. [1801–2]

Folio. Engraved frontispiece; title page (1 leaf); "conclusion" (1 leaf);
note ([1]–2); 20 cahiers, each with 1 leaf of description of the plates and
six engraved plates.

The engraver Pierre Nicolas Ransonnette (1745–1810) was a Parisian
who had been a student of Choffard and had held the appointment of
draftsman and engraver to Monsieur, brother of the king (see also No.
40). For the engraved frontispiece, see Plate LX.

    Johann Karl Krafft (1764–1833), though an Austrian, lived and
worked mostly in Paris. He says in the English portion of his note that
the

revolution, which has taken place in the arts, and particularly in architecture,
since the last twenty five years in France, has been remarked by every man
of taste.

    Knowledge, which has spread itself throughout every class of society, a
passion for traveling, and progressive improvements have brought about in
the art of building, and decorating public edifices very remarquable [*sic*]
changes. The great number of private Houses, erected in the new parts of the
town for opulent proprietors, who brought back with them from their travels
in Italy, and other Countries the taste of Novelty, and a certain propensity of
deviating from the old, servile method of Building, of freeing themselves from
many received prejudices, operated a complete change in the outward fea-

Plate LX. *From No. 64.* Frontispiece.

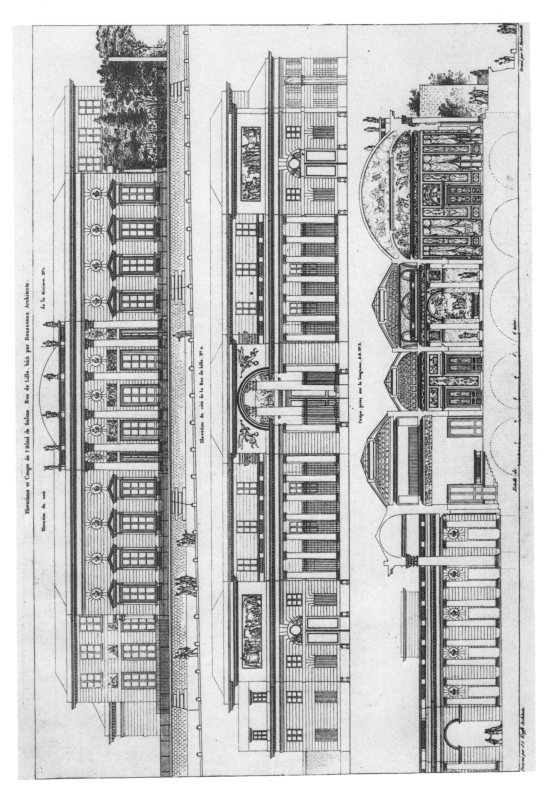

Plate LXI. *From No. 64.* "Elevations et Coupe de l'Hôtel de Salme" (Pl. 73).

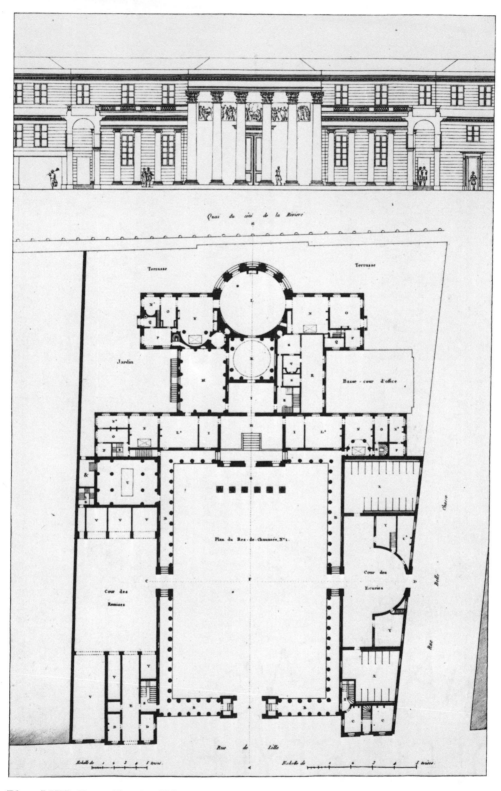

Plate LXII. *From No. 64.* "Plan Général, Elevation du côté de la Cour de l'Hôtel de Salme" (Pl. 74).

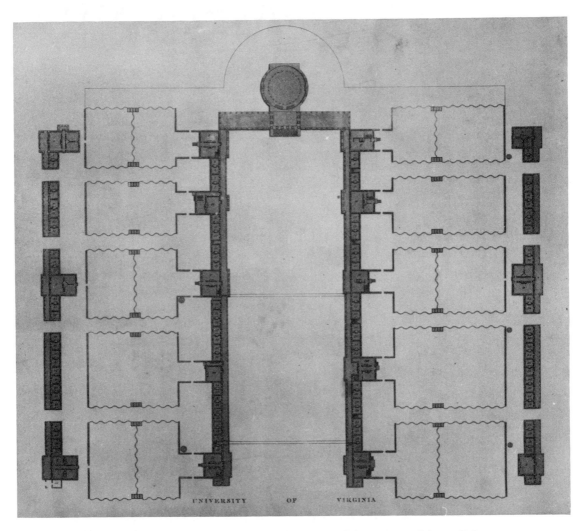

Plate LXIII. The Maverick plan of the University of Virginia, engraved from Jefferson's drawing (N-385).

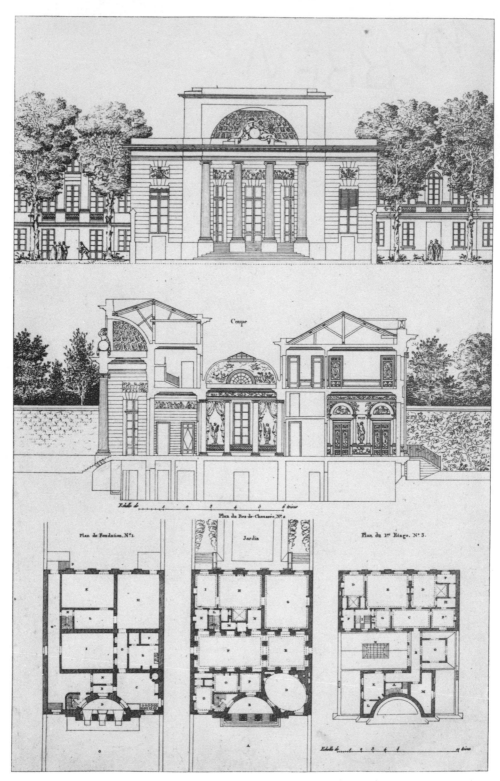

Plate LXIV. *From No. 64.* "Maison de Melle. Guimard" (Pl. 49).

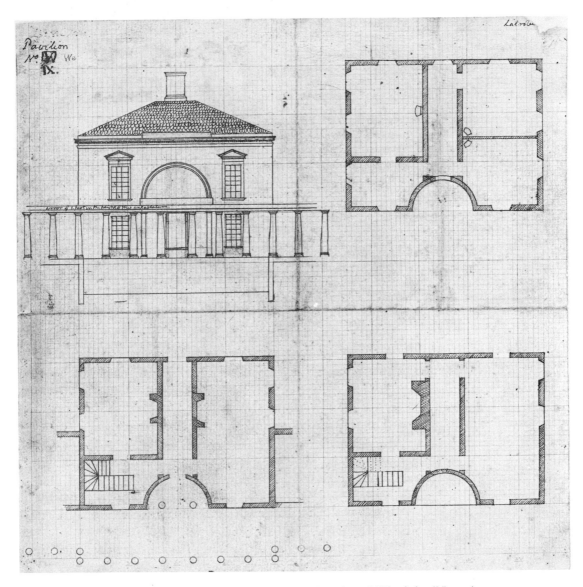

Plate LXV. Jefferson's drawing for Pavilion IX, University of Virginia (N-357).

tures of architecture; and those foreigners, who fancy they acquire a perfect idea of this art in consulting the old collections of our Buildings, or in deriving their principles from these works, which have formerly treated of this subject, are vastly mistaken.

We look upon it as an important service rendered to society to publish, what may well be called the monuments of architecture regenerated in the nineteenth Century, and those, which towards the end of the eighteenth, have prepared this regeneration.

We have, therefore, made choice of those Buildings, the most elegant, the most agreable, as well for the outward, as the inward distribution and decorations; and in order to present them the more faithfully, we have consulted the Artists themselves, under whose care they have been erected. . . .

We shall not allow ourselves the least censorious reflexion on the works of men, the greatest part of whom are still living, in order that every one may enjoy the greatest latitude of judging. . . . Moreover it appears to us, that it only belongs to the following generation, to judge impartially the preceeding one; for we often view too near our contemporaries, and can seldom disengage ourselves from the influence of our passions. We are actuated either by hatred or friendship, and we have too many examples before us of critics, who, whether severe or indulgent, have judged, without meaning so perhaps, the person of the author, while they imagined that they only judged his works. [Pp. (1)–2]

This is a surprisingly inclusive book with its illustrations of notable late eighteenth-century Parisian buildings. The work of no less than forty-three architects is represented, among them Bellanger, Boullée, Durand, Ledoux (including his own house), Legrand, Moitte, Rousseau, and Soufflot. All the years from 1762 to 1802 are represented with the exception of 1763–66, 1768–69, 1771, 1773, 1782, 1785, 1791, and 1794.

Several plates in the book seem to have possible Jeffersonian connections. That for the "House belonging to M. Vassale, situated in the street Pigalle, near by the Chausée d'Antin, built in the year 1788, by M. Henry, Architect" shows a circular building with enlongated oval, octagonal, and irregularly shaped rooms fitted within the circle. The oval rooms Jefferson later put in the Rotunda for the University of Virginia are reminiscent of this arrangement, although there seems to be a closer precedent for the Rotunda plan in the Steiglitz *Plans et dessins* (No. 117).

Two other plates, Nos. 73 and 74 (see Plates LXI and LXII), may have strengthened Jefferson's remembrance of what Krafft called "the Hotel Salm, Lille street, built in the year 1787, by Rousseau, Architect." Certainly Jefferson had known this building very well in Paris, going nearly every day to look at it, and it seems to have had a certain influence on his shaping of the Lawn at the University (see Plate LXIII). The colonnade surrounding the court of the Hotel de Salm, with a dominant portico at the end and a pavilionlike arched entrance on either side into service courts, may very well have been a remembered prototype for the Lawn.[1]

And finally there is the Krafft plate No. 49 (see Plate LXIV), the "House of Mrs. Guimard, Mont-Blanc street, built in the year 1770 by Ledoux, Architect." On the drawing Jefferson made for Pavilion IX at the University (see Plate LXV), he wrote "Latrobe," indicating that it derived from some suggestions Latrobe had sent him for the University. Jefferson's composition must certainly have derived from the Guimard house also, though the derivation may very well have been second- or thirdhand through Latrobe and possibly others. Jefferson could have seen the house during his stay in Paris; it was illustrated in this book; and both Latrobe and his pupil Robert Mills, who was also Jefferson's pupil and friend, used similar compositions.[2]

Sowerby notes that Jefferson bought the Krafft on December 24, 1804, for $40.00. During the following year he tried to get whatever further parts might have been issued, but Part XX, which he already had, was the last. His copy was later sold to Congress.

He ordered the book for the University in the section on "Architecture" of the want list, but there is no record of the library's having acquired it during his lifetime. The library's present copy is a recent purchase, the gift of the Thomas Jefferson Memorial Foundation.

U. Va.
*NA7348.P2K8.1803

M
Sowerby 4214

65. La Chausse, Michel Ange de.

Raccolta di gemme antiche figurate, incise da Pietro Santi Bartoli ed illustrate da Michelangelo Causeo de La Chausse. 2 vols. Rome, 1805.

Not now owned by the University.

[1] See William B. O'Neal, "Origins of the University Ground Plans," *University of Virginia Alumni News*, L (Nov. 1962), 6.

[2] See Emil Kaufmann, "Three Revolutionary Architects, Boulée, Ledoux, and Lequece," *Transactions of the American Philosophical Society*, n.s., XLII, pt. 3 (Oct. 1952), 491; Rich Borneman, "Some Ledoux Inspired Buildings in America," *Journal of the Society of Architectural Historians*, XIII (Nov. 1954), 15; and Frederick D. Nichols, "Two Millionth Book," *Chapter and Verse*—3, Feb. 1975, p. 3.

Michel Ange de La Chausse (fl.1700), although French, lived most of his life in Rome.

Pietro Santi Bartoli (1635–1700) was an Italian painter and engraver. As an engraver he executed plates not only from antiquity but also after pictures by Raphael, Annibale Carracci, Lanfranco, and others.

Jefferson had owned a work listed in Sowerby as *Le gemme antiche figurate di Michel Angelo Causeo de La Chausse* (Rome, 1700). Since its title page was engraved by "Petrus Sanctes Bartolus," it may very well be the first, or at least an early, edition of this work. It is described as a quarto volume with 200 engraved plates of gems.

Jefferson ordered this, the second (?), edition of the work for the University in the section on "Gardening. Painting. Scultpure. Music" of the want list, but there is no record of its ever having been received.

U. Va.   M

Sowerby 4232

66. La Faye, Polycarpe de.

RECHERCHES / *SUR* / *LA PRÉPARATION* / QUE LES RO-MAINS / *DONNOIENT* / À LA CHAUX / Dont ils se servoient pour leurs construc-/tions, & sur la composition & l'emploi / de leurs Mortiers. / *Par M.* DE LA FAYE, *Trésorier général des* / *Gratifications des Troupes.* / A PARIS, / DE L'IMPRIMERIE ROYALE. / M.DCCLXXVII.

8vo. Title page ([i]); note (iii-vi); text ([1]–83); [new pagination:] index (i-ix).

The book contains two other essays bound in, the *Mémoire sur une découverte dans l'art de bâtir* by Sr. Loriot and La Faye's *Mémoire pour servir de suite aux recherches sur la préparation que les romains donnoient à la chaux*, neither of which are a part of the previous work.

La Faye says:

Si les anciens monumens qu'offre l'Italie, ne devoient leur conservation qu'à la chaleur du climat & à la qualité particulière des sables & des pierres que le sol y produit, il ne resteroit aucuns vestiges des constructions qui ont été faites par les Romains au nord de la France & en Angleterre, avec les seules matières que le pays leur procuroit. Il semble donc que la durée & la soliditée des anciens monumens sont dûes à la qualité des matières, qu'à la façon de les employer. Cette réflexion m'a engagé à faire des recherches sur les constructions des Romains. J'ai recueilli tout ce que les Auteurs anciens ont écrit sur ce sujet,

& après avoir comparé leurs textes, j'ai reconnu qu'il s'accordoient parfaitement sur une mannière de préparer la chaux, qui est ignorée de nos jours, & qui diffère absolument de la nôtre. J'ai fait éteindre de la chaux suivant ce procédé, je l'ai mêlée avec nos sables, comme ont fait les Romains, en observant dans les divers mélanges, les proportions indiquées par les Auteurs. Les mortiers que ces effais m'ont procurés, ont acquis une si grande dureté, que j'ai cru pouvoir les employer aux différens travaux de construction & d'embellissement auxquels ils étoient propres. D'après le succès qu'ont eu mes épreuves, j'ose me flatter qu'en sy conformant, on parviendra à donner à nos constructions la même solidité que nous remarquons dans celles des Romaines. [Pp. (1)–3]

Jefferson was undecided about the classification of this book, for, as Sowerby notes, in his own catalogue he first listed it under "Technical Arts" and then transferred it to the section on "Architecture." Kimball (p. 95) says Jefferson bought his copy betwen 1785 and 1789. It was sold to Congress, where it was put back under "Technical Arts."

Jefferson ordered it for the University in the section on "Technical Arts" of the want list, but there is no record of its acquisition until the recent duplicate entered the collections. It is the gift of the Thomas Jefferson Memorial Foundation.

U. Va.   M
*TP881.L67.1777   Sowerby 1176 and 4205

67. Landon, Charles Paul.

Vol. I. ANNALES DU MUSÉE / ET DE / L'ÉCOLE MODERNE DES BEAUX-ARTS. / RECUEIL de Graveurs au trait, d'après les principaux / ouvrages de peinture, sculpture, ou projets d'archi-/tecture qui chaque année ont remporté le prix, soit / aux écoles spéciales, soit aux concours nationaux; / les productions des Artistes en tous genres, qui, aux / différentes expositions, ont été citées avec éloges; / les morceaux les plus estimés ou inédits de la galerie / de Peinture; la suite complète de celle des Anti-/ques; édifices anciens et modernes, etc. Rédigé par / C. P. LANDON, Peintre, ancien Pensionnaire de / la République, a l'école des Beaux-Arts à Rome; / membre de l'Athénée des Arts, de la Société Philo-/technique; de celle libre des Sciences, Lettres et / Arts de Paris; et Associé-Correspondant de la Société d'émulation d'Alençon. / TOME PREMIER. / A PARIS, / Chez C. P. LANDON, Peintre, au Louvre. / DE L'IMPRIMERIE DES ANNALES DU MUSÉE. / AN IX.–1801.

8vo. Half title ([i]); engraved frontispiece (1 leaf); title page ([iii]); dedication ([v]); table of contents ([vii]-xii); text, with 72 engravings inserted ([1]–148).

Vol. II.   [Not now owned by the University.]

Vol. III.   [Not now owned by the University.]

Vol. IV.   ANNALES DU MUSÉE / . . . / TOME QUATRIÈME. / A PARIS, / Chez C. P. LANDON, Peintre, quai Bonaparte, no. 23 au / coin de la rue de Bacq. / AN XII.–1803.

8vo. Half title (1 leaf); engraved frontispiece (1 leaf); title page (1 leaf); table of contents ([i]-vi); text, with 72 engravings inserted (9–152).

Vol. V.   ANNALES DU MUSÉE / . . . / TOME CINQUIÈME. / . . .

8vo. Half title (1 leaf); engraved frontispiece (1 leaf); title page (1 leaf); table of contents ([i]-vi); text, with 72 engravings inserted (9–152); dedication (1 leaf).

Vol. VI.   ANNALES DU MUSÉE / . . . / TOME SIXIÈME. / . . . / AN XII.–1804.

8vo. Half title (1 leaf); engraved frontispiece (1 leaf); title page (1 leaf); table of contents ([i]-vi); text, with 72 engravings inserted (9–151).

Vol. VII.   ANNALES DU MUSÉE / . . . / TOME SEPTIÈME. / . . . / An XII.–1803.

8vo. Half title (1 leaf); engraved frontispiece (1 leaf); title page (1 leaf); table of conents ([i]-vi); text, with 72 engravings inserted (9–151).

Vol. VIII.   ANNALES DU MUSÉE / . . . / TOME HUITIÈME. / . . .

8vo. Half title (1 leaf); engraved frontispiece (1 leaf); title page (1 leaf); table of contents ([i]-ii); subscription form (1 leaf); text, with 72 engravings inserted (9–152).

Vol. IX.   ANNALES DU MUSÉE / . . . / RECUEIL de Gravures au trait, contenant la collection / complète des peintures et sculptures du

Musée Napo-/léon; les principaux ouvrages de peinture, sculpture, / ou projets d'architecture qui, chaque année, ont rem-/porté le prix aux concours public; les productions des / Artistes en tous genres, qui, aux différentes expositions, / ont été cités avec éloges; édifices public, etc. / Rédigé . . . / TOME NEUVIÈME. / . . .

8vo. Half title (1 leaf); engraved frontispiece (1 leaf); title page (1 leaf); table of contents ([i]-v); text, with 72 engravings inserted (9–147).

Vol. X.   ANNALES DU MUSÉE / . . . / TOME DIXIÈME. / . . .

8vo. Half title (1 leaf); engraved frontispiece (1 leaf); title page (1 leaf); table of contents ([i]-v); subscription form (1 leaf); text, with 72 engravings inserted (9–148).

Vol. XI.   ANNALES DU MUSÉE / . . . / TOME ONZIÈME. / Chez C. P. LANDON, Peintre, quai Bonaparte, no. 1, au coin / de la rue du Bacq. / DE L'IMPRIMERIE DES ANNALES DU MUSÉE. / 1806.

8vo. Half title (1 leaf); engraved frontispiece (1 leaf); title page (1 leaf); table of contents ([i]-vi); dedication (1 leaf); text, with 72 engravings inserted (9–149).

Vol. XII.   ANNALES DU MUSÉE. / . . . / TOME DOUZIÈME. / · · ·

8vo. Half title (1 leaf); engraved frontispiece (1 leaf); title page (1 leaf); table of contents ([i]-vi); dedication (1 leaf); text, with 72 engravings inserted (9–150).

Vol. XIII.   ANNALES DU MUSÉE / . . . / RECUEIL de Gravures au trait, contenant la collection / complète des Peintures et Sculptures du Musée Na-/poléon et de celui de Versailles; les objets les plus / curieux du Musée des Monumens francais; les prin-/cipales productions des Artistes vivans, en peinture, / sculpture et architecture, édifices publics, etc.; avec / des notices historiques et critiques. / PAR C. P. LANDON, Peintre, ancien pensionnaire de / L'Académie de France, à Rome; membre de plusiers / Sociétés littéraires. / *Cet Ouvrage classique a obtenu une Médaille d'argent à / l'exposition publique de 1806.* / TOME TREIZIÈME. / . . . / 1807.

8vo. Half title (1 leaf); engraved frontispiece (1 leaf); title page (1 leaf); table of contents ([i]-vi); dedication (1 leaf); text, with 72 engravings inserted (9–152).

Vol. XIV. ANNALES DU MUSÉE / . . . / TOME QUATOR-ZIÈME. / . . .

8vo. Half title (1 leaf); engraved frontispiece (1 leaf); title page (1 leaf); table of contents ([i]-vi); text, with 71 (of a total of 72) engravings inserted (9–148).

Vol. XV. ANNALES DU MUSÉE / . . / TOME QUINZIÉME. / . . .

8vo. Half title (1 leaf); engraved frontispiece (1 leaf); title page (1 leaf); table of contents ([i]-iv); text, with 72 engravings inserted (9–140).

Vol. XVI. ANNALES DU MUSÉE / . . / TOME SEIZIÈME. / . . . / Chez C. P. LANDON, Peintre, rue de l'Université, no. 19, vis-à-/vis la rue de Beaune. / . . . / 1808.

8vo. Half title ([i]); engraved frontispiece ([iv]); title page ([v]); table of contents ([vii]-x); dedication (1 leaf); text, with 72 engravings inserted (3–136); note to printer (1 leaf).

Vol. XVII. PAYSAGES / ET / TABLEAUX DE GENRE / DU MUSÉE NAPOLEON; / Gravé a l'eau forte par divers artistes, et publiés par / C. P. LANDON, peintre, ancien pensionnaire de / l'Académie de France, à Rome; membre de plusiers / Sociétés littéraires. / Recueil pouvant faire suite aux Annales du Musée, par le même / Auteur; et réunissant, comme cette dernière collection, un choix / de productions modernes, avec l'explication des planches. / TOME PREMIER. / A PARIS, / Chez C. P. LANDON, Peintre, quai Bonaparte, no. 23, et chez / les principaux Libraires et Directeurs des postes. / DE L'IMPRI-MERIE DES ANNALES DU MUSÉE. / An XIII–1805.

8vo. Half title (1 leaf); engraved frontispiece (1 leaf); table of contents, misbound from another volume ([i]-vi); [new pagination:] table of contents (iii-iv); dedication (1 leaf); note to publisher (1 leaf); text, with 71 engravings inserted (9–97).
Binder's number for this is Volume I.

Vol. XVIII. ANNALES DU MUSÉE / . . . / *PAYSAGES ET TABLEAUX DE GENRE.* / TOME DEUXIÈME. / . . .

8vo. Half title (1 leaf); title page (1 leaf); table of conents ([i]-v); text, with 70 engravings inserted (5–88).
Binder's number for this is Volume II.

Vol. XIX. ANNALES DU MUSÉE / . . . / *PAYSAGES ET TAB-LEAUX DE GENRE.* / TOME TROISIÈME. / . . . / 1808.

8vo. Half title (1 leaf); title page (1 leaf); table of contents, misbound from Vol. III ([iii]-iv); [new pagination:] partial table of contents (iii); note (1 leaf); text, with 72 engravings inserted (3–76).

Binder's number for this is Volume III. Volume III of the *PAY-SAGES* series serves as both Vols. III and IV of that series, thus completing the set.

Vol. XX (?). [Not now owned by the University.]

Vol. XXI (?). ANNALES DU MUSÉE / . . . / TOME COMPLE-MENTAIRE. / . . . / 1809.

8vo. Half title (1 unnumbered p.); advertisement (1 unnumbered p.); engraved frontispiece (1 leaf); dedication [5–6]; avis ([7]–8); table of plates ([9]–14); text (15–134), with 99 engravings of which 7 are folding inserted; table generale ([135]–209).

Binder's number for this is Volume XVII.

The engravings in Vols. I–XVI are largely by Charles Pierre Joseph Normand (see No. 40) and are executed in a neoclassic line making all the works of art look as though they were by the same artist. Volumes XVII-XIX have plates in chiaroscuro.

Charles Paul Landon (1760–1826) was born at Nonant, Normandy. He studied at the atelier Regnault and at Rome. He became known both as a genre painter and for his writings on art. He issued over ten different titles, was associated with the *Journal des arts*, *des sciences*, *et de la littérature*, and was a proprietor of the *Gazette de France*.

He dedicated his first volume of his *Annales*

A MADAME BONAPARTE.
MADAME,

Vous aimez les Arts, comme votre illustre Epoux aime la gloire, avec idolâtrie! La gloire l'a récompensé; les arts vous doivent leur hommage.

Ce recueil, que j'ose vous dédier, est destiné à retrace les chefs-d'oeuvre que la France posséde. Ils se multiplieront par les encouragemens que vous prodiguez aux artistes.

Agréez avec bienveillance ce faible tribut de ma reconnaissance et de mon respect.

LANDON. [I, (v)]

The volumes contain ancient and modern examples of painting and sculpture, as well as some plates of buildings. Most notable among the buildings, perhaps, is that on Plate 68 of Vol. VII, which is the "Façade de l'hôtel de Salm." He says of this building, already discussed in No. 64: "L'hotel de Salm, aujourd'hui le palais de la Legion d'honneur, . . . est une des plus riches et des plus fastueuses habitations qui qui [*sic*] aient été érigées à Paris, depuis vingt-cinq années" (VII, 143).

Jefferson owned and sold to Congress a ten-volume set, complete only for volumes issued to 1806. His order for the University for twenty volumes in the section on "Gardening. Painting. Sculpture. Music" of the want list shows that he was aware of the supplement. Hilliard apparently filled the order with a sixteen-volume set consisting of the supplement and Vol. IV-XVI of the main set. This is the set described in the 1828 *Catalogue*. It is still in the library, but Vols. I and XXI have recently been added to it, the gift of the Thomas Jefferson Memorial Foundation. Volumes II and III are still missing, as is Vol. XX unless the double volume of Vol. XIX serves also as Vol. XX.

U. Va. M
*N2010.L3.1800 Sowerby 4244

68. Langley, Batty.

Practical Geometry / Applied to the Useful ARTS of / *Building, Surveying, Gardening and Mensuration;* / Calculated for the Service of / Gentlemen as well as Artisans, / And set to View / In FOUR PARTS, / CONTAINING, / I. Preliminaries or the Foundations of the several ARTS / above-mentioned. / II. The various Orders of Architecture, laid down and improved from / the best Masters; with the Ways of making Draughts of Buildings, Gardens, / Groves, Fountains, &c. the laying down of Maps, Cities, Lordships, Farms, &c. / III. The Doctrine and Rules of Mensuration of all Kinds, illustrated by / select Examples in Building, Gardening, Timber, &c. / IV. Exact Tables of Mensuration, shewing, by Inspection, the Super-/ficial and Solid Contents of all Kinds of Bodies, without the Fatigue of Arithme-/tical Computation: / To which is annexed, / An Account of the Clandestine Practice now generally obtaining in / Mensuration, and particularly the Damage sustained in felling Timber by Measure. / The Whole / Exemplify'd with a large Number of Folio Copper Plates, curiously / Engraven by the best Hands. / By *BATTY LANGLEY.* / The Second Edition. / *LONDON:* / Printed for Aaron Ward at the *King's-Arms* in *Little-Britain.* 1729.

Small folio. Bookseller's advertisement (1 leaf); two- color title page (1 leaf); dedication (1 leaf); preface ([i]-viii); table of contents (4 leaves); text ([1]–136); 40 engraved plates, of which 25 are double.

Batty Langley (1696–1751) was born at Twickenham, Middlesex, the son of a gardener. He worked first as a landscape gardener, but he moved to London ca.1736. There he started, with his brother Thomas, an academy of architectural drawing; one source says that his pupils were carpenters. He also had a large surveying connection and was a valuer of timber. A building he designed for Nathaniel Blackerby, son-in-law of Nicholas Hawksmoor, was called in the press "a curious grotesque temple, in a taste entirely new" (*DNB*).

He wrote no less than twenty-one books, almost all of which appeared in many editions. The *Practical Geometry* was first issued in 1726; this edition of 1729 is labeled "Second Edition," though one authority gives issues for both 1728 and 1729. The work is really a how-to-do-it book, and Langley says:

My design . . . is to treat of architecture, gardening, mensuration and Land-surveying, in a method as easy and intelligible as it is new and generally useful. I shall begin with the fundamental, or first principles of these several arts, and gradually conduct my reader from the easier parts of 'em up to the hardest, taking particular care all along to let him see the *utile* as well as the *dulce* thereof; the fruitful practice, and not the barren theory only. From a failure of authors in this point, I apprehend it is that these arts are at present much less cultivated than they merit. An author cannot do them greater justice, than to paint them as they are, most useful and delightful employments; of great importance in human life. To convince the world of this truth, as it is the design, so it wou'd be the highest recommendation of the present treatise. [P. i]

One should note that the garden designs are still formal (see Plate LXVI), although a few meandering paths do appear within the formal divisions of the plates.

Jefferson sold his copy of the 1729 edition to Congress. He did not order it for the University. The library's present copy has been recently acquired, the gift of the Thomas Jefferson Memorial Foundation.

M

*T353.L28.1729   Sowerby 4185

Plate LXVI. *From No. 68.* Entrance into a shady walk (Pl. XXXI).

69. Le Clerc, Sébastien.

Vol. I. TRAITÉ / D'ARCHITECTURE / AVEC / DES RE-
MARQUES / ET DES OBSERVATIONS / TRES-UTILES / Pour
les Jeunes Gens, qui veulent s'appliquer / à ce bel Art. / *Par* SEB. LE
CLERC, *Chevalier Romain,* / *D. & G. O. du C. du Roy.* / A PARIS, /
Chez PIERRE GIFFART, Libraire & Graveur du Roy, / rue S.
Jacques, à l'Image de Sainte Therese. / MDCCXIV. / *AVEC APPRO-
BATION ET PRIVILEGE DE SA MAJESTÉ.*

4to. Title page (1 leaf); note to reader (3 unnumbered pp.); license (3
unnumbered pp.); text ([1]–194); table of contents (1 leaf).

Vol. II. TRAITÉ / D'ARCHITECTURE / SECOND VOLUME /
Contenant / LES FIGURES.

4to. Engraved title page (1 leaf); engraved half title (1 leaf); 181 engraved plates.

Sébastien Le Clerc (1637–1714) was born at Metz. Taught by his
father, a silversmith and engraver, he began engraving at the age of
seven and at twelve astonished observers by his ability. In 1665 he went
to Paris where Le Brun took him under his protection. He was given a
flat at the Gobelins by Colbert in 1669; in 1672 he was a member of the
royal academy; a little later he was appointed professor of geometry; in
1690 he was made draftsman and engraver to the king; and in 1706 he
was created a Roman knight.

Le Clerc became the father of a son, also Sébastien (1676–1763),
a painter who in turn became the father of a son, Sébastien Jacques
(1734–85), sometimes called Leclerc des Gobelins, who was both a
painter and an engraver.

Le Clerc published many books, among them the next entry, No.
70, and at least two works on perspective. The *Traité d'architecture* was
first issued in this edition and later translated into Russian on the order
of Peter the Great. All the plates of this work were engraved by Le
Clerc, the last one executed just six months before his death.

The work was an early example of the French "cours d'architecture," written especially for the young man wishing to become a pro-
fessional architect. The plates are particularly well drawn and hand-
somely engraved (see Plate LXVII), as one would expect of a man
whom Desgodetz (No. 36) called one of the best engravers in France.

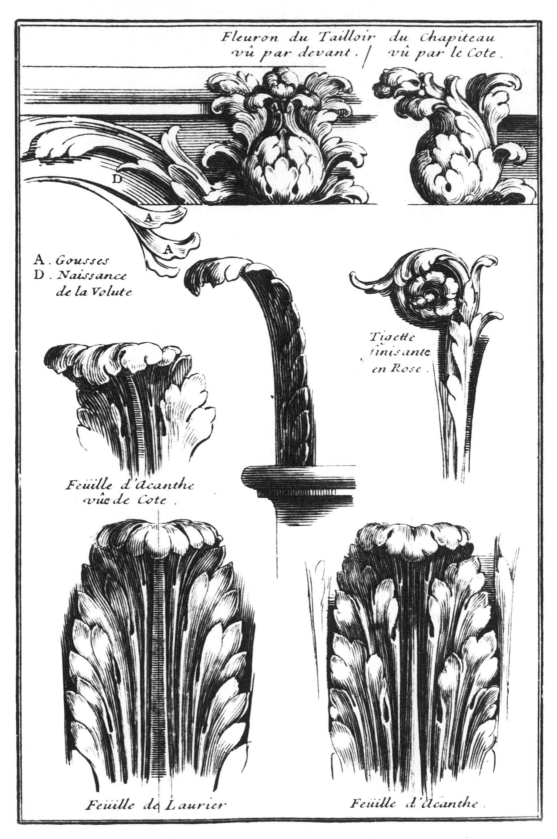

Fleuron du Tailloir du Chapiteau
vû par devant. / vû par le Cote.

D

A
A

A . Gousses
D . Naissance
de la Volute

Feüille d'Acanthe
vû de Cote .

Tigette
finisante
en Rose .

Feüille de Laurier

Feüille d'Acanthe

Plate LXVII. *From No. 69.* "Ordre Romain," details (Vol. II, Pl. 49).

Le Clerc begins his book with a series of definitions and requirements for the study of architecture:

L'Architecture en general est l'Art de bien bâtir; & cet Art se distingue en deux parties principales, l'une Civile, & l'autre Militaire.

La Civile a pour but, de mettre les hommes à couvert des injures du temps, de leur donner des demeures & des habitations solides, convenables, commodes, saines & agreables.

. . . Dans le Dessein, on fait attention à la distribution des appartemens, a leurs commoditez & usages; à la belle apparence du Bâtiment, au juste accord & rapport de ses parties, & leurs proportions & elegance. [I, (1)–2]

Cette belle & noble maniere de bâtir, est celle dont les anciens Grecs & Romains nous ont donnez les premiers idées, par les Bâtimens magnifiques qu'il élevoient pour la gloire de leurs faux Dieux, de leurs Princes, & sur-tout pour la magnificence publique. . . .

On distingue cette Architecture de la commune & de l'ordinaire, par ses ordres de Columnes & de Pilastres, par leur accompagnemens, comme les Frontons, les Niches, les Balustrades, les Vases, les Statues, & les autres ornemens. Par ce nobles & riches ordonnances de Portails, de Vestibules, de Peristyles, de Dômes, de Salons, & de Portiques que les Architects ont inventez, pour composer ces grands & pompeux Edifices, que marquent toûjours la gloire de ceux pour qui ils sont élevez. [Pp. 4–5]

Entre les Arts, celui de l'Architecture est un des plus étendus & des plus difficiles; c'est pourquoi un jeune homme qui vent s'y appliquer & s'y rendre habile, ne doit negleger aucune des connoissances qui peuvent lui ouvrir l'esprit, lui donner du genie, de l'exactitude, & du bon goût pour tout ce qui peut avoir quelque rapport aux Bâtiments.

Ces études peuvent neanmoins se réduire au Dessein, à la Geometrie, à l'Arithmetique, aux Mecaniques ou Forces mouvantes, à la Coupe des pierres, à la Perspective, au Nivellement, & aux Hydroliques. [P. 6]

The copy that Jefferson sold to Congress had the work bound in one volume. Kimball (p. 96) says Jefferson had acquired his copy between 1785 and 1789. The library still owns the set acquired on Jefferson's order in the section on "Architecture" of the want list (see Plate LXVIII). It is in two volumes, not one as specified.

U. Va.   M

*NA2515.L46.1714   Sowerby 4180

TRAITÉ
D'ARCHITECTURE
AVEC
DES REMARQUES
ET DES OBSERVATIONS
TRES-UTILES

Pour les Jeunes Gens, qui veulent s'appliquer
à ce bel Art.

Par SÉBAstien LE CLERC; *Chevalier Romain*,
D. & G. O. du C. du Roy.

A PARIS,
Chez PIERRE GIFFART, Libraire & Graveur du Roy,
rue S. Jacques, à l'Image de Sainte Therese.
_____
MDCCXIV.
AVEC APPROBATION ET PRIVILEGE DE SA MAJESTÉ.

Plate LXVIII. *From No. 69.* Title page (Vol. I). Copy received on Jefferson's order.

70. Le Clerc, Sébastien.

Traité de géométrie théorique et pratique, à l'usage des artistes. Paris, 1774.
Not now owned by the University.

For information about Le Clerc, see No. 69. Sowerby says that the 1774 edition is an octavo of 124 leaves with 54 folded engraved plates. The first edition of this work has been variously dated as either 1668 or 1669, but the 1744 edition seems to be the first with engravings.

From an examination of the 1764 edition which is on the University's shelves (*QA464.L46.1764) it would appear, in spite of the charming engravings after drawings by Cochin fils, that the book is essentially a handbook of geometry for artisans, who are, presumably, the "artistes" of the title.

Jefferson's own copy of this work was sold to Congress. Although he had not ordered it for the University, there was a copy of the 1764 edition in its collections before 1828, but it has not survived.

M
Sowerby 3710

71. Legrand, Augustin.

GALERIES / DES ANTIQUES, / OU / *ESQUISSES des Statues, Bustes et Bas-reliefs, / fruit des conquêtes de l'Armée d'Italie.* / PAR AUG. LEGRAND. / A PARIS / CHEZ ANT. AUG. RENOUARD / XI. – 1803.

8vo. Half title (1 leaf); engraved frontispiece (1 leaf); title page ([i]); dedication ([iii]); introduction ([v]-viii); text, with 92 engraved plates inserted ([1]–51).

Augustin Legrand (fl.1803–30) issued his *Galeries des antiques* to celebrate the removal to Paris of many works of art from Italy after Napoleon's conquests there. He says:

La Galerie des Antiques du Musée central des Arts de France, est un des plus superbes trophées élevés à la gloire de l'Armée d'Italie, car fort peu d'objets provenant de l'interieur de la France y ont été ajoutés.

C'est au Capitole et au Vatican que ces chefs-d'oeuvres ont été choisis par les citoyens Barthelemi, peintre, et Moitte, sculpteur, commissaires nommés par le Gouvernement, a la recherche des objets de sciences et arts . . . an exécution du traité de Tolentino. [P. (v)]

Nous offrons donc ce Recueil aux artistes, aux élèves, a tous nos concitoyens sur-tout aux étrangers comme une *réminiscence* utile et agreable. [P. viii]

In Jefferson's third manuscript catalogue of his collection of works of art, the entry concerning a statue in the hall at Monticello says "#17. a Cleopatra in marble. # see this correction pa. 11," and the correction says "see Notice de la Galerie des Antiques du Musee Napoleon. No. 60." Jefferson mistook the number, which is "59. Ariadne," in the *Galeries des antiques*, illustrated on Plate No. 5 (see Plates LXIX and LXX). Legrand says:

Cette figure est plutôt connue sous le nom de *Cléopâtre*.

Couchée sur les rochers de Naxos, ou le perfide Thésée vient de l'abandonner, *Ariadne* est ici représentée endormie, telle qu'elle était au moment où Bacchus l'appercevant, en devint amoureux, et telle que plusieuers monumens antiques de Sculptures et de Poësie nous la retracent. Sa tunique à demi-détachée, son voile négligemment jeté sur sa tête, le désordre de la draperie dont elle est enveloppée, témoignent les angoisses qui ont précédé cet instant de calm. A la partie supérieure du bras gauche, on observe un bracelet qui a la forme d'un petit serpent, et que les Anciens appelaient *ophis*. C'est ce brasselet [*sic*], pris pour un véritable aspic, qui a fait croire long-tems que cette figure représentait *Cléopâtre* se donnant la mort par la piqûre de ce reptile.

Cette statue, en marbre de *Paros*, a fait pendant trois siècles, l'un des principaux ornemens du *Belveder* du Vatican, où Jules II le fit placer; elle y décorait une fontaine, et donnait son nom au grand corridor construit par le Bramante. [P. 4]

Jefferson's own copy was sold to Congress. He ordered the work for the University in the section on "Gardening. Painting. Sculpture. Music" of the want list, and it was in the library by 1828. That set has survived until the present.

U. Va.   M
*N2030.L5.1803   Sowerby 4243

72. Leonardo da Vinci.

A / TREATISE / OF / PAINTING, / BY / *Leonardo da Vinci.* / Translated from / The Original *Italian*, / And adorn'd with a great

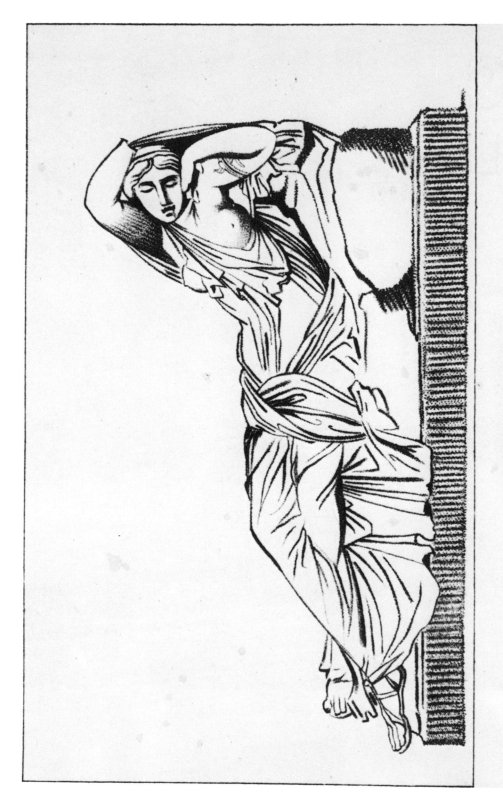

59.

ARIADNE.

Plate LXIX. *From No. 71.* "Ariadne" (Pl. 5, No. 59).

Plate LXX. Copy of *Ariadne* owned by Jefferson. See Plate LXIX.

Number of Cuts. / To which is prefix'd, / The AUTHOR's LIFE; / Done from / The Last Edition of the *French*. / *LONDON;* / Printed for J. SENEX at the *Globe* in *Salisbury* / *Court;* and W. TAYLOR, at the *Ship* in *Pater-/Noster-Row*. MDCCXXI.

8vo. Engraved frontispiece (1 leaf); two-color title page (1 leaf); dedication (2 leaves); translator's preface (5 leaves); life of Leonardo ([1]–27); text, with 34 engraved plates, of which 4 are folding ([29]–189); index (3 leaves); bookseller's advertisement (1 unnumbered p.).

John Senex (d. 1740) was a cartographer, an engraver, and a bookseller in London.

Leonardo da Vinci (1452–1519), Italian man of the Renaissance and painter, has towered above most of the other figures of the Renaissance through the subsequent centuries. His *Treatise of Painting* has had many editions in many languages. It was first issued in 1651. Sowerby notes that this edition in English is the first of this translation, which was made from the 1716 edition of the French translation by Roland Fréart de Chambray (No. 46), first issued during the same year as the first Italian edition.

According to the manuscript catalogues of Jefferson's collection of paintings and sculpture, he owned a painting copied from the *St. John* of Leonardo. The painting hung in the hall at Monticello and is described by Jefferson in his third catalogue as "a bust of the natural size. The right han[d] pointing to heaven, the left, deeply shaded, is scarcely s[een] pressing his breast which is covered by his hair flowi[ng] thickly over it. It is seen almost full face. On canv[as]. Copied from Leonardo da Vinci." In the original the hand is covered as much by St. John's hair shirt as by his own hair.

Jefferson's own copy was sold to Congress. He ordered it for the University in the section on "Gardening. Painting. Sculpture. Music" of the want list, but there is no record of its having been received. The present copy in the library is from the collection of T. W. Tottie.

U. Va.   M
*ND1130.L6.1721   Sowerby 4237

73. Le Roy, Julien David.

LES RUINES / DES PLUS BEAUX / MONUMENTS / DE LA GRECE: / *OUVRAGE DIVISÉ EN DEUX PARTIES*, / OÙ L'ON

CONSIDERE, DANS LA PREMIERE, CES MONUMENTS / DU CÔTÉ DE L'HISTOIRE; ET DANS LA SECONDE, / DU CÔTÉ DE L'ARCHITECTURE. / *Par M. LE ROY, Architecte, ancien Pensionnaire du Roi à Rome, / & de l'Institut de Bologne.* / A PARIS, / Chez / H. L. GUERIN & L. F. DELATOUR, rue Saint Jacques. / JEAN-LUC NYON, Libraire, quai des Augustins. / A AMSTERDAM, / JEAN NEAULME, Libraire. / M. DCC. LVIII. / AVEC APPROBATION ET PRIVILEGE DU ROI.

Folio. Title page ([i]); dedication (iii-iv); preface (v-viii); essay on the history of civil architecture (ix-xiv); text for Part I, with 28 engraved plates inserted (1–56); half title for Part II (1 leaf); [new pagination:] essay on the principles of civil architecture (i-vi); text for Part II, with 38 engraved plates inserted (1–25); table of contents (26–27); notes (28).

The engravers were Le Bas; Littret de Montigny; de Neufforge; and Pierre Patte (1723–1814), an architect and engraver (No. 95). The engravings in Part I are largely pictorial, while in Part II they are architectural.

Julien David Le Roy (1724–1803) was the son of Julien Le Roy, *horologer du roi*, who lived in the Louvre. Julien David won the Rome prize in architecture in 1751 and after three years in Rome spent an additional year in Greece.

His *Ruines* (see Plate LXXI) was his first published work. It had a quick success in spite of some grave errors, which were corrected in the second edition of 1770. Le Roy also published *Histoire de la disposition donnée par les chrétiens à leurs temples*, 1764, with a German translation in 1778, and *Observations sur les édifices des anciens peuples*, 1767.

In order to get to Greece, he communicated "à Rome, le projet & le plan de mon voyage, à M. l'Abbé de Canillac, Auditeur de Rote & Commandeur de l'Ordre du Saint Esprit, & à feu M. de la Bruere, chargé des affaires du Roi en cette Ville" (p. vi). Allowed by them to travel via Venice to Constantinople, he then had to obtain the permission of the Grand Seigneur before going on to Greece.

He tells why he divided the work into two parts:

J'AI CONSIDÉRÉ les Monuments que j'ai recueillis dans la Grece sous deux points de vue différents, qui forment la division naturelle de cet Ouvrage en deux Parties; dans la premiere, j'envisage ces Monuments du côté Historique; dans la second, du côté de l'Architecture; par-la je me procure un double avantage. Les détails d'Architecture étant séparés de la partie Historique, elle en deviendra moins languissante; & ces mêmes détails étant rapprochés les

LES RUINES

DES PLUS BEAUX

MONUMENTS

DE LA GRECE:

OUVRAGE DIVISÉ EN DEUX PARTIES,

Où l'on considere, dans la premiere, ces Monuments du côté de l'Histoire; et dans la seconde, du côté de l'Architecture.

Par M. LE ROY, Architecte, ancien Pensionnaire du Roi à Rome, & de l'Institut de Bologne.

A PARIS,

Chez
H. L. GUERIN & L. F. DELATOUR, rue Saint Jacques.
JEAN-LUC NYON, Libraire, quai des Augustins.
A AMSTERDAM,
JEAN NEAULME, Libraire.

M. DCC. LVIII.

AVEC APPROBATION ET PRIVILEGE DU ROI.

Plate LXXI. *From No. 73.* Title page.

uns des autres dans celle qui concerne particuliérement l'Architecture & comme réunis sous un même point de vue, rendront les comparaisons plus faciles à faire & à saisir. [P. vii]

His book is one of the earliest to deal with Greek architecture (see Plate LXXII), having been published before Stuart and Revett (No. 119) began issuing their volumes in 1762. Sowerby notes, however, that Le Roy was actually in Greece a year later than Stuart and Revett. His book is also earlier than Major's work on the Greek ruins at Paestum (No. 76), which did not appear until 1768.

The edition in Jefferson's own library is not certain, but that copy was sold to Congress. He ordered the book for the University in the section on "Architecture" of the want list without specifying the edition, but the copy in the library by 1828 was the 1758 edition. It has not survived, the copy now on the library's shelves being a recent acquisition, the gift of the Thomas Jefferson Memorial Foundation.

U. Va.   M?
*NA271.L6.1758   Sowerby 4189

74. Lipsius, Justus.

Roma illustrata . . . et Georgii Farbricii chemnicensis veteris Romae . . . Ex nova recensione Antonii Thysii. London, 1692.

Not now owned by the University.

Justus Lipsius (1547–1606) was a Belgian humanist who embraced Protestantism. He published many works of learning and history. The first edition of the *Roma illustrata* was issued at Leyden, 1645. Georg Fabricius (1516–71) was a German poet, historian, and archaeologist. Antoine Thysius (ca.1603–65) was a Dutch historian and librarian of Leyden University.

Sowerby describes this book as a small octavo of 193 leaves with an engraved frontispiece, one folded plate, and engravings in the text. Jefferson sold his copy to Congress. It was not ordered for the University.

M
Sowerby 117

Le Roy Arch.t del in itenere.

Le Bas Sculp.

Vuë du Temple de Minerve à Athene

Plate LXXII. From No. 73. "Vuë du Temple de Minerve à Athene" (Pl. IV).

75. Lubersac de Livron, Charles François de.

DISCOURS / *SUR LES* / MONUMENS PUBLICS / DE TOUS LES ÂGES / ET DE TOUS LES PEUPLES CONNUS, / *SUIVI* / D'une Description de Monument projeté à la gloire / de Louis XVI & de la FRANCE. / *TERMINÉ* / Par quelques Observations sur les principaux Monumens modernes / de la ville de Paris, & plusiers Projets de décoration / & d'utilité publique pour cette Capitale. / DÉDIÉ AU ROI. / *Par M. l'Abbé DE LUBERSAC, Vicaire genérál de Narbonne,* / *Abbé de Noirlac & Prieur de Brive.* / *A PARIS,* / DE L'IMPRIMERIE DE CLOUSIER, Rue Saint-Jacques, vis-à-vis les Mathurins. / M. DCC. LXXV.

Folio. Half title (1 leaf); frontispiece and explanation of frontispiece (2 leaves); title page (1 leaf); dedication (4 leaves); note (i-viii); text ([1]–288); 2 folding, engraved plates; [new pagination:] observations on the monuments of Paris ([i]-lxxix); license (1 unnumbered p.).

The two engravings of the front (see Plate LXXIII) and back view of a monument in the form of an obelisk are very spirited. The monument was designed by Lubersac and drawn by Touze. The plates were engraved by L. T. Masquilier, perhaps Louis-Joseph Masquelier (1741–1811).

Charles François de Lubersac de Livron (1730–84) was an *abbé* as well as an author. His *Discours sur les monumens publics* is primarily a means of flattering his monarch, but its most interesting portion is that containing a description of existing monuments.

Kimball (p. 96) says Jefferson acquired his copy, which was later sold to Congress, during his years in France. Sowerby notes that this edition was its first. Jefferson ordered the work for the University in the section on "Architecture" of the want list, and it had entered the collections before his death, but that copy has not survived. The present duplicate has been recently received, the gift of the Thomas Jefferson Memorial Foundation.

U. Va.   M
*NA9335.L83.1775   Sowerby 4210

Plate LXXIII. *From No. 75.* "Monument à la gloire du Roi et de la France"
(opp. p. 228).

76. Major, Thomas.

THE / RUINS / OF / PAESTUM, / OTHERWISE / POSIDONIA, / IN / MAGNA GRAECIA. / By *THOMAS MAJOR*, Engraver to His Majesty. / *LONDON:* / Published by T. Major, in *St. Martin's Lane*. / Printed by James Dixwell, MDCCLXVIII.

Folio. Title page (1 leaf); dedication (1 leaf); list of subscribers ([i-ii]); note ([iii]-iv); text, with 4 engraved headpieces and 1 engraved tailpiece numbered XXVI, XXVII, XXV (misnumbered for XXVIII), XXIX, and XXIX [*sic*] ([5]-39); explanation of plates (43-45); list of works of Thomas Major (1 unnumbered p.); 25 engraved plates numbered I–XVIII, XIXa, XIXb, and XX–XXIV.

The plates were all engraved by Thomas Major, but they were drawn by Magri and J. G. Soufflot in part.

Among the list of subscribers were one builder, eight doctors, ten ecclesiastics, three engravers, one mason, one painter, one plasterer, one sculptor, and one surveyor. The architects included William Chambers, Francis Hiron of Warwick, Robert Mylne, William Newton, and J. G. Soufflot. William Caslon, the letter founder (No. 20), was also a subscriber.

Thomas Major (1720–99) studied in Paris with Le Bas and Cochin. While he was there he was thrown into prison as a hostage for the French who were taken prisoner at Culloden. He returned to England in 1753 where he produced plates etched, then well finished with the graver. He was the first engraver to become an associate of the Royal Academy. In addition he was engraver to the stamp office for forty years and was appointed engraver to the king.

He says that the work "owes its Birth" to

an *English* Gentleman . . . who procured at *Naples* several fine Drawings of these Temples. The other Views were taken in Presence of his Excellency Sir James Gray, whilst His Majesty's Envoy Extraordinary and Plenipotentiary at the Court of *Naples*. The Plans, Elevations, and Measures, the Public owe to that eminent Artist, Mons. J. G. Soufflot: They were by him accurately taken on the Spot, and he has generously assisted the Engraver in this Undertaking. Thus furnished with Materials . . . the Engraver was induced to believe that this Performance, from the singular Construction of the Edifices, would prove acceptable to the Public. These Temples . . . are noble Monuments of the Magnificence of that ancient City. [Pp. (iii)-iv]

Hc gives the organization of his work: "This work is divided into three Parts. The first contains a summary Account of the Origin of *Paestum*, or *Posidonia*, and likewise of its ancient and modern State: The second, a Description of the Temples, with some occasional Remarks thereon: The third is a Dissertation upon the Coins and Medals of that City" (p. iv). And he speaks of the origin of architecture:

All Historians agree, that Architecture took its Rise in *Greece;* and that the Doric Order here described, on account of the shortness of its Columns, and the simplicity of the Entablature and Capital, comes the nearest to the Origin of Architecture: and what is here advanced appears the more probable, as these Columns have no Bases.

The Doric Order took its Rise from the simple Construction of the *Grecian* Huts, which were supported by the Trunks of Trees; in imitation whereof, the first Idea of Columns was borrowed. . . . This Order being the first and most ancient of all, and retaining more of the Structure of the primitive Huts than any other, it has also undergone the greatest Changes in its Proportions. We shall only consider it here in its first State, as being to our Purpose. The Columns were in general extremely short, they not having any fixed Rules to determine their Proportions. This appears from these Temples at *Paestum*, which are not five Diameters in height. [Pp. 20–21]

He knew both Stuart and Revett (No. 119) and Le Roy (No. 73) before he produced his *Ruins of Paestum* (see Plates LXXIV–LXXVI). This edition is its first. It was translated into French in 1769 and into German in 1781.

Jefferson ordered this work for the University in the section on "Architecture" of the want list, and it was received by 1828, but the copy has not survived. The library's copy was acquired during this century and is from the collection of William Arthur, sixth duke of Portland.

U. Va.
*NA285.P3M2.1768

77. Maps.

Collection of Plans of Towns.

Not now owned by the University.

A large folio with this binder's title was sold by Jefferson to Congress. Sowerby's note on it gives the known details. In 1805 it was bound into an atlas 16 by 25 inches. Before April 10, 1791, the collection contained

Plate LXXIV. *From No. 76.* "A View of the three Temples, taken from the East" (Tab. II).

Plate LXXV. *From No. 76.* "A View of the Hexastyle Ipteral Temple, taken from the South" (Tab. VII).

Plate LXXVI. *From No. 76.* "A View of the Hexastyle Peripteral Temple, taken from the North West" (Tab. XV).

plans of Frankfurt am Main, Karlsruhe, Amsterdam, Strasbourg, Paris, Orléans, Bordeaux, Lyons, Montpelier, Marseilles, Turin, and Milan. Some of Jefferson's later purchases of American maps are also detailed by Sowerby, though the chief group of these may have remained in Jefferson's private library until his death. Compare, for example, lot 347 in the 1829 sale catalogue, *Plans and Forts of America*, 8vo. No such group of plans was ordered for the University.

M
Sowerby 3859

78. Maréchal, Pierre Sylvain.

Vol. I. ANTIQUITÉS / D'HERCULANUM / *GRAVÉES PAR F. A. DAVID* / AVEC / LEURS EXPLICATIONS / Par P. Sylvain M. / TOME I. / *A Paris chez* David, *Graveur, rue* / *des Noyers, en face de celle des Anglois* / *Avec Privilége du Roi.* / 1781 [1780?].

4to. Engraved title page (1 leaf); historical note ([1]–7); text, with 134 engravings on 65 plates inserted (8–165); table of sizes (166–68).

Vol. II. ANTIQUITÉS / D'HERCULANUM / . . . / TOME II. / . . . / 1781.

4to. Engraved title page (1 leaf); text, with 141 engravings on 72 plates inserted ([1]–212); table of sizes (213–15).

Vol. III. ANTIQUITÉS / D'HERCULANUM / . . . / TOME III. / . . .

4to. Engraved title page (1 leaf); text, with 130 engravings on 72 plates inserted ([1]–200); table of sizes (201–3).

Vol. IV. ANTIQUITÉS / D'HERCULANUM / . . . / Par P. Sylvain Maréchal / TOME IIII / . . .

4to. Engraved title page (1 leaf); text, with 130 engravings on 72 plates inserted ([1]–116); table of sizes (117–19).

Vol. V. ANTIQUITÉS / D'HERCULANUM / . . . / TOME V. / . . .

4to. Engraved title page (1 leaf); text, with 181 engravings on 108 plates inserted ([1]–95); table of sizes (97–99).

Vol. VI.   ANTIQUITÉS / D'HERCULANUM / . . . / TOME VI. / . . . / TOM I. BRONZES.

4to. Engraved title page (1 leaf); text, with 144 engravings on 72 plates inserted ([1]–96); table of sizes (97–98).

Vol. VII.   ANTIQUITÉS / D'HERCULANUM / . . . / TOME VII. / . . . / TOM II BRONZES.

4to. Engraved title page (1 leaf); text, with 163 engravings on 108 plates inserted ([1]–101); table of sizes (102–3).

Vol. VIII.   ANTIQUITÉS / D'HERCULANUM / . . . [Maréchal's name deleted] / TOME VIII / . . .

[Printed title page:] ANTIQUITÉS / D'HERCULANUM / OU / Les *plus belles Peintures Antiques, Marbres,* / *Bronzes, Meubles, trouvés dans les Excavations* / *d'Herculanum, Stabia & Pompeïa;* / GRAVÉES PAR M. DAVID, / Graveur du Roi de Prusse, de MONSIEUR, de l'Académie / Royale de Peinture de Berlin, de celle des Sciences & / Belles-Lettres de Rouen. / *Avec leurs Explications Françoises.* / TOME VIII. / *A PARIS,* / Chez l'Auteur, M. DAVID, rue des Cordeliers, / au coin de celle de l'Observance. / M. DCC. LXXXIX. / *AVEC PRIVILÉGE DU ROI.*

4to. Engraved title page (1 leaf); printed title page (1 leaf); text, with 72 engravings on 66 plates inserted ([1]–52).

Vol. IX.   ANTIQUITÉS / D'HERCULANUM / . . . / Par P. Sylvain M. / TOME IX. / A PARIS / *Chez F. A.* David, *rue Pierre-/Sarrazin No. 13.* [1781 deleted.]

[Printed title page:] ANTIQUITÉS / D'HERCULANUM, / *Ou les plus belles Peintures antiques, et les* / *Marbres, Bronzes, Meubles, etc. etc.* / *trouvés dans les excavations d'*Herculanum, / Stabia *et* Pompeia, / GRAVÉES PAR F. A. DAVID, / AVEC LEURS EXPLICATIONS, / PAR P. S. MARÉCHAL. / TOME NEUVIÈME. / A PARIS, / Chez l'AUTEUR, F. A. DAVID, / rue Pierre-Sarrazin, no. 13. / M. DCC. LXXX [?].

4to. Engraved title page (1 leaf); printed title page (1 leaf); text, with 129 engravings on 58 plates inserted ([1]–108).

Vol. X.   ANTIQUITÉS / D'HERCULANUM / . . . / TOME X. / . . . / *Chez F. A.* David, *rue Pierre-/Sarrazin, No. 14* / [1781 deleted].

[Printed title page:] ANTIQUITÉS / . . . / TOME DIXIÈME. / . . . / rue Pierre-Sarrazin, no. 14. / M. DCC. XCVII.

4to. Engraved title page (1 leaf); printed title page (1 leaf); text, with 59 engravings on 59 plates inserted ([1]–86).

Vol. XI.   ANTIQUITÉS / D'HERCULANUM / . . . / TOME XI. / . . .

[Printed title page:] ANTIQUITÉS / . . . / TOME ONZIÈME. / . . . / AN VI.

4to. Half title (1 leaf); engraved title page (1 leaf); printed title page (1 leaf); text, with 28 engraved plates inserted and 29 engraved plates following ([1]–44); index (45–58).

Vol. XII.   ANTIQUITÉS / *PEINTURES ANTIQUES / D'HERCU-* LANUM / et celles du Tombeau / des Nasons / AVEC / LEURS EXPLICATIONS / TOM. XII. / A PARIS / *Chez* David, *Rue de Vaugirard, No. 1202.* / AN XI. (1803)

[Printed title page:] ANTIQUITÉS / OU / LES PLUS BELLES / PEINTURES ANTIQUES / D'HERCULANUM / Envoyées par S. M. le Roi de Naples et / des Deux-Siciles au Gouvernement Français en l'an XI (1803), / et celles / DU TOMBEAU DES NASONS; / Gravées par F. A. DAVID, / *AVEC des explications et des recherches relatives à* / *l'Histoire, à la Mythologie, aux Usages anciens* / *et à l'Art.* / TOME DOUZIÈME. / A PARIS, / Chez DAVID, rue de Vaugirad, no. 1202. / An XI. (1803.)

4to. Half title (1 leaf); engraved title page (1 leaf); printed title page (1 leaf); text, with 34 engraved plates inserted ([1]–46); index (47–48).

The engraver was François-Anne David (1741–1824), a Parisian who studied with Le Bas and became engraver to the king of Prussia. David was a member of the Royal Academy of Painting of Berlin, as well as that of Sciences and Letters at Rouen.

Pierre Sylvain Maréchal (1750–1803) seems to have been known as a pornographic writer, a result, perhaps, of his association with Herculaneum.

The first five volumes of this work are devoted to painting, Vols. VI and VII are concerned with bronzes, Vol. VIII with objects and furniture, Vols. IX–XI with lamps (see Plate LXXVII), and the twelfth volume with paintings.

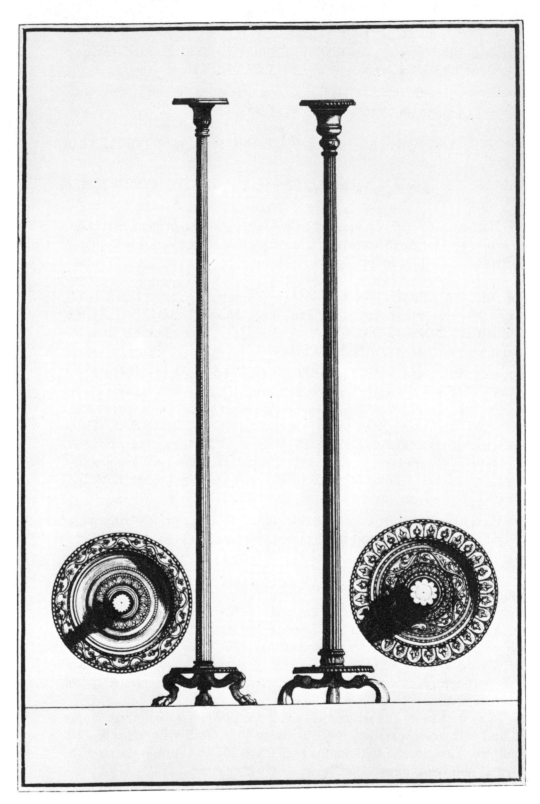

Plate LXXVII. *From No. 78.* Two lamps (Vol. XI, Pl. 45).

This edition of the *Antiquités d'Herculanum* was entered by Brunet under the name of its engraver, François-Anne David, and though it was issued in both quarto and in octavo, there still remains some doubt as to whether the quarto set was the one Jefferson had in mind when he ordered, in the section on "Architecture" of the want list, a seven-volume set for the University. One thing, however, is certain: this edition is what Jefferson got from his order, because the 1828 *Catalogue* acknowledges the presence of the twelve-volume set. Of this, only the first nine volumes have survived.

The library has recently acquired a second set of twelve volumes. The information on the title pages and contents has been taken from this second set. The indifference to exact binding orders in the eighteenth and early nineteenth centuries is well illustrated by these two sets. The first set is bound in the following order: engraved title, title page, text, and engravings. The engraved titles and the title pages for this first set are late and were evidently bound in the earlier volumes after publication of Vol. VIII. On the other hand, the second set lacks printed title pages for the first seven volumes, some of which must certainly have been published in the years between 1780(?) and 1789. This second set is the gift of the Thomas Jefferson Memorial Foundation.

U. Va.
*DG70.H5M2.1780

79. Mascheroni, Lorenzo.

Nuove ricerche sull'equilibrio della volte. Bergamo, 1785.

Not now owned by the University.

Lorenzo Mascheroni (1750–1800) was a mathematician and professor of philosophy who worked at Bergamo, Milan, and Paris.

Kimball (p. 96) says Jefferson acquired this book between 1785 and 1789. Sowerby quotes a letter from Jefferson in which he says the book "appears to be a very scientifical work." This edition is the first.

Jefferson's copy was sold to Congress. It was not ordered for the University. The library has several of Mascheroni's books on geometry but has not yet acquired this work.

M
Sowerby 4203

80. Maucomble, Jean Francois Dieudonné de.

HISTOIRE / *ABRÉGÉE* / DE LA VILLE / DE NÎMES, / *AVEC* / LA DESCRIPTION / DE SES ANTIQUITÉS. / *PREMIERE PARTIE.* / . . . . . . *Quod adest, memento* / *Componere aequus* . . . . . Hor. Od. 23. Lib. 3. / À AMSTERDAM. / M. DCC. LXVII.

and

HISTOIRE / . . . / *SECONDE PARTIE,* / *CONTENANT* / LA DESCRIPTION DE SES ANTIQUITÉS. / *Considére le terrible pouvoir des années! Rome semble ensévélie / sous ses propres débris, & n'offre aux yeux que des voutes / ébranlées & des temples ruinés.* Pope, épit. a M. Addison. / . . .

8vo. Half title, Part I (1 leaf); title page (1 leaf); text ([1]–158); table of contents (2 leaves); half title, Part II (1 leaf); title page (1 leaf); preface (1 leaf); [new pagination:] text ([1]–28); 9 engravings, all folding.

One engraving is signed by C. L. Verdier as both delineator and engraver. All the engravings are rather poor.

Jean François Dieudonné de Maucomble (1735–68) started a projected series of city histories which was abandoned when this one (see Plate LXXVIII) was given a bad critical reception. Nevertheless this had a second edition in 1806.

He gives the origins of the name of Nîmes in this passage: "NIMES, destiné à jouir de tous les honneurs des Villes célèbres, a, ainsi qu'elles, son origine fabuleuse. Plusieurs Ecrivains, d'après Parthenius & Etienne de Bisance, lui ont donné pour Fondateur *Nemausus*, un des Héraclides; mais d'autres, avec plus de raison, ne l'etablissant qu'après la ville de Marseille, prennent l'etymologie de ce nom *Nemausus*, dans le mot celtique *Nemos*, qui signifie *lieu consacré à la Religion*" (p. (1)).

Sowerby points out that Jefferson called the "Maison Quarrée," described on pages 11–13 of this book and illustrated in Figs. 13 and 14, "one of the most beautiful & precious morsels of architecture left us by antiquity" in a letter to James Madison, September 20, 1785; that he called it "the most perfect remains of antiquity which exist on earth" in a letter to Thomas Shippen, September 29, 1788; that he visited it in 1787; but that in his memorandum of his visit to Nîmes he inexplicably

HISTOIRE

ABRÉGÉE

DE LA VILLE
DE NÎMES,

AVEC

LA DESCRIPTION

DE SES ANTIQUITÉS.

PREMIERE PARTIE.

...... *Quod adeſt*, *memento*
Componere æquus...... Hor. Od. 23. Lib. 3.

À AMSTERDAM.

M. DCC. LXVII.

Plate LXXVIII. *From No. 80.* Title page.

made no mention of the temple. And, of course, he used the temple as precedent for the Capitol in Richmond (see No. 29).

Jefferson sold his own copy of this book to Congress. He did not order it for the University. The library's present copy has been recently acquired, the gift of the Thomas Jefferson Memorial Foundation.

M

*DC801.N71M3.1767   Sowerby 3886

81. Meinert, Friedrich.

Die Schöne Landbaukunst oder Neue Ideen und Vorschriften. Leipzig, 1798.

Not now owned by the University.

Although there was earlier uncertainty over the identification of this work, the above information seems correct from a comparison of the plates mentioned by Jefferson. On the drawing of garden temples reproduced in Kimball as No. 161, there is a note in Jefferson's hand: "No. 1 maybe a Gothic for design see Meinert No. 8.37.38.45." Meinert is also mentioned by Jefferson on two of his other drawings reproduced as Nos. 164 and 165 in Kimball. This rather fugitive book contains suggestions for a series of very simple, neoclassic and neoGothic buildings, primarily for rural areas.

Sowerby, who had no copy for inspection, points out that Jefferson paid $16.80 for his copy, purchased in 1805 at the same time as Nos. 11 and 117. He spent a further $2.50 to have it bound.

Jefferson sold his copy of the book to Congress. He ordered it for the University in the section on "Architecture" of the want list, but there is no record of the library's ever having received a copy.

U.Va.   M

Sowerby 4224

82. Migneron de Brocqueville.

Description du pont de Brienne, construit à Bordeaux. Bordeaux, 1788?.

Not now owned by the University.

Sowerby describes this book as a quarto pamphlet of eleven leaves with a folding engraving of the bridge at the end. Jefferson sold it to Congress, but did not order it for the University.

M
Sowerby 4200

83. Milizia, Francesco.

Vol. I.   PRINCIPJ / DI / ARCHITETTURA CIVILE / DI / FRAN-CESCO MILIZIA / *TERZA EDIZIONE VENETA* / Riveduta, emen-data, ed accresciuta de Figure disegnate / ed incise in Roma / DA / GIO. BATTISTA CIPRIANI SANESE. / *TOMO PRIMO.* / *BAS-SANO* / DALLA TIPOGRAPHIA GIUSEPPE REMONDINI E FI-GLI / 1813.

8vo. Title page ([1]); note to reader (3–4); life of Milizia (5–9); note (10); text (11–277); table of contents (278–80); 10 engraved plates, all folding.

Vol. II.   PRINCIPJ / . . . / *TOMO SECONDO.* / . . .

8vo. Title page ([1]); text ([3]–304); table of contents (305–8); 12 en-graved plates, all folding.

Vol. III.   PRINCIPJ / . . . / *TOMO TERZO* / . . .

8vo. Title page ([1]); text, with folding table at p. 169 and 8 folding plates at p. 161 ([3]–259); table of contents (260–63); 5 engraved plates, all folding.

For Cipriani, see No. 93. Francesco Milizia (1725–98) was a critic and a theoretician of neoclassicism. After settling in Rome in 1761, he be-came a member of the circle of friends which revolved around Anton Raphael Mengs and Johann Joachim Winckelmann. He published no less than twelve books and two translations, many of them appearing in several editions, while his *Vita di' piu celebri architetti*, in turn, was translated into both French and English. The first edition of the *Principi di architettura civile* was in 1781. He says:

L'ARCHITETTURA è l'Arte di fabbricare: e prende denominazioni differenti secondo le diversità de'suoi oggetti. Si chiama ARCHITETTURA CIVILE, si il suo ogetto si raggira intorno alla costruzione delle fabbriche destinate al comodo, ed ai varj usi degli uomini raccolti in Civil Societa. [I, 11]

Qualunque fabbrica per potersi dire COMPITÀ, deve sempre avere i tre requisiti seguenti. 1. BELLEZZA, 2. COMODITÀ, 3. SOLIDITÀ. . . . Nella prima parte si tratterà della BELLEZZA, nella seconda della COMODITÀ, e nella terza della SOLIDITÀ dell'Architettura. [I, 15]

La Belezza dell'Architettura dipende da quattro principj, che sono 1. ORNATO, 2. SIMMETRIA, 3. EURITIMIA, 4. CONVENIENZA. . . .

Per *Ornato* s'intende tutto quel pulimento, che s'impiega, o se soprappone al vivo d'una fabbrica.

I principali Ornati sono gli *Ordini*, le *Sculture*, le *Pitture*, i *Marmi*, gli *Stucchi* ec. [I, 17]

La Simmetria e una proporzionata quantità di misura, che le parti debbono avere fra loro, e col tutto. [I, 160]

La parola euritmia è quasi fuori d'uso, e il suo significato si è impropriamente unito alla voce simmetria, la quale già si è veduto, che cosa è.

L'euritmia consiste nella uniforme corrispondenza delle parti simili, le quali debbono essere tali, e tante da un lato, come dall'altro, e similmente disposte, acciocchè il tutto faccia un grato aspetto. [I, 189]

La *Convenienza*, che da taluni viene anche chiamata decoro, costume, o proprietà, deve guidicarsi come il primo principio dell'Arte de fabbricare.

La convenienza prescrive a ciascun genere di edificio il suo carattere distinto, e retalivo all sua grandezza, disposizione, ricchezza, o semplicità. [I, 198]

La Comodità di qualunque edificio comprende tre oggetti principali che sono. 1. La sua situazione. 2. La sua forma. 3. La distribuzione delle sue parti. [II, 3]

Questa sei condizioni sono necessarie per una buona situazione; 1. bontà di terreno, 2. l'aria, 3. l'acqua, 4. esposizione sana, 5. comodità di luogo, 6. amenità di veduta. [II, 5]

. . . Sempre colla mira a questo triplice vantaggio va considerata la varia eleganza delle forme, le quali non possono essere che di tre genere, curve, rette, e miste. [II, 15]

. . . Onde nell'Architettura la distribuzione è di due sorti; l'una ha per oggetto il terreno, o la pianta di un edificio qualunque ripartito nei suoi pezzi interni; l'altra riguarda il ripartimento esterno dell'elevazione di qualunque edificio, o sia della decorazione delle facciate. [II, 21]

He introduces the third volume, largely concerned with the nature and strengths of materials, by saying: "Il più essenzial requisito degli edificj è la *Solidità*, senza di cui la bellezza, la comodità, la magnificenza divengono un nulla" (III, 3).

Although this work came into Jefferson's hands late in his life, in 1824, he decided to have it used for "a course of lectures" on architecture at the University when that institution was opened, as he states in his letter of October 24, 1824, to Joseph Coolidge (U. Va. Library): "I ought sooner to have thanked you for the valuable work of Milizia, on Architecture. Searching as he does, for the sources and prototypes of our ideas of beauty in that fine art, he appears to have elicited them with more correctness than any author I have read, and his work, as a text book, furnishes excellent matter for a course of lectures on the subject, which I shall hope to have introduced into our institution." In addition, on a drawing for a proposed observatory for the University, which may be dated after October 24, 1824, he wrote "See Observatory of Paris. 2. Milizia. pa. 187. pl IX. c." (see Plates LXXIX and LXXX). A comparison of Jefferson's drawing with Vol. II, Plate IX, Figs. C and D in Milizia shows striking similarities, especially in the use of octagonal towers. Milizia labels Fig. C as "Pianta terrena dell' Osservatorio di Parigi" and Fig. D as "Metà della pianta del secondo piano."

Milizia has this to say about the observatory:

L'osservatorio è ordinariamente un edificio quadrato, situato, ed elevato bene in alto con un terrazzo in cima per le osservazioni astronomiche. Sovente su questo terrazzo si construisce un padiglione per contenere gli strumenti al coperto. Quando questo edificio è internamente isolato da qualunque altro, deve avere gran basamento, contenere più stanze per professore, per i custodi, per le macchine, e molti terrazzi, rastremandosi a misura, che s'inalza. La sua decorazione esteriore sia semplice, ma d'un genere egregio, e d'un carattere deciso ricavato dal destino della fabbrica. Vale più l'osservatorio di Parigi, che tutte le piramidi, e i tempi dell'Antichità. [II, 187]

There was a set of this edition in Jefferson's private library at the time of his death. It was sold as lot 720 in the 1829 sale. The order from Jefferson for the University in the section on "Architecture" of the want list was presumably for this edition, the latest he could have known of, since he is not likely to have heard of the 1825 reprint (edition?) and would probably have preferred the 1813 edition to any of the earlier ones. There is no record of the library's ever having received the set. The library's present set is a recent acquisition, the gift of the Thomas Jefferson Memorial Foundation.

U.Va.   M
*NA1111.M55.1813

84. Mitchell, Robert.

PLANS, AND VIEWS IN PERSPECTIVE, / WITH / DESCRIP-TIONS, / OF / BUILDINGS / *ERECTED IN ENGLAND AND*

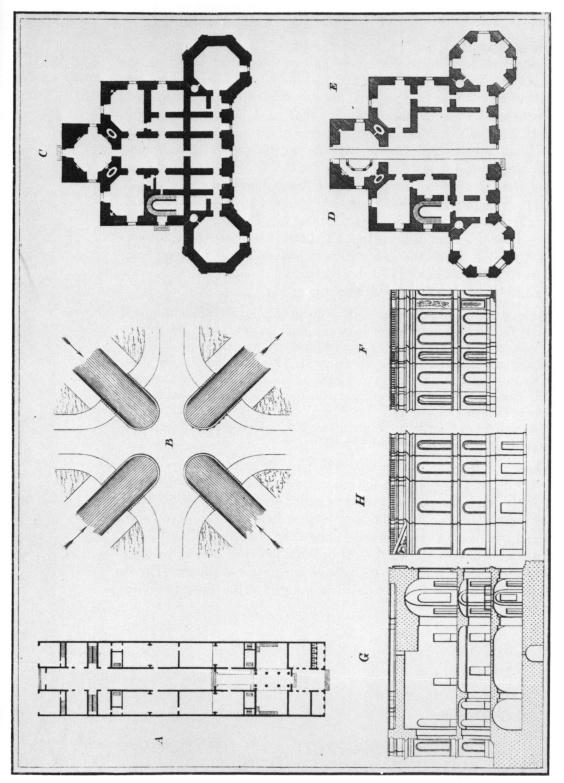

Plate LXXIX. *From No 83*. Observatory at Paris (Vol. II, Pl. IX).

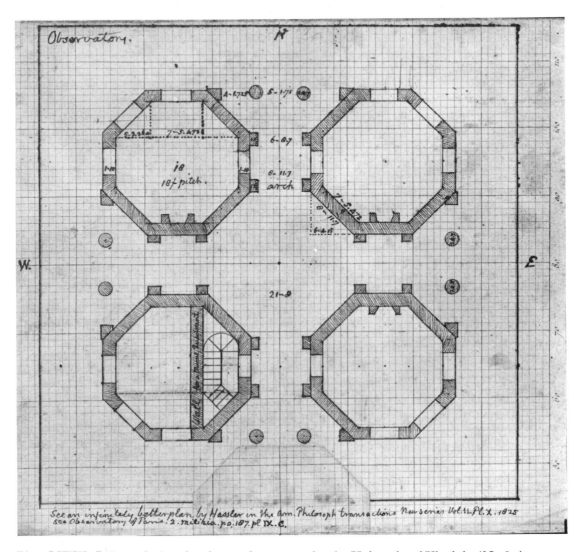

Plate LXXX. Jefferson's drawing for an observatory for the University of Virginia (N-381).

SCOTLAND: / AND ALSO / AN ESSAY, / TO ELUCIDATE / THE GRECIAN, ROMAN AND GOTHIC ARCHITECTURE, / ACCOMPANIED WITH DESIGNS. / By ROBERT MITCHELL, Architect. / PLANS, DESCRIPTIONS, ET VUES EN PERSPEC-TIVE, / DES / EDIFICES / *ERIGÉS EN ANGLETERRE ET EN ECOSSE:* / SUIVI / D'UN ESSAI / SUR / L'ARCHITECTURE GREQUE, ROMAINE ET GOTHIQUE, / AVEC / DES DESSEINS ILLUSTRATIFS, / Par ROBERT MITCHELL, Architecte. / London: / *Printed, at the* Oriental Press, *by* Wilson & Co. *for the Author:* / AND SOLD BY J. TAYLOR, ARCHITECTURAL LI-BRARY, HIGH HOLBORN; R. FAULDER, NEW BOND-STREET; / J. AND T. CARPENTER, OLD BOND-STREET; T. EVANS, PALL-MALL: AND J. WHITE, FLEET-STREET. / 1801.

Folio. Frontispiece, a colored aquatint (1 leaf); title page (1 leaf); introduction (1 leaf); description of plates ([1]–8); essay ([9]–15); description of plates in French ([17]–24); essay in French ([25]–32); 16 aquatint plates, of which 11 are colored (of a total of 18, numbering the frontispiece; Plate 14, "A Section of the Rotunda in Leicester Square," is missing).

Robert Mitchell (fl.1800) was an architect who lived in London. He exhibited in the Royal Academy for the years 1782, 1796, 1797, and 1798. He designed the Rotunda in Leicester Square for Robert Barker and his panoramas.

He was one of the early proponents of the Gothic Revival, and he explains why he wrote the book, as well as the beauties of Gothic architecture, by saying:

The Plates in this Work are a representation of a portion of the Buildings which he [the author] has been employed in constructing, the four last Plates excepted, which are Designs intended to elucidate an Essay on Architecture. This Dissertation upon the Three Styles of Architecture he is desirous may be read with attention, and particularly what relates to the Gothic Architecture. . . . If what has been advanced can contribute to remove those prejudices which have long prevailed against a style of Architecture that is the source of much pleasure to many, his intentions will be fully answered, and his wishes completely gratified. [Introduction]
Architecture, as an art connected with science, had not existence till the invention of the column, and its application in the construction of buildings.

It must be confessed that this is the prominent feature which possesses such real beauty and elegance as cannot admit of any substitute.

Whoever will investigate the subject will, it is apprehended, find, that there never has existed, in any age or nation, but three styles of Architecture, the Grecian, the Roman, and the Gothic; as all other forms which have been introduced, shew Architecture, either in the progress which it afterwards attained, or on its decline. [P. 9]

The Gothic is a style of Architecture truly original. Whoever will attentively examine it, as found in buildings in its purest style, will certainly find that it has not anything in common with either the Grecian or Roman Architecture, in whatever constitutes their principles, or wherein they are distinguished by their forms. [P. 11]

In viewing a Gothic building, all the parts are found united, whilst, in the Grecian or Roman Architecture, they are cut asunder by the horizontal lines. The striking effects of a Gothic building are produced by taking in the whole, in all its relations; but, in the Greek and Roman, chiefly by examining the elegance and fine proportions of their parts. [P. 11]

. . . When we reflect that a style of Architecture, as is the case in the Gothic, has since been invented, and established in practice, in which correct forms, or strict proportions, have been disregarded; and, notwithstanding which, effects are produced in this style of Architecture, which, in certain cases, make stronger impressions upon the mind than can be effected by the Greek or Roman—it will then be confessed, that, in the whole circle of human knowledge, there is no example of so astonishing a revolution taking place in any art or science. . . .

The Greek and Roman Architecture will ever charm, from their beautiful forms, all persons of real taste; but compositions in these styles, from being the result of positive rules, are easily comprehended, and soon lose the attraction of novelty. Whilst the Gothic edifices are found to possess infinite variety, their compositions require more ingenuity and science to produce them, and are more difficult to be comprehended: from these circumstances it is that we never return to examine a Gothic structure without finding new subjects for contemplation. [Pp. 13–14]

To demonstrate his thesis Mitchell shows a residential plan and perspectives of Greek, Roman, and Gothic exteriors for it. The other buildings of his own design, however, are very Regency in feeling (see Plate LXXXI), including his plates for the Leicester Square Rotunda.

Although Kimball (p. 96) says Jefferson received his copy of this book sometime between 1801 and 1805, Sowerby points out that the evidence for the latter date as quoted by Kimball is nonexistent. The earlier date, of course, stands since it was the date of publication. Jefferson's own copy was sold to Congress.

He ordered this book for the University in the section on "Architecture" of the want list, but there is no evidence of its having entered the library. The library's present copy, a presentation copy from the author to the Right Honorable Lord Witeworth, has been recently acquired, the gift of the Thomas Jefferson Memorial Foundation.

U. Va.   M
*NA2620.M5.1801   Sowerby 4208

Plate LXXXI. *From No. 84.* "Staircase and Music Gallery in the House of Selwood Park" (Pl. 4).

85. Mitford, William.

PRINCIPLES OF DESIGN / IN / ARCHITECTURE / *TRACED IN OBSERVATIONS ON BUILDINGS* / PRIMEVAL, EGYPTIAN, PHENICIAN OR SYRIAN, / GRECIAN, ROMAN, GOTHIC OR CORRUPT ROMAN, / ARABIAN OR SARACENIC, OLD ENG-LISH EC-/CLESIASTICAL, OLD ENGLISH MILITARY AND / DOMESTIC, REVIVED ROMAN, REVIVED GRECIAN, /CHI-NESE, INDIAN, MODERN ANGLO-GOTHIC, AND / MODERN ENGLISH DOMESTIC: / *IN A SERIES OF LETTERS TO A FRIEND.* / London: / Printed by Luke Hansard & Sons, near Lincolns-Inn Fields; / FOR T. CADELL & W. DAVIES IN THE STRAND. / 1809.

8vo. Title page ([i]); table of contents ([iii]-vi); errata (1 leaf); text ([1]–293).

William Mitford (1744–1827) was educated at Cheam School, Surrey, Queen's College, Oxford, and Middle Temple. He never practiced law, however, and was principally a historian.

He wrote *An Essay on the Harmony of Language*, 1774 and 1804; *A History of Greece*, which went into many editions beginning in 1784; *Considerations . . . on the Corn Laws*, 1791; and *Observations on the History . . . of Christianity*, 1823.

This book was first issued in 1809 and again in 1824. It is written in the form of letters which are conversational in tone. Mitford is very clear in his definition of terms, so that the reader is able to follow his arguments without difficulty. These definitions seem to be the most interesting part of the book:

Architecture, in all its branches, originating from the wants of mankind, the first Principle of DESIGN in building must be UTILITY. [P. 4]

But this first essential and characteristical purpose, [of utility] . . . being attained, the mind of man would soon begin to look farther. [P. 8]

Hence would arise a second Principle of Design in architecture: it would be desired, with the useful to connect the graceful, the splendid, the awful, and to avoid the offensive and the mean. [P. 9]

Of the picturesk and beautiful, Gratification of the Mind through the Eye is the ultimate object. But, of architecture, Use is the first object; gratification of the mind through the eye but secondary. [P. 12]

. . . But those forms which among infinitely varying tastes, the general sense of mankind reckons beautiful, have all, I am inclined to believe, a natural and necessary and intimate connection with the useful. I say those forms which the general sense of mankind has agreed to call beautiful: because, after the various attempts of very ingenious, very learned, and very able men to analyze and define beauty, there is yet no complete agreement. [Pp. 12–13]

Architecture is essentially among the useful arts. Through its power to impress ideas of the sublime and beautiful, it becomes associated among the ornamental arts, or those commonly called the fine arts. Hence arise two distinct characters of Design in architecture, the useful and the ornamental. The term Design certainly may be properly applicable to both. But, in the practice of language it is more commonly limited to Architecture considered as one of the fine arts, the sister of Painting, than extended to it as simply a useful art. [Pp. 13–14]

In a chapter called "Sense and Nonsense in Architecture," he says: "Nonsense in architecture is principally observable in the misapplication of forms, invented for use, where they are strickingly useless intruders; or sometimes, where they are even inconvenient, and obviously adverse to use" (p. 256).

Kimball (p. 97) says Jefferson's copy of Mitford came into his hands after 1819, misdating the publication year as 1819 instead of 1809. Since this was in Jefferson's library at the time of his death and is not noted in Sowerby, it probably entered his collection after the sale of his large library to Congress in 1815. The book, which was not ordered for the University, was sold after Jefferson's death as lot 730 in the 1829 sale. The University's present copy is a recent acquisition, the gift of the Thomas Jefferson Memorial Foundation.

M

*NA2750.M6.1809

86. Montfaucon, Bernard de.

Vol. I. ANTIQUITY / EXPLAINED, / And REPRESENTED in / SCULPTURES, / BY THE / Learned Father *MONTFAUCON,*/ Translated into *English* by / *DAVID HUMPHREYS*, M. A. / And Fellow of *Trinity-College* in *Cambridge*. / VOLUME *the* FIRST. / *LONDON:* / Printed by J. TONSON and J. WATTS. / MDCCXXI.

Folio. Two-color title page (1 leaf); dedication (1 leaf); preface (5 leaves); table of contents (21 unnumbered pp.); introduction (7 unnumbered pp.); text, with 98 engravings, of which 20 are double, inserted ([1]–260).

Vol. II.   ANTIQUITY / . . . / VOLUME *the* SECOND. / . . .

Folio. Two-color title page ([1]); text, with 61 engravings, of which 1 is folding and 16 double, inserted ([3]–284).

Vol. III.   ANTIQUITY / . . . / VOLUME   *the*   THIRD. / . . . / MDCCXXII.

Folio. Two-color title page ([1]); text, with 63 engravings, of which 12 are double, inserted ([3])–227).

Vol. IV.   ANTIQUITY / . . . / VOLUME *the* FOURTH. / . . .

Folio. Two-color title page ([1]); text, with 46 engravings, of which 28 are double, inserted ([3]–193).

Vol. V.   ANTIQUITY / . . . / VOLUME *the* FIFTH. / . . .

Folio. Two-color title page ([1]); text, with 51 engravings, of which 19 are double, inserted ([3]–165).

Vol. VI.   THE / SUPPLEMENT / TO / ANTIQUITY / EX-PLAINED, / And REPRESENTED in / SCULPTURES / By THE / Learned Father *MONTFAUCON.* / Translated into *English* by *DAVID HUMPHREYS*, M. A. / And Fellow of *Trinity College* in *Cambridge.* / In FIVE VOLUMES. / VOLUME *the* FIRST. / *LONDON:* / Printed by J. TONSON and J. WATTS. / MDCCXXV.

and

THE / SUPPLEMENT / TO / ANTIQUITY / EXPLAINED, / And REPRESENTED in / SCULPTURES. VOLUME the SECOND.

Folio. Two-color title page (1 leaf); preface (3 leaves); table of contents (6 leaves); text, with 31 engravings, of which 6 are double, inserted ([1]–132); title page ([133]); text, with 23 engravings (numbered 32–54), of which 1 is folding and 2 are double, inserted ([135]–256).

Vol. VII.   THE / SUPPLEMENT / . . . / VOLUME   the   THIRD.
and

THE / SUPPLEMENT / . . . / VOLUME the FOURTH.
and

THE / SUPPLEMENT / . . . / VOLUME the FIFTH.

Folio. Title page ([257]); text, with 26 engravings (numbered 55–80), of which 6 are double, inserted ([259]–386); title page ([387]); text, with 23 engravings (numbered 81–103), of which 8 are double, inserted ([389]–482); title page ([483]); text, with 25 engravings (numbered 104–128), of which 1 is double, inserted ([485]–571).

Bernard de Montfaucon (1655–1741) began life as a soldier, but after an early military career he entered the Benedictine order in 1675. In 1687 he was called to Paris where the order had a collection of medals, and in 1698 he was sent to Italy. He was a member of the Académie des Inscriptions, 1719, and wrote altogether some thirteen books. The present work was issued in French between 1719 and 1724.

Montfaucon himself tells the origin of his work and something of its organization:

About four and thirty Years ago, my Superiors appointed me to put out an Edition of the *Greek* fathers: I presently applied my self to those Studies which would enable me to do it with Success. I perceived immediately that profane Learning was absolutely requisite, in order to a full Understanding of the Fathers of the Church. . . . I therefore applied my self to a serious Study of Antiquity . . . and . . . began to make a Collection of Drawings and antique Pieces about six and twenty Years ago. [I, i]

I have reduced into one Body all Antiquity. By the Word *Antiquity* I mean only what may be the Object of the Sight, and may be represented by Figures; and this alone is of a vast Extent. [I, iii]

. . . The first Volume . . . which treats of the Gods of the *Greeks* and *Romans*, and contains almost all their Mythology. . . .

The Second Volume contains the religious Worship of the *Greeks* and *Romans* and the Gods and Religion of the Barbarious Nations. . . .

The Third Volume was thought a fit place to speak of the Ancients Hunting, and Fishing before the Instruments of the Arts. [I, iv]

The second volume has two plates of the Pantheon (see Plate LXXXII) and no less than eight concerning the Maison Carrée, while Plates 14, 15, and 16 are also especially architectural. Volume III shows some public buildings (see Plate LXXXIII); Vol. IV, which deals with military matters and roads, contains a good many illustrations of military architecture; Vol. V, which deals with funerals and lamps, also has a number of architectural illustrations. The supplemental volumes contain only a few architectural illustrations, but, of course, the entire work is full of illustrations taken from coins and statues.

Jefferson, perhaps ignorant of the last volume, ordered a nine-volume edition for the University in the section on "History-Civil-Antient" of the want list, but there is no record that any of the volumes were received during his lifetime. The library's present set has been

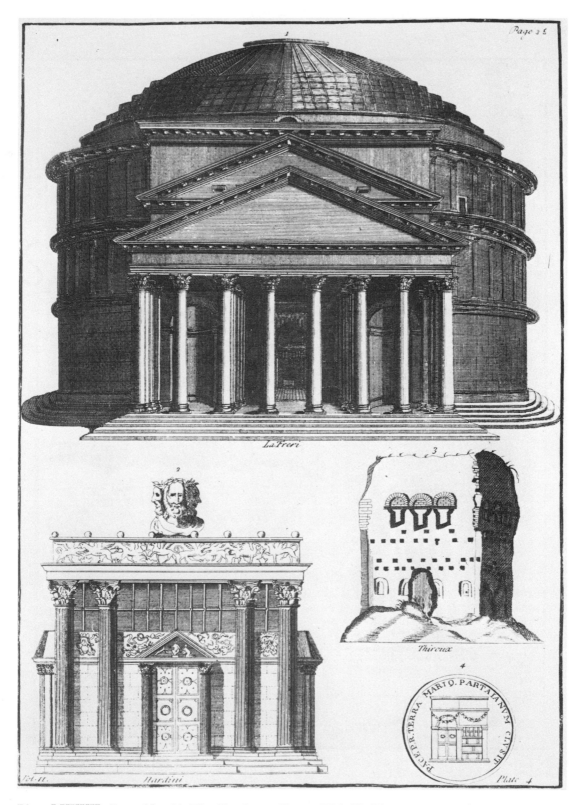

Plate LXXXII. *From No. 86.* The Pantheon, Rome (Vol. II, Pl. 4, opp. p. 35).

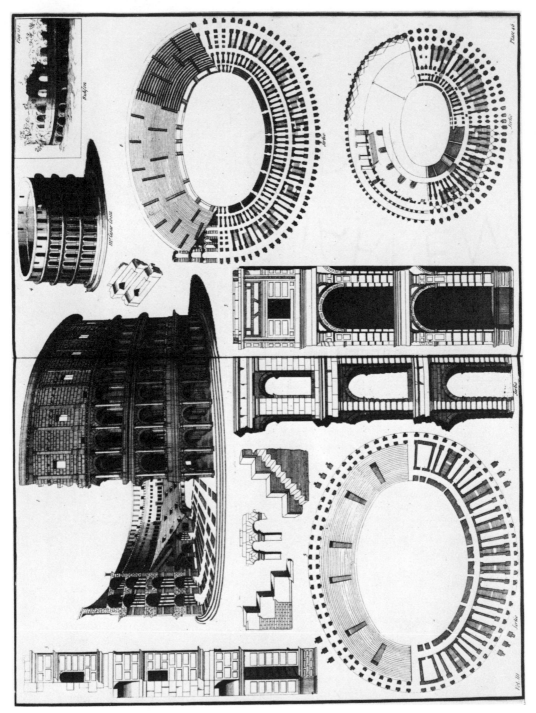

Plate LXXXIII. *From No. 86.* The Colosseum, Rome (Vol. III, Pl. 46, opp. p. 162).

recently acquired, the gift of the Thomas Jefferson Memorial Foundation.

U. Va.
*DE57.M79.1721

87. Morris, Robert.

SELECT / ARCHITECTURE: / BEING / REGULAR DESIGNS / OF / PLANS and ELEVATIONS / Well suited to both TOWN and COUNTRY; / IN WHICH / The Magnificence and Beauty, the Purity and Simplicity of DESIGNING / For every Species of that Noble Art, / Is accurately treated, and with great Variety exemplified, / From the Plain TOWN-HOUSE to the stately HOTEL, / And in the Country from the genteel and convenient FARM-HOUSE / to the PAROCHIAL CHURCH. / With Suitable Embellishments. / ALSO / BRIDGES, BATHS, SUMMER-HOUSES, &c. to all which such REMARKS, EXPLANA-/TIONS and SCALES are annexed, that the Comprehension is rendered easy, and / Subject most agreeable. / *Studium sine divite vena.* Hor. / *Illustrated with* FIFTY COPPER PLATES, *Quarto.* / By *ROBERT MORRIS*, Surveyor. / LONDON: / Sold by ROBERT SAYER, opposite Fetter-Lane, in Fleet-Street. MDCCLV. / Price 10 *s.* 6 *d.*

4to. Two-color title page (1 leaf); preface (1 leaf); introduction (4 leaves); explanation of plates (1–8); list of subscribers ([i]-iv); 50 engraved plates.

The plates were drawn by Morris and engraved by Richard Parr (fl.1755), English.

The subscribers included one attorney, seven bricklayers, twenty-one carpenters, three carvers, one glazier, two instrument makers, four joiners, seven masons, five painters, one plasterer, and six surveyors. The architects subscribing were John Adam, Sr., John Adam, Jr., Robert Adam, James Horn, William Jones, and John Sanderson, while the engraver Richard Parr was also listed.

Robert Morris (fl.1754) was an architect "of Twickenham," as he described himself in one of his books, as well as a surveyor, according to the title page of *Select Architecture*. He had trained with his kinsman Roger Morris, the carpenter and principal engineer to the Board of Ordinance. Robert Morris was associated with both the earl of Burlington and John Carr, as well as with his relative.

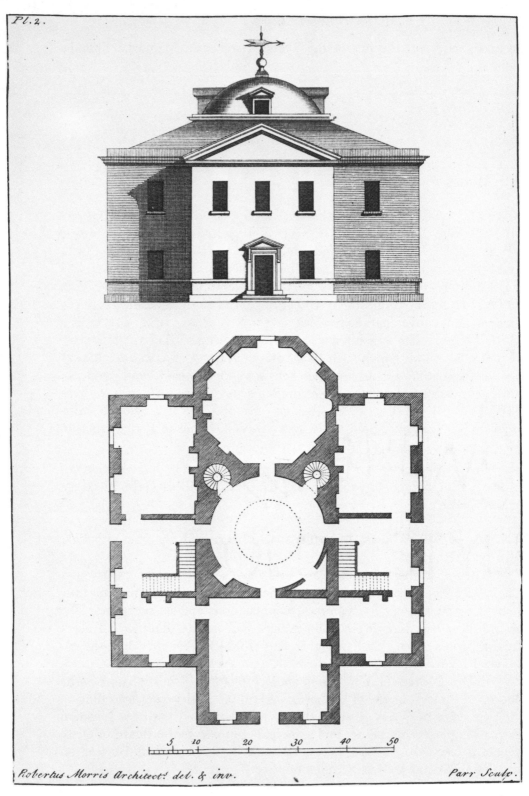

Robertus Morris Architect! del. & inv.

Parr Sculp.

Plate LXXXIV. *From No. 87.* House with a "Back Break for Part of the Octogon" (Pl. 2).

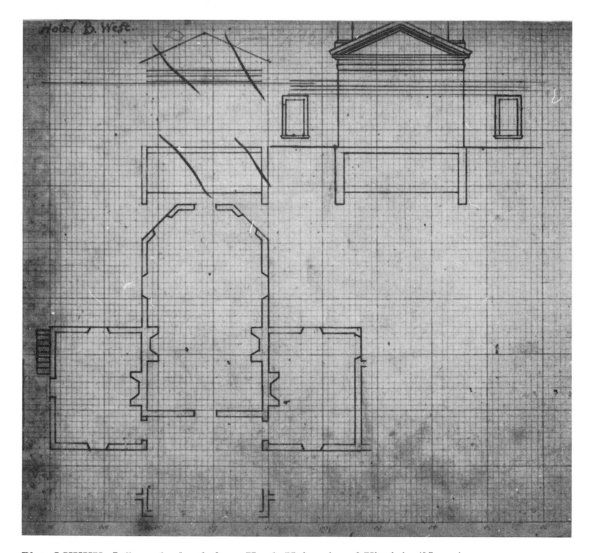

Plate LXXXV. Jefferson's sketch for a Hotel, University of Virginia (N-359).

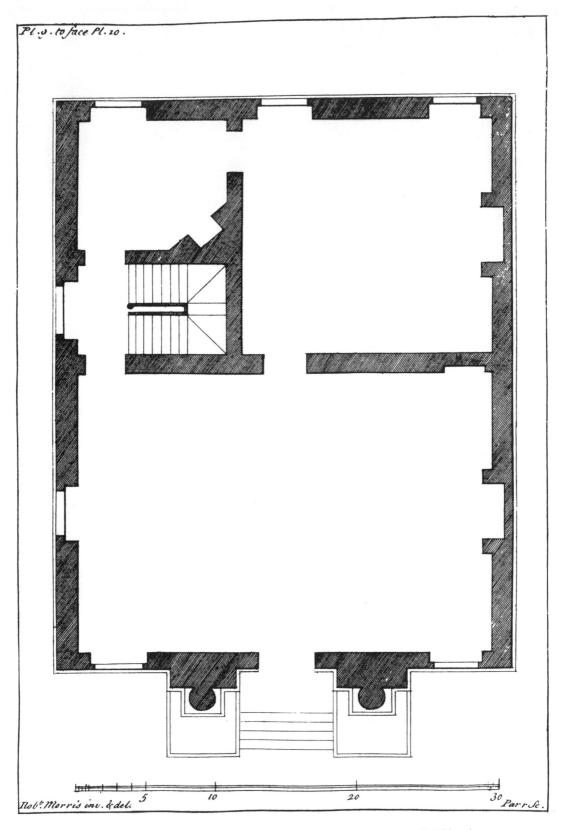

Pl. 9. to face Pl. 10.

Rob.ͭ Morris inv. & del.

5   10   20   30   Parr Sc.

Plate LXXXVI. *From No. 87.* "A Plan . . . of a Little Garden-House" (Pl. 9).

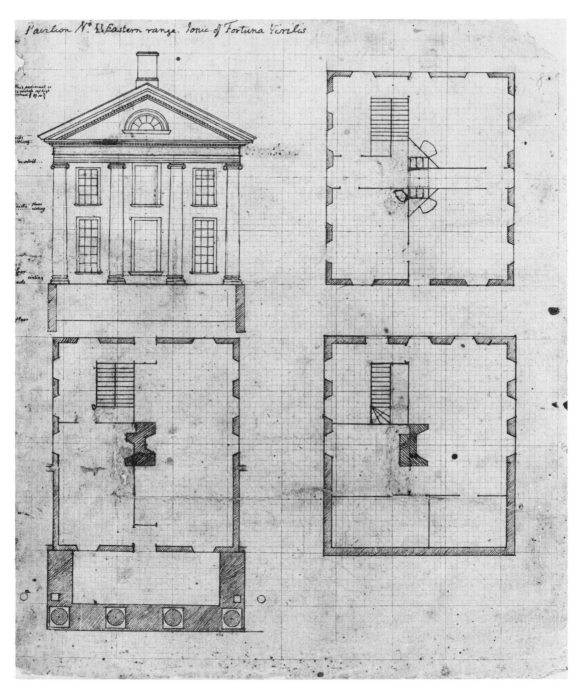

Plate LXXXVII. Jefferson's drawing for Pavilion II, University of Virginia (N-321).

He wrote, in addition to this work which was first issued in 1755 and again in 1759, the following: *An Essay in Defense of Ancient Architecture*, 1728; *Lectures on Architecture*, 1734, with a second part issued in 1736, and a second edition of the first part in 1759, a book which was based on lectures given between October 1730 and January 1735 for the Society for the Improvement of Knowledge in Arts and Sciences, which he had founded; *Rural Architecture*, 1750; *The Architectural Remembrancer*, 1751; *Architecture Improved*, 1755; and, with T. Lightoler and John and William Halfpenny, *The Modern Builder's Assistant*, 1742, with a second edition in 1757.

Morris wrote *Select Architecture* because he thought that there were "so *few Persons* residing in the *Country*, that are capable of *Designing*, something of this Nature might be acceptable." He goes on to say:

Most who have wrote on this Subject, have raised nothing but *Palaces*, glaring in *Decoration* and *Dress;* while the *Cottage*, or plain little *Villa*, are passed by unregarded. *Gaiety, Magnificence*, the rude *Gothic*, or the *Chinese unmeaning Stile*, are the Study of our modern Architects; while *Grecian* and *Roman Purity* and *Simplicity* are neglected.

As an *Admirer* of those *last* mentioned, I place myself and my following *Designs*, before you. [Preface]

The Ground Work of the Whole arises from the Beauty or Purity, and Simplicity, of Designing: By *Purity*, I mean, free from being corrupted, Exactness, and Unmixedness; and by *Simplicity*, Plainness, and without Disguise.

. . . Unnatural Productions are the Things I would mark out for avoiding in Design, so as to make the Reverse more to be studied, and every Structure, to whatever End raised, to be considered as to its *Use, Situation and Proportion;* and to make Art fit and tally with Nature in the Execution, so they may be equally subservient to each other. [Introduction]

Kimball (p. 97) says Jefferson had a copy of *Select Architecture* as early as 1783. As Clay Lancaster has pointed out, it was a book well used by Jefferson.[1] It is uncertain whether he owned a copy at the time of building operations at the University of Virginia, but he undoubtedly remembered Morris's use of arcades, and his liking for the projecting semioctagon, so frequently illustrated in Morris, as in Plate 2 (see Plate LXXXIV), is reflected in an unfinished sketch for one of the hotels of the University (see Plate LXXXV). Lancaster (p. 10) has suggested that the plan of Pavilion II at the University was derived from Plate 9 of *Select Architecture*, a plan for what Morris calls "a little Garden-House. . . . The Dress is plain and Simple" (see Plate LXXXVI). A comparison of Jefferson's drawing for this pavilion (see Plate LXXXVII) and

[1] Lancaster, "Jefferson's Architectural Indebtedness to Robert Morris," *Journal of the Society of Architectural Historians*, X (March 1951), 2–10.

Plate 9 in Morris tends to show differences, however, rather than similarities.

Lancaster (p. 10) has also suggested Morris as a source for the arcades of East and West Ranges at the University. He describes them as having "long arcades of brick set on square piers. The model for these passages onto which open the students' rooms may well have been a *Select Architecture* plate [plate 38] showing the front elevation of a 'Green House.' This is an open gallery adjoining three rooms with doors and windows only at the rear of the building. The plinth and projecting course at the necking of each pier appear on the students' quarters, which, like Morris' greenhouse, are hipped-roofed." But it should be noted that the piers of the arcades of the Ranges are rectangular, not square as in Morris's plate, and the roofs of the Range dormitories were originally flat, not hipped as Lancaster describes and as they appear in Morris's plate. Thus, the resemblance between the Morris and Jefferson designs is considerably weakened, and it is problematical whether Palladio (No. 92b), or Morris might be the major source for Jefferson's designs.

The direct use of Palladio by Jefferson as he designed the University is discussed at No. 92b, but it may be pointed out here that although Plates 16, 17, 29, 38, and 44 in Morris show arcades, in no case does he show an arcade of the length of the Ranges, whereas Palladio shows one with the same number of bays as the longest arcade on the Ranges.

On the other hand, one cannot help wondering if Jefferson's drawing for an octagonal chapel (N-419), perhaps intended for Williamsburg, might not have been inspired by the Morris Plates 31 and 32 (see Plates LXXXVIII and LXXXIX) in spite of Jefferson's reference on the drawing to "Pallad. B. 4. Pl. 38. 39," designs which show a circular rather than an octagonal building.

Jefferson sold his copy of Morris to Congress. It was not ordered for the University. The library's present copy was acquired during the twentieth century.

M
Sowerby 4219

*NA7328.M6.1755

88. Nicholson, Peter.

THE / *Carpenter and Joiner's Assistant;* / CONTAINING / PRACTICAL RULES / FOR / MAKING ALL KINDS OF JOINTS, AND

Pl. 31. to face Pl. 32.

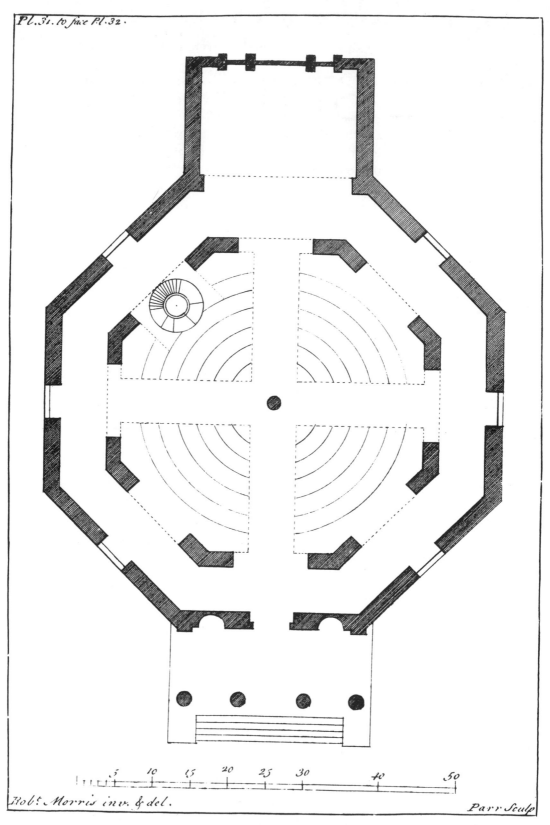

Plate LXXXVIII. *From No. 87.* An octagonal temple or chapel (Pl. 31).

Pl.32.

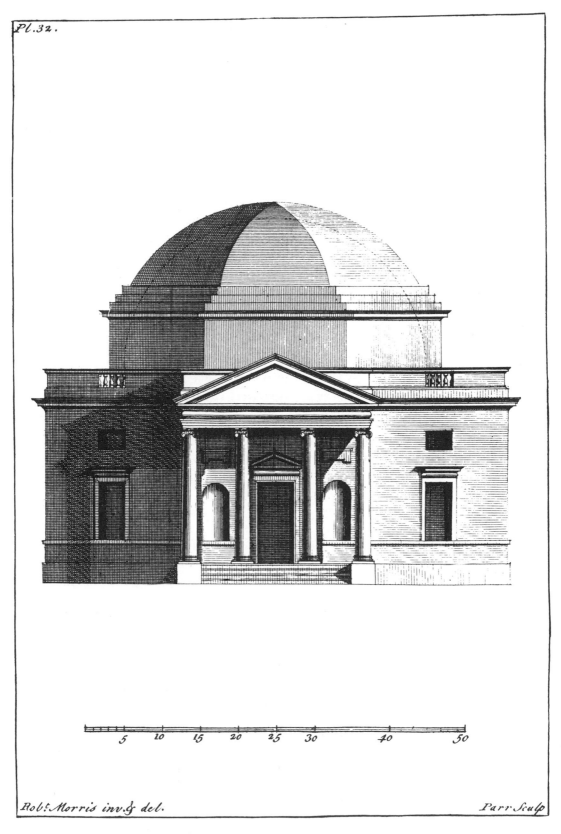

5   10   15   20   25   30   40   50

Robt Morris inv.& del.   *Parr Sculp*

Plate LXXXIX. *From No. 87.* An octagonal temple or chapel (Pl. 32).

VARIOUS METHODS / OF HINGEING THEM TOGETHER; / FOR HANGING OF DOORS ON STRAIGHT OR CIRCULAR PLANS; / For Fitting up WINDOWS and SHUTTERS to answer various Purposes, / with rules for hanging them: / For the Construction of *Floors, Partitions, Soffits, Groins, Arches for Masonry;* / for constructing *Roofs*, in the best Manner from a given Quantity of Timber: / For placing of *Bond Timbers;* with various Methods for adjusting *Raking* / *Pediments*, enlarging and diminishing of Mouldings; *taking Dimensions* for / Joinery, and for setting out *Shop Fronts.* / With a new Scheme for constructing *Stairs* and *Hand-rails*, and for Stairs / having a Conical Well-hole, &c. &c. / TO WHICH ARE ADDED, / EXAMPLES OF VARIOUS ROOFS EXECUTED, / WITH THE SCANTLINGS, FROM ACTUAL MEASUREMENTS. / With Rules for MORTICES and TENONS, and for fixing IRON STRAPS, &c. / Also Extracts from *M. Belidor, M. du Hamel, M. de Buffon*, &c. / On the STRENGTH OF TIMBER, with Practical Observations. / Illustrated with SEVENTY-NINE PLATES, and copious Explanations. / By PETER NICHOLSON, / AUTHOR OF THE CARPENTER'S NEW GUIDE, &c. / *LONDON:* / printed for I. and J. TAYLOR, at the architectural library, / opposite great-turnstile, holborn. / 1797.

4to. Title page ([i]); preface ([iii]-viii); table of contents ([ix]-xi); explanation of plates, with 79 engraved plates, of which 5 are folding, inserted ([1]–79).

Peter Nicholson (1765–1844) was born in East Lothian, the son of a stonemason. He was educated at the village school and apprenticed to a cabinetmaker. As a journeyman he went to Edinburgh where he studied mathematics. At twenty-four he was in London where he set up a night school for mechanics. He moved about a great deal, going to Carlisle in 1805, Glasgow in 1806 where he worked as an architect, to London again in 1810, to Morpeth in 1829, and to Newcastle-on-Tyne in 1832 where he set up another school. He died at Carlisle. He had received the gold medal of the Society of Arts in 1814.

He issued some twenty-four other books in related fields besides the three here examined (see also Nos. 89 and 90). This particular work was first issued in 1792, and again in 1793, 1797 (see Plate XC), 1798, and 1810. He says:

It may be proper for me here again to observe, that this book will not supersede or render useless my former publication *The Carpenter's New Guide* [No. 89], by no means; the subjects, a few instances only excepted, are totally

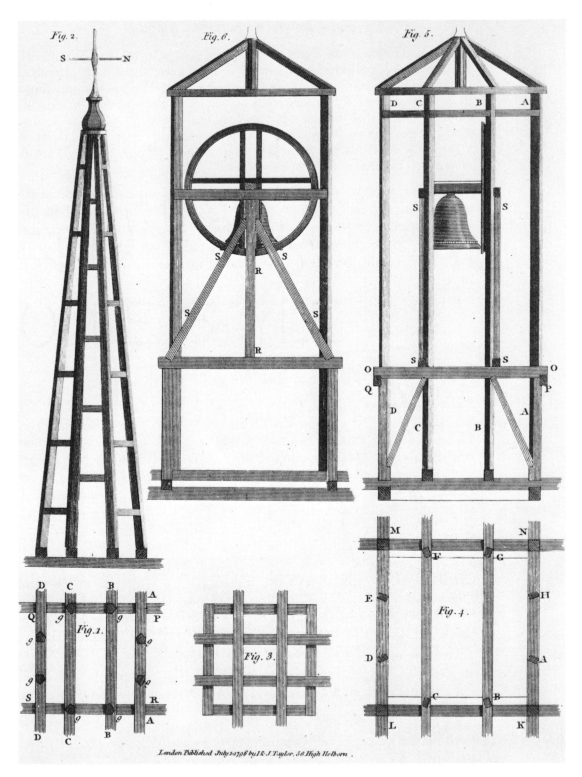

London Published July 1 1796 by I & J Taylor, 56 High Holborn.

Plate XC. *From No. 88.* "Design for a Spire" (Pl. 75).

different: the two volumes will form a complete treatise on the Carpenter and Joiner's business; besides, the Elements or Principles, as the basis of practice, laid down in the beginning of the Carpenter's Guide, I earnestly recommend to be well understood by every one who wishes to attain to eminence and accuracy in the profession; for whoever shall attempt the practical parts of the Carpenter's business without a due knowledge of the principles, will be like a ship at sea without rudder or compass, the port may be obtained, but the labour will be great and the event doubtful. [P. vi]

Jefferson ordered the book in 1825 for the University in the section on "Technical Arts" of the want list, but there is no record of its ever having been received by the library during his lifetime. The duplicate presently on the shelves has recently entered the collections, the gift of the Thomas Jefferson Memorial Foundation.

U. Va.
*TH5605.N6.1797

89. Nicholson, Peter.

THE / Carpenter's New Guide: / BEING A / COMPLETE BOOK OF LINES / FOR / CARPENTRY AND JOINERY. / TREATING FULLY ON / Practical Geometry, Soffits, Brick and Plaister Groins, Niches of every Descrip-/tion, Sky-lights, Lines for Roofs and Domes, with a great Variety of Designs / for Roofs, Trussed Girders, Floors, Domes, Bridges, &c.;—Stair-cases and / Hand-Rails of various Constructions; Angle Bars for Shop Fronts, &c.; / and Raking Mouldings; with many other Things entirely new. / The whole founded on true Geometrical Principles; and the Theory and Practice / well explained, and fully exemplified / ON SEVENTY-EIGHT COPPER-PLATES, / CORRECTLY ENGRAVED BY THE AUTHOR. / INCLUDING / SOME OBSERVATIONS AND CALCULATIONS ON THE / STRENGTH OF TIMBER. / BY / *PETER NICHOLSON*. / LONDON: / PRINTED FOR I. AND J. TAYLOR, / AT THE ARCHITECTURAL LIBRARY, No. 56, HIGH HOLBORN. / MDCCXCIII.

4to. Title page ([iii]); preface ([v]-viii); list of plates ([ix]-xii); text, with 78 engraved plates inserted ([1]–76); [new pagination:] catalogue of books ([1]–4).

For information on Peter Nicholson, see No. 88. About this book Nicholson says:

To a book intended merely for the use of Practical Mechanics, much Preface is not necessary. . . .

In this Second Edition the arrangement is gradual and regular, such as a student should pursue who wishes to attain a thorough knowledge of his profession; and as it is Geometry that lays down all the first principles of building, measures, lines, angles, and solids, and gives rules for describing the various kinds of figures used in buildings; therefore, as a necessary introduction to the art treated of, I have first laid down, and explained in the terms of workmen, such problems of Geometry as are absolutely requisite to the well understanding and putting in practice the necessary lines for Carpentry. [P. v]

In that nice and elegant branch of the Building Art, called Joinery, Stairs and Hand-rails take the lead; and notwithstanding the great importance of this subject, I am sorry to find it has been treated, by authors in general, in a very clumsy and slovenly manner. For Stair-cases, in general, I have laid down right methods, on principles entirely new, and which, since the publication of the former edition of this work, I have the satisfaction to say, have been put in practice, and found to answer well. [P. vii]

In this Second Edition the arrangement of the subjects is progressive and regular; and besides eighteen additional plates, many of the others have been re-engraved, the subjects, in some, made more intelligible, and, in others, multiplied: So that this edition may be considered as a New Work. [P. viii]

The Carpenter and Joiner's Assistant (No. 88) was meant to be a work complementary to this one.

Jefferson in ordering this for the University in the section on "Technical Arts" of the want list did not specify in the way of edition anything more than "London," and there were London editions in 1792, 1793, 1797, 1801, 1805, and 1808 that he could have meant. There is no record of any edition having been received by the library in Jefferson's lifetime. After 1808, the book was issued again in London in 1835, 1854, and 1856.

The library's recently acquired copy, the gift of the Thomas Jefferson Memorial Foundation, is well worn and has carpenters' drawings on some of its blank pages. What is more interesting is the four-page catalogue for the Architectural Library bound in at the end with its listing of over 100 titles in stock at the shop of that name in London.

U. Va.?
*TH5605.N62.1793

90. Nicholson, Peter.

Vol. I.   THE / PRINCIPLES / OF / ARCHITECTURE, / CONTAINING THE / FUNDAMENTAL RULES OF THE ART, / IN / GEOMETRY, ARITHMETIC, & MENSURATION; / *With the Ap-*

plication of those Rules to Practice. / THE TRUE METHOD OF / Drawing and Ichnography and Orthography of Objects, / *GEOMET-RICAL RULES FOR SHADOWS*, / ALSO THE / FIVE ORDERS OF ARCHITECTURE; / WITH A GREAT / *VARIETY OF BEAU-TIFUL EXAMPLES*, / SELECTED FROM THE ANTIQUE; / AND / MANY USEFUL AND ELEGANT ORNAMENTS, / WITH RULES FOR PROJECTING THEM. / *By P. NICHOLSON*, *Archi-tect.* / Illustrated with Two Hundred and Sixteen Copper-plates, en-graved in a / superior Manner by *W. Lowry*, from original Drawings by the Author. / IN THREE VOLUMES. / THE SECOND EDI-TION WITH ADDITIONS, / REVISED AND CORRECTED BY THE AUTHOR. / VOL. I. / London: / PRINTED FOR J. BAR-FIELD, WARDOUR-STREET, / AND T. GARDINER, PRINCES-STREET CAVENDISH SQUARE. / 1809.

8vo. Title page ([i]); preface ([iii]-xii); table of contents ([xiii]-xxxiii); half title (1 leaf); text, with 49 engraved plates inserted ([1]–53); half title ([55]); text ([57]–149); half title ([151]); text, with 9 engraved plates, numbered 50–58, inserted ([153]–266); advertisement (1 un-numbered p.).

Vol. II. THE / PRINCIPLES / . . . / VOL. II. / . . .

8vo. Title page ([i]); preface ([iii]-viii); table of contents ([ix]-xvi); text, with 44 engraved plates, numbered 59–102, of which 1 is folding, inserted ([1]–81).

Vol. III. THE / PRINCIPLES / . . . / VOL. III. / . . .

8vo. Title page ([i]); preface ([iii]-xi); table of contents (4 leaves); text, with 114 engraved plates, numbered 112–216, of which 1 is folding, inserted ([1]–114); directions to binder (1 leaf).

For information about Wilson Lowry, the engraver, see No. 32. For in-formation on Peter Nicholson, see No. 88. Nicholson tells us:

Although a number of publications have at different times appeared, professing to treat of the *Principles*, or *Elements of Architecture*, it is justly complained of them, that they do not fully correspond to their title. For not sufficiently entering into those mathematical principles, on which this noble art ultimately rests, and from which indeed it derives its very existence, they may rather be said to consider it *merely* as an *art*, than as a *science* also; and are more calculated to instruct the Student in drawing Architectural Plans, than to point out and elucidate those unalterable rules, and first principles, which, however unperceived, must enter into the very essence of every plan that is correct and practicable. [I, (iii)-iv]

In this Volume, the PRINCIPLES only are laid down. The GEOMETRI-CAL part is first attended to. [I, vii]

Number, as well as magnitude, being concerned in Architecture, ARITH-METIC follows next. [I, ix-x]

MENSURATION itself is then explained. This, showing the proportion one magnitude bears to another of the same kind, is necessary to enable the architect to proportion the scantlings of his timber, and to give strength and stability to his design. [I, xi-xii]

In the first volume I have very fully treated on PRACTICAL GEOMETRY. This it is the object of the present volume to apply, in the solution of various useful problems, in the several branches of our art.

I have first shown the method of describing ARCHES of every kind. [II, (iii)]

I have next explained the manner of describing both Grecian and Roman MOULDINGS, by applying the general principles of the Ellipsis, Parabola, and Hyperbola, to this particular subject. [II, iv]

The ICHNOGRAPHY AND ELEVATION OF OBJECTS being necessary to represent their true outline in all the varieties of position to the projecting plane, I have given instructions for them, and then proceed in the last place to treat of the PROJECTION OF SHADOWS: A subject hitherto entirely neglected by writers on Architecture, notwithstanding its importance in orthographical or geometrical designs. [II, vi-vii]

I NOW submit the third and last volume of this Work. . . . It treats of the Decorative parts of Architecture. . . .

On this subject many able authors have already written; but the plan I have followed is different from theirs. It has not been so much my object to entertain the eye by a multitude of descriptive Drawings, as to enable the learner to understand and imitate those he meets with. This purpose I have thought would be most effectually answered, by first explaining those mathematical principles, to which all chaste ornament owes its beauty and permanence; and then showing the exemplification of them in those specimens of ancient magnificence, which have escaped the ravages of time. [III, (iii)-iv]

Greece indeed has been long in the possession of barbarians, which, till of late, has occasioned it to be greatly neglected, few people caring to risk their lives among them. At length, however, Monsieur Le Roy [No. 73], a traveler of great assiduity, and repute, took the trouble to make drawings from the remaining antiquities of that ancient repository of arts and learning: and the world have [*sic*] since been still more indebted to the united labors of Stuart and Revett [No. 119], for those accurate representations with which they have elucidated this subject.

Grecian Architecture being thus happily recovered from the ruins in which it was concealed, it is found far preferable to the Roman, both in the beauty of its designs, and the elegance and proportion of their parts [see Plate XCI; compare with Plate CXXXIII]. The numerous members of the latter render their profiles trifling and confused; their overloaded cornices make

Plate XCI. *From No. 90.* "Grecian Architecture: From the Temple of Theseus at Athens" (Vol. III, Pl. 128).

them clumsy and inelegant; . . . while the boldness of the Grecian commands the attention of the spectator; the grandeur of its parts, and the graceful curvature of its mouldings; producing the most happy variety of light and shade upon its surfaces. [III, vi-vii]

An artificial arrangement of leaves, branches, fruit, flowers, drapery, &c. either singly or combined in any manner with each other, are [*sic*] called ornaments in architecture. [III, (1)]

This eminently interesting work, with its emphasis on the importance of mathematics in architecture, went through at least five editions, in 1795–98, 1809, 1836, 1841, and 1848. The engraved plates in all the volumes are especially beautiful, even those which are purely diagrammatic.

Jefferson, in ordering this book for the University in the section on "Architecture" of the want list, specified only a three-volume edition in octavo, which could have referred to the original edition of 1795–98 or the 1809 edition. There is no record that either edition was received by the library before Jefferson's death. The library's present set has been recently acquired, the gift of the Thomas Jefferson Memorial Foundation.

U. Va.
*NA2520.N58.1809

91. Palladio, Andrea.

[Half title:] BIBLIOTHEQUE / PORTATIVE / D'ARCHITEC-TURE / ÉLÉMENTAIRE, / A L'USAGE DES ARTISTES / Divisée en six Parties. / SECONDE PARTIE. / Contenant / L'Architecture de Palladio.

[Title page:] ARCHITECTURE / DE / *PALLADIO*, / CONTE-NANT / *Les cinq Ordres d'Architecture, suivant / cet Auteur, ses observations sur la maniere / de bien bâtir, & son Traité des grands / Chemins & des Ponts, tant de charpente / que de maçonnerie.* / NOU-VELLE ÉDITION / A PARIS, RUE DAUPHINE, / Chez Jombert, Libraire du Roi pour l'Artillerie / & le Génie, à l'Image Notre-Dame. / M. DCC. LXIV.

8vo. Half title ([i]); engraved frontispiece (1 leaf); title page ([iii]); advertisement (v-vii); table of contents (viii-x); life of Palladio (xi-xii); preface (xiii-xvi); text, with 75 engraved plates inserted, of which 1 is double ([1]–149); approbation (150); privilege of the king (150–51); registration (152).

For information about Palladio, see No. 92a. This book is Part II of the *Bibliothèque portative d'architecture élémentaire . . .* which Charles-Antoine Jombert began publishing in 1764 at Paris. For further information on the *Bibliothèque* and the other three parts that were published, see Nos. 46, 111c, and 123a.

Sowerby notes that Jefferson wrote on the flyleaf of his copy

$$
\begin{array}{lcr}
 & & \mathbf{D} \\
\text{prime cost supposed} & 15 = & 2.75 \\
\text{worth in the US} & & 4.81
\end{array}
$$

That copy was sold to Congress. Jefferson ordered the entire *Bibliothèque* for the library in the section on "Architecture" of the want list, but there is no record of its having been received. The present copy on the University's shelves has been recently acquired, the gift of the Thomas Jefferson Memorial Foundation.

U. Va.   M
*NA2515.P253.1764   Sowerby 4215

92a. Palladio, Andrea.

Vol. I.   THE / ARCHITECTURE / OF / A. PALLADIO; / IN FOUR BOOKS. / CONTAINING, / A short TREATISE of the FIVE ORDERS, and the most / necessary Observations concerning all Sorts of BUILDING, / *AS ALSO* / The different Construction of PRIVATE and PUBLICK HOUSES, / HIGH-WAYS, BRIDGES, MARKET-PLACES, XYSTES, and / TEMPLES, with their Plans, Sections, and Uprights. / *To which are added several Notes and Observations made by* INIGO JONES, / *never printed before.* / Revis'd, Design'd, and Publish'd / *By* GIA-COMO LEONI, *a* Venetian; *Architect to his most* / SERENE HIGHNESS, the / ELECTOR PALATINE. / *Translated from the* Italian *Original.* / *LONDON:* / Printed by *John Watts,* for the AUTHOR. / M DCC XV.

Folio. Engraved portrait of Palladio (1 leaf); engraved frontispiece (1 leaf); title page (1 leaf); biography of Palladio (1 unnumbered p.); translator's preface (3 unnumbered pp.); Palladio's preface (2 leaves); list of subscribers (1 leaf); text, with plates I-VII and XXXVII inserted (1–54); title page in French (1 leaf); biography of Palladio in French (1 unnumbered p.); translator's preface in French (3 unnumbered pp.);

[new pagination:] Palladio's preface in French (1–3); text in French (3–33); title page in Italian (1 leaf); biography of Palladio in Italian (1 leaf); Palladio's preface in Italian (i-ii); text in Italian (iii-xxx); plates VIII-XLIII, except for XXXVII which is inserted in English text.

Vol. II. THE / ARCHITECTURE / OF / A. PALLADIO; / BOOK *the* SECOND. / CONTAINING / The DESIGNS of several Houses which he has Built / either in TOWN, or in the COUNTRY. / WITH / Some other DESIGNS of the Manner of Building amongst the / GREEKS and ROMANS. / Revis'd, Design'd, and Publish'd / *By* GIACOMO LEONI, . . . / . . . / Printed by *John Watts*, for the AUTHOR.

Folio. Title page (1 leaf); dedication in Italian (2 leaves); text (1–37); title page in French (1 leaf); [new pagination:] text in French ([1]–23); title page in Italian (1 leaf); text in Italian (i-xxi); 61 engraved plates.

Vol. III. THE / ARCHITECTURE / . . . / BOOK *the* THIRD. / Wherein is treated / Of Ways, Streets, Bridges, Squares, Basilicas or Courts / of Justice, Xistes, or Places of Exercise, &c. / The Whole Revis'd, Design'd, and Publish'd / . . .

Folio. Title page (1 leaf); preface (1–3); text (4–37); title page in French (1 leaf); [new pagination:] preface in French (1–2); text in French (2–23); title page in Italian (1 leaf); dedication in Italian (1 leaf); list of new subscribers in English (1 leaf); preface in Italian (i-ii); text in Italian (ii-xxii); 22 engraved plates of which 1 is double.

Vol. IV. THE / ARCHITECTURE / . . . / BOOK *the* FOURTH. / PART *the* FIRST. / Wherein is treated / Of the Antient Temples in *Rome*, and some others to / be seen in *Italy*, and other Parts of *Europe* / . . .

Folio. Title page (1 leaf); preface ([1]–2); list of new subscribers (1 leaf); text (3–33); title page in French (1 leaf); [new pagination:] preface in French (1–2); text in French (2–20); title page in Italian (1 leaf); dedication in Italian (1 leaf); preface in Italian (i-ii); text in Italian (ii-xx); 54 engraved plates, of which 7 are double and mostly multinumbered.

Vol. V. THE / ARCHITECTURE / . . . / BOOK *the* FOURTH. / PART *the* SECOND. / . . . / *CUM PRIVILEGIO.*

Folio. Title page (1 leaf); Leoni's preface to the reader (1 leaf); text (1–17); table of contents (4 unnumbered pp.); license (1 unnumbered p.); title page in French (1 leaf); [new pagination:] text in French

(1–12); title page in Italian (1 leaf); text in Italian (i-xii); 50 engraved plates, numbered LV–CIV, of which 7 are double and mostly multi-numbered.

The plates were all drawn by Leoni and were engraved by Thomas Cole (perhaps I. Cole who flourished ca.1720); John Harris (No. 48); Bernard Picart (1632–1721), a pupil of his father and of Sébastien Le Clerc (No. 69) who worked in Holland where he became one of the best of the engravers during the first part of the eighteenth century; and Van der Gucht (No. 37).

The subscribers listed in the first volume included one attorney, one carpenter, one engineer, and two booksellers. Sir Christopher Wren was the only architect mentioned. Those mentioned in the third volume included two bricklayers, two carpenters, four clerks of His Majesty's works, one draughtsman, two gardeners, one joiner, four masons, one stone carver, and one surveyor. The earl of Burlington and James Gibbs were in this volume. In the fourth volume the new subscribers included two booksellers, one bricklayer, four carpenters, one clerk of His Majesty's works, and two masons.

Andrea Palladio (1508 or 1518–80), born in Vicenza, became one of the most eminent architects, and a major influence in the architectural field, especially in England and America, for a very long period of time. His *I quattro libri del' architettura* was first published in Venice in 1570 and has since been translated into many languages and has had many editions. For portraits of Palladio, see Plates XCII and XCIII.

For information on Inigo Jones, see No. 59a.

Giacomo Leoni (1686–1746) redrew all the plates in this book. He is supposed to have come to England for that purpose at the instigation of the earl of Burlington, and he remained there until his death.

Nicholas du Bois was the translator of the text into both French and English. He says in his preface in the first volume:

Among those great Masters of Civil *Architecture*, *Palladio* whose Work I have undertaken to translate, is doubtless the most eminent. If therefore the Book of that Learned Man has been admir'd all over *Europe*, tho his *Designs* have only been coursly [sic] engrav'd in *Wooden Cuts;* will any one deny that the generous Foreigner, who has spent several years in preparing the *Designs*, from which the following *Cuts* have been engrav'd, makes a very considerable Present to the Publick? . . .

Every one may rest satisfied that the two new Translations publish'd in this Volume, and join'd to the *Italian* Original, are very faithful, and that I have left nothing unattempted to make them as perfect as could be wish'd,

Plate XCII. *From No. 92a.* Frontispiece (Vol. I).

ANDREAS PALLADIVS VICENTINVS.

Plate XCIII. *From No. 92a.* Portrait of Andrea Palladio (Vol. I).

and answerable to the Beauty of the *Cuts*, with which they are attended, and which have been engrav'd by the best Masters. . . .

It were an endless thing to enumerate all the absurdities, which many of our Builders introduce every day into their way of building. I shall be contented to apply to them what the ingenious Mr. *Campbell* says of the Architecture of Boronimi [*sic*], in his *Vitruvius Britannicus*. . . . *They are*, says he, *chimerical beauties, where the Parts are without proportions, solids without their true bearing, heaps of materials without strength, excessive ornaments without grace.* I add, and a ridiculous mixture of *Gothick* and *Roman*, without Judgment, Taste, or *Symmetry*. . . .

I hope this work will meet with a general approbation: if those, who have no skill in Architecture, read it, their curiosity will perhaps move them to learn an Art, which several great Princes did not think unworthy of their application. Those who begin to study Architecture, and whose taste is not come yet to its perfection, will be cur'd of their wrong notions; and finding in this Work a method no less experienc'd than beautiful and safe, they will learn by it to work with good success, and without any fear of being mistaken. As for those Learned architects, who are better known by the reputation of their works, than by any thing I could say of them, tis not doubted but they will be glad to see *Palladio* come out under a form more suitable to the nobleness of his *Designs*, and the great Esteem the Publick has always had for him.

> Nicholas Du Bois, *Architect,*
> *and one of his Majesty's*
> *Engineers.*

Leoni tells of the work of executing the drawings and his failure to get permission to use Jones's notes in his preface to the last volume:

After five Years continual Labour, I have at last happily finish'd the Edition. . . . I have not only made all the draughts my self . . . but also made so many necessary Corrections with respect to shading, dimensions, ornaments, &c. that this Work may in some sort be rather consider'd as an Original, than an Improvement. As for the *Notes* of the excellent *Inigo Jones*, I was not able to get them from the Gentleman in whose possession they are, either by my own intreaty or the intercession of my Friends: But if any persons, who have a greater interest with him can obtain this favour, I promise to print them with the utmost exactness, and to distribute the Copies to all my Subscribers gratis.

Kimball (p. 97) says a copy of this edition of Palladio, the first with the Leoni plates, was in Jefferson's hands before 1783. There is no question that Palladio was a major influence in Jefferson's architectural life, but since the second edition of the Leoni *Palladio* may be more easily connected by documents to Jefferson's designs, the extent of that influence will be discussed in No. 92b.

This edition of the Leoni Palladio was in the library Jefferson sold to Congress. It was not ordered for the University. The library's present copy was acquired during the twentieth century.

*NA2517.P3.1715

M
Sowerby 4175

92b. Palladio, Andrea.

Vol. I. THE / ARCHITECTURE / OF / A. PALLADIO; / IN FOUR BOOKS / CONTAINING / A short TREATISE of the FIVE ORDERS, and the most / necessary Observations concerning all Sorts of / BUILDING; / AS ALSO / The different Construction of PRIVATE and PUBLICK HOUSES, / HIGH-WAYS, BRIDGES, MARKET-PLACES, XYSTES, and / TEMPLES, with their Plans, Sections, and Uprights. / Revis'd, Design'd, and Publish'd / *By* GIACOMO LEONI, *a* Venetian; *Architect to His most* / SERENE HIGHNESS, *the Late* / ELECTOR PALATINE. / *Translated from the* Italian *Original.* / In TWO VOLUMES. / The SECOND EDITION. / *LONDON,* / Printed by JOHN DARBY for the AUTHOR, and all the Plates by / JOHN VANTACK. M. DCC. XXI.

and

THE / ARCHITECTURE / OF / A. PALLADIO; / BOOK *the* SECOND. / CONTAINING / The DESIGNS of several Houses which he has / Built either in TOWN, or in the COUNTRY. / WITH / Some other DESIGNS of the Manner of Building amongst the / GREEKS and ROMANS. / Revis'd, Design'd, and Publish'd / *By* GIACOMO LEONI, *a* Venetian; *Architect to His Most* / SERENE HIGHNESS, *the Late* / ELECTOR PALATINE. / *Translated from the* Italian *Original.* / Printed for the AUTHOR.

Folio. Engraved frontispiece (1 leaf); title page (1 leaf); dedication (1 leaf); list of subscribers and errata (1 leaf); Leoni's preface (1 unnumbered p.); biography of Palladio (1 unnumbered p.); engraved portrait of Palladio (1 leaf); Palladio's preface (2 leaves); text, with 43 engraved plates inserted ([1]–54); title page ([55]); text, with 61 engraved plates inserted (57–93).

bound with

Vol. II. THE / ARCHITECTURE / . . . / BOOK *the* THIRD./ Wherein is Treated of / Ways, Streets, Bridges, Squares, Basilicas or Courts / of Justice, Xistes or Places of Exercise, *&c.* / The Whole Revis'd . . .

and

THE / ARCHITECTURE / . . . / BOOK *the* FOURTH. / Wherein is Treated / Of the Antient Temples in *Rome*, and some others to / be seen in *Italy*, and other parts of *Europe*. / The Whole Revis'd . . .

Folio. Title page (1 leaf); preface (1–3); text with 22 engraved plates, of which 1 is double, inserted (4–37); title page ([39]); preface (41–42); text with 104 engraved plates, of which 14 are double and mostly multinumbered, inserted (43–90); table of contents (2 leaves).

Although the title page says "all the Plates by JOHN VANTACK," it clearly means they were printed by him, since they are identical with those in No. 92a.

The subscription list includes one apothecary, two attorneys, four booksellers, three bricklayers, five carpenters, one clerk of the works, two doctors, an order for twelve copies from the draughtsman to the office of His Majesty's Ordnance, one ecclesiastic, four engineers, six joiners, three masons, thirteen merchants, one pattern drawer, one plasterer, one printseller, one schoolmaster, and one surveyor.

In this second edition of the Leoni *Palladio* the text has been considerably rearranged, with the French and Italian versions omitted. The English text is the same as that in the 1715 edition, but it has been reset. Leoni's preface makes no reference to the notes of Inigo Jones.

Palladio, when describing the Villa Emo, says that "people may go under shelter every where about this House, which is one of the most considerable conveniencies that ought to be desir'd in a Country-house" (I, 82). This was a statement that Jefferson put into practice in at least three instances—at Monticello, at Edgemont, and at the University of Virginia. At the University he may very well have derived the form of the arcades of the Ranges from Palladio as well (see No. 87), and we know that he checked the proportions of the arches against Palladio in his specifications for the arcades.[1]

Jefferson ordered the capitals for Pavilions II, III, and V at the University from Italy and specified that they be carved after particular plates in Leoni's *Palladio*, 1721 (see plates XCIV–CII).[2] Since the order at Pavilion II is based on Palladio's plates of the temple of Fortuna Virilis, it is reasonable to suppose that the entablature for Pavilion IX, which is based on the same order, is also derived from Palladio. Even the

[1] See "Operations at & for the College," a manuscript notebook in Jefferson's hand, p. 14, U. Va. Library.

[2] Jefferson to Thomas Appleton, April 16, 1821, U. Va. Library.

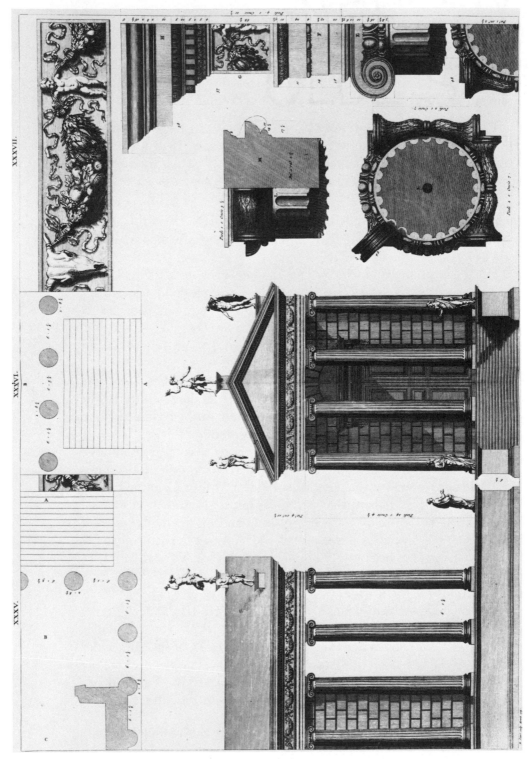

Plate XCIV. *From No. 92b.* "Of the Temple of Fortuna Virilis or Manly Fortune"
(Vol. II, Bk. IV, Pls. XXXV, XXXVI, and XXXVII).

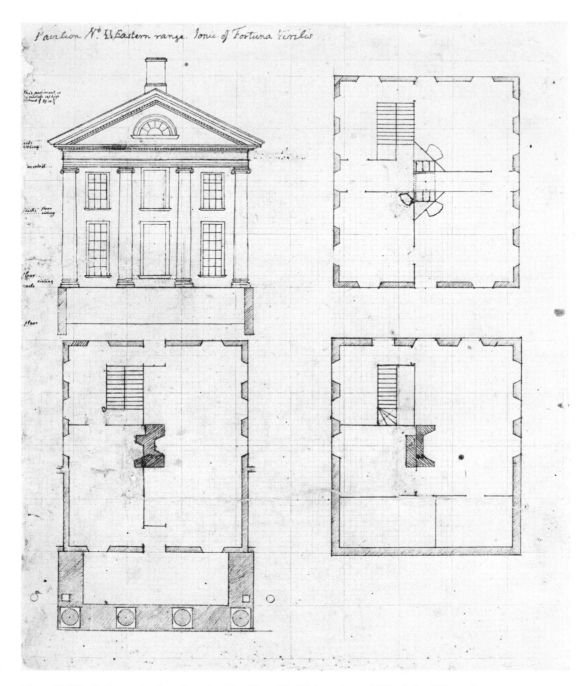

Plate XCV. Jefferson's drawing for Pavilion II, University of Virginia (N-321).

Plate XCVI. *From No. 92b.* "Of the Corinthian Order" (Vol. I, Bk. I, Pl. XXVI,
opp. p. 31).

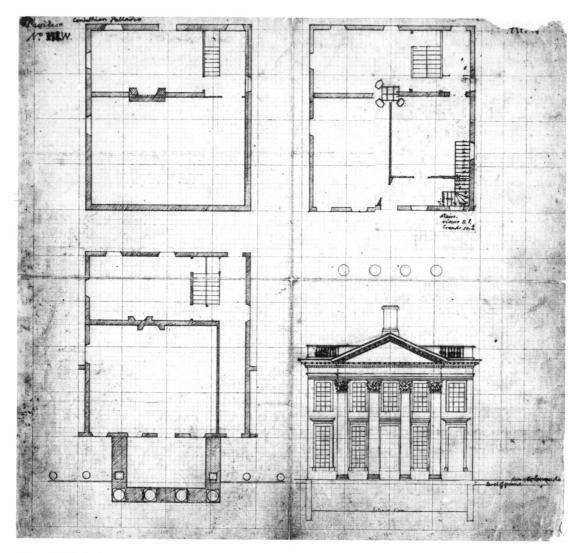

Plate XCVII. Jefferson's drawing for Pavilion III, University of Virginia (N-316).

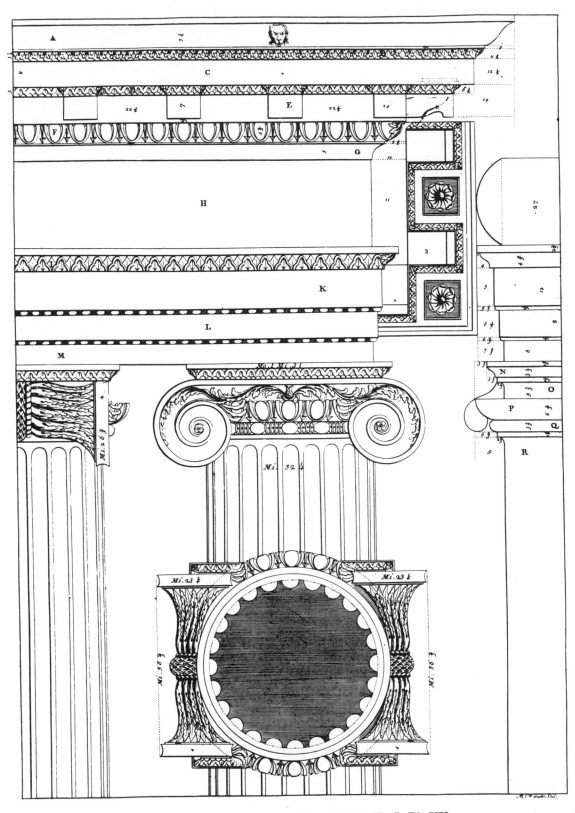

Plate XCVIII. *From No. 92b.* "Of the Ionick Order" (Vol. I, Bk. I, Pl. XX, opp. p. 28).

Plate XCIX. *From No. 92b.* "Of the Ionick Order" (Vol. I, Bk. I, Pl. XXI, opp. p. 29).

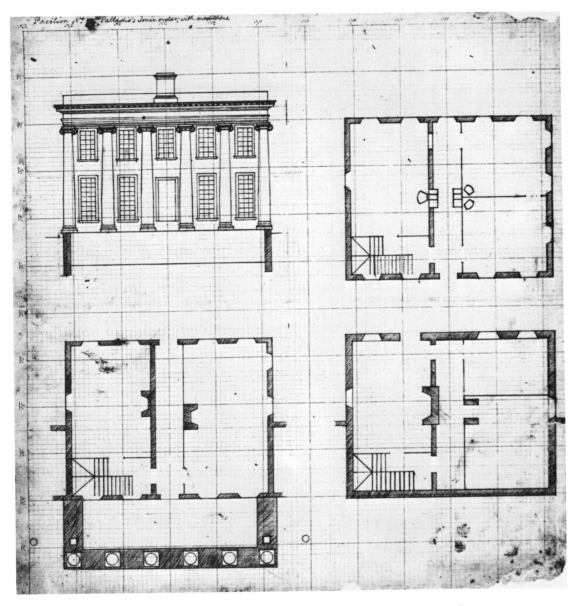

Plate C. Jefferson's drawing for Pavilion V, University of Virginia (N-356). See Plates XCVIII and XCIX.

Plate CI. *From No. 92b.* Elevation "Of the Pantheon, now call'd the Rotunda" (Vol. II, Bk. IV, Pls. LVI and LVII).

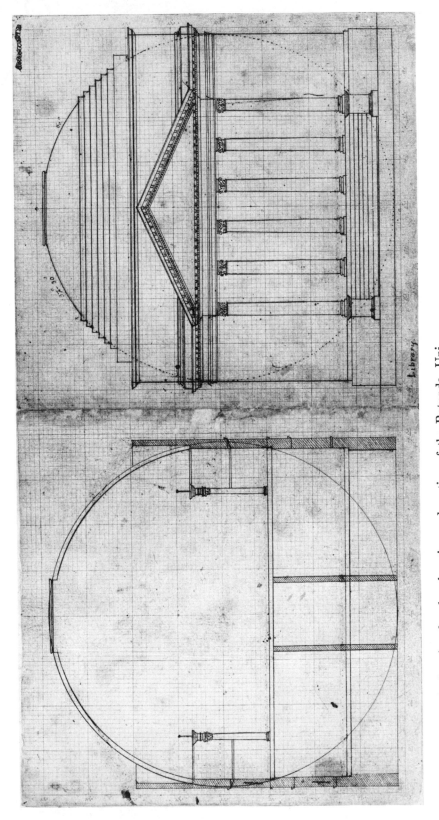

Plate CII. Jefferson's drawing for the elevation and section of the Rotunda, University of Virginia (N-328). See Plate CI.

order for Pavilion VII is derived from Palladio via Fréart de Chambray (No. 46).

Jefferson also ordered the capitals for the columns of the Rotunda from Italy, again citing Palladio as the model.[3] At the time of the design of the Rotunda, the best reference available to Jefferson concerning the Pantheon, which he used as his precedent as he notes on his drawing of the plan for the dome room (N-331), was Leoni's *Palladio*, 1721.[4]

These many uses of Palladio at the University of Virginia hardly substantiate the statement that "from Morris [No. 87] came practically as many designs as from Palladio."[5]

One has only to add the many other allusions to Palladio, and especially to the Villa Rotunda, in Jefferson's *oeuvre* to begin to understand the strong underlying Palladian basis in his design vocabulary, a basis which can hardly be too much emphasized.

The case for arguing that this edition of Palladio was the one recorded by Kean as being in the University's collection in 1825, though physically then "at Monticello," rests on the certainty, as noted above, that this was one of the editions used during the construction of the University. The volumes apparently never got back from Monticello because they do not appear in the 1828 *Catalogue*. The copy now in the library was the gift of Thomas Nelson Page.

U. Va.
*NA2517.P3.1721

92c. Palladio, Andrea.

Vol. I. THE / ARCHITECTURE / OF / A. PALLADIO; / IN FOUR BOOKS. / CONTAINING / A short TREATISE of the FIVE ORDERS, and / the most necessary Observations concerning / all sorts of BUILDING: / AS ALSO / The different Construction of PRIVATE and PUBLICK HOUSES, / HIGH-WAYS, BRIDGES, MARKET-PLACES, XYSTES, and / TEMPLES, with their Plans, Sections, and Uprights. / Revis'd, Design'd, and Publish'd / By *GIACOMO LEONI*, a *Venetian*, / *Architect to His Most* SERENE HIGHNESS, *the Late* / ELECTOR PALATINE. / *Translated from the* Italian *Original.* / THE THIRD EDITION, CORRECTED. / With NOTES and REMARKS of / *INIGO JONES:* /

[3] Jefferson to Thomas Appleton, Oct. 8, 1823, U. Va. Library.
[4] O'Neal, *Jefferson's Buildings*, pp. 2–3.
[5] Lancaster, "Jefferson's Architectural Indebtedness to Robert Morris," *Journal of the Society of Architectural Historians*, X (March, 1951), 10.

Now first taken from his Original Manuscript in *Worcester* College Library, *Oxford*. / AND ALSO, / An APPENDIX, containing the ANTIQUITIES of *ROME*. / Written by *A. PALLADIO*. / And a DISCOURSE of the FIRES of the Ancients. / Never before Translated. / IN TWO VOL UMES. / *LONDON:* / Printed for A. WARD, in *Little-Britain;* S. BIRT, in *Ave-Mary-Lane;* D. BROWNE, / without *Temple-Bar;* C. DAVIS, in *Pater-noster-Row;* T. OSBORNE in / *Gray's-Inn;* and A. MILLAR, against St. *Clement's* Church in the *Strand*. / M. DCC. XLII.

and

THE / ARCHITECTURE / OF / A. PALLADIO; / BOOK *the* SECOND. / CONTAINING / The DESIGNS of several Houses which he has / Built either in TOWN, or in the COUNTRY / WITH / Some other DESIGNS of the Manner of Building among / the GREEKS and ROMANS. / Revis'd, Design'd, and Publish'd / *By* GIACOMO LEONI, *a* Venetian, *Architect to His Most* / SERENE HIGHNESS, *the Late* / ELECTOR PALATINE. / *Translated from the* ITALIAN *Original*. / With NOTES, by *INIGO JONES*. / . . .

and

THE / ARCHITECTURE / . . . / BOOK *the* THIRD. / Wherein is Treated of / Ways, Streets, Bridges, Squares, Basilicas or Courts / of Justice, Xistes or Places of Exercise &c. / The Whole Revis'd, Design'd, and Publish'd / . . . / VOL. I.

Folio. Engraved frontispiece (1 leaf); two-color title page ([i]); advertisement (iii); Leoni's preface to the second edition and biographical note on Palladio (iv); engraved portrait of Palladio (1 leaf); Palladio's preface (v-vii); text (1–37); Jones's notes (38–40); 53 engraved plates; title page Book II ([41]); text (43–69); Jones's notes (70–72); 61 engraved plates; title page, Book III ([73]); preface (75–77); text (78–102); Jones's notes (103–4); 22 engraved plates.

Vol. II. THE / ARCHITECTURE / . . . / BOOK *the* FOURTH. / Wherein is Treated / Of the Ancient Temples in *Rome*, and some others / to be seen in *Italy*, and other parts of *Europe*. / . . . / VOLUME *the* SECOND. / . . .

and

APPENDIX. / THE / ANTIQUITIES / OF / ROME. / BY / ANDREA PALLADIO. / To which is added, / A Discourse of the FIRES of the Ancients. / Now first Translated from the ITALIAN. / *LONDON:* / . . . / VOL. II.

Folio. Title page, Book IV ([1]); preface (3–4); text (5–41); Jones's notes (42–53); table of contents (54–56); 104 engraved plates; title page, Appendix ([57]); note to reader ([58]); text (59–100).

At last it was possible for Leoni to include in this edition the notes left by Inigo Jones, for:

THE late Dr. CLARKE, Member of Parliament for the University of *Oxford*, being possess'd of an old Edition of PALLADIO's *Architecture*, (on which were wrote, by the Famous INIGO JONES, Notes and Remarks on the Plates;) bequeath'd it, with the rest of his Library, to *Worcester-College*. The Proprietors being inform'd of this, apply'd to the President of the said College, for Liberty to get a Copy of those *Notes* and *Remarks*. This Favour was granted, on condition a Person well skilled in *Architecture* should be sent thither. Mr. JAMES LEONI was prevail'd upon to undertake this, went to *Oxford* accordingly, and transcribed the *Notes* and *Remarks* from the *Manuscript-Copy* of INIGO JONES. Some few of these are placed in the Side-margin, and the rest (which make several Sheets) are added at the end of each Book. This, no doubt, will be esteemed a very great Advantage to this Edition, by all who are Lovers of *Architecture*, and have a value for the Memory of the *Celebrated Architect* who made the Remarks. [I, iii]

As for the appendix, we are told: "AT the end of the Second Volume is added, by way of Appendix, a Tract written by A. PALLADIO, intitled, *The Antiquities of* Rome, &c. now first translated from the Italian" (I, iii).

Palladio says of Rome:

The consideration that almost every body is highly desirous to know and enquire into the Antiquities and sumptuous Works of this most celebrated City, have incited me to compile this small Treatise, in the concisest manner possible, out of the best ancient and modern Writers, who have treated this Subject at large. . . . Read therefore this new Work of mine over and over, if you are desirous to taste that exquisite and amazing pleasure, which is to be reap'd from a perfect Knowledge of so great a City as *Rome*, and so famous for her magnificent Structures, Nobility, and Renown. [II, 58]

The text of the *Four Books*, though reset, is identical with the English text of both the 1715 and 1721 editions. The plates are also the same. The remarks of Inigo Jones are mostly corrections of dimensions or usages of classical elements by Palladio. It is said Jones traveled about the Vicentine area carrying his copy of Palladio with him as a reference.

Kimball (p. 97) says Jefferson probably had a copy of this edition before 1769. That copy was sold to Congress. It was not ordered for the University. The library's present set is a recent acquisition, the gift of the Thomas Jefferson Memorial Foundation.

M

*NA2517.P3.1742   Sowerby 4147

92d. Palladio, Andrea.

LES QVATRE LIVRES / DE L'ARCHITECTVRE / D'ANDRÉ PALLADIO. / *Mis en François;* / Dans lesquels, / a prés vn petit Traité des / cinq Ordres, auec quelques-/vnes des plus necessaires ob-/serua-tions pour bien bastir, / Il parle de la construction des / maisons par-ticulieres, des grand / chemins, des Ponts, des Pla-/ces publiques, des Xystes, / des Basiliques, & des / Temples. / A PARIS, / De l'Im-primerie d'EDME MARTIN. / ruë S. Iacques, au Soleil d'or. / M. DC. L.

Folio. Title page (1 leaf); translator's note (1 leaf); text with many woodcut illustrations (1–329).

It should be noted that the illustrations are woodcuts and not engravings as stated in Sowerby.

For information on Roland Fréart de Chambray, the translator, see No. 46. His estimation of Palladio was high: "Je diray donc seulement tout en un mot, auec le consentement uniuersel des intelligens, qu'il est premier entre ceux de sa profession, & qu'on peut tenir ce Liure comme un Palladium de la uraye Architecture" (Translator's note). This trans-lation of Palladio by Fréart de Chambray was first issued in this edition of 1650 (see Plates CIII-CVI; compare Plates CV and CVI with Plate XCIV).

Jefferson sold his copy to Congress. Kimball (p. 98) says it had entered his library between 1785 and 1789. It was not ordered for the University, whose present copy has recently entered its collections, the gift of the Thomas Jefferson Memorial Foundation.

M

*NA2515.P254.1650   Sowerby 4181

93. Palladio, Andrea.

I CINQUI ORDINI / DELL'ARCHITETTURA / DI ANDREA PALLADIO / *ILLUSTRATI* / *E RIDOTTI A METODO FACILE* / UMILIATI / A S. E. IL SIG. CAVALIERE / D. DOMENICO AN-TONIO DI SOUZA / COUTINHO / INVIATO STRAORD. E MINISTRO PLENIP. DI S. M. F. / PRESSO S. M. IL RE DI SARDEGNA / &c. &c. &c. / *DA GIO. BATTISTA CIPRIANI* / *SANESE* / ROMA / CON PERMESSO / 1801

and

REGINA VIRTVS

LES QVATRE LIVRES
DE L'ARCHITECTVRE
D'ANDRE' PALLADIO.

Mis en François.

Dans lesquels,
prés vn petit Traitté des
cinq Ordres, auec quelques-
vnes des plus necessaires ob-
seruations pour bien baftir,
Il parle de la construction des
maisons particulieres, des grands
chemins, des Ponts, des Places publiques, des Xystes,
des Bafiliques, & des
Temples.

A PARIS,
De l'Imprimerie d'EDME MARTIN,
ruë S. Iacques, au Soleil d'or.

M. DC. L.

Plate CIII. *From No. 92d.* Title page.

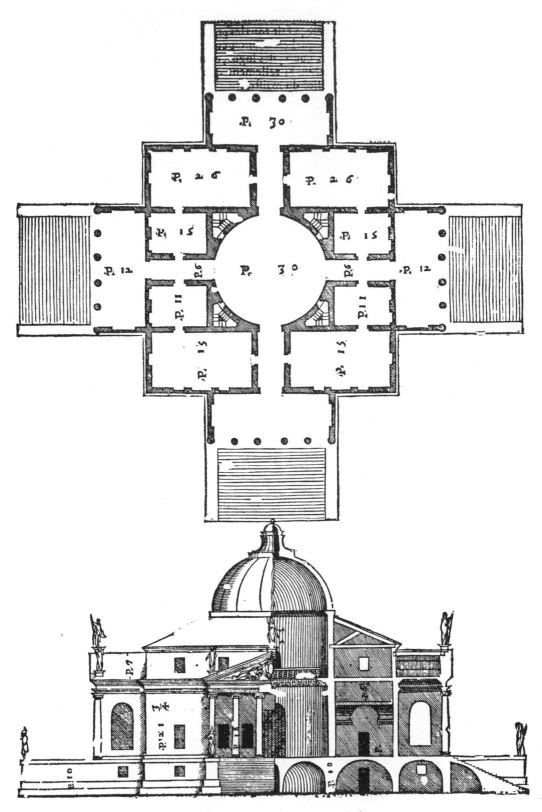

Plate CIV. *From No. 92d.* Villa Rotunda (woodcut on p. 87).

Plate CV. *From No. 92d.* Temple of Fortuna Virilis (woodcut on p. 241).

Plate CVI. *From No. 92d.* Temple of Fortuna Virilis (woodcut on p. 242).

SCELTA / DI ORNATI / ANTICHI.E MODERNI / *DISEGNATI ED INCISI* / *DA* / GIO. BATT. CIPRIANI / ROMA / CON PERMESSO / 1801.

4to. Engraved title page (1 leaf); dedication (1 leaf); note (1 leaf); text (1–24); 25 engraved plates; title page (1 leaf); 30 engraved plates.

For information about Palladio, see No. 92a. Giovanni Battista Cipriani (1727–1785 or 1790) was born in Florence but died in London where he had studied and worked. He was a pupil of Bartolozzi and became a member of the Royal Academy, for which he designed the certificate of admission. He restored, or was in charge of the restoration of, the Rubens ceiling in the Banqueting House, Whitehall.

The posthumously issued *Cinque ordini* is a handsome but straightforward book of the orders with a supplement of ornament. All the plates are beautifully drawn and engraved, as one would expect of Cipriani. (see Plate CVII)

This quarto edition of Cipriani is known from the Kean list to have been in the library at a time when only Jefferson controlled the acquisitions. Later records of this volume (e.g., 1828 *Catalogue* entries on pp. 105 and 108) make one wonder whether there were two copies of this edition in the library; or, if there was only one, whether it was given to Jefferson for the library by Joseph Coolidge or James Madison. In any case no copy survived. The library's present copy has been recently acquired, the gift of the Thomas Jefferson Memorial Foundation.

U. Va.
*NA2810.P3.1801

94. Palladio, Andrea.

THE / FIRST BOOK / OF / Architecture, / BY / *ANDREA PALLADIO* / Translated out of *ITALIAN:* / With an *Appendix* Touching / DOORS and WINDOWS, / By *Pr. LE MUET* Architect to the *French* King. / Translated out of *French* by *Godfrey Richards:* / The whole Illustrated with above Seventy Copper Cutts. / ALSO, / *Rules* and *Demonstrations*, with several Designs for the Framing / of any manner of *Roofs*, either above *Pitch* or under *Pitch*, / whether *Square* or *Bevel*, / never Published before by that In-/genious Architect Mr. *William Pope* of *London.* / WITH / Designs of *Floors*, of Variety of small Pieces of Wood Inlayed, / lately made in the Pallace [sic] of Queen

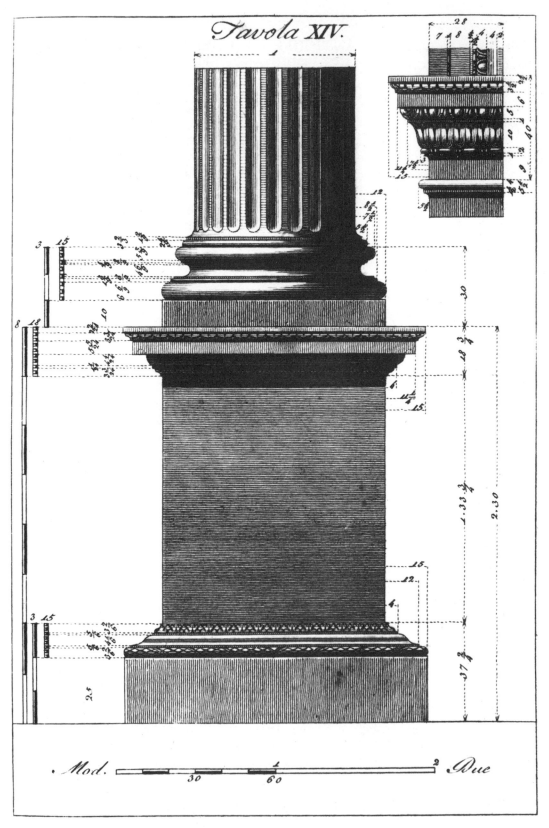

Plate CVII. *From No. 93.* Base and pedestal (Tab. XIV).

Dowager, at *Sommerset-/House;* a Curiosity never practiced in *England* before. / The *Sixth Edition Corrected* and *Enlarged* with the new *Model* of the *Cathedral* of St. *Pauls* in *London.* / *LONDON,* / Printed for *Tho. Braddyll,* and *Eben. Tracy* on *Lon-/don-Bridge,* MDCC.

8vo. Engraved frontispiece (1 leaf); title page (1 leaf); Richards's preface (1 leaf); text, with 66 (not 70) engraved plates, of which 4 are folding, inserted (1–237).

Pierre Le Muet (1591–1669) was born at Dijon. By 1616 he was the holder of the first of a series of offices before becoming, in 1628, *Architecte ordinaire du roi.* After Lemercier's death he was associated with the building of the church of Val-de-Grace in Paris. His books included *Manière de bien bastir pour toutes sortes de personnes, etc.* (Paris, 1623 and 1647); *Traité des cinq ordres d'architecture dont se sont servi les anciens, traduit du Palladio augmenté de nouv. inventions pour l'art de bien bastir etc.* (Paris, 1645 and Amsterdam, 1682); and *Augmentations de nouveaux bastimens faicts en France par les ordres et desseins de Sieur L. M.* (Paris, 1647).

Godfrey Richards, the translator, points up the scarcity of English architectural books at the turn of the eighteenth century when he tells us about this edition of Palladio's Book I:

The Subject of this Translation, being *Architecture,* doth in the opinion of Sr. Hen. Wotton, need no Commendation, where there are Noble Men or Noble Minds. . . . To these [designs of Palladio] are added Designs of *Doors* and *Windows,* by *Pr. Le Muet,* Architect to the *French* King which I thought good to present (*Palladio* only discoursing them) they being well approved by all Artists, both for their Manner and Proportions, and the same which are at the *Louvre* at *Paris;* and out of him I have given the Proportion of *Halls* and *Chambers,* though a little different from *Palladio,* because most agreeing to the present practice both in *England* and *France.* And for the same Reason, I do, instead of *Monsieur Muet's* Designs of Frames of Houses, put in such as are used in *England,* by the direction of some of our ablest *Architects.* . . . We have but few Books which we can recommend to you besides the excellent Discourses of Sir *H. Wotton* and *John Evelin,* Esq.; the former on the Elements of Architecture, and the latter in his accompt of Architecture and Architects (added to his Elegant Translation of the Parallel [No. 46]) where they have comprised fully the most weighty Observations of the Art. [Richards's preface]

That Jefferson owned a copy of this work is clear from the annotation "Palladio's 1st book of architecture, with Le Muet on doors & windows" (see Plate CVIII) in his manuscript library catalogue now at the Massachusetts Historical Society, but the copy apparently did not

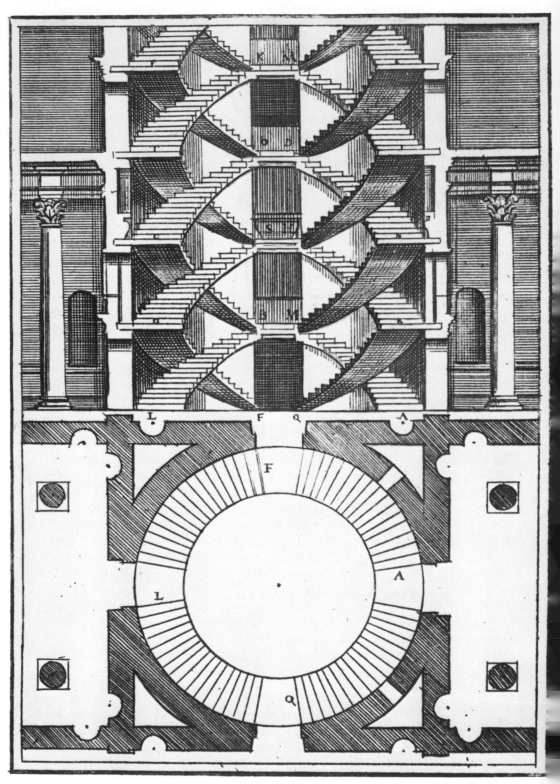

Plate CVIII. *From No. 94.* Double staircase (p. 213).

go to Congress in 1815, and there is no record of it in the 1829 sale. Perhaps it was never returned after it had been loaned to James Oldham, the contractor, as stated in Jefferson's letter to him of December 24, 1804, and quoted in Sowerby (4175): "There never was a Palladio here [in Washington] even in private hands till I brought one: . . . I send you my portable edition, which I value because it is portable. It contains only the 1st book on the orders which is the esesential part."

Kimball (pp. 97–98) says this book entered Jefferson's library between 1785 and 1789. Which edition Jefferson owned, however, is a matter of speculation. Kimball listed as possibilities the first, second, third, seventh, and twelvth editions (of 1663, 1668, 1676, 1708, and 1733 respectively, though he misprinted two of these dates). The edition now at the University, the gift of the Reverend Lee M. Dean, is as likely as any other, so far as is now known. It was not ordered for the University.

M

*NA2517.P3.1700

95. Patte, Pierre.

MONUMENS / ÉRIGÉS EN FRANCE / A LA GLOIRE / DE LOUIS XV, / Précédés d'un TABLEAU du progrès des Arts & des Sciences sous / ce règne, ainsi que d'une DESCRIPTION des Honneurs & des / Monumens de gloire accordés aux grands Hommes, tant chez les / Anciens que chez les Modernes; / *Et suivi d'un choix des principaux Projets qui ont été proposés, pour placer la* / STATUE du ROI dans les *différens quartiers de Paris:* / Par M. PATTE, Architecte de S. A. S. Mgr. le Prince PALATIN, Duc-règnant / DE DEUX-PONTS. / *Ouvrage enrichi des Places du Roi, gravées en taille-douce.* / Praesenti tibi maturos largimur honores. *HOR. lib. II, ep. l.* / A PARIS, / Chez / L'AUTEUR, rue des Noyers, la sixième porte cochère, à droite, en entrant / par la rue Saint Jacques. / DESAINT, / SAILLANT, / Libraires, rue Saint-Jean de Beauvais. / M. DCC. LXV. / *AVEC APPROBATION ET PRIVILÈGE DU ROI.*

Folio. Title page (1 leaf); preface (1 leaf); engraved floor plan (1 leaf); text, with 39 engraved plates, of which 6 are folding, inserted ([1]–229); table of contents (230–32); 18 engraved plates numbered XL-LVII, all folding; supplement (233–36); license, errata, and note to binder (1 leaf).

It is notable that one of the engraved headpieces in this book was designed by Boucher and engraved by Cochin, with the exception of the portrait of Louis XV which appears in it and which was engraved by Le Mire (see Plate CIX). The engravers of the plates were C. Frussotte (fl.1765), French; Nöel Le Mire (1724–1800), who studied with Le Bas and de Descamps and became, though working in Paris, a member of the Académie Royale et Imperiale des Beaux-Arts of Vienna, 1768; Loyer (fl.1760), French; Martin Marvie, or Marvye, (1713–1813), French; and Pierre Patte (see below).

Pierre Patte (1723–1814) was born in Paris but died in Nantes. He was both an architect and an engraver (see No. 73). His book is adulatory (see Plate CX) as he says in his preface:

> J'Eprouve une satisfaction délicieuse, quand je pense que je vais jouir du bonheur si précieux & si rare, de célébrer un bon Prince, un vrais héros de l'humanité; que je vais montres à tout l'Univers les marques éclatantes de l'allégresse de ses peuples, les monumens de leur amour & de leur reconnaissance.
>
> Rien n'a été négligé pour parvenir à donner à cet ouvrage la perfection & la magnificence dont il pouvoit être susceptible. Puisse-t-il être un nouveau monument, digne à la fois de mon Prince & de ma Nation!

Kimball (p. 98) says a copy of this work had entered Jefferson's library between 1785 and 1789. That copy was sold to Congress, but Jefferson also ordered it for the University in the section on "Architecture" of the want list. It was received by the library, but that copy has not survived. The library's present copy is a recent acquisition, the gift of the Thomas Jefferson Memorial Foundation.

U. Va.   M
*NA1046.P3.1765   Sowerby 4211

96a. Perrault, Claude.

ORDONNANCE / DES CINQ ESPECES / DE COLONNES / SELON LA METHODE / DES ANCIENS. / *Par M. PERRAVLT de l'Academie Royale des / Sciences, Docteur en Medecine de la Faculté / de Paris.* / A PARIS, / Chez JEAN BAPTISTE COIGNARD Imprimeur & Libraire / ordinaire du Roy, ruë S. Jacques, à la Bible d'or. / M. DC. LXXXIII. / *AVEC PRIVILEGE DE SA MAJESTÉ.*

Folio. Title page (1 leaf); dedication (2 leaves); license, (1 leaf); preface (i-xxvii); table of contents (xxviii); text (1–124); 6 engraved plates.

LUDOVICO XV. PATRI PATRIÆ.

Dessiné par Boucher.

Gravé par Cochin, Fit le Portrait du Roi fait par le Mire.

Plate CIX. *From No. 95.* Headpiece.

COLONNE   LUDOVISE.

Echelle de   1   2   3   4   Toises.

Plate CX. *From No. 95.* "Colonne Ludovise," from a project for the Place Dauphine
(Pl. XLIII).

The engravers were Louis de Chastillon (see No. 36); Sébastien Le Clerc (see Nos. 36 and 69); and Pierre Le Pautre (see No. 36).

Claude Perrault (1613–88) was educated as both a mathematician and a physician. He continued in both fields all his life and, indeed, died of a malady contracted while dissecting a camel at the Jardin du Roi. He was the architect of both the east colonnade of the Louvre and the Observatory and became a member of the Académie Royale d'Architecture.

He tells how he organized his book:

Cet ouvrage est divisé en deux Parties, dans la premiere j'établis les regles generales des proportions communes à tous les Ordres, telles que sont celles des Entablemens, des hateurs des Colonnes, des Piedestaux [see Plate CXI], &c. . . . Dans la seconde Partie je determine les grandeurs & les caracteres particuliers des membres dont toutes les Colonnes sont composées dans tous les Ordres. . . . Or bien que ce que je rapporte de l'Antique soit une chose plus difficile à verifier que ce que j'ay pris dans les Modernes, le Livre que Mr. Desgodets [No. 36] a depuis peu fait imprimer des Anciens Edifices de Rome, donnera une grande facilité aux Lecteurs qui seront curieux de s'instruire de ces choses, de mesme qu'il m'a servi pour sçavoir au juste les differentes proportions qui ont esté prise par cet Architecte, avec une tres grande exactitude. [Pp. xxvi–xxvii]

This edition was the first for this work, but it was later translated into English and quotations will be given primarily from that version (see No. 96b). Jefferson ordered this French edition for the University in the section on "Architecture" of the want list, and it was received but did not survive. The present copy is a recent acquisition, the gift of the Thomas Jefferson Memorial Foundation.

U. Va.
*NA2812.P38.1683

96b. Perrault, Claude.

A / TREATISE / OF THE / FIVE ORDERS / IN / ARCHITEC-TURE. / To which is Annex'd A / Discourse concerning Pilasters: / and of several ABUSES introduc'd into / ARCHITECTURE. / Written

Plate CXI. *From No. 96a.* "De l'Ordre Corinthien" (Pl. V).

in FRENCH / By *CLAUDE PERRAULT*. / OF THE / ROYAL ACADEMY of *PARIS*, / And made ENGLISH / By JOHN JAMES of *Greenwich*. / *The* SECOND EDITION. / To which is added, / An ALPHABETICAL EXPLANATION of all the TERMS in ARCHITECTURE, / which occur in this WORK. / *London:* / Printed for J. SENEX, and R. GOSLING in *Fleet-street;* W. TAYLOR in *Pater-noster-Row;* / W. and J. INNYS in St. *Paul's Church-Yard;* and J. OSBORN in *Lombard-street*. / M. DCC. XXII.

Folio. Title page (1 leaf); engraved title page (1 leaf); John James's dedication, engraved (1 leaf); Perrault's dedication (2 leaves); preface (i-xxi); table of contents ([xxii]); text, with 6 engraved plates inserted ([1]–131); [new pagination:] glossary ([i]-xii).

The engraver for this edition was John Sturt (1658–1730), English, who worked on a large number of religious and artistic books of the time.

For information on Claude Perrault, see No. 96a. For information on John James, see No. 37.

Perrault says:

It was not without Reason the *Ancients* thought that the Rules of those Proportions, which make the Beauty of Buildings, were taken from the Proportions of human Bodies, and that as Nature has given a stronger Make to Bodies fit for Labour, and a slighter to those of Activity and Address; so there are different Rules in the Art of Building, according as a Fabrick may be design'd massy or more delicate. Now these different Proportions, accompanied with their proper Ornaments, make the Differences of the Orders of Architecture; in which, the most visible Characters which distinguish them, depend on the Ornaments, as the most essential Differences consist in the Proportions that their Parts have in regard of each other.

These Differences of the Orders, taken from their Proportions and Characters, without much exact Punctuality, are the only things that Architecture has well determined: all the rest, which consists in the precise Measures of the several Members, and a certain Turn of their Figures, has, as yet, no certain Rules in which all Architects agree. [Pp. i-ii]

'Tis certain, then, that there are some Beauties in Architecture, which are positive, and some that are only arbitrary, tho' they seem positive through prejudice, from which it is very difficult to guard ourselves. 'Tis also true, that a good judgment is founded on the Knowledge of both these Beauties; but it is certain, that the Knowledge of arbitrary Beauties, is most proper to form what we call a right Tast [*sic*], and 'tis that only which distinguishes true Architects from those that are not so; because common Sense alone is sufficient for knowing the greatest part of positive Beauties. [P. x]

As Architecture, as well as Painting and Sculpture, has been often handled by Men of Letters, so it has been govern'd by this Humour more than the other Arts; they have taken all their Arguments from Authority, imagining that the Authors of the admirable Works of *Antiquity*, did nothing but for good Reasons, though we cannot find them out.

But those who will not allow that the Reasons which cause those beautiful Works to be admir'd, are incomprehensible, after having examin'd all that belongs to this Subject, and been instructed by the most able Persons; will be convinc'd, if they consult good Sense, that 'tis no great Absurdity to think that those Things, for which no Reason can be found, are really without any that contributes to their Beauty, and that they have no other Foundation than Chance, and the Humour of the Workmen, who sought for no Reason to guide them in the Determination of those things, the Preciseness of which, was of no Importance. [Pp. xv-xvi]

Now, tho' the Truth of what I mention of the *Antique*, be a Thing more difficult to be prov'd, than what I have taken from the *Moderns*, the Book which Mons. *Desgodets* [No. 39] has lately printed of the *Ancient* Buildings of *Rome*, will be a great Assistance to such Readers as are curious to be instructed in these things, as it was very servicable to me in finding precisely the different Proportions, which that Architect has taken with the greatest Exactness. [P. xxi]

ORDONANCE, according to *Vitruvius*, is that which regulates the Size of all the Parts of a Building, with respect to their Use. . . .

AN Order of Architecture, then, is that which is regulated by the Ordonance, when it prescribes the Proportions of intire Columns, and determines the Figure of certain Parts which are proper to them, according to the different Proportions which they have. [Pp. (1)–2]

John James, in the glossary, gives two very interesting definitions:

GOTHICK, or Modern Architecture, is that which is far removed from the Manner and Proportions of the *Antique*, having its *Ornaments* Wild and Chimerical, and its *Profiles* incorrect: However, it is oftentimes found very strong, and appears very rich and pompous, as, particularly in several of our English Cathedrals. This Manner of Building came Originally from the North, whence it was brought by the *Goths* into *Germany*, and has since been introduced into other Countries. [New pagination: p. v]

SYMMETRY, comes from the Greek *Symmetria*, with Measure, and signifies the Relation of Parity, both as to Height, Depth and Breadth which the Parts have, in order to form a Beautiful Whole. In Architecture we have both Uniform Symmetry, and Respective Symmetry; in the Former, the Ordonnance is pursued in the same Manner throughout the whole Extent; whereas in the Latter, only the Opposite Sides correspond to each other. [New pagination: p. ix]

Kimball (p. 98) says this book entered Jefferson's library between 1785 and 1789. It was sold by him to Congress. Sowerby notes that

Kimball identifies Jefferson's copy wrongly as the 1708 first edition. It was not ordered for the University, whose present copy is a recent acquisition, the gift of the Thomas Jefferson Memorial Foundation.

*NA2812.P4.1722

M
Sowerby 4182

97. Perrier, François.

ILLmo. D. D. ROGERIO DV PLESSEIS / DNO. DE LIANCOVRT MARCHI-/ONI DE MONTFORT, COMITI DE / LA ROCHEG-VION &. a. VTRIVSQVE / ORDINIS CHRISTIANISSIMAE / MAIESTATIS E QVITI REGIIS A / CUBICVLIS PRIMARIO. / *Heroi Virtutum et magnarum arti-/um eximio cultori.* / *Auorum pace belloque praestantium / Et aeui melioris decora referenti;* / SEG-MENTA *nobilium signorum e statuaru, / Quae temporis dentem inui-dium euasere / Vrbis aeternae ruinis erepta / Typis aeneis abse commissa / Perpetuae uenerationis monumentum. / Franciscus Perrier.* / D. D. D. / M.D.C. XXXVIII / *Romae, superiorum permissu.* / *Cum privilegio summi / Pontificis.*

Folio. Engraved title page (1 leaf); 100 engraved plates, of which 2 are folding; engraved index (2 leaves).

All the plates were drawn and engraved by Perrier, the first plate bearing a full signature and the others being initialed.

François Perrier, who worked under the name François Perrier Le Bourguigon or Perrier Le Bourguigon (1584–1656), studied in Rome with Lanfranco. He returned to Mâcon and Paris, but being unsuccessful, he went back to Rome where he stayed for some ten years.

This book is a first edition. It contains views of sculpture found in Rome (see Plate CXII), sometimes several views of the same statue.

Jefferson's own copy was sold to Congress. He ordered it for the University in the section on "Gardening. Painting. Sculpture. Music" of the want list, but there is no record of its having been received. The library's present copy has been recently acquired, the gift of the Thomas Jefferson Memorial Foundation.

U. Va.
*NB86.P45.1638

M
Sowerby 4231

Plate CXII. *From No.* 97. Laocoön (Pl. I).

98a. Pilkington, Matthew.

A / DICTIONARY / OF / PAINTERS / FROM THE REVIVAL OF THE ART TO THE PRESENT PERIOD; / BY / THE REV. M. PILKINGTON, A. M. / A / NEW EDITION, / WITH CONSIDERABLE ADDITIONS, AN APPENDIX, AND AN INDEX; / BY / HENRY FUSELI, R. A. / STAT SUA CUIQUE DIES: BREVE ET INREPARABILE TEMPUS / OMNIBUS EST VITAE: SED FAMAM EXTENDERE FACTIS, / HOC VIRTUTIS OPUS. VIRGIL. AENEID. LIB. X. / *LONDON:* / PRINTED FOR J. WALKER; WILKIE AND ROBINSON; R. LEA; J. STOCKDALE; SCATCHERD / AND LETTERMAN; CUTHELL AND MARTIN; VERNOR, HOOD, AND SHARPE; LONGMAN, / HURST, REES, AND ORME; CADELL AND DAVIES; LACKINGTON, ALLEN, AND CO.; / BLACK, PARRY, AND KINGSBURY; W. MILLER; J. HARDING; J. MAWMAN; J. MURRAY; / CROSBY AND CO.; J. FAULDER; AND J. JOHNSON AND CO. / 1810.

4to. Title page ([i]); dedication, dated 'Dublin, 1770' ([iii]); preface ([v]-xii); bibliography ([xiii]-xiv); glossary ([xv]-xx); editor's note (1 leaf); note to new edition (1 leaf); text ([1]–658); index ([659]–78).

The title page of this copy is inscribed: 'Presented by C. B. Ogle Esq. to G. Hayter, 1813.' The bookplate is inscribed: 'To / Angelo C. Hayter, / From his affectionate Father, / Sir George Hayter. / 1864.'

Matthew Pilkington (1700?–1784) was born in Dublin and educated at Trinity College there. He became the vicar of Donobate and Portrahan, county Dublin, about 1722. His *Dictionary of Painters* was the first such work in English.

Pilkington speaks of his work and of painting in general in his preface:

I persuade myself, that an endeavour to acquire a taste for the polite arts; a desire to obtain a thorough knowledge of them; and a zeal to diffuse that knowledge more extensively through these kingdoms; cannot appear an improper employment for the leisure hours of an Ecclesiastic. [P. vii]

As painting is the representation of nature, every spectator, whether judicious or otherwise, will derive a certain degree of pleasure from seeing nature happily and beautifully imitated; but, where taste and judgment are combined in a spectator who examines a design conceived by the genius of a Raphael, and touched into life by his hand, such a spectator feels a superior, and enthusiastic, a sublime pleasure, whilst he minutely traces the merits of the work, and the eye of such a connoisseur wanders from beauty to beauty, till he feels himself rising gradually from admiration to ecstasy. [Pp. viii–ix]

It is only by a frequent and studious inspection into the excellencies of the artists of the first rank, that a true taste can be established; for, by being attentively conversant with the elevated ideas of others, our own ideas imperceptibly become refined. [P. xi]

This book has a long publishing history. It was first issued in London in 1770. There was a new edition, emended by James Barry, the painter, in 1798; another with additions by John Wolcott, M.D., in 1799; one in 1805, and again in 1810 with additions by Henry Fuseli, the painter and keeper of the schools of the Royal Academy; this was corrected by Watkins for an edition of 1824; in 1829 Richard Davenport made additions; in 1840 Alan Cunningham did the same; in 1851 there was a new issue of the Davenport version; and finally in both 1852 and 1857 Davenport and Cunningham combined forces on editions.

Fuseli points out, in a note to his 1805 edition, the additions of articles he made and his emendations. In his 1810 edition Fuseli says he had added over three hundred names, especially of the Spanish school.

It was the 1810 edition which Jefferson ordered for the University in the section on "Gardening. Painting. Sculpture. Music" of the want list, but it was not supplied. It is worth noting that half a century later, in 1871, Lowndes was still saying that the 1810 edition was the "best." The University's present copy has come into the collections recently, the gift of the Thomas Jefferson Memorial Foundation.

U. Va.
*ND35.P6.1810

98b. Pilkington, Matthew.

Vol. I. A GENERAL / DICTIONARY OF PAINTERS; / CONTAINING / MEMOIRS / OF / THE LIVES AND WORKS / OF THE MOST EMINENT / Professors of the Art of Painting, / FROM ITS REVIVAL, BY CIMABUE, / IN THE YEAR 1250, / TO THE PRESENT TIME. / BY MATTHEW PILKINGTON, A. M. / A NEW EDITION, / REVISED AND CORRECTED THROUGHOUT, WITH NUMEROUS ADDITIONS, / PARTICULARLY OF THE MOST DISTINGUISHED ARTISTS / OF THE BRITISH SCHOOL. / —Reperire, apta atque reperta docendum / Digerere, atque suo quaeque ordine ritè locare, / Durus uterque Labor. VIDA, Lib. 2. Poetic. / Ut Plurimis prosimus, enitimur. CICERO. / IN TWO VOL-

UMES. / VOL. I. / London: / PRINTED FOR THOMAS M'LEAN, 26 HAYMARKET. / 1824.

8vo. Half title ([i]); title page ([iii]); dedication ([v]); editor's preface ([vii]-xvii); bibliography ([xix]-xxvii); glossary ([xxix]-xxxvi); text ([1]-543).

Vol. II. A GENERAL / DICTIONARY OF PAINTERS; / . . . / VOL. II. / . . .

8vo. Half title (1 leaf); title page (1 leaf); text ([1]-533); supplement ([535]-68).

For information about Pilkington, see No. 98a. The editor of this edition takes a dim view of English painting during the third quarter of the eighteenth century when he says: "When this Dictionary was first undertaken, there existed nothing of the kind in our language; nor were there any helps for such a compilation to be obtained, except in foreign tongues, the Art of Painting being at that time as low as it well could be in this country" (I, [vii]).

This was the edition revised and corrected by Watkins and the one supplied to the University despite Jefferson's order for the 1810 edition. The set originally received has not survived, but a duplicate set has been recently acquired, the gift of the Thomas Jefferson Memorial Foundation.

U. Va.
*ND35.P6.1824

99. Piranesi, Giovanni Battista.

VARIE VEDUTE / DI ROMA / *Antica e Moderna / Disegnate e Intaglia / te da Celebri Autori / In* ROMA *1748. / A spese di Fausto Amidei Librario al'Corso*

Small folio. Engraved title page (1 leaf); 83 engraved plates.

The engravers included in this volume are Paolo Anesi (ca.1700–after 1761), a landscape painter and an engraver of views and portraits who worked in Rome; Jerome-Charles Bellicard (1726–86), a Parisian who won the Prix de Rome, 1747, and became a professor at the Académie in 1762, but who was ruined by gambling; F. Pierre Duflos (eighteenth century), a painter and engraver who worked at Rome; Jean-Laurent Le Geay, an architect, painter, and engraver who won the Prix de Rome, 1732, and worked in Germany after leaving Rome; and Piranesi.

Giovanni Battista Piranesi (1720–78), though a Venetian who trained with Lucchesi and Zucchi, worked primarily in Rome as both an architect and an engraver, his engravings forming by far the greater part of his life's work.

The present volume, which has recently come into the University's collections, has a title more or less matching that given in Jefferson's want list for the University, in the section on "Architecture." Although the book includes some engravings by other hands, there are some thirty-seven with an engraved "Piranesi F" signature and a good many more with an inked imitation of that signature. Among these is that for the temple of Fortuna Virilis, whose beautiful Ionic order was later used at the University (see No. 92b). The title page is dated 1748, but the seven plates by Bellicard are dated 1750, which might mean that this volume was expanded by the inclusion of plates by others after the 1748 date.

The title of this book matches that given by Sowerby. It is something of a composite, which will surprise no one familiar with the bibliography of Piranesi. The restrikes from the Piranesi plates have been so numerous and so unsystematized that it is difficult to determine either what Jefferson was ordering for the University or what he himself bought for his private library. He recommended that the University get a single-folio volume which he called "Vedute di Roma antica et moderna del Piranesi." The volume in his own library, which, according to Kimball (p. 98), entered it in 1805 and was later sold to Congress, was described in 1840 as a Rome, 1748, quarto edition with the binder's title *Varie Vedute di Roma antica e Moderna*, but the volume is not now known to be in existence and thus escapes further analysis.

It seems clear enough that Jefferson did not own the two-volume folio edition of the 1760s issued by Piranesi, the 127 plates of which were to make up Vols. XVI and XVII of the 1800 collected restrike.

The copy now on the library's shelves is the gift of the Thomas Jefferson Memorial Foundation.

U. Va. M
*NA1120.P78.1748 Sowerby 4197

100. Piroli, Tommaso.

Vol. I. ANTIQUITÉS / D'HERCULANUM, / GRAVÉES / PAR TH. PIROLI, / ET PUBLIÈES / PAR F. ET P. PIRANESI, FRÉRES. / TOME PREMIER. / PEINTURES. / À PARIS, / CHEZ /

PIRANESI, Frères, place du Tribunat, no. 1354; / LEBLANC, Imprimeur-Libraire, place et maison / Abbatiale St.-Germain-des-Prés, no. 1121. / AN XII. = 1804.

Large 4to. Half title (1 leaf); title page ([i]); dedication ([iii-iv]); publisher's note ([v]-viii); 48 engraved plates, each with page of text inserted.

Vol. II. ANTIQUITÉS / D'HERCULANUM, / . . . / PEINTURE. / TOME II. / . . .

Large 4to. Half title (1 leaf); title page (1 leaf); 48 engraved plates, each with a page of text inserted; errata (1 leaf).

Vol. III. ANTIQUITÉS / D'HERCULANUM / . . . / TOME III. / PEINTURES. / . . . / AN XIII. = 1805.

Large 4to. Half title (1 leaf); title page (1 leaf); 60 engraved plates, each with a page of text inserted; table of contents (4 leaves).

Vol. IV. ANTIQUITES / D'HERCULANUM / . . . / TOME IV. / BRONZES. / . . .

Large 4to. Half title (1 leaf); title page (1 leaf); note (1 leaf); 48 engraved plates, each with page of text inserted; table of contents (2 leaves).

Vol. V. [Not now owned by the University.]

Vol. VI. [Not now owned by the University.]

[*Note:* In the University's second set of the *Antiquités* the title pages for Vols. V and VI are as follows:

Vol. V. ANTIQUITÉS / D'HERCULANUM, / . . . / TOME V. / BRONZES.–TOME II. / . . . / AN XIV. = 1805.

bound with

Vol. VI. ANTIQUITÉS / D'HERCULANUM, / . . . / TOME VI. / LAMPES ET CANDÉLÂBRES. / . . . / LEBLANC, Imprimr.-Libre., rue de la Paix, maison / Abbatiale Saint-Germain-des-Pres, no. I. / AN XIV. = 1806.]

Tommaso Piroli (ca.1752–1824) was born in Rome, studied in Florence, and worked as an engraver in both Rome and Paris. His publisher said of him and his plates for this work:

La gravure, exécuté à l'eau-forte par THOMAS PIROLI, conserve par-tout la grâce, l'esprit et le sentiment des productions originales. Chaque planche est accompagnée d'une page de texte, qui indique le lieu et l'époque des découvertes, la dimension du sujet, les traits mythologiques qui s'y rapportent et l'opinion qui paraît la plus admissible sur son explication. . . . On peut donc considérer cet Ouvrage comme devant être une source d'agrément pour l'amateur et d'instruction pour l'artiste: c'est, en effet, une mine inépuisable à exploiter; un sentiment exquis, une grâce enchanteresse, un style noble et pur, offrent, dans tous ces précieux restes, des modèles à suivre. [I, (v)-vii]

The volumes are, essentially, picture books. The first three are devoted to paintings, the fourth and fifth to bronzes, and the sixth to lamps and candlebra. In spite of the publisher's avowal, the plates do not preserve "la grâce, l'esprit et le sentiment des productions originales" quite as well as one might suppose, a certain awkwardness appearing in the draughtsmanship occasionally.

The library still has the first four of the six volumes acquired on Jefferson's original order made in the section on "Gardening. Painting. Sculpture. Music" of the want list. In addition it has a complete set bound in three volumes.

U. Va.
*DG70.H5P6.1804

101. Plumier, Charles.

L'ART / DE TOURNER, / OU / DE FAIRE EN PERFECTION TOUTES / SORTES D'OUVRAGES AU TOUR. / DANS LE-QUEL, / Outre les principes & élemens du Tour qu'on y enseigne méthodiquement pour tourner tant le / bois, l'ivoire &c. que le fer & tous les autres métaux, on voit encore plusieurs belles machi-/nes à faire des Ovales, tant simples que figurées de toutes grandeurs; la maniere de tourner le / globe parfait, le rampant, l'excentrique, les pointes de dia-mant, les facettes, le panier ou échi-/quier, la couronne ondoyante, la rose à raiseau, les manches de couteaux façon d'Angleterre, / les ovaires, la torse à jour ondée & goderonnée, les globes concentriques, la massuë à pointes, les / tabatieres barlongues de toutes figures, le bâton rompu, les cannelures, les écailles &c. & géné-/ralement toutes les methodes les plus secrettes de cet art, avec la disposition des Tours, &c. / OUVRAGE TRES CURIEUX, ET TRES NECESSAIRE / à ceux qui s'exercent au Tour. / *Composé en François & on Latin en faveur des Etrangers, & enrichi de prés de / quatre-vingt Planches.* / Par le R. P. CHARLES

PLUMIER, *Religieux Minime*. / A PARIS, RUE S. JACQUES, / Chez CLAUDE JOMBERT, au coin de la ruë des Mathurins, / vis-à-vis l'Eglise, à l'Image de Nostre Dame. / M. D. CCI. / AVEC PRIVILEGE DU ROY.

Folio. Engraved half title (1 leaf); two-color title page (1 leaf); dedication (3 unnumbered pp.); preface (13 unnumbered pp.); table of contents (3 leaves); licenses (3 unnumbered pp.); list of plates (1 unnumbered p.); text (1–187); engraved plates 1–65, 73, 80, and another 15 without numbers (making a total of 82), of which 1 is folding.

A slip of paper has been pasted over the words 'A LYON' and an illegible address on the title page.

The engravers were A. Bouchet, an eighteenth-century engraver at Lyon; T. Buys; Michel-François Demaso (1654–?), an engraver and painter who was born at Lyon; and Sébastien Le Clerc (Nos. 36 and 69).

Although Charles Plumier (1646–1706) wrote several works, the *Art de tourner* does not seem to have been a major one among his *oeuvre*. He entered orders at sixteen and became a botanist and traveler, having journeyed to the Antilles in 1689 and to America between 1693 and 1695.

This work, somewhat outside his interests, sets forth the process and the machinery necessary for turning a great variety of objects (see Plate CXIII). It is of particular interest for its advice on balusters, moldings, and finials, as well as the layout of the shop necessary for the operation. When he speaks of profiles he says: "J'appelle le profil un simple contour; & le bon goût cet agrément à la vûë qui d'abord satisfait l'esprit par le seul port & aspect de l'ouvrage. Veritablement il est bien difficile de pouvoir expliquer ce bon goût, & d'en établir des regles précises, puisqu'il dépend plutôt de l'idée & du genie des gens que d'aucune methode certain. L'oeil seul en droit prescrire les regles & les lois" (p. 133).

Jefferson sold his copy of the book to Congress. It was not ordered for the University. The library's present copy has been recently acquired, the gift of the Thomas Jefferson Memorial Foundation.

M

*TT201.P73.1701   Sowerby 1183

102. Potter, John.

Vol. I. Archaeologia Graeca, / OR THE / ANTIQUITIES OF GREECE: / BY / JOHN POTTER, D. D. / LATE ARCHBISHOP

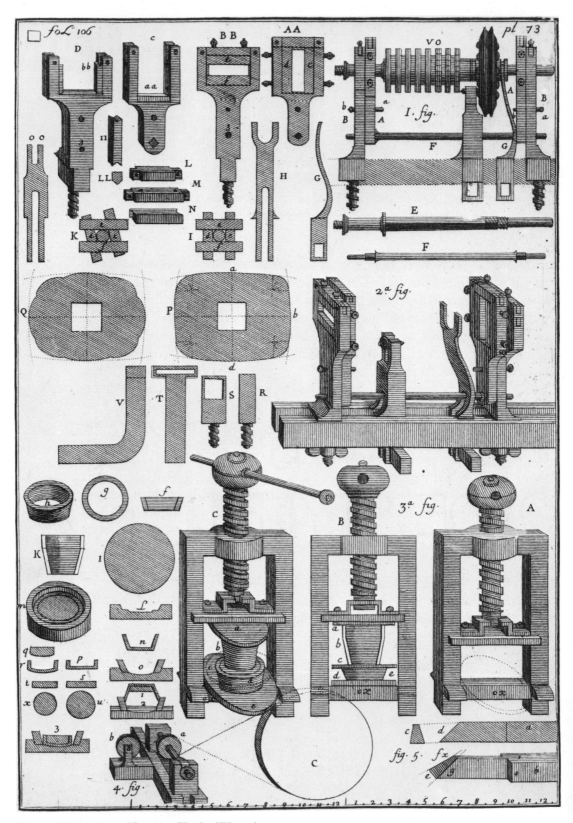

Plate CXIII. *From No. 101.* Tools (Pl. 73).

OF CANTERBURY. / A NEW EDITION; / WITH / A LIFE OF THE AUTHOR, / BY ROBERT ANDERSON, M. D. / AND / AN APPENDIX, / CONTAINING / A CONCISE HISTORY OF THE GRECIAN STATES, / AND A SHORT ACCOUNT OF THE LIVES AND WRITINGS OF THE / MOST CELEBRATED GREEK AUTHORS; / BY GEORGE DUNBAR, F. R. S. E. / AND PROFESSOR OF GREEK IN THE UNIVERSITY OF EDINBURGH. / IN TWO VOLUMES. / VOL. I. / *—Antiquam exquirite Matrem—*VIRG. / *—Vos exemplaria Graeca / Nocturna versate manu, versate diurna.—*HORAT. / EDINBURGH: / PRINTED FOR STIRLING & KENNEY; AND FOR LONGMAN, HURST, / REES, ORME, BROWN, & GREEN; J. NUNN; BALDWIN, CRADOCK, / & JOY; HARDING & CO.; J. CUTHILL; G. & W. B. WHITTAKER; R. / SCHOLEY; R. SAUNDERS; HURST, ROBINSON, & CO.; T. & J. ALLMAN; / W. GINGER, LONDON; WILLIAMS, ETON; AND PARKER, OXFORD. / 1824.

8vo. Engraved folding map; title page (1 leaf); life of Potter ([i]-xii); table of contents ([viii]-xv); directions for binding plates (unnumbered p.); text, with 9 engraved plates inserted ([1]–527).

Vol. II. Archaelogia Graeca, / . . . / VOL. II. / *—Simili froudescit virga metallo.—*VIRG. / *Quis reprehendit nostrum otium, qui in co non modo nosmetipsos hebescere et languere / nolumus, sed etiam, ut plurimus prosimus, enitimur?—*CIC. / . . .

8vo. Title page (1 leaf); table of contents ([i]-iv [misnumbered 'vi']); text, with 23 engraved plates inserted ([1]–422); [new pagination:] text of general history (1–112); index (4 leaves); index of Latin words (1 leaf); index of Greek words (6 leaves).

The engravings are by Daniel Lizars (d. 1812), who turned to engraving after his father's death in order to maintain his brothers and sisters, and by William Home Lizars (1788–1859), his son and pupil.

John Potter (1674?–1747), born in Wakefield, Yorkshire, was the son of a linen draper. He was educated first at the local grammar school, but entered University College, Oxford, at 14. He earned his B.A. in 1692, his M.A. in 1694, his B.D. in 1704, and his D.D. in 1706. He was ordained in the priesthood in 1699 and pursued a brilliant ecclesiastical career. He became Regius professor of divinity at Oxford in 1707, bishop of Oxford in 1715, and archbishop of Canterbury in 1737.

He was the author of many learned works. The *Archaeologia Graeca* was a rather early one, Vol. I being issued first in 1697 and its second volume in 1698. It subsequently went into many editions.

The text, which is concerned mainly with the laws, customs, and habits of the ancient Greeks, contains a few descriptions of temples and a few plates of illustrations of them from which architectural information may be gained.

Ordered by Jefferson for the University in the section on "History-Civil-Antient" of the want list, this set was in the library by 1828, but the original copies have not survived. The library's present set was the gift of R. L. Harrison.

U. Va.
*DF76.P86.1824

103. Preti, Francesco Maria.

Elementi di architettura. Venice, 1780.

Not now owned by the University.

Francesco Maria Preti (1701–74), born at Castelfranco, was an architect, mathematician, and tract writer.

Sowerby describes the *Elementi di architettura* as a quarto of thirty-five leaves with four engraved plates, all folding, and gives the above date for its first edition. Kimball (p. 99) says the book entered Jefferson's library between 1785 and 1789.

Jefferson sold his copy to Congress. It was not ordered for the University.

M
Sowerby 4202

104. *The Repertory of Arts and Manufactures.*

Vol. I.   THE / REPERTORY / OF / ARTS AND MANUFAC-TURES: / CONSISTING OF / ORIGINAL COMMUNICATIONS, / SPECIFICATIONS OF PATENT INVENTIONS, / AND / SELECTIONS OF USEFUL PRACTICAL PAPERS / FROM THE / TRANSACTIONS / OF THE / PHILOSOPHICAL SOCIETIES / OF ALL NATIONS, &c. &c. / VOL. I. / *LONDON:* / PRINTED FOR G. AND T. WILKIE, AND G. G. AND J. ROBERTSON, / PATERNOSTER-ROW: P. ELMSLY, STRAND; / W. RICHARD-

SON, CORNHILL; J. DEBRETT, PICADILLY; / AND J. BELL, NO. 148, OXFORD-STREET. / 1794.

8vo. Title page ([i]); table of contents (iii-vii); list of plates (viii); [new pagination:] note (i-iv); text, with 25 engraved plates inserted (1–432); index (433–40).

Vol. II. THE / REPERTORY / . . . / VOL. II. / . . . / 1795.

8vo. Title page ([i]); table of contents (iii-vii); list of plates (viii); text, with 24 engraved plates inserted (1–432); index (433–40).

Vol. III. THE / REPERTORY / . . . / VOL. III. / . . . / PRINTED FOR THE PROPRIETORS; / AND SOLD BY T. HEPTINSTALL, NO. 131, FLEET-STREET; / G. G. AND J. ROBINSON, PATER-NOSTER-ROW; P. ELMSLY, / STRAND; W. RICHARDSON, CORNHILL; J. DEBRETT, / PICADILLY; AND J. BELL, NO. 148, OXFORD-STREET. / . . .

8vo. Title page ([i]); table of contents (iii-vii); list of plates (viii); text, with 24 engraved plates inserted (1–432); index (433–40).

Vol. IV. THE / REPERTORY / . . . / VOL. IV. / . . . / 1796.

8vo. Title page ([i]); table of contents (iii-vii); list of plates (viii); text, with 23 engraved plates inserted (1–432); index (433–40).

Vol. V. THE / REPERTORY / . . . / VOL. V. / . . .

8vo. Title page ([i]); table of contents (iii-vii); list of plates (viii); text, with 23 engraved plates inserted (1–432); index (433–40).

Vol. VI. THE / REPERTORY / . . . / VOL. VI. / . . . / 1797.

8vo. Title page ([i]); table of contents (iii-vii); list of plates (viii); text, with 22 engraved plates inserted (1–432); index (433–40).

Vol. VII. THE / REPERTORY / . . . / VOL. VII. / . . . / AND SOLD BY H. LOWNDES, No. 77, FLEET-STREET / T. HEPTIN-STALL, NO. 304, HOLBORN; / . . .

8vo. Title page ([i]); table of contents (iii-vii); list of plates (viii); text, with 21 engraved plates inserted (1–432); index (433–40).

Vol. VIII. THE / REPERTORY / . . . / VOL. VIII. / . . . / PRINTED FOR THE PROPRIETORS; / AND SOLD BY H. LOWN-DES, NO. 77, FLEET-STREET; / G. G. AND J. ROBINSON, PA-

TERNOSTER-ROW; P. ELMSLY, / STRAND; W. RICHARDSON, CORNHILL; J. DEBRETT, / PICADILLY; AND J. BELL, NO. 148, OXFORD-STREET. / 1798.

8vo. Title page ([i]); table of contents (iii-vii); list of plates (viii); text, with 22 engraved plates inserted (1–432); index (433–40).

Vol. IX. THE / REPERTORY / . . . / VOL. IX. / . . .

8vo. Title page ([i]); table of contents (iii-vii); list of plates (viii); text, with 18 engraved plates inserted (1–432); index (433–440).

Vol. X. THE / REPERTORY / . . . / VOL. X. / *LONDON:* / PRINTED FOR, AND SOLD BY, THE PROPRIETORS, / NO. 182, FLEET-STREET; WHERE COMMUNICATIONS FOR / THIS WORK ARE REQUESTED TO BE ADDRESSED. / 1799.

8vo. Title page ([i]); table of contents (iii-vii); list of plates (viii); text, with 21 engraved plates inserted (1–432); index (433–40).

Vol. XI. THE / REPERTORY / . . . / VOL. XI. / . . . / PRINTED BY JOHN NICHOLS, / RED-LION-PASSAGE, FLEET-STREET, / FOR, AND SOLD BY, THE PROPRIETORS, NO. 182, FLEET-/ STREET; WHERE COMMUNICATIONS FOR THIS / WORK ARE REQUESTED TO BE ADDRESSED. / . . .

8vo. Title page ([i]); table of contents (iii-vii); list of plates (viii); text, with 19 engraved plates inserted (1–432); index (433–40).

Vol. XII. THE / REPERTORY / . . . / VOL. XII. / . . . / 1800.

8vo. Title page ([i]); table of contents (iii-vii); list of plates (viii); text, with 19 engraved plates inserted (1–432); index (433–40).

Vol. XIII. THE / REPERTORY / . . . / VOL. XIII. / . . .

8vo. Title page ([i]); table of contents (iii-vii); list of plates (viii); text, with 18 engraved plates inserted (1–432); index (433–40).

Vol. XIV. THE / REPERTORY / . . . / VOL. XIV. / . . . / 1801.

8vo. Title page ([i]); table of contents (iii-vii); list of plates (viii); text, with 20 engraved plates inserted (1–432); index (433–40).

Vol. XV. THE / REPERTORY / . . . / VOL. XV. / . . .

8vo. Title page ([i]); table of contents (iii-vii); list of plates (viii); text, with 20 engraved plates inserted (1–432); index (433–40).

Vol. XVI.   THE / REPERTORY / . . . / VOL. XVI. / . . . / 1802.

8vo. Title page ([i]); table of contents (iii-vii); list of plates (viii); text, with 16 plates inserted (1–432); index (433–40).

Of the engraved plates, a few are folding in each volume.

At the very beginning of this journal the publishers say:

OF the work now offered to the public, one of the principle objects is, to establish a vehicle, by means of which new discoveries and improvements, in any of the useful Arts and Manufactures, may be transmitted to the public; particularly to Artists, Manufacturers, and others, who, from various circumstances frequently attending those discoveries and improvements, (such as their being announced in a bulky or expensive publication, or in a foreign language) might otherwise have but little chance of ever becoming acquainted with them. Yet, though novelty will be regarded as an important consideration, the general utility of a subject will always be looked upon as one of equal if not of greater, consequences. [I, (new pagination:) i]

In the sixteen volumes there are some fifty-three articles that relate, mostly in a utilitarian way, to the fine arts. The architectural and building subjects include such things as heat, materials, bridges of iron, and colors. There are articles on stucco (III, 1); on fireplaces (IV, 226); on boring wooden water pipes or aqueducts, a problem which was to concern Jefferson quite a lot during the building of the University (IX, 45); on laying water pipes (X, 251); on water closets (XI, 237); on the making of bricks (XIII, 148); on bridges, warehouses, etc., without wood, i.e., out of cast iron (XIV, 145); on a speedy elevator (XV, 26); and on painting with milk (XV, 411). Count Rumford (see No. 109) has a good many articles, some on heat, which seems to have been a favorite subject with the *Repertory*.

The nonarchitectural and nonpainterly articles cover a considerable range. A typical one is "Specifications of Mr. UNWIN's Patent for rendering Soap-suds, after being used in scouring, &c. capable of serving again" (IV, 168).

Jefferson's order for the University in the section on "Technical Arts" of the want list called for fifteen volumes only. He was apparently thinking only of the first series, or else was ignorant of the fact that the journal ran much longer. As a result of the original order, the University actually received more than the sixteen volumes in its first years of operation. Of the first series of the original set a mutilated copy of the fourth volume survives. The library, however, has recently acquired a duplicate set of the sixteen volumes, the gift of the Thomas Jefferson Memorial Foundation.

U. Va.
*T1.R4

105. Roland Le Virloys, Charles François.

Vol. I.   DICTIONNAIRE / *D'ARCHITECTURE,* / CIVILE, MILI-TAIRE ET NAVALE, / ANTIQUE, ANCIENNE ET MODERNE, / *ET DE TOUS LES ARTS ET MÉTIERS QUI EN DÉPENDENT;* / Dont tous les Termes sont exprimés, / EN FRANÇOIS, LATIN, ITALIEN, ESPAGNOL, ANGLOIS ET ALLEMAND. / *Enrichi de cent une Planches de Figures en Taille-douce,* / POUR EN FACILITER L'INTELLI-GENCE, / AUQUEL ON A JOINT / *Une Notice des* ARCHITECTES, INGÉNIEURS, PEINTRES, SCULPTEURS, / GRAVEURS *& autres Artistes les plus celebres,* / *dont on rapporte les principaux Ouvrages.* / PAR M. C. F. ROLAND LE VIRLOYS, / ci-devant Architecte du Roi de Prusse, & depuis de l'Impératrice-Reine. / TROIS VOLUMES IN-QUARTO. / *TOME PREMIERE.* / *A PARIS.* / Chez les LIBRAIRES Associés. / M. DCC. LXX. / *AVEC APPROBATION ET PRIVI-LEGE DU ROI.*

4to. Half title (1 unnumbered p.); list of associated bookshops (1 un-numbered p.); title page (1 leaf); dedication ([i-ii]); preface ([iii]-iv); text ([1]–648).

Vol.   II.   DICTIONNAIRE / *D'ARCHITECTURE* / . . . / *TOME SECOND* / . . .

4to. Half title (1 leaf); title page (1 leaf); text (1–671).

Vol.   III.   DICTIONNAIRE / *D'ARCHITECTURE* / . . . / *TOME TROISIEME.* / . . . / M. DCC. LXXXI. / . . .

4to. Half title (1 leaf); title page (1 leaf); text (1–152); 99 engraved plates, of which 36 are folding and 5 are double; [new pagination:] half title ([1]); vocabularies in Latin, Italian, Spanish, English, and German ([3]–290); errata (291–98); licenses (1 leaf).

Charles François Roland Le Virloys (1716–72) was a French architect who was, at one time, architect to the king of Prussia.

His *Dictionnaire* has many handsome engravings illustrating its subjects (see Plate CXIV), including even the monograms of engravers. Its definition of the word *art* is especially useful for us since it includes the contemporary shades of meaning, which are not always understood today:

ART, f. m. Lat. *Ars.* It. & Esp. *Arte*, Ang. *Address*, All. *Kunst.*
Est en général ce qui se fait par l'industrie & l'address des hommes; c'est aussi la méthode de bien une chose: ce qui a donné lieu à une division de l'art, en *Arts libéraux*, & *Arts Méchaniques.*

 Les *Arts libéraux* . . . dont l'exercice est noble & honnête, sont ceux où l'esprit travaille plus que la main; tels sont l'Architecture civile, militaire & navale, la Peinture, la Sculpture, la Musique, la Poésie, la Médecine, &c.

 Les *Arts Méchaniques* . . . sont ceux où le corps travaille plus que l'esprit, comme la Maçonnerie, la Charpenterie, la Serrurerie, la Menuiserie, la Vitrerie, Plomberie, Marbrerie, Horlogerie, Fonderie, &c. [I, 109]

 Kimball (p. 99) says Jefferson bought his set between 1785 and 1789. It was bound in two volumes and was later sold to Congress. The book was not ordered for the University, whose present set has been recently acquired, the gift of the Thomas Jefferson Memorial Foundation.

M

*NA31.R6.1770   Sowerby 4206

106. Rondelet, Jean Baptiste.

Vol. I. TRAITÉ / THÉORIQUE ET PRATIQUE / DE / L'ART DE BÂTIR, / PAR J. RONDELET, / *Architecte de l'Eglise de Sainte-Geneviève; Membre du Comité / consultatif des Bâtimens de la Couronne, et du Comité / des Bâtimens Civils auprès du Ministre de l'Intérieur; / Professeur de Stéréotomie à l'Ecole spéciale d'Architecture; / de l'Académie des Sciences, Belles-Lettres et Arts de / Lyon, et de plusieurs autres Sociétés savantes.* / TOME PREMIERE. / PARIS, / CHEZ L'AUTEUR, ENCLOS DU PANTHÉON. / M DCCC XII.

4to. Half title ([i]); title page ([iii]); avant-propos ([v]-xvi); text, 1st book ([1]–228); text, 2d book ([229]–432); summary ([433]–42); list of subscribers (443–48).

Vol. II. TRAITÉ / . . . / TOME DEUXIÈME. / . . . / DE L'IMPRIMERIE DE GILLÉ. / M DCCC XIV.

4to. Half title (1 leaf); title page (1 leaf); text, 3d book ([1]–172); text, 4th book ([173]–345); summary ([346]–49).

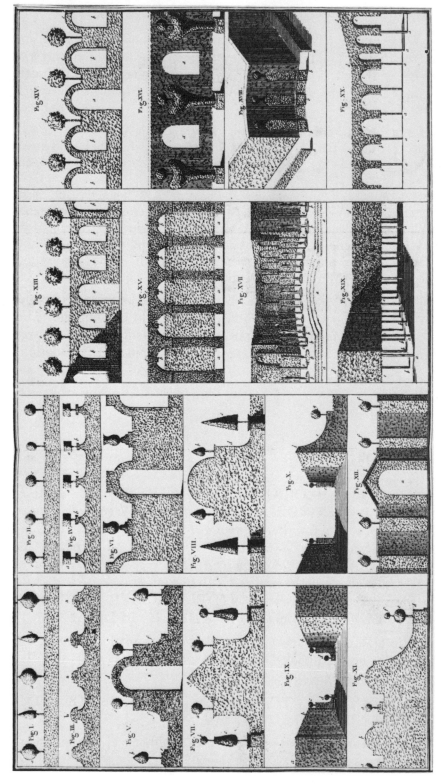

Plate CXIV. *From No. 105.* Topiary work (Vol. III, Pl. LXXXIX).

Vol. III. TRAITÉ / . . . / TOME TROISIÈME. / CINQUIÈME LIVRAISON. / . . .

4to. Half title (1 leaf); title page (1 leaf); text, 5th book ([1]–400); summary ([401]–12); supplement (2 leaves).

Vol. IV. TRAITÉ / . . . / TOME QUATRIÈME. / PREMIÈRE PARTIE. / CHARPENTE, AVEC 60 PLANCHES. / PARIS, / CHEZ L'AUTEUR, ENCLOS DU PANTHÉON. / M DCCC X.

and

TRAITÉ / . . . / TOME QUATRIÈME. / DEUXIÈME PARTIE. / COUVERTURE, MENUISERIE ET SERRURERIE, AVEC 31 PLANCHES. / . . . / DE L'IMPRIMERIE DE GILLÉ. / M DCCC XIV.

4to. Half title, [Part I] (1 leaf); title page (1 leaf); text, 6th book ([1]–382); [new pagination:] supplement (1–2); summary ([3]–7); errata (1 unnumbered p.); half title, [Part II] (1 leaf); title page (1 leaf); [old pagination:] text, 7th book (383–557); summary ([559]–62); errata (1 leaf).

Vol. V. TRAITÉ / . . . / TOME QUATRIÈME. / TROISIÈME PARTIE. / . . . / DE L'IMPRIMERIE DE FAIN, PLACE DE L'ODÉON. / M DCCC XVII.

4to. Half title (1 leaf); title page (1 leaf); text, 8th book ([561]–886); 10 folding tables; [new pagination:] appendix ([1]–80); summary ([81]–93); errata (1 leaf).

Vol. VI.   [No title page.]

4to. 92 engraved plates, of which 19 are folding, the rest double.

Vol. VII.   [No title page.]

4to. 96 engraved plates numbered XCIII-CLXXX and A-H, of which 57 are folding and the rest double.

The engravers were Adam; Aubertin; Louis-Pierre Baltard (see No. 40); Antoine-Joseph Gaitte (see No. 40); Hibon; A. Mosy; C. Normand (see No. 40); B. Rondelet; P. B. Rondelet; P. B. Rondelet, the nephew; J. E. Thierry; Thierry, fils; and Thierry, the nephew.

The subscribers included eighty-two architects, among them Jacques Guillaume Legrand, Jean-Nicolas-Louis Durand, and Johann Karl Krafft; thirty-two engineers also subscribed. One hundred and twenty-five copies were taken by the office of the Minister of the Interior, as well as fifty copies by the office of the Minister of War.

Jean Baptiste Rondelet (1743–1829) was the son of a master mason. He was educated by the Jesuits, by his father, and by Jean-François Blondel at the Académie d'Architecture. He then became an inspector for the Panthéon under Soufflot. After further study in Italy, he returned to become a professor of construction at the Beaux-Arts and a member of the Institute.

Rondelet says in his preface:

> Le but essentiel de l'art de bâtir est de construire des édifices solides, en y employant une juste quantité de matériaux choisis et mis en oeuvre avec art et économie.
>
> Cet art comprend deux parties principales, qui sont la *théorie* et la *pratique;* la perfection de l'art de bâtir dépend de la réunion de ces deux parties.
>
> La pratique, qui est la plus ancienne, est l'art d'extraire les matériaux, de les transporter, de les façonner et de les mettre en oeuvre pour l'exécution d'un ouvrage quelconque.
>
> La théorie est une science qui dirige toutes les opérations de la pratique. Cette science est le résultat de l'experience et du raisonnement fondé sur les principes de mathématiques et de physiques appliqués aux différentes opérations de l'art. C'est par le moyen de la théorie qu'un habile constructeur parvient à detérminer les formes et les justes dimensions qu'il faut donner à chaque partie d'un édifice, en raison de sa situation et des efforts qu'elle peut avoir a soutenir, pour qu'il en résulte perfection, solidité et economié. . . . Ce sont ces différentes connaissances que j'ai tâché de réunir dans mon ouvrage, afin d'en former un traité qui tout ce qui est essentiellement utile à un architecte, et en général à tous deux qui sont chargés de faire exécuter des travaux relatifs à l'art de bâtir.
>
> Ce nouveau Traité se divise en six livres; le premier commence par un exposé général de l'architecture. . . . Le second livre traite des compositions et des préparations que l'art a imaginé pour supplier aux pierres dans les pays où elles sont rare et difficiles à travailler. . . . Le troisième livre traite des constructions en pierres de tailles posées sans mortier, à la manière des anciens, et avec mortier comme les modernes. . . . Le quatrième livre traite de la coupe des pierres, et des principes de géométrie sur lesquels elle est fondée. . . . Le cinquième livre a pour objet l'application des principes de la théorie à la construction des édifices, pour leur procurer le degré de solidité qu'ils doivent avoir. . . . Le sixième livre traite de la traite de la charpente. [I, (v)-xiv]

Parts of this work were first issued in 1802, but it was not finally completed until Blouet contributed three volumes in 1847, 1848, and 1852. The plates are very handsome, especially those for framing and for marquetry. There are illustrations of Egyptian, Greek, Roman, and

Gothic buildings, and much information on stereotomy. Not only does Plate CLXXV (see Plate CXV) show the Coalbrookdale bridge, but several other *iron* bridges are shown. The second volume of plates illustrates chiefly carpentry, framing, and parquetry.

Jefferson ordered this set for the University, in the section on "Technical Arts" of the want list, but there is no record of its ever having been received. The University's present set, with Vol. IV bearing an earlier imprint than the other volumes, is a recent acquisition, the gift of the Thomas Jefferson Memorial Foundation.

U. Va.
*NA2521.R7.1817

107. Rossi, Filippo de.

RITRATTO / DI ROMA ANTICA, / NEL QVALE SONO FI- / GVRATI / I principali Tempij, Theatri, Anfiteatri, Cerchi, Nau- / machie, Archi Trionfali, Curie, Basiliche, / Colonne, Ordine del Trionfo, Dignità / Militari, e Ciuili, Riti, Cerimonie / & altre cose notabili. / *Ag- / giuntoui di nuouo le Vite, & Effigie de'primi / Rè di essa, e le Grandezze dell'Imperio Ro- /mano; con l'Esplicationi Istoriche de' / più celebri Anti- quarij* / IN ROMA / Appresso Filippo de'Rossi. M. DC. LIV. / *Con li- cenza de'Superiori.*

Small 8vo. Engraved half title (1 leaf); title page (1 leaf); dedication (1 leaf); note to reader (1 unnumbered p.); list of contents (4 leaves); text (1–413); sonnet (1 unnumbered p.); ode (1 unnumbered p.); colophon (1 unnumbered p.); 126 engraved plates inserted, and numerous wood-cut tailpieces.

Filippo de Rossi (fl.1654) was an Italian architect about whom not much is known. His *Roma antica* is, in actuality, a guide to ancient Rome with many illustrations, including one of the Pantheon.

Kimball (p. 99) says the book entered Jefferson's library between 1785 and 1789. His copy was sold to Congress. See Sowerby for a comment on Kimball's effort to redate it 1645.

Jefferson ordered it for the University in the section on "Architecture" of the want list, but there is no record of the library's having acquired it. The library's present copy is a recent acquisition, the gift of the Thomas Jefferson Memorial Foundation.

U. Va.
[Not yet catalogued]

M
Sowerby 4192

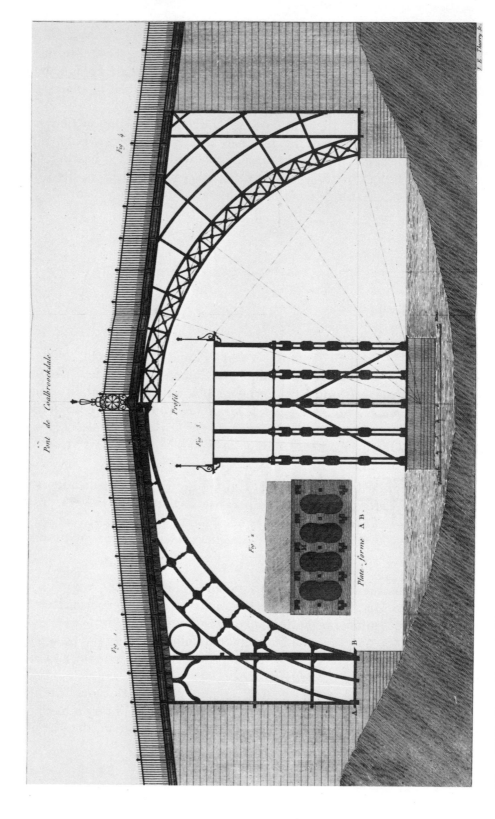

Plate CXV. *From No. 106.* "Pont de Coalbroockdale" (Vol. VII, Pl. CLXXV, p. 588).

108. Rossi, Filippo de.

RITRATTO / DI ROMA MODERNA, / NEL QVALE SONO EF-FIGIATI / Chiese, Corpi Santi, Reliquie, Indulgenze, Monasterij, / Hospedali, Oratorij, Compagnie de' Secolari, / Collegij, Seminarij, Palazzi, Fabbriche, Archi-/tetture, Pitture, Scolture, Librarie, Musei, Giar-/ dini, Fontane, e Ville sì dentro la Città, come / fuori, Pontefici, Cardinali, e Principi, che / l'hanno illustrata, & altre cose notabili. / *Distinto in sei giornate da diuersi Autori, con le Dichia-/rationi Historiche di quanto in' esso si contiene / in questa nuoua Editione accresciuto, e / migliorato in molti luoghi.* / IN ROMA, / Appresso Filippo de' Rossi, MDCLII. / *Con licenza de' Superiori.*

12mo. Engraved title page missing, but photostat inserted (1 leaf); dedication (2 leaves); index (12 leaves); text, with many engraved illustrations on the text pages ([1]–560).

For Filippo de Rossi, see No. 107. In spite of this book's title, many classical Roman buildings are illustrated, especially if they had been put to some contemporary use. The Pantheon, for example, is among this number.

Kimball (p. 99) says this book entered Jefferson's library between 1785 and 1789. Jefferson sold his copy to Congress. He ordered it for the University in the section on "Architecture" of the want list, but there is no record of the library's having acquired it during his lifetime. The library's present copy has been recently purchased, the gift of the Thomas Jefferson Memorial Foundation.

U. Va.   M
*DG62.5.R65.1652   Sowerby 4193

109. Rumford, Benjamin Thompson, Count.

Vol. I ESSAYS, / *POLITICAL, ECONOMICAL,* / AND / *PHILO-SOPHICAL.* / BY BENJAMIN COUNT OF RUMFORD, / KNIGHT OF THE ORDERS OF THE WHITE EAGLE, AND ST. STANISLAUS; / *Chamberlain, Privy Counsellor of State, and Lieutenant-General in the Service / of his Most Serene Highness the* ELECTOR PALATINE, *Reigning* DUKE / *of* BAVARIA; *Colonel of his Regiment of*

Artillery, and Commander in / Chief of the General Staff of his Army;
F. R. S. Acad. R. / Hiber. Berol. Elec. Boicoe. Palat. et Amer. Soc. /
The First American, / From the Third London, Edition. / *VOL*. I. /
BOSTON: / Printed by MANNING & LORING, / For DAVID WEST.
Sold at his Book-store, No. 56, / *Cornhill;* by EBENEZER S. THOMAS,
Charleston, S. Carolina; / and by SOLOMON COTTON & Co. *Baltimore.* /
March, 1798.

8vo. Engraved portrait ([ii]); title page ([iii]); dedication ([v-vi]); table
of contents ([vii]-xxiii); text, with 6 woodcut plates inserted between pp.
376–87 ([1]–464).

Vol. II. ESSAYS / . . . / *VOL*. II. / . . . / AUGUST, 1799.

8vo. Title page (1 leaf); note (1 leaf); table of contents (7 leaves); text,
with 11 engraved plates inserted, of which 1 is folding ([1]–496).

Vol. III. ESSAYS / . . . / A NEW EDITION. / Vol. III. / Boston: /
PRINTED FOR WEST AND GREENLEAF, / No. 56, CORNHILL. /
1804.

8vo. Title page (1 leaf); note ([i]-iv); partial table of contents ([v]-vii);
remainder of contents (3 leaves); text, with 8 engraved plates inserted,
of which 1 is folding, and with many woodcut figures in the text and 5
woodcut plates inserted ([1]–498).

Benjamin Thompson (1753–1814) was born in Woburn, Massachusetts.
He was educated in Woburn, Byfield, and Medford and showed an early
aptitude for drafting and mathematics. Although he was apprenticed to
an importer, he continued his scientific studies with the Rev. Thomas
Banerd of Salem. A Loyalist, he went over to England in 1776. He was
knighted there in 1784 and given the title of Count of the Holy Roman
Empire in 1791 by the Elector of Bavaria. He chose the name of Rumford, which was the old name of Concord, New Hampshire, to accompany this honor. He later married Mme. Lavoisier, the widow of the
physicist, but they were soon separated. He remained, however, in Paris
until his death.

Rumford's principal work was in the fields of food, thermodynam-
ics, the absorption of moisture, and gunpowder. He was a member of the
academies of Berlin, Munich, and Mannheim; he helped found the Royal
Institution in London; he was a foreign honorary member of the American Academy of Arts and Sciences; and he was offered the post of super-
intendent of West Point. When his will was read, it was found that he
had left a professorship to Harvard and $5,000 for a medal to the Ameri-
can Academy of Arts and Sciences.

His *Essays* were first published in 1796 and had an edition as late as 1880 as well as a reprint in 1969. The edition of 1798–1804 was the first American one.

Jefferson owned the first two volumes, later sold to Congress, and some of the chapters had a notable influence on him as a practicing architect; e.g., "Essay IV. Of CHIMNEY FIRE-PLACES, WITH PROPOSALS for Improving them to save FUEL; to render Dwelling-houses more COMFORTABLE and SALUBRIOUS, and effectually to prevent CHIMNIES from SMOKING" (I, [301]–87), first published in the *Bibliothèque Britannique* in Geneva in 1796 and again in the same year in Vol. I of the London edition of Rumford's *Essays, Political, Economical, and Philosophical*, and "Essay I. OF THE MANAGEMENT OF FIRE, AND THE ECONOMY OF FUEL" (II, [1]–196). From these essays Jefferson derived his peculiar but efficient forms for fireplaces so evident at Monticello (see Plates CXVI and CXVII).

In 1799 Wilson Cary Nicholas asked Jefferson for the dimensions of the Rumford fireplaces. Jefferson replied on May 2 saying he had used them "with great satisfaction," although he had changed Rumford's proportions of the back opening from one-third the front to one-half, which would allow him to burn wood rather than coal. There is also an undated memorandum on "Count Rumford fireplaces" (N-146b) in which Jefferson specifies the proportions of the fireplaces in the two "square rooms" of the first floor of Monticello, added after 1796.

All three volumes of the American edition were ordered by Jefferson for the University in the section on "Technical Arts" of the want list, but there is no evidence that they had been received by 1828. The library has acquired a set of the books in the twentieth century.

U. Va.   M
*Q113.R92.1798   Sowerby 1182

110. Sanvitali, Federico.

ELEMENTI / DI / ARCHITETTURA / CIVILE / *DEL PADRE* / FEDERICO SANVITALI / DELLA COMPAGNIA DI GESU. / *OPERA POSTUMA.* / IN BRESCIA. / Dalle Stampe di GIAMMARIA RIZZARDI. / MDCCLXV. / *CON LICENZA DE' SUPERIORI.*

4to. Engraved portrait (1 leaf); title page ([i]); dedication ([iii]-viii); text (1–105); advertisement (106); 4 engraved plates, all folding.

Federico Sanvitali (1704–61) was an Italian architect and mathematician. He divided his *Elementi* into three parts—"solidità," "comodità,"

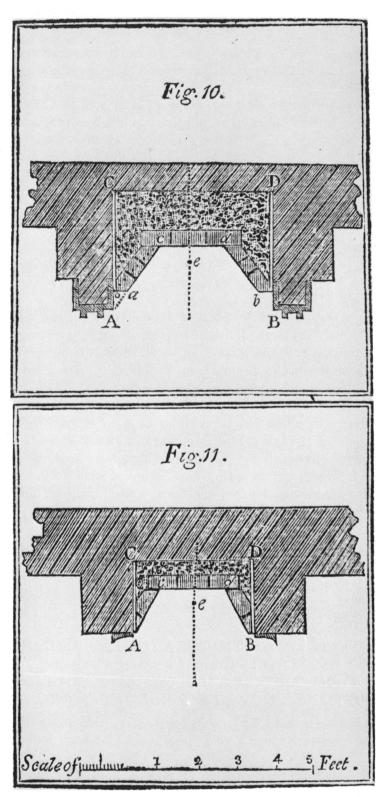

Plate CXVI. *From No. 109.* Plans of fireplaces (Vol. I, p. 385).

Plate CXVII. Fireplace in Martha Jefferson Randolph's bedroom, Monticello.

and "venustà." Each part is further divided into definitions and problems with their solutions given.

Kimball (p. 99) says Jefferson acquired this book between 1785 and 1789. His copy was sold to Congress. It was not ordered for the University, whose present copy has been recently acquired, the gift of the Thomas Jefferson Memorial Foundation.

M

*NA2515.S2.1765   Sowerby 4201

111a. Scamozzi, Vincenzo.

LES / CINQ ORDRES / D'ARCHITECTURE / DE / VINCENT SCAMOZZI, / VINCENTIN, / ARCHITECTE DE LA REPUBLI-QUE DE VENISE: / Tirez du sixième Livre de son Idée generale d'Architecture: / *AVEC LES PLANCHES ORIGINALES.* / *Par* AU-GUSTIN CHARLES D'AVILER, *Architecte.* / A PARIS, / Chez JEAN BAPTISTE COIGNARD, Imprimeur du Roy, / ruë Saint Jacques, à la Bible d'or. / M. DC. LXXXV. / *AVEC PRIVILEGE DE SA MAIESTÉ.*

Folio. Title page (1 leaf); preface (2 leaves); table of contents (1 leaf); Latin-French glossary of terms (1 leaf); text, with 37 engraved plates inserted (1–143).

Vincenzo Scamozzi (*ca.*1552–1616) was Italian. He had studied the works of Palladio (Nos. 91, 92a-d, 93, and 94) and finished the Teatro Olimpico in Vicenza after Palladio's death. *His L'idea dell'architettura,* from which this work is taken, was first published in Venice, 1615. It was translated into German and published in Nuremberg as *Grundregeln der Baukunst* in 1647; into French as *Oeuvres d'architecture* (Paris, 1685); and English as *The Mirror of Architecture* (London, 1690).

Augustin Charles D'Aviler (1655–1700) was a French architect who translated here only the sixth book of Scamozzi's work. It is, of course, the one dealing with the orders (see Plate CXVIII). He says in the preface:

Or ce qu'il y a de plus remarquable dans l'Architecture de Scamozzi, c'est qu'elle est fondée sur les raisons les plus vraysembles de la nature, sur la doctrine de Vitruve, & sur les exemples des plus excellens Edifices de l'Antiquité: sa maniere de profiler est Geometrique, mais elles est si contrainte par les figures dont il se sert pour décrire ses moulures, que la grace du dessein

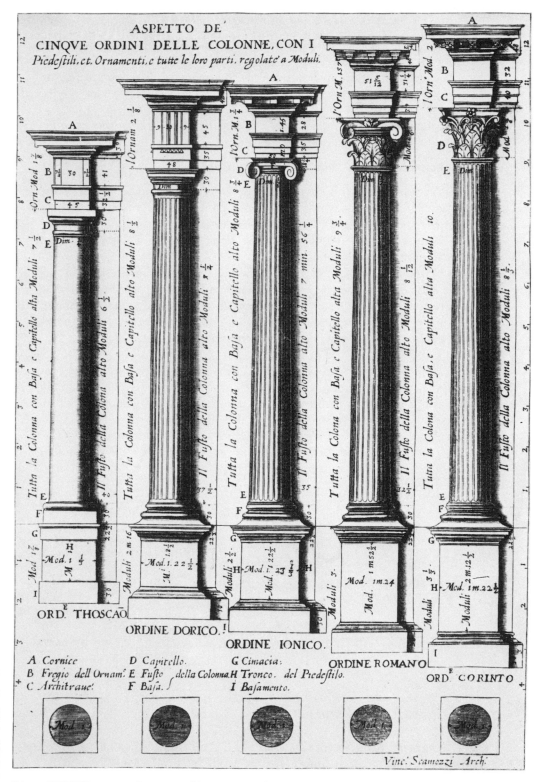

Plate CXVIII. *From No. 111a.* "Aspetto de cinque ordini delle colonne" (plate before p. 1).

n'y a presque point de part; ce qui a donné à cet Auteur la reputation d'avoir une maniere seche, qui provient de la quantité des moulures qui entrant dans ses profils, dont il y en a plus de rondes que de quarrées, & de ce qu'elles ne sont point meslécs alternativement, ainsi qu'il est necessaire pour les rendre plus variées. . . .

Parce qu'on s'est servi dans cette edition des planches originales, elles sont telles que Scamozzi les avoit fait graver.

Scamozzi begins by defining the term *order:*

LES Ancien Architectes sont dignes de loüange en beaucoup de choses; mais particulierement plus avoir trouvé & mis en usage les Ordres d'Architecture avec les ornemens de toutes les parties, dont le corps de chaque Ordre est composé. Pour traiter ce sujet avec methode, nous parlerons d'abord des corps entiers, & ensuite de leurs parties.

Le mot d'Ordre pris en general signifie beaucoup de choses; mais en Architecture on l'employe pour exprimer l'harmonie & la composition de diverse choses proportionnées les unes aux autres, & relatives & unies ensemble, comme sont les Piedestaux, les Colonnes & les Entablements, parceque toutes les parties & tous les membres ont une structure bien reglée & bien ordonnée. [P. 1]

La difference d'un Ordre à l'autre, consiste dans la proprieté des Modules, qui dépend de la juste distribution des grandeurs des parties, & dans la belle disposition de leurs membres, qui fait paroistre la solidité dans un Ordre, & la delicatesse dans un autre.

Ces choses doivent estre reglées par l'example de la Nature, qui a donné à l'homme né pour le travail des membres forts & robustes, & qui formé le corps de la femme avec une delicatesse convenable à son sexe. [P. 2]

Kimball (p. 99) says Jefferson acquired this edition of Scamozzi between 1785 and 1789. Sowerby points out that Jefferson had it bound with a Vignola (No. 123b), and a Serlio (No. 113). He sold his copy to Congress.

This edition was not ordered by Jefferson for the University, whose copy has been recently purchased, the gift of the Thomas Jefferson Memorial Foundation.

M

*NA2812.S2.1685   Sowerby 4178

111b. Scamozzi, Vincenzo.

THE / Mirror of Architecture: / OR THE / Ground Rules of the / Art of Building. / Exactly laid down by / *VINCENT SCAMOZZI,* / Master-Builder of / *VENICE.* / Whereby the principal Points of *Architec-*/*ture* are easily and plainly / demonstrated for the Benefit of all Lovers and Ingenious Practi-/tioners in the said Art. / With the Description and Use of a *Joint-Rule*, fitted with Lines for / the ready finding the, *Lengths* and *Angles* of *Rafters*, and *Hips*, and / *Collar-Beams*, in any Square or Bevelling *Roofs* at any pitch; and the ready drawing the *Archi-trave*, *Frize*, and *Cornice* in any Order. / With other useful Conclusions by the said Rule. By *John Brown.* / The SEVENTH EDITION. / Whereunto is Added, *A Compendium of the Art of Building.* Giving / a Brief Account of the Names, Natures, and Rates of all the Ma-/terials, belonging to the Erection, of an Edifice: And what Quan-/tity of each sort will be needful for the Building of any House. / Whereby Estimates, Valuations and Contracts may be made be-/tween Builder and Work-man, without Damage to either. And / how to measure the Works of the several Artificers belonging / to Building; and what Methods and Cus-toms are observ'd therein. / By *WILLIAM LEYBUBN* [sic]. / *LON-DON.* / Printed for *B. Sprit*, 1734.

Small 4to. Engraved portrait (1 leaf); title page (1 leaf); note (1 leaf); engraved plate and description (1 leaf); text of *The Mirror of Architec-ture*, with 51 engraved plates, of which 3 are folding, inserted (1–56); half title ([57]); text of *Compendium*, with 1 engraved plate inserted (58–[112]).

For information about Scamozzi, see No. 111a. Sir Henry Wotton (1568–1639), who wrote the *Compendium of the Art of Building*, was an English diplomat and poet. The curious spelling "Leybubn" on the title page is a misprint for Leybourn. William Leybourn (1626–1700?) was a mathematician.

The note for this book says:

There having been many Masters who have with great Care and Industry brought this Art to a great Perfection, among whom the Famous Master *Vincent Scamozzi*, Chief Builder of the Magnificent City of *Venice*, deserves to be plac'd in the First and Chiefest Rank by the consent of all Judicious Artists. Therefore for the benefit of our own Nation, and that it may be made most useful for all Artificers in Building, and Lovers and Practitioners in this most useful Art, and for the greater Splendor and Glory of Princes Courts, Gentlemens Seats, and whole Cities, especially the most Famous City of *London*, you have the larger book reduc'd into a smaller Volume, and the Author has given Parts [see Plate CXIX], divided into Minutes; whereby the Principal Rules of *Architecture* are made plain to ordinary Capacities, by *Joachim Schuym*, an Ingenious Artist.

Plate CXIX. *From No. 111b.* "The Ornament of A Corinthian Doare or window" (Pl. 35).

Kimball (p. 99) says this work may have entered Jefferson's library about 1778, and may have come from the sale of William Byrd's library. It should be noted that this is the seventh edition. Jefferson sold his copy to Congress.

The book was not ordered for the University by Jefferson. The library's present copy, the gift of the Thomas Jefferson Memorial Foundation, bears the bookplate of John Adam.

M

*NA2515.S3.1734 Sowerby 4179

111c. Scamozzi, Vincenzo.

OEUVRES / *D'ARCHITECTURE* / DE / *VINCENT SCAMOZZI*, / Architecte de la République de Venise. / NOUVELLE ÉDITION. / Revue & corrigée exactement sur l'original Italien. / A PARIS, RUE DAUPHINE, / Chez Jombert, Libraire du Roi pour l'Artillerie / & le Génie à l'Image Notre-Dame. / M. DCC. LXIV.

Large 8vo. Engraved frontispiece ([ii]); title page ([iii]); preface (v-xi); table of contents (xii-xviii); life of Scamozzi (xix-xxix); errata (xxx-xxxi); binding order for plates (xxxii); text ([1]–240); 82 engraved plates, of which 2 are folding, inserted, and several woodcut tailpieces.

The frontispiece (see Plate CXX) was engraved by Grégoire Huret (1606–70), who was born at Lyons. He worked there at first then went to Paris where he became a member of the Académie Royale de Peinture et Sculpture in 1663. The frontispiece is engraved "Oeuvres d'architecture de Scamozzi: A Paris chez Jombert rue Dauphine 1764." Although the frontispiece is undated, its inscription is obviously superimposed over the earlier engraving.

See No. 111a for information about Scamozzi. The book is Part III of the *Bibliothèque portative d'architecture* issued by Jombert. See No. 46 for further information about this series. The *Oeuvres* consists of three divisions devoted to the orders and one to houses, mostly palaces, by the author.

Jefferson ordered the book for the University in the section on "Architecture" of the want list, but there is no record of its having been received. The library's present copy has been recently acquired, the gift of the Thomas Jefferson Memorial Foundation.

U. Va.
*NA2810.S35.1764

OEUVRES·
D'ARCHI
TECTURE
de
S·CAMOZZI

A PARIS
chez JOMBERT
rue Dauphine
.1764.

Gr: Huret. f:

Plate CXX. *From No. 111c.* Frontispiece.

112. Scamozzi, Vincenzo.

DISCORSI / SOPRA / L'ANTICHITÀ DI ROMA / DI / VICENZO SCAMOZZI / ARCHITETTO VICENTINO / Con XL. Tauole in Rame. / IN VENETIA, / Appresso francesco ziletti. MDLXXXIII.

4to. Engraved title page (1 leaf); dedication, etc. (6 leaves); table of contents (8 leaves); text (42 unnumbered pp.); 40 double-page engravings.

The plates are signed either "Battista P" or "B. P. V. F.," as Giovanni Battista Pittoni, called Vicentino (1520–83), frequently signed his work. Pittoni was born and worked in Vicenza, producing chiefly landscapes with ruins or mythological subjects. Some of the plates carry the date 1581. For the engraved title page, see Plate CXXI.

For information about Scamozzi, see No. 111a. Each plate of this book is accompanied by a careful description written by Scamozzi of the ancient buildings shown. The plates give views of Rome, and are rather spirited and energetic (see Plate CXXII).

Kimball (p. 99) says Jefferson bought this book some time between 1785 and 1789. Sowerby, who had not seen a copy, describes it as a folio volume. Jefferson's own copy was sold to Congress.

He ordered it for the University in the section on "Architecture" of the want list, but there is no record of its having been received. The library's present copy is the gift of Julian P. Boyd.

U. Va.   M
*NA310.S3.1583   Sowerby 4194

113. Serlio, Sebastiano.

IL SETTIMO LI-/BRO D'ARCHITETTV-/RA DI SEBASTIANO SERGLIO / BOLOGNESE. NEL QVAL SI / *TRATTA DI MOLTI ACCIDENTI*, / *che possono occorrer' al Architetto, in diuersi luoghi, &* *istrane for-/me de siti, è nelle restauramenti, o restitutioni di case, è come* / *habiamo à far, per siruicij de gli altri edifici è simil'* / *cose, come nella* *sequente pagina si lege.* / Nel fine visono aggiunti sei palazzi, con le sue piante è fazzate, in diuersi modi fat-/te, per fabricar in villa per gran Prencipi. Del sudetto autore, / Italiano è Latino. / Sebastiani Serlij

DISCORSI
SOPRA
L'ANTICHITÀ DI ROMA
DI
VICENZO SCAMOZZI
ARCHITETTO VICENTINO
Con XL. Tauole in Rame.

INTER OMNES

IN VENETIA
APPRESSO FRANCESCO
ZILETTI. M DL XXXIII

Plate **CXXI.** *From No. 112.* Title page.

HAEC HABET TEMPLVM IOVIS TONANTIS, TEMPLVM, VT QVIDAM PVTANT, CONCORDIAE, ARCVM SEPTIMII TEMPLVM IOVIS STATORIS, ET PARTEM COLLIS PALATINI.

BATISTA F.V.

Plate CXXII. *From No. 112.* "Il Tempio di Giove Tonante" (Pl. 2).

Bononiensis Architecturae liber septimus. / *IN QVO MVLTA EX-PLICANTVR, QVAE ARCHITE-/cto variis locis possunt occurrere, tum ob inusitatam situs rationem, tum si quando instau-/rare siue restituere aedes, aut aliquid pridem factum in opus adbibere, aut caetera / huiusmodi facere necesse fuerit: prout proxima pagina indicatur.* / Ad finem adiuncta sunt sex palatica, ichnographia & orthographia variis rationibus descripta, quae / ruri à magno quopiam Principe extrui possint. Eodem autore. / Italicè & Latinè. / Ex. MUSAEO IAC. DE STRADA S. C. M. ANTIQVARII, CIVIS ROMANI. / *Cum S. C. M. Priuilegio:* & *Regis Galliarum.* / FRANCOFVRTI AD MOENVM, / Ex officina typographica Andreae Wecheli. / M. D. LXXV.

Folio. Title page (1 unnumbered p.); synopsis (1 unnumbered p.); dedication (3 unnumbered pp.); notes to readers (5 unnumbered pp.); licenses (1 leaf); text, with 120 full-page woodcut plates inserted (1–243).

Sebastiano Serlio (1475–1552 or 1554) worked first as a painter in perspective. He then studied with Peruzzi in Rome and thereafter worked as an architect. He died at Fontainebleau, where he had worked for some time.

His *Trattato di architettura* was published piecemeal, in haphazard order, and in various locations. Book IV was first with a Venice, 1537 edition; it was followed by Book III, 1540; Books I and II, 1545; Book V, 1547; Book VI, 1551; and Book VII, 1575 in Frankfurt.

Book VII contains illustrations of villas, palaces, fireplaces, city gates, window frames (see Plate CXXIII) and other details, multi-shaped plans, and various mannerist compositions. It should be noted that this book is one of the earliest of any of the architectural works in Jefferson's library.

Kimball (p. 100) says the *Settimo Libro* entered Jefferson's library between 1785 and 1789. Sowerby notes that it was bound with a Scamozzi (No. 111a) and a Vignola (No. 123b). Jefferson sold his copy to Congress. He did not order it for the University. The library's present copy is a recent acquisition, the gift of the Thomas Jefferson Memorial Foundation.

M

*NA2717.S51.1575

Sowerby 4176

Plate CXXIII. *From No. 113.* "Delle finistre & usci" (p. 77).

114a. Smeaton, John.

A / NARRATIVE OF THE BUILDING / AND / A DESCRIPTION of the CONSTRUCTION / OF THE / EDYSTONE LIGHTHOUSE / *WITH STONE:* / TO WHICH IS SUBJOINED, / AN APPENDIX, giving some Account of the LIGHTHOUSE on the SPURN POINT, / BUILT UPON A SAND. / BY JOHN SMEATON, *CIVIL ENGI-NEER*, F.R.S. / LONDON: / PRINTED FOR THE AUTHOR, BY H. HUGHS: / *SOLD BY G. NICOL,* / BOOKSELLER TO HIS MAJ-ESTY, PALL-MALL. 1791.

Folio. Title page with engraving ([i]); dedication ([iii-iv]); preface (v-vi); table of contents (vii-xiv); text (1–184); appendix (185–92); description of plates (193–98); 23 engraved plates, of which 1 is folding.

The engravers were A. or O. Birrel (fl.1786–1800), who worked at London; William Faden; John Record (fl. 1768–90), English; Henry Roberts (d. ca.1790), an English engraver who died at about age 80; Edward Rooker (see No. 3); Charles Reuben Ryley (1752–98), a native of London who became a history painter and an engraver; and Sam Ward.

Many of the plates in this work are dated; the dates range from 1761 to 1790.

John Smeaton (1724–92) was born near Leeds, the son of an attorney. He was educated at Leeds Grammar School and his father's office. He went to London to further his legal studies, but he abandoned the law and became a philosophical instrument maker. By 1750 he was a Fellow of the Royal Society.

The new Edystone Lighthouse (1756–59) was built of stone by Smeaton. Replacing an earlier wooden one, it made use of an ingenious system of interlocking stones in order to withstand the force of the waves. The engraving on the title page is a very romantic and Turneresque view (see Plate CXXIV).

Jefferson would have had a special interest in the chapter "Containing Experiments to Ascertain a Complete Composition for Water Cements; with Their Results," since he had at least one other work on the same subject (No. 42).

Kimball (p. 100) says this book entered Jefferson's library between

A

NARRATIVE OF THE BUILDING

AND

A DESCRIPTION of the CONSTRUCTION

OF THE

EDYSTONE LIGHTHOUSE

WITH STONE:

TO WHICH IS SUBJOINED,

An APPENDIX, giving some Account of the LIGHTHOUSE on the SPURN POINT,

BUILT UPON A SAND.

By JOHN SMEATON, *CIVIL ENGINEER*, F.R.S.

A   B   C

The MORNING after A STORM at S.W.

See § 17, u, w, 301, and Technical References.

LONDON:

PRINTED FOR THE AUTHOR, BY H. HUGHS:

SOLD BY G. NICOL,

BOOKSELLER TO HIS MAJESTY, PALL-MALL. 1791.

Plate CXXIV. *From No. 114a.* Title page.

1785 and 1789, but Sowerby quotes a letter of May 11, 1791, from Jefferson thanking Benjamin Vaughan for it. Jefferson's copy was sold to Congress. This edition was not ordered for the University. The library's present copy has been recently acquired, the gift of the Thomas Jefferson Memorial Foundation.

M

*TC375.S63.1791   Sowerby 4213

114b. Smeaton, John.

A / NARRATIVE OF THE BUILDING / AND / A DESCRIPTION OF THE CONSTRUCTION / OF THE / EDYSTONE LIGHT-HOUSE / WITH STONE: / TO WHICH IS SUBJOINED, / AN APPENDIX, / GIVING SOME ACCOUNT OF / THE LIGHTHOUSE ON THE SPURN POINT, / BUILT UPON A SAND. / BY JOHN SMEATON, CIVIL ENGINEER, F. R. S. / THE SECOND EDITION. / *LONDON:* / PRINTED BY T. DAVISON, LOMBARD-STREET, WHITEFRIARS; / FOR LONGMAN, HURST, REES, ORME, AND BROWN, PATERNOSTER-ROW. / 1813.

Folio. Title page ([i]); dedication ([iii-iv]); preface ([v]-vi); table of contents ([vii]-xiv); text ([1]–184); appendix ([185]–92); description of plates ([193]–98); 23 engraved plates.

For information about John Smeaton, see No. 114a. The contents of this edition are the same as those in the edition of 1791.

Kean's catalogue of May 1825 shows that the University library owned a copy of Smeaton's *Narrative;* the 1828 *Catalogue* annotation of the copy identifies it as likely to be this 1813 edition. Nevertheless, Jefferson included the *Narrative* in the section on "Architecture" of the want list. Since he owned a copy of the 1791 edition, it may have been that edition that he was ordering for the University. He is presumed, however, to have been a party to the acquisition of the 1813 edition and may simply have forgotten that the title had already been acquired. The library's copy did not survive, but a duplicate has recently entered the University collections, the gift of the Thomas Jefferson Memorial Foundation.

U. Va.
*TC375.S63.1791a

115. Society for the Improvement of Naval Architecture.

The Report of the Committee for Conducting Experiments of the Society. London, 1800.

Not now owned by the University.

Jefferson ordered a copy of this *Report* for the University in the section on "Technical Arts" of the want list, but there is no record of the library's ever having received a copy.

U. Va.

116. Spence, Joseph.

POLYMETIS: / OR, / An ENQUIRY concerning the / AGREEMENT / Between the WORKS of the / ROMAN POETS, / And the RE- MAINS of the / ANTIENT ARTISTS. / BEING / An ATTEMPT to illustrate them mutually from / one another. / IN TEN BOOKS. / By the Revd. Mr. SPENCE. / Omnes artes, quae ad humanitatem pertinent, habent quoddam commune vinculum; / & quasi cognatione quâdam inter se continentur. Cicero; pro Arch. / The Verse and Sculpture bore an equal part; / And Art reflected images to Art. / Pope, of Poetry and Statuary. / —Each from each contract new strength and light. / Id. of Poetry and Painting. / LONDON: / Printed for R. DODSLEY; at Tully's- Head, Pall-Mall. / M.DCC.XLVII.

Folio. Title page ([i]); preface (iii-v); list of subscribers (vii-xii); text, with 41 engraved plates, of which 2 are folding and 2 double, inserted ([1]–327); description of plates ([329]–36); index of figures ([337]– 40); classical index ([341]–51); index (353–61); binder's directions and errata ([362]).

The engraver for this book was Louis-Phillipe Boitard (d. after 1770), who worked in both France and England. His engravings for the *Polymetis* formed his most considerable work.

Joseph Spence (1699–1768) was born in Hampshire, the son of a rector. He was educated at Eton, Winchester, Magdalen Hall, Oxford, and New College, Oxford. He received his B.A. in either 1723 or 1724, took holy orders in 1724, and was given his M.A. in 1727. He was professor of poetry from 1728 to 1738 and was appointed Regius professor of modern history in 1742. He traveled abroad as companion to several noblemen. Dr. Johnson said of him that "his learning was not very great, and his mind not very powerful; his criticism, however, was commonly just; what he thought, he thought rightly, and his remarks were recommended by coolness and candour" (*DNB*).

He explains his interest in and the origin of his work by saying:

THE following work is the result of two very different scenes of life, in which I have happened to be engaged. The one, was my having been Professor of Poetry, in the University of Oxford, for ten years; and the other, my being abroad, for above half that space of time. The former obliged me to deal in Poetical Criticism; as the latter, (and particularly the considerable stay that I made, both at Florence, and at Rome,) led me naturally enough into some observation and love for the fine remains of the antient artists. As these two periods of my life happened partly to coincide, this put me on the thoughts of joining these studies together: and in doing this indeed I found very little difficulty; for, (as Cicero says in the motto to my book,) there is a natural connexion between all the polite arts: and consequently, they may rather seem to meet one another, than to have been brought together by any contrivance. [P. iii]

MY confining myself to the Roman writers only, or such of the Greeks as were quite Romanized; has been of great use to me, toward making the whole work the less perplexed. My chief stock was laid in from all the Roman poets, quite from Ennius down to Juvenal; and from several of their prose-writers, from Varro down to Macrobius. Had I gone lower, the authorities would have grown still weaker and weaker; and my subject would have been the more liable to have been confused. [P. v]

The book is cast in the form of dialogues between Polymetis, a fictitious person, and his guests who have retired to a villa. This edition is the first, but by 1777 it was in a fourth edition. As late as 1802 it was issued in an abridged form.

Jefferson knew this book as early as 1771, for he made a notation that year in a want list of works of art: "Diana Venetrix (see Spence's Polymetis)" (Kimball, fig. 79). Spence illustrates the Diana Venatrix in Plate XIII, Fig. IV (see Plate CXXV), and describes it as "DIANA VENATRIX: an Onyx; in Senator Buonaroti's collection, at Florence" (p. 330). He further says:

OF all the various characters of this goddess, there is no one more known, than that of her presiding over woods; and delighting in hunting. The Diana Venatrix, or goddess of the chace, is frequently represented as running on, and with her vest as flying back with the wind; notwithstanding its being shortened, and girt about her, for expedition. She is tall of stature; and her

Plate CXXV. *From No. 116*. Diana Venatrix (Pl. XIII, Fig. IV).

face, tho' so very handsome, is something manly. Her legs are bare; very well shaped, and very strong. Her feet are sometimes bare too; and sometimes adorned with a sort of buskin, which was worn by the huntresses of old. She often has her quiver on her shoulder; and sometimes holds a javelin, but more usually her bow, in her right hand. It is thus she makes her appearance in several of her statues; and it is thus the Roman poets describe her: particularly, in the epithets they give this goddess; in the use of which they are so happy, that they often bring the idea of whole figures of her into your mind, by one single word.

I BELIEVE there is scarce any one of all the little circumstances I have mentioned, which has escaped the poets. Her javelin and bow are as frequent in them, as in the antiques which represent her. Ovid takes notice of the shape of her leg; and Virgil is so good as to inform us, even what color her buskins were of.

THE statues of Diana were very frequent in woods. She was represented there, all the different ways they could think of. Sometimes, as hunting; sometimes, as bathing; and sometimes, as resting herself after her fatigue. Statius gives us a very pretty description of the latter; which I should be very glad to see well executed in marble, or colours. [P. 100]

Spence uses quotations from Ovid, Virgil, and Statius to annotate this passage.

The copy of *Polymetis* that Jefferson sold to Congress was this edition. The library's present copy is the one ordered by Jefferson in the section on "Gardening. Painting. Sculpture. Music" of the want list. The 1828 *Catalogue* entry indicating that the one Hilliard sent was an 1813 edition is an error, brought about by an accidental transfer of imprint from the preceding item.

U. Va.
*N5613.S7.1747

M
Sowerby 4230

117. Steiglitz, Christian Ludwig.

PLANS ET DESSINS / TIRÉS DE LA / BELLE ARCHITEC-TURE / OU / REPRESENTATIONS / D'EDIFICES EXECUTÉS OU PROJETTÉS / EN 115 PLANCHES / AVEC / LES EXPLICA-TIONS NÉCESSAIRES / LE TOUT ACCOMPAGNÉ / D'UN / TRAITÉ ABRÉGÉ / SUR / LE BEAU / DANS L'ARCHITEC-TURE / PAR / *Dr. C. L. STIEGLITZ.* / LEIPZIG / *CHEZ VOSS ET COMPAGNIE* / MOSCOU /*CHEZ RISS ET SAUCET* / 1800.

Folio. Engraved frontispiece (1 leaf); title page (1 leaf); dedication (1 leaf); note (1 leaf); preface (1 leaf); text ([1]–14); 113 engraved plates with descriptions inserted.

Note: There is some doubt that the Stieglitz is the proper identification of Jefferson's order for the "Portfeuille des artistes, ou dessins de chateaux, etc. (4to) Leips. 1800." for the University. In Jefferson's own memorandum on garden temples (N-182), he cites among various sources for a Gothic temple Plate XXX from the "Leipsic Portefeuille." Plate XXX in Stieglitz shows a residence whose central feature is an Ionic portico screening an apsidal entrance space. The only Gothic structures in the work are two pavilions shown on Plates LXXIII and LXXIV.

On the other hand, if one accepts the Stieglitz as the "Leipsic Portefeuille," there is an interesting, but undocumented, connection with Jefferson's architectural work, as pointed out below. Until further information is available it seems worthwhile to investigate the Stieglitz here.

The engravers were Gottlieb Böttger (fl.1796), who worked at Leipzig; Philibert Boutrois (fl.1775–1814), who worked in Paris; Coquet (see No. 40); Johann-Adolph Darnsteds, or Darnstadt (1769–1844), who was in Dresden by 1784, a member of the academy at Dresden by 1811, and who later worked in Berlin, Milan, and Copenhagen; Delettre; Gustave-Georg Endner (1754–1824), who was born at Nuremberg and died near Leipzig; Carl Frosch (b.1771), who worked in Leipzig; C. Frussotte (see No. 95); Antoine-Joseph Gaitte (see No. 40); Grünter; Heluis, or Helvis (fl.1799), who worked in Paris; Hullmann; Jean-Baptiste Liénard (1750–1807), French; Claude-Alexandre Moisy (1763–ca.1827), French; Piquet; Pierre Nicolas Ransonnette (see No. 40); Jean-Baptiste Réville (see No. 40); Johann Friedrich Schröter (1770–1836), a native of Leipzig and engraver to Leipzig University after 1813; and van Mael.

Christian Ludwig Stieglitz (1756–1836), a jurist and an architectural historian, was educated at Leipzig. He published nineteen works from 1787 until his death.

He says of architecture and the beautiful in architecture:

Les amateurs et surtont [*sic*] les connoisseurs recevront donc ici, un ouvrage, principalement dévoué à la beauté de cet art. [Preface]

La forme dans les productions de l'architecture est déterminée par le but de l'oeuvre, au quel il faut necessairement qu'elle corresponde, sans quoi elle seroit sans utilité. Ce qui fait que les formes dans l'architecture sont bien diférentes de celles qu'on observe dans le dessein, la sculpture et la peinture. [P. 2]

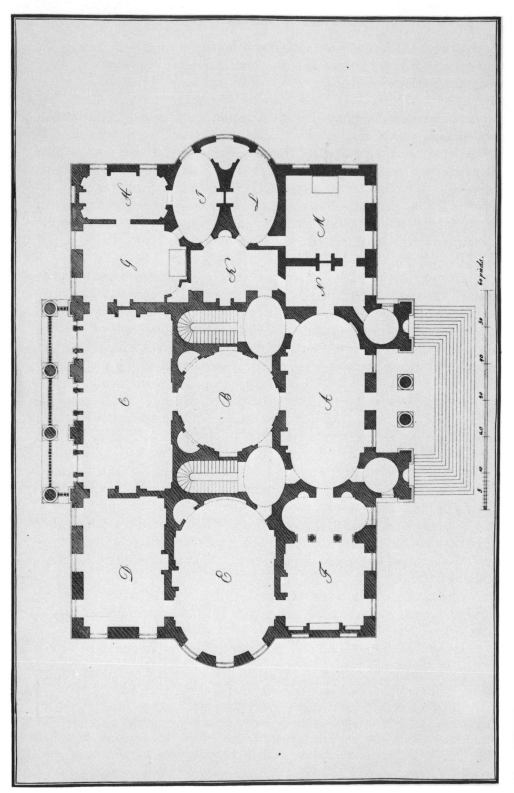

Plate CXXVI. *From No. 117.* Plan of a country house (Pl. XIII).

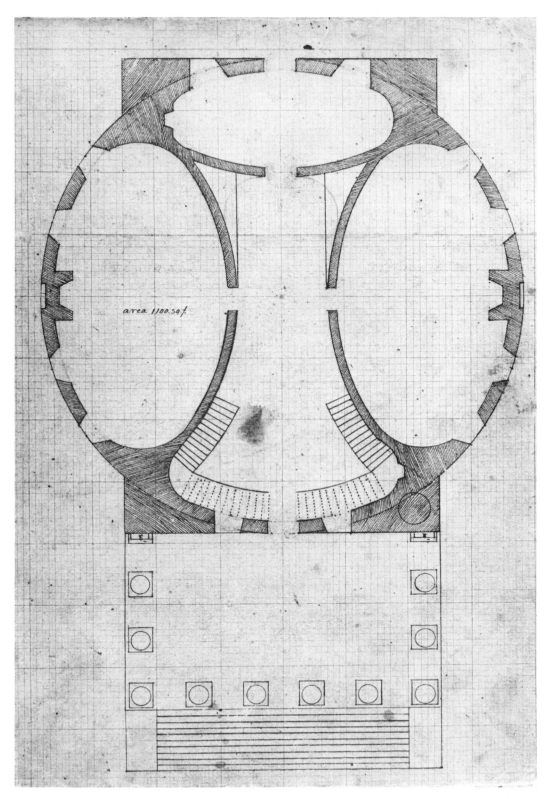

area 1100.5q.f.

Plate CXXVII. Jefferson's drawing for the plan of the main floor of the Rotunda, University of Virginia (N-330).

Le beau dans l'architecture, ne peut donc naître que de la beauté de la forme. Or le but de l'oeuvre déterminant cette forme, il ne sauroit lui communiquer aucune beauté. [P. 3]

Le beau nait premierement de l'ordre, qui exige que la disposition des parties d'un bâtiment ne soit rien moins qu'arbitraire, mais soumise absolument à de certaines regles, soit orizontalement, soit perpendiculairement. . . .

L'ordre et la symétrie sont donc dans un bâtiment deux titres pour prétendre à la beauté; cependant ils ne suffisent pas encore pour atteindre à la beauté des formes, c'est la proportion de qui on peut l'obtenir. [P. 4]

Comme il y a diverses especes de bâtiments, il y a aussi les divers caracteres, qui y conviennent, que l'artiste ne doit pas négliger par ce qu'ils exigent tout son attention. . . .

Voici donc les principales especes de caracteres: le *majestueux*, le *sérieux*, le *magnifique*, le *terrible*, le *gracieux* et le *merveilleux*. [P. 6]

This edition is the first of this beautiful neoclassic work of plates of designs for buildings, chiefly country houses. There were two later Paris editions, in 1801 and 1809. It seems to have been an international production with its Leipzig and Paris editions, its French and German engravers, its text in French, and its agents in Leipzig and Moscow.

Plate XIII shows a plan of a country house which has oval rooms fitted within a circular space at one end of the building (see Plate CXXVI). The house is described as follows: "La magnificence et la simplicité se trouvent réunies dans le bâtiment réprésenté ici. Les avant-corps des deux façades sont magnifiques tandis qu'une modeste simplicité caractérise les parties reculées." The layout of this house bears a striking resemblance to the oval rooms fitted into the circular plan of the Rotunda of the University of Virginia by Jefferson on his drawing for the Rotunda's first floor, a drawing dated about March 29, 1821, or before (see Plate CXXVII). The Stieglitz plan may have been a remembered prototype for the Rotunda plan, if, indeed, the volume has been correctly identified.

Kimball (p. 98) says Jefferson bought his copy of the "Portfeuille des artistes, ou dessins de chateaux etc." between 1800 and 1805. Sowerby pinpoints the date to June 21, 1805, quoting the correspondence between Jefferson and his bookseller Reibelt, and notes its cost as $14.40 with a binding cost of $2.50.

That Jefferson made his desideratum note for the University in the section on "Architecture" of the want list from a recollection of the copy he sold to Congress seems certain. That copy, however, has not survived. Hilliard never found a copy for the University, and Sowerby despaired of identifying the book. The University's recent acquisition of the

Stieglitz lessens the doubt that this is the volume Jefferson specificied, although he described it as quarto instead of folio. The library's present copy is the gift of the Thomas Jefferson Memorial Foundation.

U. Va.?   M?
*NA2600.S69.1800   Sowerby 4222

118a. *Stowe.*

STOWE: / A / DESCRIPTION / Of the Magnificent / HOUSE and GARDENS / Of the Right Honourable / George Grenville Nugent Temple, / Earl TEMPLE, / Viscount and Baron *COBHAM*, / One of the four Tellers of his Majesty's Exchequer. / Lord Lieutenant and Custos Rotulorum of the County of / Buckingham, / Colonel of the Militia for the said County; / And one of his Majesty's most Honorable Privy Council. / *Embellished with a* General Plan *of the* Gardens. / And also a separate Plan of the House, and of each / Building, with Perspective Views of the same. / A NEW EDITION, / With all the Alterations and Improvements that have / been made therein, to the present Time. / With the Description of the Inside of the House. / Where Order in Variety we see, / And where, tho' all Things differ, all agree,— / Nature shall join you, Time shall make it grow, / A Work to wonder at— perhaps a Stowe. Pope. / BUCKINGHAM, / Printed and Sold by B. Seeley. / Sold also by J. Fielding, No. 23, Pater-noster-Row, London; and / T. Hodgkinson, at the New Inn at Stowe. / M DCC LXXXIII.

Small 8vo. Folding engraved frontispiece (1 leaf); title page ([1]); list of plates ([2]); dedication ([3]); ode (5–6); text, with 12 engraved plates, of which 2 are folding, inserted (7–39); explanation of plans ([40]); 7 engraved plates of plans.

The plans were delineated by B. Seeley and engraved by Gabriel(?) L. Smith (1724–83), a Londoner who had studied both in London and Rome.

This little volume is a simple guidebook to a very early example of the "English garden," which was designed in part by William Kent (see No. 59a). The first edition of *Stowe* was published in 1745 or 1747.

The plates are important for their illustrations of meanders in plan (see Plate CXXVIII), a feature Jefferson used in his own garden at Monticello. Sowerby notes that Jefferson, when he visited Stowe, de-

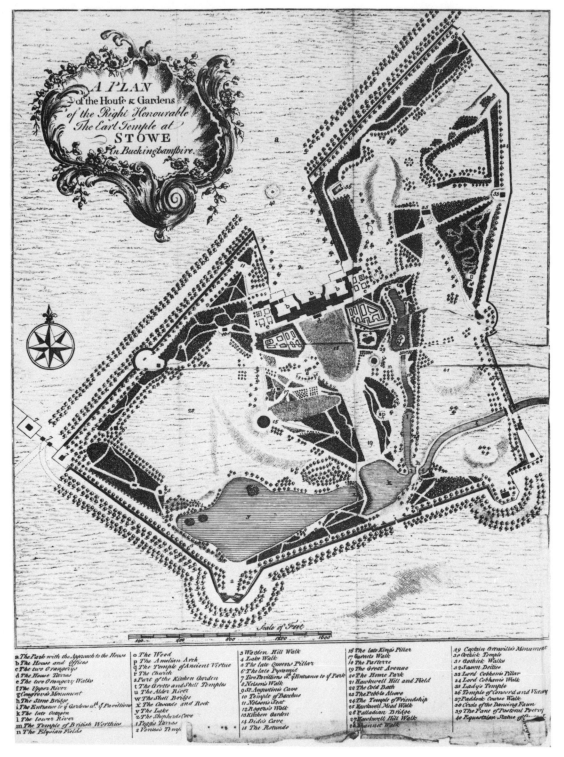

Plate LXIII. *From No. 118a.* "A Plan of the House & Gardens . . . at Stowe" (frontispiece).

scribed it in the following terms: "*Stowe* . . . 15. men and 18. boys employed in keeping pleasure grounds. Within the walk are considerable portions separated by inclosures & used for pasture. . . . The inclosure is entirely by ha! ha!"

The edition of 1783 is the one Jefferson sold to Congress. It was not ordered for the University. The library's recently acquired copy is the gift of the Thomas Jefferson Memorial Foundation.

M

*DA664.S8.1783   Sowerby 4229

118b. *Stowe.*

STOWE. / *A Description* / of the / *HOUSE and GARDENS* / of the / *Most Noble & Puissant Prince,* / *GEORGE-GRENVILLE-NUGENT-TEMPLE* / Marquis of Buckingham. / *Printed and Sold by J. Seeley, Buckingham, Sold also by* / *J. Edward's Pall Mall, & L. B. Seeley Paternoster Row, London* [1797]

4to. Engraved frontispiece ([2]); title page ([3]); list of plates ([5]); engraved plate ([8]); text, with 23 engraved plates inserted ([9]–63); references to plans ([64]); 7 engraved plates of plans, of which 2 are folding.

The plates were drawn and engraved by Thomas Medland (d. after 1822), an English landscapist and engraver. They bear the inscription "Published July 17th 1797, by J. Seeley, Buckingham."

For general information about *Stowe*, see No. 118a. This new edition has completely new engravings. The contrast in the descriptions of the same features of the gardens may be seen in the examples quoted here. No. 118a says of the Grotto (see Plate CXXIX) that it "stands at the Head of the *Serpentine* River, and on each side a Pavilion, the one ornamented with Shells, the other with Pebbles and Flints broke to Pieces. The Grotto is furnished with a great number of Looking-glasses both on the Walls and Ceiling, all in Frames of Plaster-work, set with Shells and Flints. A Marble Statue of Venus, on a Pedestal stuck with the same." The later No. 118b describes the Grotto (see Plate CXXX) as having "trees which stretch across the water, together with those which back it, and others which hang over the cavern, form[ing] a scene singularly perfect in its kind. . . . In the upper [end] is placed

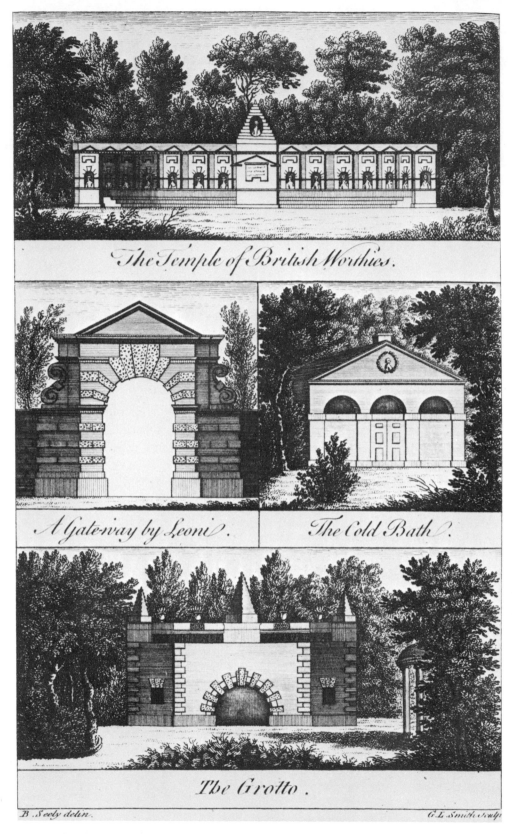

The Temple of British Worthies.

A Gateway by Leoni.

The Cold Bath.

The Grotto.

B. Seely delin.

G.L. Smith Sculp.

Plate CXXIX. *From No. 118a.* Garden pavilions (Pl. VI).

GROTTO.

Drawn & Engraved by I. Merkland Bayly on Street Westminster.

Published July 6th 1825 by I. Nodes Buckingham.

Plate CXXX. *From No. 118b.* "Grotto" (opp. p. 25).

a fine marble statue of Venus rising from her bath, and from this the water falls into the lower bason."

In 1825 Jefferson ordered only a single octavo volume for the University in the section on "Gardening. Painting. Sculpture. Music" of the want list. Under this specification the library acquired the 1797 edition. The copy received then survives.

U. Va.
*DA664.S8.1797

119. Stuart, James, and Nicholas Revett.

Vol. I.   THE ANTIQVITIES OF / ATHENS. / MEASURED AND DELINEATED / BY JAMES STVART F.R.S. AND F.S.A. / AND NICHOLAS REVETT. / PAINTERS AND ARCHITECTS. / VOLVME THE FIRST / LONDON / PRINTED BY JOHN HABERKORN, MDCCLXII.

Folio. Engraved portrait (1 leaf); title page (1 leaf); dedication (1 leaf); list of subscribers (3 leaves); engraved, folding map; preface ([i]-viii); engraved, folding plate; description of preceding plate (ix-x); text, with 70 engraved plates, of which 1 is folding, inserted ([1]–52); errata (1 leaf).

Vol. II.   THE ANTIQVITIES OF / ATHENS / . . . / VOLVME THE SECOND / . . . / PRINTED BY JOHN NICHOLS. / MDCCLXXXVII.

Folio. Title page (1 leaf); note to reader (i); introduction (iii-iv); half title (1 unnumbered p.); advertisement (1 unnumbered p.); folding, engraved plate; [new pagination:] explanation of preceding plate (iii-iv); double, engraved plan; explanation of plan (v-vii); text, with 72 engraved plates of which 1 is folding, inserted (1–46).

Vol. III.   THE ANTIQVITIES OF / ATHENS / . . . / VOLVME THE THIRD. / . . . / PRINTED BY JOHN NICHOLS, MDCCXCIV.

Folio. Title page ([i]); preface (iii-xviii); 2 engraved plates, of which 1 is folding; [new pagination:] description of plates ([i]-vi); folding, engraved plate; list of ancient place names (vii-xxv); text, with 72 engraved plates, of which 1 is folding and 1 is double, inserted (1–64); errata (1 leaf).

Vol. IV. THE ANTIQVITIES OF / ATHENS / . . . / VOLVME THE FOVRTH. / LONDON: / PRINTED BY T. BENSLEY, FOR J. TAYLOR, HIGH-HOLBORN, MDCCCXVI.

Folio. Engraved portrait (1 leaf); title page (1 leaf); preface ([i]-xvii); notes (xviii-xx); memoirs of Stuart and Revett (xxi-xxxi); text, with 87 engraved plates inserted ([1]–36); errata (37–42); index (43–44).

Vol. V. [Outside this study.]

The engravers for Vol. I were James Basire (see No. 3); I. or J. Cole (fl.1750), English; Pierre Fourdrinier (see No. 21); James Green (1755–ca.1800), English; Charles Grignion (see No. 23); Charles Knight (1743–1826), who worked in London; Conrad Martin Metz (1749–1827), who was born in Bonn, studied with Bartolozzi (see No. 3) in London, and went to Rome in 1802; W. Palmer (fl.1750), English; Edward Rooker (see No. 3); Sir Robert Strange (1721–92), who studied in Edinburgh and in Paris with Le Bas, and who later went to Italy and became a member of the academies of Rome, Florence, Bologna, Parma, and Paris; and A. Walker (see No. 3).

The engravers for Vol. II were François-Germain Aliament (1734–90), who had studied with his brother Jacques and had set up a school in London; Daniel Lerpinière (1745–85), of French descent but born in London; James Newton (1748–ca.1804), pupil of his father Edward; William Sharp (1749–1824), who worked in London; and Samuel Smith (1745–1808), who also worked in London.

The engravers for Vol. III were Lerpinière; Newton; William Blake (1757–1827), who studied with James Basire (see No. 3), Ryland, and at the Academy of Paris in London and who later became known for his beautiful, mystical books; John Hall (1739–97), who was engraver to George III; John Harding (fl.1790), English; John Landseer (1769–1852), who worked in London and was the father of the more famous Edwin; Wilson Lowry (see No. 32); Thomas Medland; John Record (see No. 114a); William Skelton (1763–1848), pupil of James Basire and William Sharp; and John Walker (fl.1794), a nephew of Anthony Walker (see No. 3).

The engravers for Vol. IV were Lerpiniere; Record; Thomas Baxter (1782–1821), English; James Davis; Peter Mazell (see No. 63); Henry Moses (see No. 47); Henry Taylor; James Taylor (1745–97), London; and Edmond Turrell (fl.1815–20), London.

The subscribers' list in Vol. I contains the names of three builders, two carpenters, eleven doctors, twenty-three ecclesiastics, one joiner, two lawyers, ten painters, one plasterer, and three sculptors. The architects listed are John Adam, Robert Adam, James Adam, Lancelot Brown, Henry Flitcroft, David Hiorne, James Payne, William Robinson, John Smeaton, and Vanvitelli. James Basiere, the engraver; David Garrick, the actor; and Uvedale Price, the writer on taste, were also subscribers.

James Stuart (1713–88) was born in London, the son of a mariner who died early, leaving his son to support the family by painting fans for Louis Goupy, many with classical scenes. Stuart was given a premium at age thirteen or fourteen at the Society of Arts for a self-portrait. He went to Rome in 1741 where he met Revett. They went on to Athens in 1750–51 and returned to England in 1755. Stuart was F.R.S. and F.S.A., as well as a member of the Society of Dilettanti.

Nicholas Revett (1720–1804) was born in Suffolk. He was in Rome by 1742, studying painting. After the publication of the first volume of the *Antiquities of Athens*, he quarreled with Stuart, sold his rights to the publication to Stuart, and had no connection with succeeding volumes. He went to Asia Minor in 1764–66 and later published *The Antiquities of Iona*, Vol. I, 1769, and Vol. II, 1797.

Stuart tells why and how he and Revett went to Athens and how they divided their labors on the book:

THE ruined Edifices of Rome have for many years engaged the attention of those, who apply themselves to the study of Architecture. . . . Many representations of them . . . have been published. . . .

But altho' the World is enriched with Collections of this sort already published, we thought it would be a Work not unacceptable to the lovers of Architecture, if we added to those Collections, some Examples drawn from the Antiquities of Greece. [I, (i)]

We were then at Rome, where we had already employed 6 or 7 years in the study of Painting, and there it was that towards the end of the year 1748, I first drew up a brief account, of our motives for undertaking this Work, of the form we proposed to give it, and of the subjects of which we then hoped to compose it. [I, v]

We did not set out from Rome till the month of March 1750. . . . On the 19 January, 1751, we embarked on board an English Ship [from Venice]. . . . We arrived safely on March 11, N.S. at Corinth . . . and on the 17 at night anchored in the Pireus. [I, vi-vii]

The Architectural Prints compose, I imagine, the most useful and interesting part of this Work; and at the same time, that, which I apprehend is least liable to censure: for our joint endeavours were here diligently employed, and my Friend Mr. Revett wholly confined his attention to this part. [I, vii]

The Antiquities of Athens must have one of the longest publishing histories on record, with its first planning in 1748, its first volume appearing in 1762, and its fifth, and last (though it was earlier thought the fourth would be the last), not being issued until 1830. There was a second edition of Vols. I-III between 1825 and 1830 and a third edition of these three volumes in 1841. The editor of Vol. IV says:

It has been the singular fate of this work that only the first volume was published by the author, and that each succeeding one has been ushered into the world by a different editor. The first appeared in 1762; the second bears 1787 on the title page, but was not published till after Stuart's death, which happened in February, 1788, when the arrangements were completed by Mr. Newton; and in 1794, Mr. Revely appears as the editor of the third. After a further interval of twenty years, the papers put into my hands by Mr. Taylor, enable me to offer to the public the fourth and last volume. [IV, (i)]

The appearance of Vol. I caused what was called "Grecian gusto" to reign supreme. In spite of Le Roy (No. 73), who did not visit Athens until 1754 after Stuart and Revett had finished there, but who published *Les ruines* in 1758, and in spite of Dalton's inaccurate views of Athens of 1749, Stuart and Revett "may fairly claim to have been pioneers of classical archaeology" and their work to have been "the commencement of the serious study of Classical art and antiquities" (*DNB*). Nor can one underestimate the importance of their plates detailing the various buildings discussed (see Plates CXXXI and CXXXII), especially those dealing with the columns of the Parthenon and Theseum (see Plate CXXXIII; compare with Plate XCI), for they seem to have been the direct ancestors of the books treating of the Greek orders of many later authors, both in England and the United States.

Jefferson owned only the first volume of this work, which Kimball (p. 100) says came into his collections between 1785 and 1789, but he does not seem to have been much influenced by it. He later sold it to Congress.

Jefferson ordered the first four volumes, all that had been published before his death, for the University in the section on "Architecture" of the want list. There is no record, however, that the library acquired a set before 1828. The library's present set of all 5 volumes was the gift of G. Harris.

U. Va.   M
*NA280.S9.1762   Sowerby 4190

120. Toulongeon, François Emmanuel Toulongeon, vicomte de.

Vol. I. MANUEL / DU / MUSÉUM FRANÇAIS, / Avec une description analytique et raisonné de / chaque tableau, indiqué au trait par

Plate CXXXI. *From No. 119.* "A View of the Tower of the Winds in its present Condition" (Vol. I, Chap. III, Pl. I).

Plate CXXXII. *From No. 119.* "The Elevation of the Tower of the Winds" (Vol. I, Chap. III, Pl. III).

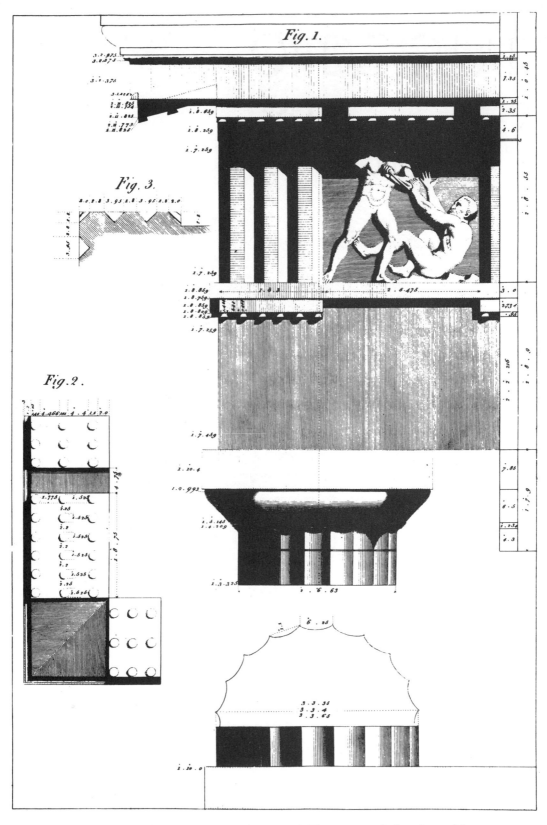

Plate CXXXIII. *From No. 119.* "Of the Temple of Theseus: capital and entabla-ture" (Vol. III, Chap. I, Pl. VI).

une gra-/vure à l'eau forte, tous classés par *Écoles*, et / par *OEuvre* des grands artistes. / PAR F. E. T. M. D. L. I. N. / A PARIS, / Chez TREUTTEL et WÜRTZ, Libraires, / quai Voltaire, no. 2. / Et à STRASBOURG, grand'rue, no. 15. / AN X.–1802.

and

MANUEL / . . . / *ÉCOLE ITALIENNE.* / OEUVRE DU *DOMINI-QUIN* / ET DE *SPADA.* / . . . / AN XI.–1802.

8vo. Title page (1 leaf); introduction (3 leaves); text, with 18 engraved plates inserted (34 leaves); half title for "Seconde Livraison" (1 leaf); title page (1 leaf); text, with 20 engraved plates inserted (35 leaves).

Vol. II. MANUEL / . . . / *ÉCOLE FLAMANDE.* / OEUVRE DE *RUBENS.* / . . . / AN XI.–1803.

and

MANUEL / . . . / *ÉCOLE ITALIENNE.* / OEUVRE DE *RAPH-AËL.* / . . . / AN XII.–1803.

8vo. Half title for "Troisième Livraison" (1 unnumbered p.); advertisement (1 unnumbered p.); title page (1 leaf); text, with 48 engraved plates inserted (64 leaves); half title for "Quatrième Livraison" (1 unnumbered p.); advertisement (1 unnumbered p.); title page (1 leaf); text, with 39 engraved plates inserted (74 leaves); errata (1 leaf).

Vol. III. MANUEL / . . . / *ÉCOLE FRANÇAISE.* / OEUVRE DE *LEBRUN.* / . . . / AN XII.–1804.

and

MANUEL / . . . / *ÉCOLE FLAMANDE.* / OEUVRE / DE VAN OSTADE, / DE GERARD DOW, / DE VAN DYK. / A PARIS, / Chez TREUTTEL et WÜRTZ, Libraires; / Et à STRASBOURG, même adresse / AN XII.–1804.

8vo. Title page (1 leaf); text, with 34 engraved plates, of which 3 are folding, inserted (50 leaves); half title for "Sixième Livraison" (1 leaf); title page (1 leaf); text, with 49 engraved plates inserted (67 leaves).

Vol. IV. MANUEL / . . . / *ÉCOLE FRANÇAISE.* / OEUVRE DE VERNET. / A PARIS / Chez TREUTTEL et WÜRTZ, Libraires, / rue de Lille, no. 703; / Et à STRASBOURG, même Maison de Commerce. / AN XIII.–1805.

and

MANUEL / . . . / *ÉCOLE VÉNITIENNE.* / OEUVRE DU TITIEN. / A PARIS / Chez TRUETTEL et WÜRTZ, Libraires, / rue de Lille, derrière les Théatins. / . . . / 1805.

8vo. Half title for "Septième Livraison" (1 unnumbered p.); advertisement (1 unnumbered p.); title page (1 leaf); text ([1]–72); 29 engraved plates; half title for "Huitième Livraison" (1 unnumbered p.); advertisement (1 unnumbered p.); title page (1 leaf); text, with 25 engraved plates, of which 1 is folding, inserted (37 leaves).

Vol. V. MANUEL / . . . / *ÉCOLE ITALIENNE.* / OEUVRE DE PAUL VÉRONÈSE. / . . . / rue de Lille, no. 17, derrière les Théatins. / . . . / 1806.

and

MANUEL / . . . / *ÉCOLE FRANÇAISE.* / OEUVRE DE LESUER. / *GALERIE D SAINT-BRUNO*, / Exposée au Luxembourg; décrite et analysée par M. L. R. F. / . . . / 1808.

8vo. Half title for "Neuvième Livraison" (1 unnumbered p.); advertisement (1 unnumbered p.); title page (1 leaf); text, with 17 engraved plates, of which 1 is folding, inserted (37 leaves); prospectus (1 leaf); half title for "Galerie de Saint-Bruno" (1 unnumbered p.); advertisement (1 unnumbered p.); title page (1 leaf); text, with 26 engraved plates, of which 2 are folding, inserted (47 leaves).

François Emmanuel Toulongeon, vicomte de Toulongeon (1748–1812), had a military and political career although he cultivated the sciences, letters, and the arts. He became a member of the Institute des Sciences Morales et Politiques in 1797, and he left many literary works.

He gives his definition of beauty in his introduction in Vol. I:

LA beauté dans les arts est ou naturelle ou de convention; celle-ci tient à la perfection du travail, à certaines règles établis et convenues, que l'étude a fait deriver de la nature corrigée et embellie; c'est ce qu'on appelle le Beau-idéal, qui souvent n'est pas à la portée du vulgaire, dont le mérite peut être perdu pour celui qui n'a pas appris à le connaître et à l'apprécier. . . . Les beautés naturelles sont l'imitation vraie de la nature; elles sont d'un effet sûr et général.

Sowerby notes that Jefferson purchased his copy of this work in 1805. This set was in four volumes, all that were published in 1805, but was later bound into three.

Jefferson made direct use of it in at least six instances during the compilation of his final catalogue of his collections of painting and sculpture, a catalogue in which he gave the location of each object at Monticello, and which is now at the University of Virginia. These instances were:

[Parlor, middle tier.] 36. A Transfiguration. Copied from Raphael. Whole length figures of 6.I. On Canvas. The subject Matt. 17.1.–8. See 4. Manuel du Museum. Pl. 1. [See Plate CXXXIV]

[Parlor, lower tier.] 51. A Descent on Copper. The Christ is of about 10.I. Behind him is the virgin weeping. On each side angels. It is copied from Vandyke by Diepenbec. See Rubens management of the same subject. 3. Manuel du Museum. 483. [See Plate CXXXV]

[Dining room, upper tier.] 68. Diogenes in the market of Athens. Laertius in the life of this philosopher tells us that appearing in a public place in midday with a lanthorn in his hand he was asked by the crowd what he was doing? He answered he was seeking if he could find a man. This anecdote is the subject of this piece. It is a groupe [*sic*] of 6. figures, half lengths, of full size on canvas. Copied from Rubens. See 3. Manuel du Museum. 495. [See Plate CXXXVI]

[Dining room, upper tier.] 72. An Ascension of St. Paul into the third heaven. From Dominiquin. On canvas. The original is in the collection of the king of France. The principal figure is 22.I. The head is inspired. The Saint sees the heavens open and expands his arms towards the glorious light he sees. He is supported by angels. The groupe is no longer ascending, but in a state of rest to give him time to contemplate the scene. See 2 Manuel. 778. [See Plate CXXXVII]

[Dining room, upper tier.] 73. The holy family copied from Raphael on canvas. The figures are whole lengths. the Virgin & infant Jesus, Joseph, Elizabeth & the infant John & 2 angels. See the 4. Manuel du Museum Pl. 3. [See Plates CXXXVIII and CXXXIX]

[Dining room, upper tier.] 75. A Flagellation of Christ, a groupe of 10 figures, the principal of which is 21.I. He is bound to a post, two soldiers whipping him with bundles of rods, and a third binding up another bundle. On the right are the Superintendants & Spectators. The subject Matt. 27.26. It is copied on wood from Devoes. See the same subject treated very similarly by Rubens. 3. Manuel du Musee. 501. [See Plate CXL]

As an example of the way Jefferson was influenced by the *Manuel*, compare item 72 above with Toulongeon's text for the *Ascension of St. Paul:*

Ce tableau paraît avoir inspiré celui de l'assomption de la Vierge par le Poussin. Le Dominiquin avait pensé le premier qu'une scène qui se passe au troisième ciel doit être d'une couleur nette, brillante et point vaporeuse. La tête de St.-Paul est inspirée; il voit les cieux ouverts et tend les bras vers la lumière glorieuse qu'il aperçoit: il faut étudier le bel engencement de toutes les différentes parties de la figure de St.-Paul. La belle disposition des draperies; la manière savante dont les anges sont placés; le groupe ne monte plus;

Plate CXXXIV. *From No. 120.* "*La Transfiguration.* Raphael" (Vol. II, Pt. 4, opp. sig. b-5).

Plate CXXXV. *From No. 120. "J.-C. mort sus les genoux de sa Mère.* Rubens"
(Vol. I, Pt. 3, No. 483).

Plate CXXXVI. *From No. 120. "Diogène cherchant un homme.* Rubens" (Vol. II, Pt. 3, No. 495).

Plate CXXXVII. *From No. 120. "Le Ravissement de Saint Paul. Dominiquin"*
(Vol. I, Pt. 2, No. 778).

Plate CXXXVIII. *From No. 120. "La Ste. famille de Jèsus Christ.* Raphael" (Vol. II, Pt. 4, opp. sig. c-5).

Plate CXXXIX. Copy of Raphael's *Holy Family*, owned by Jefferson.

Plate CXL. *From No. 120. "La Flagellation.* Rubens" (Vol. II, Pt. 3, No. 501).

il est en repos pour donner au saint le loisir de contempler. Ce tableau est surtout remarquable par sa touche ferme et assurée; il n'y a pas un coup de pinceau qui ne soit de maître; rien n'est essayé; tout est posé en place, net, franc, arrêté. [I, 2d Pt., No. 778]

Jefferson's own set was sold to Congress. He ordered the work for the University in the section on "Gardening. Painting. Sculpture. Music" of the want list, and the library still has the set acquired on his order.

U. Va.   M
*N2030.T7.1802   Sowerby 4245

121. Tredgold, Thomas.

ELEMENTARY PRINCIPLES / OF / CARPENTRY: / A TREA-TISE / ON THE PRESSURE AND EQUILIBRIUM OF BEAMS AND TIMBER FRAMES; / THE RESISTANCE OF TIMBER; AND THE CONSTRUCTION OF / FLOORS, ROOFS, CENTRES, BRIDGES, &c. / *WITH PRACTICAL RULES AND EXAMPLES.* / TO WHICH IS ADDED, / AN ESSAY ON THE NATURE AND PROPERTIES OF TIMBER, / INCLUDING THE METHODS OF SEASONING, AND THE CAUSES AND PREVENTION OF DE-CAY, / WITH DESCRIPTIONS OF THE KINDS OF WOOD USED IN BUILDING. / ALSO, / NUMEROUS TABLES / OF THE SCANTLINGS OF TIMBER FOR DIFFERENT PURPOSES, THE SPECIFIC GRAVITIES OF MATERIALS, &c. / *ILLUSTRATED BY TWENTY-TWO ENGRAVINGS.* / BY THOMAS TRED-GOLD. / —While we give ourselves infinite trouble to pursue investiga-tions relating to the motions and masses of / bodies which move at im-measurable distances from our planet, we have never thought of de-termining the forces / necessary to prevent the roofs of our houses from falling on our heads. EDIN. REV. vol. vi. p. 386. / LONDON: / PRINTED FOR J. TAYLOR, / AT THE ARCHITECTURAL LI-BRARY, No. 59, HIGH HOLBORN. / 1820.

4to. Title page ([iii]); dedication ([v]); preface ([vii]-xiv); table of contents ([xv]-xx); text ([1]-238); index ([239]-50); errata (1 leaf); 22 engraved plates.

The engraver was James Davis, about whom nothing is known.

Other than the evidence of this book, there is little known about

Thomas Tredgold. The delineator for the twenty-two plates, he gives his reasons for publishing this treatise as follows:

IN the course of the last century several treatises on Carpentry have appeared; but in none of them is to be found any thing on the mechanical principles of the art, except it be a few rules for calculating the strength of timber; and these are founded upon erroneous views of the subject, and therefore are not to be relied upon. The greater part of the works on Carpentry are confined almost wholly to what is termed "finding the lines;" a branch of science to which the celebrated Monge gave the name of Descriptive Geometry: and in the works of Mr. P. Nicholson [Nos. 88, 89, and 90], this part of Carpentry has been so ably handled, that little more seems to be required on the subject.

But the knowledge of practical and descriptive geometry is not the only part of science that a Carpenter ought to acquire; for when it is considered that the art of Carpentry is directed chiefly to the support of weight or pressure, it will be obvious that a considerable knowledge of the principles of mechanics is required to practise it with success. And it is not to carpenters alone that the study of the mechanical principles of Carpentry should be confined; for in the modern practice of building, it forms one of the most important departments of the science of construction; and a knowledge of construction is so essential to the art of design, in Architecture, that it is difficult to believe how much it has been neglected, and how little it is esteemed by the students of that profession. [P. vii]

As the mechanical principles of Carpentry have never been published in a separate form, I have attempted in the following pages, to supply that defect. [P. viii]

THE Elementary Principles of Carpentry being a title which includes all that is essential to the art, it therefore embraces a wider range than I have attempted to fill; and to avoid promising more in a title than is performed in the work, I have omitted the definite article, and made it "ELEMENTARY PRINCIPLES OF CARPENTRY.

Lord Kames made a like limitation to his "Elements of Criticism," which of course suggested this. [P. x]

The *Elements* is divided into ten sections—nature and laws of pressure; results of experiments; construction of floors; roofs; domes; partitions; centers for bridges; wooden bridges; construction of joints and straps; nature and properties of timber.

The book was ordered by Jefferson for the University in the section on "Technical Arts" of the want list, but there is no record that it was received during his lifetime. A recently acquired copy has now entered the library's collections, the gift of the Thomas Jefferson Memorial Foundation.

U. Va.
*TH5604.T8.1820

122. Vasari, Giorgio.

Vol. I.   DELLE VITE / De' più Eccellenti / PITTORI, SCVLTORI, / ET ARCHITETTI. / *DI GIORGIO VASARI* / Pittore, & Architetto, Aretino. / *PARTE PRIMA, E SECONDA.* / *In questa nuoua edizione diligentemente reuiste, ricoret-/te, accresciute d'alcuni Ritratti, & arricchite / di postille nel margine.* / AL SERENISSIMO / FERDINANDO II. / GRAŃ DVCA / DI TOSCANA. / IN BOLOGNA, MDCXLVIII. / Per gli Eredi di Euangelista Dozza. Con licenza de' Superiori.

4to. Half title (1 leaf); title page (1 leaf); dedication (1 leaf); table of contents (1 leaf); editor's note (3 unnumbered pp.); poems (5 unnumbered pp.); text (1–432).

Vol. II.   DELLE VITE / . . . / PARTE TERZA / Secondo Volume. / *In questa nuoua edizione diligentemente corrette, accresciute d'alcuni / Ritratti, e postille nel margine, con nuoua aggiunta.* / IN BOLOGNA / Presso gli Heredi di Euangelista Dozza. M.DC.LXIII. / *Con licenza de'Superiori.*

4to. Half title (1 leaf); title page (1 leaf); note on Vasari (3 unnumbered pp.); table of contents (1 unnumbered p.); letter from Marcello Adriani to Vasari (18 leaves); text (1–407); license ([408]); index (66 leaves).

Vol. III.   DELLE VITE / . . . / PARTE TERZA / Primo Volume. / . . .

4to. Half title (1 leaf); title page ([1]); preface (3–6); [new pagination:] table of contents (5–6); text (7–543).

The Parte Terza, Secondo Volume, is misbound in Vol. II, while the Parte Terza, Primo Volume, is misbound in Vol. III. All through the volumes there is a series of woodcut portraits of the artists at the head of each biography.

Giorgio Vasari (1511–74) studied painting in Florence with Andrea del Sarto, Baccio Bandinelli, G. B. Rosso, and Francesco Salvaiti. He went to Rome in 1531 with Cardinal Ippolito de Medici. While there he studied the works of Michelangelo and became one of his acquaintances.

Vasari decided to write *Le vite* in 1546 and a first edition was issued in 1550. The title above was given to the 1568 edition. The work has gone through innumerable editions in many languages during the intervening centuries.

Sowerby notes that Jefferson, in a letter of August 28, 1814, mentions Vasari in a discussion of the copies of portraits of Columbus and Vespuccius at Monticello.

This edition, which is both the one Jefferson sold to Congress and the one he ordered for the University in the section on "Gardening. Painting. Sculpture. Music" of the want list, has its dedication signed by Carlo Menolessi. There is no record of Jefferson's order for the University having been filled, but a duplicate of the set has been recently acquired, the gift of the Thomas Jefferson Memorial Foundation.

U. Va.   M
*N6922.V3.1648   Sowerby 4240

123a. Vignola, Giacomo Barozzio da.

[Half title:] BIBLIOTHEQUE / PORTATIVE / D'ARCHITECTURE / ÉLÉMENTAIRE, / A L'USAGE DES ARTISTES. / *Divisée en six Parties.* / PREMIERE PARTIE. / Contenant / Les cinq Ordres d'Architecture de Vignole.

[Title page:] REGLES / DES / *CINQ ORDRES* / D'ARCHITECTURE. / *Par* Jacques Barrozzio de Vignole. / NOUVELLE ÉDITION, / *Traduite de l'Italien & augmentée de Remarques.* / A PARIS, RUE DAUPHINE, / Chez Jombert, Libraire du Roi pour l'Artillerie / & le Génie, à l'Image Notre-Dame. / M. DCC. LXIV.

8vo. Half title (1 leaf); engraved frontispiece ([ii]); title page ([iii]); advertisement (v-viii); preface (ix-xii); table of contents (xiii-xiv); license (xv-xvi); engraved half title (1 unnumbered p.); text (1–72); 67 engraved plates, of which 6 are folding.

The frontispiece was drawn by I. B. Corneille and engraved by I. Mariette. The plate is very worn and is certainly an earlier plate with the inscription for this new book superimposed. For the title page, see Plate CXLI.

I. B. (Jean-Baptiste) Corneille (1649–95), born in Paris, studied with his father, Michel, and Charles d'Errard (see No. 46) as well as in Rome. He married Madeleine Mariette, sister of Jean Mariette.

Jean (or I.) Mariette (1660–1742), born in Paris, was the son of a family of painter-engravers. He studied with his brother-in-law, Corneille and was advised by Charles Le Brun to concentrate on engraving. His

REGLES
DES
CINQ ORDRES
D'ARCHITECTURE.

Par Jacques Barrozzio de Vignole.

NOUVELLE ÉDITION,

Traduite de l'Italien & augmentée de Remarques.

A PARIS, RUE DAUPHINE,

Chez Jombert, Libraire du Roi pour l'Artillerie
& le Génie, à l'Image Notre-Dame.

M. DCC. LXIV.

Plate CXLI. *From No. 123a.* Title page.

son Pierre-Jean (or I.) Mariette (1694–1774) had a greater reputation and became, as well as an engraver, a notable collector of drawings.

Giacomo Barozzio, or Barocchio, da Vignola, called Vignola (1507–73), came under the influence of Serlio (No. 113). He worked in Rome from 1530; was in France, 1541–43; returned to Bologna, 1543–50; and was in Rome again from 1550. His work both as architect and writer has had immense influence in the world of architecture.

He published his *Due regole della prospettiva pratica* in 1538. The first edition of the *Regola delli cinqui ordini* was 1562. It has had many editions, translations, and adaptations since.

In the preface Vignola says:

Mon intention, cher Lecteur, est de vous exposer en peu de mots les motifs qui m'ont déterminé à composer cet Ouvrage, pour le bien public, & pour la satisfaction des personnes qui d'adonnent à l'Architecture.

Ayant exercé cet Art pendant bien des années dans les différens pays où je me suis trouvé, j'ai toujours pris plaiser à examiner soigneusement les sentiments des divers Auteurs qui ont écrit sur les proportions & les ornemens des Ordres, en les comparant entr'eux & avec les monumens qui nous restent de l'Antiquité, dans le dessin d'en tirer une regle certaine dans laquelle on puisse avoir confiance, & qui fût approuvée par les Maîtres de l'Art, sinon dans son tout, du moins en sa plus grande partie. Mon unique intention étoit alors de me faciliter la connoissance de ces proportions, pour en faire usage quand l'occasion s'en présenteroit. [P. ix]

The book, which is Part I of the *Bibliothèque portative d'architecture* issued by Jombert in 1764 (see No. 46), consists mostly of the study of orders, but there are many details besides. These show paving patterns, interior entablatures, pedestals "extraordinaires," vaulting, and symbolic columns.

Jefferson, who had owned only Part IV of the *Bibliothèque* before the sale of his library to Congress, managed to obtain all four parts of the set before his death. That set was sold as lot 723 in the 1829 sale.

He ordered the complete set for the University in the section on "Architecture" of the want list, but there is no record of the library's having acquired it. The present copy of the Vignola has come into the collections recently, the gift of the Thomas Jefferson Memorial Foundation.

U. Va.   M
*NA2810.V55.1764

123b. Vignola, Giacomo Barozzio da.

Regola delli cinque Ordini / D'ARCHITETTVRA / *Di M. GIACOMO* BAROZZIO DA VIGNOLA. / Con la nuova aggionta di Michel-Angelo Buonaroti. / Regel van de vüf Ordens der Architecture / Ghestelt by M. Iacob Barozzio van Vignola. / Met een nieu byvoegsel van *Michel Angelo Buonaroti*. / Reigle des cinq Ordres / D'ARCHITECTVRE, / *De M. Iacques Barozzio de Vignole*. / Avec une augmentation nouvelle de Michel Angelo Bonaroti. / Regel der funff orden von Architectur / Ghestelt durch M. Iacob Barozzio von Vignola. / Auffs news vermehrt mit etliche herliche Gebäwen von *Michel Angelo Bonaroti*. / 't AM-STERDAM, / Ghedruct by Willem Ianssz, woonende op't Water by de / oude Brugghe inde gulden Sonnewyser. / *Ao*. M. DC. XIX.

Folio. Title page ([1]); engraved portrait ([3]); dedication (5); note to reader (7–11); text, with 42 engraved plates inserted (12–94).

For information about Vignola and the *Regola*, see No. 123a. See also Plates CXLII and CXLIII.

The text of this edition is in Italian, French, Dutch, and German. Jefferson sold his copy to Congress. Sowerby notes that it was bound together with Serlio (No. 113) and Scamozzi (No. 111a) for Jefferson. It was not ordered for the University. The library's present copy of this edition has recently entered its collections, the gift of the Thomas Jefferson Memorial Foundation.

M

*NA2810.V552.1619

Sowerby 4177

124. Visconti, Ennio Quirino.

A LETTER / FROM THE / CHEVALIER ANTONIO CANOVA: / AND / TWO MEMOIRS / READ TO THE ROYAL INSTITUTE OF FRANCE / ON THE / SCULPTURES / IN THE COLLEC-TION / OF / THE EARL OF ELGIN; / BY THE / CHEVALIER E. Q. VISCONTI, / MEMBER OF THE CLASS OF THE FINE ARTS, AND OF THE / CLASS OF HISTORY AND ANCIENT LITERATURE; / AUTHOR OF THE ICONOGRAPHIE GREQUE, / AND OF THE MUSEO PIO-CLEMENTINO. / TRANSLATED

Plate CXLII. *From No. 123b*. Engraved portrait.

ALEXANDER FARNESIVS
CAR. S. R. E. VICECANCEL.

Palmi. 11

Palmi Romani con li quali e fatto il presente disegno.

XXXI

Plate CXLIII. *From No. 123b.* Door from the Villa Caprarola (p. 73).

FROM THE FRENCH AND ITALIAN. / LONDON: / PRINTED FOR JOHN MURRAY, ALBEMARLE-STREET, / BY W. BULMER AND CO. CLEVELAND-ROW. / 1816.

Large 8vo. Title page ([i]); catalogue of the Elgin marbles, vases, casts, and drawings (iii-xx); Canova's letter (xxi-xxii); half title: 'MEMOIR / ON THE / SCULPTURES / WHICH BELONGED TO / THE PARTHENON / AND TO SOME OTHER EDIFICES / OF / THE ACROPOLIS, / AT ATHENS. / READ AT A PUBLIC MEETING OF THE TWO CLASSES OF / THE ROYAL INSTITUTE OF FRANCE, / IN THE YEAR 1815.' (1 leaf); memoir (1–176); half title: 'MEMOIR / ON A / GREEK EPIGRAM WHICH / SERVED FOR AN EPITAPH ON THE TOMB / OF THE / ATHENIAN WARRIORS KILLED AT POTIDAEA. / READ TO THE CLASS OF HISTORY AND ANCIENT / LITERATURE OF THE ROYAL INSTITUTE OF FRANCE, / IN THE MONTH OF SEPTEMBER 1815' (1 leaf); memoir (179–205); index (207–21).

Antonio Canova (1757–1822), the celebrated sculptor, was also a painter, though his paintings are not much remembered today. He was born at Possagno, near Bassano, and died at Venice. He studied with indifferent masters, from nature, and from the antique. He became a leader in neoclassicism and was twice called to Paris by Napoleon.

Thomas Bruce, seventh earl of Elgin and eleventh earl of Kincardine (1766–1841), educated at Harrow, Westminster, St. Andrews University, and in Paris, entered the army, and later the diplomatic service. In 1799 he was sent to the Ottoman Porte, where he became interested in Greek art. He sent artists to Athens in 1800 to record the monuments and in 1801 received a firman from the Porte to "fix scaffolding round the antient Temple of the Idols, and to mould the ornamental sculpture and visible figures thereon in plaster and gypsum," as well as "to take away any pieces of stone with old inscriptions or figures thereon."

He spent £74,000 on removing his collection and was given £35,000 in 1816 for it by the English government after an inquiry as to his ownership. Previous to that he had opened it to the public at his house in Park Lane and then in Burlington House.

Ennio Quirino Visconti (1751–1818), born in Rome, worked at the Vatican, became president of the Istituto Nazional delle Scienze e delle Arti, Rome, and after his move to France the administrator of antiquities at the Louvre. His studies of the iconography of Greece and Rome brought together for the first time all such material and examined it scientifically. He was also a great enthusiast of the Elgin marbles.

The letter from Canova is a letter of thanks to the earl of Elgin for allowing him to see the marbles. He says:

I can never satisfy myself with viewing them again and again: and although my stay in this metropolis must of necessity be extremely short, I am still anxious to dedicate every leisure moment to the contemplation of these celebrated relics of ancient art. I admire in them the truth of nature combined with the choice of beautiful forms: everything about them breaths animation, with a singular truth of expression, and with a degree of skill which is the more exquisite, as it is without the least affectation of the pomp of art. [Pp. (xxi)-xxii]

Visconti's memoirs are a rather pompous display of erudition.

Jefferson ordered this book for the University in the section on "History-Civil-Antient" of the want list, and a copy was received before 1828, but it has not survived. The library's present copy has been recently acquired, the gift of the Thomas Jefferson Memorial Foundation.

U. Va.
*NB92.E6.1816

125a. Vitruvius Pollio.

ABREGÉ / DES DIX LIVRES / D'ARCHITECTURE / DE / VITRUVE. / A PARIS, / Chez Jean Baptiste Coignard, / ruë S. Jacques, à la Bible d'or. / M. DC. LXXIV. / *AVEC PRIVILEGE DU ROY.*

12mo. Title page (1 leaf); note (1 leaf); table of contents (4 leaves); text (1–224); note (1 unnumbered p.); 11 engraved plates with explanations; glossary (25 unnumbered pp.); license and errata (1 unnumbered p.).

Marcus Vitruvius Pollio, who lived at the time of Augustus, was a Roman architect whose codification of the art of architecture is one of the earliest documents in the field to come down to us. The rediscovery of a copy of his treatise caused great excitement. It was first printed in 1486, only some thirty years after the use of movable type became known.

The translator of this edition says:

On a autrefois imprimé quelques abregez de Vitruve, mais il n'y en a point où l'on ait suivi le dessein que Philibert de l'Orme en a donné dans son troisième livre: Il souhaitte qu'en abregeant Vitruve, l'on mette en ordre les matieres que cet Auteur a traittées confusement, & que ce qui se trouve despersé en plusieurs endroits appartenant à un mesme sujet, soit amassé en un seul chapitre. Cette methode que la pluspart des anciens Ecrivans ont negligée, a esté suivie dans ce Traitté. [Translator's note]

A copy of either the Paris, 1674 or the Amsterdam, 1681 edition (both translated by Perrault) was in Jefferson's library at the time of his death and was sold as lot 722 in the 1829 sale. Kimball (pp. 100–101) says it was purchased in 1819 and identifies it as the Paris, 1674 edition, but there is nothing in the sale catalogue to indicate which of the duodecimo editions it actually was.

Jefferson did not order it for the University. The library's copy of the Paris, 1674 edition is a recent acquisition, the gift of the Thomas Jefferson Memorial Foundation.

M?

*NA2515.V742.1674

125b. Vitruvius Pollio.

Architecture générale de Vitruve. Amsterdam, 1681.
Not now owned by the University.

See No. 125a for information about Vitruvius and about this edition.
Jefferson did not order this book for the University.

M?

125c. Vitruvius Pollio.

[First half title:] M. VITRUVII POLLIONIS / DE ARCHITEC-
TURA / LIBRI DECEM. / TOMUS I.

[Second half title:] (M. VITRUVII POLLIONIS / DE ARCHITEC-
TURA / LIBRI DECEM. / TOMUS II.

[Title page missing: DE ARCHITECTURA LIBRI DECEM. OPE
CODICIS GUELFERBYTANI, EDITIONIS PRINCIPIS, CETERO-
RUMQUE SUBSIDIORUM RECENSUIT, ET GLOSSARIO IN
QUO VOCABULA ARTIS PROPRIA GERM. ITAL. GALL. ET

ANGL. EXPLICANTUR, ILLUSTRAVIT AUGUSTUS RODE. Berlin, 1800–1801.]

4to. Half title (1 leaf); half title (1 leaf); note to reader (2 leaves); notes on Vitruvius (6 leaves); table of contents (2 leaves); text (1–264); [new pagination:] half title ([1]); glossary ([3]–72); geographical and historical index (73–80).

For information on Vitruvius Pollio, see No. 125a.

    This edition of Vitruvius, with its text in Latin and with no illustrations, was ordered by Jefferson for the University in the section on "Architecture" of the want list, but was never received. The library's present copy was a gift of the Virginia Chapter of the American Institute of Architects.

U. Va.
*NA2515.V5.1800

125d. Vitruvius Pollio.

LES DIX LIVRES / D'ARCHITECTURE / DE / VITRUVE / CORRIGES ET TRADVITS / *nouvellement en François, avec des Notes / & des Figures.* / Seconde Edition reveuë, corrigée, & augmentée. / *Par M.* PERRAULT *de l'Academie Royalle des Sciences, Docteur en Medecine / de la Faculté de Paris.* / A PARIS, / Chez JEAN BAPTISTE COIGNARD, / Imprimeur ordinaire du Roy, ruë S. Jacques, à la Bible d'or. / M. DC. LXXXIV. / *AVEC PRIVILEGE DE SA MAJESTÉ.*

Folio. Engraved frontispiece (1 leaf); title page (1 leaf); dedication (3 unnumbered pp.); note (1 unnumbered p.); preface (6 leaves); text, with 67 engraved plates, of which 9 are double, inserted and with many woodcut figures ([1]–354); index, errata, and license (7 leaves).

The engravers were Gerard Edelinck, or Edelink (1640–1707), a Fleming who worked in Paris after having been called there by Colbert in 1665, eventually becoming engraver to Louis XIV and a member of the academy; Estienne Gantrel (1646–1706), born at Metz but working in Paris where he was made engraver in ordinary to the king; Jacques Grignon (ca.1640–after 1698), often called *le vieux*, who was perhaps an ancestor of Charles Grignon I and Charles Grignon II (see No. 23); Sébastien Le Clerc (Nos. 36 and 69); Pierre Le Pautre (see No. 36); I.

Patiany; either Nicolas Pitau I (1632–71), the son of Jean Pitau, a silversmith and the master of Gérard Edelinck, or Nicolas Pitau II (1670–1724), a pupil of Edelinck; Gérard Scotin (1643–1715), the son of the sculptor Pierre Scotin and the father and grandfather of engravers; Jean Jacques Tournier (see No. 36); and P. Vanderbanc.

For information on Virtuvius Pollio, see No. 125a. For information of Claude Perrault, see No. 96a.

The quality of this edition may be judged by the quality of the engravers who worked on it (see Plates CXLIV and CXLV). They were mostly associated with the court, as was Perrault, and some of them were considered at the top of their profession.

Kimball (p. 100) says Jefferson had this book before 1775. Sowerby notes that a letter written by Jefferson August 13, 1813, makes a specific reference to it: "Perrault, in his edition of Virtuvius, Paris 1684. fol. Plates 61.62." He later sold his copy to Congress.

Jefferson ordered this book for the University in the section on "Architecture" of the want list, and it was in the library by 1828, but it has not survived. The library's present copy is a recent acquisition, the gift of the Thomas Jefferson Memorial Foundation.

U. Va.   M
*NA2517.V85.1684   Sowerby 4173

126a. Ware, Isaac.

A / COMPLETE BODY / OF / ARCHITECTURE. / ADORNED WITH / PLANS and ELEVATIONS, / FROM / ORIGINAL DESIGNS. / By ISAAC WARE, Esq. / Of His MAJESTY's Board of Works. / In which are interspersed / Some DESIGNS of INIGO JONES, never before published. / LONDON: / Printed for T. OSBORNE and J. SHIPTON, in Gray's-Inn; / J. HODGES, near London-Bridge; L. DAVIS, in Fleetstreet; J. WARD, in Cornhill; / And R. BALDWIN, in Pater-Noster-Row. / MDCCLVI.

Folio. Engraved frontispiece (1 leaf); two-color title page (1 leaf); preface (5 unnumbered pp.); list of plates (3 unnumbered pp.); table of contents (4 leaves); text, with 122 engraved plates, of which 4 are folding and 3 are double, inserted ([1]–748); index (2 leaves).

The engravers were R. Benning (fl.1714–56), English; Samuel Boyce (d.1775), English; Butler Clowse (d.1782), English; B. Cole (fl.1756),

Plate CXLIV. *From No. 125d.* Frontispiece.

LES DIX LIVRES

D'ARCHITECTURE

DE

VITRUVE

CORRIGEZ ET TRADVITS
nouvellement en François, avec des Notes
& des Figures.

Seconde Edition reveuë, corrigée, & augmentée.

Par M. PERRAULT *de l'Academie Royalle des Sciences, Docteur en Medecine*
de la Faculté de Paris.

A PARIS,

Chez JEAN BAPTISTE COIGNARD,

Imprimeur ordinaire du Roy, ruë S. Jacques, à la Bible d'or.

M. DC. LXXXIV.

AVEC PRIVILEGE DE SA MAJESTE'.

Plate CXLV. *From No. 125d.* Title page.

English; I. (or J.) Couse; Matthew Darly (fl.1756–72), engraver and caricaturist, whose wife was also an engraver; R. Edwards (fl.1756), English; Pierre Fourdrinier (see No. 21); Charles Grignion (see No. 23); James Hill (d.1803), who was English but later worked in America; I. (or J.) Mynde (see No. 48); I. (or J.) Noual (see No. 24); F. Patton (see No. 3); W. Proud (fl.1756–60), English; Henry Roberts; and I. Ware, who was also the delineator.

Isaac Ware (d.1766) was a chimney-sweep's boy who was found sketching on the walls of Inigo Jones's Banqueting House, Whitehall. His evident talent persuaded Burlington to send him to Italy, and his subsequent career justified this gesture. By 1728 he was clerk of the works at the Tower of London; the next year he held the same post at Windsor; in 1735 he was draughtsman and clerk itinerant to the Board of Works; in 1736 he was secretary and draughtsman to the board at Windsor and at Greenwich; in 1738 he was clerk of the works to His Majesty's palace; and in 1763 he was Master of the Carpenter's Company.

He was active in the publishing field, too. He did the drawings and one or two engravings for Ripley's *Houghton*, 1735, and the engravings for *Rookby*, 1735. He published the *Designs of Inigo Jones and Others* in 1735(?), and again in 1743 and 1756(?); a translation of *Palladio*, 1738; another of Sirrigatti's *Practice of Perspective*, 1756; and an edition of Brook Taylor's *Method of Perspective*, 1766.

Ware says of his *Complete Body of Architecture:*

. . . We propose, in this undertaking, to collect all that is useful in the works of others, at whatsoever time they have been written, or in whatever language; and to add the several discoveries and improvements made since that time by the genius of others, or by our own industry. By this means we propose to make our work serve as a library on this subject to the gentleman and the builder; supplying the place of all other books: as it will contain whatsoever there is in them worthy regard, and, together with this, whatever we have been able to invent or obtain that is curious and useful.

Those who have studied these things, have in general considered the magnificence of building, rather than its use. Architecture has been celebrated as a noble science by many who have never regarded its benefits in common life: we have endeavoured to join these several parts of the subject, nor shall we fear to say that the art of building cannot be more grand than it is useful; nor its dignity a greater praise than its convenience. From the neglect of this consideration, those who have written to inform others of its excellence, have been too much captivated by its pomp, and have bestowed in a manner all their labour there, leaving the more serviceable part neglected. [Preface]

As might be expected from this note, the book is filled with strong, sturdy, mid-Georgian designs. The *DNB* gives "1735?" as the date of the first edition of this work and tends to identify it with Ware's 1735(?) edition of *Designs of Inigo Jones*, while giving 1756 and 1767 as the dates of subsequent editions. Kimball (p. 101), however, calls the 1767 edition the second rather than the third. An examination of the three volumes seems to corroborate Kimball, for the *Designs of Inigo Jones*, 1735(?), is a small quarto with plates from Jones's designs delineated by Ware and engraved by Pierre Fourdrinier (see No. 21) and with no text at all. *A Complete Body of Architecture*, while incorporating some designs of Inigo Jones, is a folio volume with an extended text and a series of folio plates (see Plates CXLVI and CXLVII). In addition, the Jones designs are supposed to have been "never before published" according to the title page of the *Complete Body of Architecture*, 1756.

There was a copy of either the 1756 or 1767 edition in Jefferson's private library at the time of his death. It came into his possession after 1815 (Kimball, p. 101), and it was sold as lot 721 in the 1829 sale. The copy Jefferson ordered for the University in the section on "Architecture" of the want list can be identified as either of these two editions from the title, though there is no record of the library's ever having received it. The University's present copy has been recently acquired, the gift of the Thomas Jefferson Memorial Foundation.

U. Va.?   M?
*NA2517.W3.1756

126b. Ware, Isaac.

A / COMPLETE BODY / . . . / LONDON: / Printed for J. RIVINGTON, L. DAVIS and C. REYMERS, R. BALDWIN, / W. OWEN, H. WOODFALL, W. STRAHAN, and B. COLLINS. / MDCCLXVII.

Folio. Engraved frontispiece (1 leaf); two-color title page (1 leaf); preface (5 unnumbered pp.); list of plates (3 unnumbered pp.); table of contents (4 leaves); text, with 122 engraved plates, of which 11 are folding, inserted ([1]–748).

For information on Isaac Ware, see the preceding entry.

Except for the change in the arrangement in the plates, there is little difference between this edition and the preceding entry. See that entry for fuller information on it.

Plate CXLVI. *From No. 126a.* "Variations in the Doric Entablatures" (Pl. 16).

Plate CXLVII. *From No. 126a.* "Of the several kinds of windows" (Pl. 67).

The library's present copy is the gift of the Thomas Jefferson Memorial Foundation.

U. Va.?   M?
*NA2517.W3.1767

127a. Whately, Thomas.

OBSERVATIONS / ON / MODERN GARDENING, / ILLUS-TRATED BY / DESCRIPTIONS. / Where Wealth, enthron'd in Nature's pride, / With Taste and Bounty by her side, / And holding Plenty's horn, / Sends Labour to pursue the toil, / Art to improve the happy soil, / And Beauty to adorn. F. / THE SECOND EDITION. / LONDON, / Printed for T. PAYNE, at the Mews-gate. / MDCCLXX.

8vo. Title page (1 leaf); table of contents (3 leaves); text ([1]–257).

Thomas Whatley (d.1772) was a politician and a student of literature. He wrote widely, especially on politics. He says about gardening in general:

GARDENING, in the perfection to which it has been lately brought in England, is entitled to a place of considerable rank among the liberal arts. It is as superior to landskip painting, as a reality to a representation: it is an exertion of fancy; a subject for taste; and being released now from the restraints of regularity, and enlarged beyond the purposes of domestic convenience, the most beautiful, the most simple, the most noble scenes of nature are all within its province: for it is no longer confined to the spots from which it borrows its name, but regulates also the disposition and embellishments of a park, a farm, or a riding; and the business of a gardener is to select and to apply whatever is great, elegant, or characteristic in any of them; to discover and to shew all the advantages of the place upon which he is employed; to supply its defects, to correct its faults, and to improve its beauties. For all these operations, the objects of nature are still his only materials. His first enquiry, therefore, must be into the means by which those effects are attained in nature, which he is to produce; and into those properties in the objects of nature, which should determine him in the choice and arrangement of them.

Nature, always simple, employs but four materials in the composition of her scenes, *ground*, *wood*, *water*, and *rocks*. The cultivation of nature has introduced a fifth species, the *buildings* requisite for the accommodation of men. Each of these again admits of varieties in figure, dimensions, color, and situation. Every landskip is composed of these parts only; every beauty in a landskip depends on the application of their several varieties. [Pp. (1)–2]

Of terror as an agreeable sensation he says:

THIS river [the Derwent] would be better suited to a scene characterised by that terror, which the combination of greatness with force inspires, and which is animating and interesting, from the exertion and anxiety attending it. The terrors of a scene in nature are like those of a dramatic representation; they give an alarm; but the sensations are agreeable, so long as they are kept to such as are allied only to terror, unmixed with any that are horrible and disgusting; art may therefore be used to heighten them, to display the objects which are distinguished by greatness, to improve the circumstances which denote force, to mark those which intimate danger, and to blend with all, here and there a cast of melancholy. [P. 106]

But disgust may stem from another characteristic:

IF regularity is not entitled to a preference in the environs or approach to a house, it will be difficult to support its pretensions to a place in any more *distant parts* of a park or a garden. Formal slopes of ground are ugly; right or circular lines bounding water, do not indeed change the nature of the element; it still retains some of its agreeable properties; but the shape given to it is disgusting. [P. 144]

BUT regularity can never attain to a great share of beauty, and to none of the species called *picturesque;* a denomination in general expressive of excellence. [P. 146]

And he defines *picturesque* in the following way:

The term picturesque is therefore applicable only to such objects in nature, as, after allowing for the differences between the arts of painting and of gardening, are fit to be formed into groupes, or to enter into a composition, where the several parts have a relation to each other; and in opposition to those which may be spread abroad in detail, and have no merit but as individuals. [P. 150]

The book is divided into sections on ground, wood, water, rocks, buildings, art, picturesque beauty, character, the farm, the park, the garden, the riding, and the seasons. It uses the following gardens as examples—Moor Park, Ilam, Claremont, Esher, Blenheim, Wotton, Middleton, Matlock, Bath, Dovedale, Enfield Chace, Tintern Abbey, Caversham, Leasowes, Wolvern farm, Painshill, Hagley, Stowe, Persfield.

The book had its first edition in 1770, and a second that same year. It had gone into a fourth edition by 1777, a fifth in 1793, and an expanded edition in 1801. A French translation appeared in 1771 and exerted considerable influence on later French authors.

Although Kimball (p. 101) says Jefferson had his copy of the *Observations on Modern Gardening* before 1783, Sowerby (4227) says his copy was bought in 1785 from the Rev. Samuel Henley. That he had a copy before March 1786 we know from a note made by Jefferson, quoted in Sowerby:

Memorandums made on a tour to some of the gardens described in England by Whatley in his book on gardening. While his descriptions in point of style are models of perfect elegance and classical correctness, they are as remarkable for their exactness. I always walked over the gardens with his book in my hand, examined with attention the particular spots he described, found them so justly characterised by him as to be easily recognized, and saw with wonder, that his fine imagination had never been able to seduce him from the truth. My enquiries were directed chiefly to such practical things as might enable me to estimate the expence of making and maintaining a garden in that style. My journey was in the months of March and April 1786.

As can be seen the importance of this book in the Jefferson canon is very great, and its influence on his feeling for garden design cannot be overestimated.

This is the edition Jefferson sold to Congress. Although he had another copy of this book at the time of his death, it is not known whether it was this edition or that of 1777. The library's present copy of the second edition has recently entered its collections, the gift of the Thomas Jefferson Memorial Foundation. It is uncertain whether it was this edition or that of 1777 which was ordered for the University.

U. Va.?
*SB471.W55.1770

M
Sowerby 4227

127b. Whately, Thomas.

OBSERVATIONS / ON / MODERN GARDENING, / . . . / THE FOURTH EDITION. / . . . / Printed for T. Payne and Son, at the Mews-Gate. / M DCC LXXVII.

8vo. Title page (1 leaf); table of contents (3 leaves); text ([1]–257).

For general information on this work and its author, see No. 127a. Although reset, this edition's material is the same as that in the 1770 edition.

Jefferson did not specify in the section on "Gardening. Painting. Sculpture. Music" of the want list which edition of this book he wanted for the University, but this is the one Hilliard supplied him with, though the copy has not survived. It is perhaps also this edition that was in Jefferson's private library at the time of his death and was sold as lot 727 in the 1829 sale (see also No. 127a). The library's present copy has been recently acquired, the gift of the Thomas Jefferson Memorial Foundation.

U. Va.?   M?
*SB71.W55.1777

128a. Winckelmann, Johann Joachim.

Vol. I.   STORIA / DELLE / *ARTI DEL DISEGNO* / PRESSO GLI ANTICHI / *DI* / GIOVANNI WINKELMANN / *Tradotta dal tedesco* / CON NOTE ORIGINALI DEGLI EDITORI. / *TOMO PRIMO.* / IN MILANO. MDCCLXXIX. / Nell' Imperiale Monistero di s. Ambrogio Maggiore. / *CON APPROVAZIONE.*

4to. Half title ([i]); title page ([iii]); dedication ([v]); editor's note ([vii]-xii); preface ([xiii]-xxxviii); eulogy of Winckelmann ([xxxix]-liv); index (lv-lxiv); text ([1]–347); 17 engraved plates, all folding.

Vol. II.   STORIA / . . . / *TOMO SECONDO.* / . . .

4to. Title page ([1]); text ([3]–336); table of plates (337); table of headpieces and tailpieces (338–42); index (343–55); list of subscribers (5 unnumbered pp.); 1 engraved plate.

The engravers were Domenico Aspari (1745–1831), painter and engraver after the manner of Piranesi and the father of Carlo Aspari, also an engraver; Domenico Cagnoni, who worked in Milan during the second half of the eighteenth century; and Hier-Manrelli.

Johann Joachim Winckelmann (1717–68) was born in Brandenburg, the son of a poor shoemaker. He was educated in Berlin, Salzwedel, and Halle, where he was a student of theology in 1738. His interest was in Greek art and literature, but he went to Jena as a medieval student. He then became a tutor and a librarian. In 1754 he was librarian to Cardinal Passionei. In 1755 he went to Rome as librarian to Cardinal Archinto and was later librarian to Cardinal Albani. He is buried at Trieste, where, on his way back from a visit to the court of Maria Teresa, he was murdered by a man named Arcangeli.

He had an unrivaled knowledge of ancient art, and his book sets forth its history and its principles. It is said that to his contemporaries it came as a revelation and exercised a profound influence on the best minds of the age. His book was first issued as *Geschichte der Kunst des Altertums*, 1764.

The present book is a first edition of the translation by Carlo Amoretti (1741–18??). It is the edition Jefferson sold to Congress. The library's copy is a recent acquisition, the gift of the Thomas Jefferson Memorial Foundation. Jefferson did not order it for the University.

M

*N5330.W77.1779   Sowerby 4247

128b. Winckelmann, Johann Joachim.

Vol. I. *STORIA* / DELLE / ARTI DEL DISEGNO / PRESSO GLI ANTICHI / *DI* / GIOVANNI WINKELMANN / *Tradotta dal Tedesco* / E IN QUESTA EDIZIONE CORRETTA E AUMENTATA / DALL' ABATE / CARLO FEA / GIURECONSULTO / *TOMO PRIMO.* / IN ROMO / DALLA STAMPERIA PAGLIARINI / MDCCLXXXIII. / *CON LICENZA DE' SUPERIORI.*

4to. Half title (1 leaf); engraved frontispiece (1 leaf); title page (1 leaf); dedication ([i]-iv); note to reader ([v]-xvi); note of Milanese monastery ([xvii]-xxii); note of Viennese editors ([xxiii]-lx); eulogy of Winckelmann ([lxi]-lxxxii); index (lxxxiii-xcvi); text, ([1]–451); license (1 unnumbered p.); 18 engraved plates.

Vol. II. *STORIA* / DELLE / ARTI DEL DISEGNO / . . . / *TOMO SECONDO.* / . . .

4to. Half title ([1]); title page ([3]); text ([5]–427); 11 engraved plates.

Vol. III. *STORIA* / DELLE / ARTI DEL DISEGNO / . . . / *TOMO TERZO.* / . . . / MDCCLXXXIV. / . . .

4to. Half title ([i]); title page ([iii]); editor's note ([v]-xii); preface ([1]–14); table of contents (15–16); text ([17]–514); index of monuments (515–36); index of authors (537–51); index (552–604); [new pagination:] half title for rebuttal of Carlo Fea to Onofrio Boni on Vol. III ([1]); text ([3]–40); 23 engraved plates.

The engravers for Vol. I were Carlo Baroni (fl.1761–75), who worked at Rome; Benigo Bossi (1727–ca.1793) or (probably) Giacomo Bossi (fl.1782–98), who worked at Rome; Girolamo Caretoni; L. Cunego;

Alessandro Mochetti (1760–1810), who worked at Rome; Giovanni Petrini, who worked during the second half of the eighteenth century in Rome; M. di Pietro; Carmine Pignatari (fl.1760–83), who worked at Naples and Herculanum; Francesco Rastaini (b.1750), who worked at Rome; Christoforo Silvestrini (1750–ca.1813), a Roman; and Camillo Tinti (ca.1738–96), who studied with Domenico Cunego (see No. 3) and worked at Rome. The engravers for Vol. II were Benigo Bossi, Caretoni, Mochetti, and Giovanni Battista Dassori (fl.1783–92). The engravers for Vol. III were Benigo Bossi and Caretoni, or Carattoni, together with Ferdinando, Pietro, or Vincenzo Campana, and Francesco Faccendo (1750–1820), a Roman.

For information about Winckelmann and this book, see No. 128a. This new edition of the *Storia delle Arti* is the one Jefferson ordered for the University in the section on "Gardening. Painting. Sculpture. Music" of the want list, but there is no record of its ever having been received. The library's present copy was the gift of the Virginia State Library.

U. Va.
*N5330.W77.1783

129. Wood, Robert.

THE / RUINS / OF / BALBEC, / OTHERWISE / HELIOPOLIS / IN / COELOSYRIA. / LONDON: / PRINTED IN THE YEAR MDCCLVII.

Folio. Title page (1 leaf); text ([1]–16); explanation of plates (17–28); 46 engraved plates, of which 10 are folding.

The engravers for this volume were Pierre Foudrinier (see No. 21) and Thomas Major (No. 76).

Robert Wood (1717?–71) was born in Riverstown Castle, county Meath. His education is a little obscure, but he traveled in the Middle East as early as 1742–43. He was in Asia Minor again in 1749–50 when he went to Palmyra and Balbec. He had met Stuart and Revett (No. 119) in Athens and helped them later with the publication of their *Antiquities of Athens*. Wood was under secretary of state from 1756 to 1763 and became a member of the Society of Dilettanti in 1763.

The Ruins of Balbec was first published in 1757 (see Plate CXLVIII). A French translation came out that same year and a second English edition in 1827. Gibbon characterized this book and the *Ruins*

Plate CXLVIII. *From No. 129.* "View of the hexagonal court" (Tab. IX).

of Palmyra as "the magnificent descriptions and drawings of Dawkins and Wood, who have transported into England the ruins of Palmyra and Balbec." (*DNB*).

Wood tells why he has published the *Ruins of Balbec* and the adventurous time he and Dawkins had gathering the material for it

THE Specimen of our Eastern Travels, which we have already given the publick in the RUINS of PALMYRA, has met with such a favorable reception as seems to call for the Sequel. . . .

Having observed that descriptions of ruins, without accurate drawings, seldom preserve more of their subject than it's confusion, we shall, as in the RUINS of PALMYRA, refer our reader almost entirely to the plates; where his information will be more full and circumstantial, as well as less tedious and confused, than could be conveyed by the happiest precision of language. [P. 1]

We therefore set out for Balbec March 31st. [1751] and arrived at Ersale in seven hours. The greatest part of this journey was across the barren ridge of hills called Antilibanus. . . .

We could not avoid staying here all night; but, impatient to leave a place of so much danger, we set out early the next morning, and in five hours and a half arrived at Balbec. . . .

This city . . . is now commanded by a person . . . who . . . was called Emir Hassein. [P. 3]

We had been advised to distrust the Emir. . . . New demands were every day made, which for some time we thought it adviseable to satisfy; but they were so frequently, and at last so insolently repeated, that it became necessary to give a peremptory refusal. . . .

Frequent negociations produced by this quarrel . . . ended in an open declaration, on his side, that we should be attacked and cut to pieces in our way from Balbec. When he heard that those menaces had not the effect he expected, and that we were prepared to set out with about twenty armed servants, he sent us a civil message, desiring that we might interchange presents and part friends, and allow his people to guard us as far as mount Libanus; to which we agreed. Not long after this he was assassinated by an emissary of that rebellious brother whom we have mentioned, and who succeeded him in the government of Balbec. [P. 4]

Having now finished this Second Volume, I beg leave to separate myself a moment from my fellow-traveller, to acknowledge, as editor of this work, that I alone am accountable for the delay of it's publication.

When called from my country by other duties, my necessary absence retarded, in some measure, it's progress. Mr. Dawkins, with the same generous spirit, which had so indefatigably surmounted the various obstacles of our voyage, continued carefully to protect the fruits of those labours which he had so chearfully shared: he not only attended to the accuracy of the work, by having finished drawings made under his own eye by our draughtsman, from the sketches and measures he had taken on the spot, but had the engravings so far advanced as to be now ready for the public under our joint inspection. [P. 16]

Kimball (p. 101) says *The Ruins of Balbec* entered Jefferson's library between 1785 and 1789. This copy Jefferson sold to Congress.

He ordered the book for the University in the section on "Architecture" of the want list, and it was received before 1828 but has not survived. The library's present copy was the gift of G. Harris.

U. Va.   M
*NA335.B2W8.1757   Sowerby 4188

130. Wood, Robert.

THE / RUINS / OF / PALMYRA, / OTHERWISE / TEDMOR, / IN THE / DESART. / LONDON: / PRINTED IN THE YEAR M DCC LIII.

Folio. Title page (1 leaf); publisher's note (2 leaves); engraved, folding plate; text, with 3 engraved plates inserted ([1]–35); explanation of plates ([36]–50); 56 engraved plates, of which 1 is folding.

The engravers were Pierre Fourdrinier (see No. 21); T. Gibson, perhaps the T. Gibson (1680–1751?) who was primarily a painter; Thomas Major (No. 76); Johann Sebastien Müller (see No. 26); and T. M. Müller, Jr., perhaps the son of Tobias and nephew of Johann Müller.

For information on Robert Wood, see No. 129. Wood tells of the inception of this book, the rigors of the journey, and the entourage necessary for it in his text.

Two gentlemen . . . thought, that a voyage . . . to the most remarkable places of antiquity, on the coast of the Mediteranean, might produce amusement and improvement to themselves, as well as some advantage to the publick.

As I had already seen most of the places they intended to visit, they did me the honour of communicating to me their thoughts upon that head, and I with great pleasure accepted their kind invitation to be of so agreeable a party. . . .

It was agreed, that a fourth person in Italy, whose abilities, as an architect and draftsman we were acquainted with, would be absolutely necessary.

We met our ship at Naples in the spring. She brought from London a library, consisting chiefly of all the Greek historians and poets, some books of antiquities, and the best voyage writers, what mathematical instruments we thought necessary, and such things as might be proper presents for the Turkish Grandees, or others, to whom, in the course of our voyage, we should be obliged to address our selves.

We visited most of the islands of the Archipelago, part of Greece in Europe; the Asiatick and European coasts of the Hellespont, Propontis and Bosphorus, as far as the Black-sea, most of the inland parts of Asia Minor, Syria, Phoenicia, Palestine and Egypt. . . .

Inscriptions we copied as they fell our way, and carried off the marbles whenever possible; for the avarice or superstition of the inhabitants made that task difficult and sometimes impracticable. . . .

Architecture took up our chief attention. . . . All lovers of that art must be sensible that the measures of the antient buildings of Rome, by Monsieur Desgodetz [No. 36], have been of the greatest use: We imagined that by attempting to follow the same method in those countries where architecture had its origin, or at least arrived at the highest degree of perfection it has ever attained, we might do service. . . .

How much the loss of such a person [as Mr. Bouverie] must have broke in upon the spirit of our party, may easily be supposed. Had he lived to have seen Palmyra we should, no doubt, have less occasion to beg indulgence for such inaccuracies as may be found in the following work.

. . . If anything could make us forget that Mr. BOUVERIE was dead, it was that Mr. DAWKINS was living.

If the following specimen of our joint labours should . . . rescue from oblivion the magnificence of Palmyra, it is owing entirely to this gentleman, who was so indefatigable in his attention to see every thing done accurately, that there is scarce a measure in this work which he did not take himself. [Publisher's note]

OUR account of Palmyra is confined merely to that state of decay in which we found those ruins in the year 1751. [P. 1]

We set out from Haffia the 11th of March 1751, with an escort of the Aga's best Arab horsemen, armed with guns and long pikes, and travelled in four hours to Sudud. [P. 33]

We . . . proceeded after dinner . . . to a Turkish village called Howareen (where we lay) three hours from Sudud. . . .

We set out from Howareen the 12th, and in three hours arrived at Carietein. . . .

We left Carietin [*sic*], the 13th, about ten o'clock, which was much too late. . . . This bad management exposed us to the heat of two days, before our cattle could get either water or rest. . . .

Our caravan was now encreased to about two hundred persons, and about the same number of beasts for carriage, consisting of an odd mixture of horses, camels, mules and asses. [P. 34]

The fourteenth about noon we arrived at the end of the plain . . . when the hills opening discovered to us, all at once, the greatest quantity of ruins we had ever seen, all of white marble, and beyond them towards the

Plate CXLIX. *From No. 130.* "View of the arch from the east" (Tab. XXVI).

Plate CL. *From No. 130.* "View of the arch from the west" (Tab. XXXV).

Euphrates a flat waste, as far as the eye could reach, without any object which shewed either life or motion. It is scarce possible to imagine any thing more striking than this view: So great a number of Corinthian pillars, mixed with so little wall or solid building, afforded a most romantic variety of prospect. [P. 35; see Plates CXLIX and CL]

The Ruins of Palmyra first appeared in 1753. There was a French translation that same year, and other French editions in 1819 and 1829. There was a second English edition in 1827.

Jefferson ordered the book for the University in the section on "Architecture" of the want list and it was received by 1828, but it has not survived. The library's present copy was the gift of G. Harris.

U. Va.
*NA335.P2W8.1753

Appendix
Index

Appendix

The nineteen books on music, painting, and sculpture in Jefferson's personal library not included in this study are listed here in order to complete the record of Jefferson's fine arts collection.

Those owned by the University:

Christ, [Johann Friedrich]. *Dictionnaire des Monogrammes, Chiffres, Lettres Initiales, Logogryphes, Rébus, &c. Sous lesquels les plus célèbres Peintres, Graveurs & Dessinateurs ont dessiné leurs Noms.* Traduit de l'Allemand. De M. Christ, Professeur dans l'Université de Leipsick, & augmenté de plusieurs Supplémens. Par M++. de l'Acad. Imp. & de la Société Royale de Londres. A Paris: chez Guillyn, MDCCLXII. Avec Approbation, & Privilege du Roi. [1762.]   8vo. 248 leaves, etc.

*N45.C55.1762

M
Sowerby 4241

Geminiani, F[rancesco]. *Rules for playing in a true Taste on the Violin German Flute Violoncello and Harpsicord particularly the Thorough Bass exemplify'd in a variety of Compositions on the Subjects of English, Scotch, and Irish Tunes.* By F. Geminiani Opera VIII Printed with His Majesty's Royal License. [N.p., n.d.; 1739?.] *The Art of playing on the Violin containing all the Rules necessary to attain to a Perfection on that Instrument, with great variety of Compositions, which will also be very useful to those who study Violoncello, Harpsichord, &c.* Composed by F. Geminiani. Opera IX. London, MDCCLI. Printed for the Author by J: Johnson. [1751.]   Folio. 2 vols. bound in 1. 10 leaves, etc.; 5 leaves, etc.

*MT262.G32.1751

M
Sowerby 4255

Pasquali, Nicolo. *The Art of Fingering the Harpsichord. Illustrated with Examples in Notes. To which is Added, an approved Method of Tuning that Instrument.* By Nicolo Pasquali. London: Price 3 sh. Printed and Sold by R:Bremner opposite Somerset House in the Strand. Where may be had, Thorough Bass made Easy by the same Author, 7 sh. 6d. [N.d.] Small and oblong folio. 16 leaves, etc.

*MT252.P3.1760

M
Sowerby 4258

Pasquali, Nicolo. *Through-Bass made Easy: or, Practical Rules for finding & applying its Various Chords with little Trouble: Together with Variety of Examples in Notes, shewing the manner of accompanying Concertos, Solos, Songs, and Recitatives.* By Nicolo Pasquali. Price 7 sh.6d. London: printed and sold by R. Bremner, the Assigney of Sig: Pasquali, at his Music-Shop in the Strand. [N.d.] Small and oblong folio. 24 leaves, etc.

*MT252.P3.17–

M
Sowerby 4259

Walpole, Horatio, earl of Orford. *Aedes Walpolianae: or, A Description of the Collection of Pictures at Houghton Hall in Norfolk, the Seat of the Right Honorable Sir Robert Walpole, Earl of Orford.* The Second Edition . . . London: printed in the Year MDCCLII. [Printed by John Hughs, near Lincoln's-Inn-Fields. 1752.] 4to. 72 leaves, etc.

*(No. not given)

M
Sowerby 4238

Zuccari, Carlo. *The true Method of Playing an Adagio Made Easy by Twelve Examples First in a plain Manner with a Bass Then with all their Graces Adapted for those who Study the Violin.* Composed by Carlo Zuccari of Milan. London: Printed by R. Bremner, at the Harp and Hautboy, opposite Somerset House in the Strand, [N.d.] Oblong folio. Engraved.

*M221.Z83.17–

M
Sowerby 4260

Those represented on the University's shelves in different editions:

[Gilpin, William.] *An Essay upon Prints: containing Remarks upon the Principles of picturesque Beauty, the Different Kinds of Prints, and the Characters of the most noted Masters; illustrated by Criticisms upon particular Pieces; to which are added, Some Cautions that may be useful in collecting Prints.* . . . London: printed for J. Robson, Bookseller to the Princess Dowager of Wales, MDCCLXVIII. [1768.] 8vo. 136 leaves.

M

*NE840.G48.1781; *ND1340.G5.1792   Sowerby 4235

Webb, Daniel. *An Inquiry into the Beauties of Painting; and into the Merits of the most celebrated Painters, Ancient and Modern.* By Daniel Webb, Esq; The Third Edition . . . London: printed for J. Dodsley, MDCCLXIX. [1769.] 8vo. 108 leaves.

M

*ND1130.W4.1760; *PN1031.W4.1762   Sowerby 4234

Those not now owned by the University:

Atkinson, John Augustus, and James Walker. *A Picturesque Representation of the Manners, Customs, and Amusements of the Russians, in one hundred coloured plates; with an accurate Explanation of each Plate in English and French. In Three Volumes.* By John Augustus Atkinson, and James Walker, Vol. I[-Vol. III]. London: printed by W. Bulmer and Co. for the Proprietors; and sold by them at No. 8, Conway-Street; Messrs. Boydell; Mr. Alici, St. Petersburg; and Messrs. Riss and Saucet, Moscow, MDCCCIII. [1803.] Folio. 3 vols.

M

Sowerby 4246

Bremner, Robert. *The Rudiments of Music: or, A Short and Easy Treatise on that Subject. The Third Edition. With considerable Additions; particularly, Instructions for Song; and, A Plan for teaching a Number of Persons collectively the four Parts of psalmody.* By Robert Bremner. *To which is annexed, A Collection of the best Church-tunes,*

Canons, and Anthems. London: Printed for the Author, and sold at his Music-shops at the Harp and Hautboy in London, and in Edinburgh. MDCCLXIII. Where may be had, the Church-Tunes separate, in four Parts. Price 1 s, in two Parts. Price 6d. [1763.] Small 8vo. 40 leaves, etc.

M
Sowerby 4252

Guerin, [Nicolas]. *Description de l'Academie Royale des Arts de Peinture et de Sculpture*. Par feu M. Guerin, Secretaire perpetuel de ladite Academie. A Paris: chez Jacques Collombat, imprimeur ordinaire du Roy & de l'Academie Royale de Peinture & de Sculpture, MDCCXV. Avec approbation & Privilege du Roy. [1715.] 12mo. 138 leaves, etc.

M
Sowerby 4249

Hoegi, Piere. *A Tabular System whereby the Art of Composing Minuets is made so Easy that any Person, without the least knowledge of Musick, may compose ten thousand, all different, and in the most Pleasing and Correct Manner*. Invented by Sigr. Piere Hoegi. London: Printed at Welcher's Musick Shop in Garrard Street St. Anns Soho, Where may be had Just Publish'd, for the Violin with a thorough Bass for the Harpsichord, *Six Solos* by Sigr. Tartini, *Six Solos* by Sigr. Chabran, *Six Solos* by Sigr. Mazzinghi, *Six Trios* by Sigr. Galleotti. For the Flute, *Six Sonatas* by Androux, *Six Duetts* by Sigr. Noferi, *Six Duets* by Sigr. Asuni. For the Harpsichord, *Six Concertos* by Sigr. Wagenseil, *Four Grand Concertos* by Sigr. Pellegrini, *Eight easy Lessons* by Mr. Bates. [N.d.] Oblong folio. Engraved.

M
Sowerby 4261

Holden, John. *An Essay towards a Rational System of Music*. By John Holden . . . Entered in Stationers Hall. Glasgow: printed for the Author. London: Sold by R. Baldwin, MDCCLXX. [1770.] Small oblong 4to. 78 leaves, etc.

M
Sowerby 4250

Jackson, William. *A Scheme demonstrating the Perfection and Harmony of Sounds Wherein is discover'd the true Coincidence of Tones into Diapasons and where all Musical Intervals unite and Incorporate to the Minutest part & their exact Proportions agreeable to the Proportions of Numbers Likewise the Exact Difference betwixt greater and lesser Intervals and how they are Compounded together in Musical Concordance. As also where greater and lesser Tones and Semi-Tones take place in the Diatonick Scale and how greater & lesser Semi-Tones arise in the Chromatick Scale.* To Edward Barker of ye Inner Temple London Esqr. This Scheme is Humbly inscribed by the Author William Jackson. [London?, 1726.]   Folio, engraved chart.

M
Sowerby 4251

Notice des Statues, Bustes et Bas-Reliefs, de la Galerie des Antiques du Musée Central des Arts. Paris, 1803.   12mo.

M
Sowerby 4242

Notice des Statues, Bustes et Bas-Reliefs, de la Galerie des Antiques du Musée Napoléon, ouverte pour la premier fois le 18 Brumaire an 9. Prix 1 franc 25 cent. A Paris: de l'Imprimerie des Sciences et Arts, An XI. [1802–3.]   12 mo. 94 leaves including the half title and the last blank.

M
Sowerby 4233

The Perfect Painter; or, A Complete History of the Original Progress, and Improvement of Painting. London, 1730.   12 mo. Possibly by François Perrier (see Eleanor Berman, *Thomas Jefferson among the Arts.* New York: Philosophical Library, 1947. Index.)

M
Sowerby 4239

[Prelleur, Peter.] *The Compleat Tutor for the Harpsichord or Spinnet wherin is Shewn the Italian manner of Fingering with Suits of Lessons*

*for Beginners & those who are already Proficient on that Instrument &
the Organ: with Rules for tuneing the Harpsichord or Spinnet.* Printed
for & sold by Peter Thompson Musical Instrument Maker at ye Violin,
Hautboy, & German Flute, ye West end of St. Pauls Church Yd. London. Where Books of Instructions for any Single Instrument may be
had. Price 1s & 6d. [N.d.]   8vo. 19 leaves.

M

Sowerby 4257

Richardson, [Jonathan]. *An Essay on the Theory of Painting.* By Mr.
Richardson . . . London: Printed by W. Bowyer, for John Churchill,
1715.   8vo. 120 leaves.

M

Sowerby 4236

Index

Authors, titles, and buildings by Jefferson are listed by page number and illustration number (the latter in roman numerals). Entries under such classifications of books as Architecture and Gardening are by entry number, not page number.

DATE DUE

GAYLORD			PRINTED IN U.S.A